Visual Storytelling
Infographic Design in News

Liu Yikun   Dong Zhao

Visual Storytelling
Infographic Design in News

images
Publishing

CONTENTS

007 Visual Storytelling Infographic Design in News

008 A Origin and Characteristics of Data Journalism
- 008 Origin of News Data
- 008 Characteristics of Data Journalism

011 D Data Journalism Design
- 011 Basic Elements of Data Journalism Design
- 014 Traditional Design Methods
- 022 Other Descriptive Methods
- 024 Multidimensional Data Journalism Design
- 028 Interactive Data News Design

008 **B** Forms of Data Journalism

009 **C** Data Journalism in the Media: Case Studies

- The Guardian — 009
- The New York Times — 010
- Bloomberg News — 010

032 **Case Studies**

- Finance and Economy — 034
- Sport News — 069
- Politics and Military — 100
- Entertainment News — 114
- Society and Science — 136

238 **Index**

Visual Storytelling
Infographic Design in News

We are now in the age of New Media, in which journalism's role and influence are being transformed, and digital news agencies and digital reporting are booming. Mobile platforms and social media are changing the way news content is produced and disseminated, and one of the hottest new developments is the arrival of Big Data.

With the diversification of communication channels, the development of citizen journalism is playing an increasingly important role in affecting the timeliness of news delivery. The influence of traditional print media and broadcast news has declined, and traditional news coverage often falls short of the expectations of mass audiences for increasingly diverse information. Data journalism is helping to bridge this gap.

Data journalism is a new kind of news storytelling enabled by the vast amounts of digital information collected by companies and governments. Using such data, relationships—between people, organizations, and governments—can be quantified and visualized.

Data journalism contains two kinds of innovation. The first of these is the use of graphics and the opportunity for the reader to interact with the information they contain. The other innovation concerns content. Data journalism collects, filters, and presents information in new ways, discovering new, more meaningful patterns and relationships. A small amount of information in an isolated event often lacks obvious meaning, but if viewed in larger clusters, from new angles, data can reveal more important significance. Diverse presentation techniques of data journalism not only enrich the types of news coverage, but make the presentation more concise and intuitive. Data journalism has a far-reaching impact on news production, since news collecting and editing is not limited to a single form, but needs updated skills, including data journalism design, so as to adapt to the changing times.

Data journalism is the future of journalism. With improvements in data analysis, information extraction and data mining technology, journalism is better placed to add depth to the issues it covers and to deliver the news in more creative ways. This innovative dimension is mainly reflected in three areas—investigative journalism, data visualizing narration, and data-driven application. From everyday social issues to deep social trends, it helps to provide reliable insights and predictions. News presented in graphic form aids comprehension and can help create an emotional response from the reader.

A. Origin and Characteristics of Data Journalism

Origin of News Data

According to the Pew Research Center's Internet and American Life Project, more than 90% of the world's news data in recent years was generated by government, institutions, enterprises (including the media), and Internet users. The content created includes text, images, audio and video, and location information. The data has four notable features—velocity, variety, volume, and value.

Characteristics of Data Journalism

1. Data journalism enables traditional news stories to be told using digital information. Specialist data journalists can help traditional journalists tell a complex story through engaging infographics; and open paths to new kinds of stories.

2. Data journalism can help explain how a story relates to the individual, as the BBC and the *Financial Times* now routinely do with their interactive budget reports (in which readers can find out how a particular budget affects them). It can also open up the news-gathering process itself, as *The Guardian* does so successfully in sharing data, context, and questions in its Data blog. News today is increasingly related to data and numbers, and the media's role is to report and explain it.

3. New journalism enables a journalist to report stories that have not previously been reported and to report them from new angles. This is done by finding and visualizing large amounts of data, thus reporting stories from new perspectives. Data journalism requires deep data mining through repeated extraction, screening, and reorganization, focusing on specific information to filter the data, and interpreting the information in order to visualize it and produce news stories.

4. The core of data journalism is data processing, which tends to have the following characteristics: it aims to serve the public interest; is based on open data; relies on special software for data processing to find news stories hidden in abstract data; and presents news in visual and interactive ways.

B. Forms of Data Journalism

There are three main forms of data-based news: data visualization, graphic-based news, and data maps.

1. Data visualization is a very broad concept, referring mainly to graphical methods to clearly and effectively distribute and communicate information.

2. There is no clear boundary between graphic-based news and data visualization, because graphic news is data visualization in the broadest sense. The difference between them is that news graphics simply illustrate the essential details of the traditional news story,

while data visualization always focuses on statistics and presentation of digital information.

3. Data maps usually integrate a variety of information but are mainly used in the reporting of disasters such as earthquakes, tsunamis, and landslides.

The media tend to report data-based news visually because it is a more effective way to communicate such information. Taking advantage of computer technology, data journalism visualization differs from the style of graphics traditionally used in news reporting. To these innovative new forms of graphical presentation the media have added multimedia, which combines video, text, and interactive graphics. These forms and delivery platforms not only encourage readers to engage with the information, they perfectly suit the fast-paced, multi-platform nature of the Internet.

Data journalism has transformed the way traditional journalism is done and consists of four steps: digging deep into data, filtering the data to find specific information, visualizing the data, and writing the story.

Data Journalism in the Media: Case Studies

The Guardian

The Guardian is a pioneer in introducing and developing data journalism, and has had a big impact on other successful global news media, including the BBC, *The New York Times*, *Bloomberg News*, *The Wall Street Journal*, *Financial Times*, *The Associated Press*, *Texas Tribune* and *Mother Jones*, which have all launched their own data journalism columns.

The Guardian has produced thousands of pieces of data news, covering politics, the economy, sports, war, disaster, the environment, culture, fashion, science, technology, health and other fields. These take the form of charts, maps, and a variety of interactive renderings. Data news generally has the following features:

1. Participation
The newspaper opens the data platform and invites users to participate in data news coverage. *The Guardian* has been aware of the need for new forms of news delivery (namely 'open news') for a long time. Alan Rusbridger, editor-in-chief for 20 years, defines 'open media' as news that is fully woven into existing information networks in the world. It is connected to this network; it screens and filters data from the network; works closely with the network; and better explains the world using materials published and shared by ordinary people.

2. An Open Technology Platform
The Guardian invites third-party developers to participate in the value-added development of data, offering large amounts of content free of charge for their commercial use. This includes millions of articles,

photographs, and videos created since 1999, as well as a lot of public database information.

3. Enhance Advertising Effectiveness
The Guardian signed a cooperation agreement with the emerging targeting network advertising company Quantcast, planning to subdivide advertising audiences with the help of big data mining and analysis techniques. The goal was to assist advertisers to target their advertisements more accurately, improving their return on investment.

The New York Times

In April 2014 *The New York Times* launched a new column, The Upshot, which uses data analysis and presentation to help readers understand the meaning behind complex political and economic events. As well as serious political topics, it also introduced a number of sports-themed works, covering the World Cup, football, baseball, soccer, and the NBA. From these works, we can see the following features:

1. Individualization
Individual readers can engage with a piece of data news through interaction. For example, the article 'Is it better to rent or buy?' relates macro data such as the rise and fall of house prices to the life of every reader through interaction. This feature is also available in other sections of *The New York Times* as well as many other news organizations.

2. Functionality
Ideally, data visualization pieces should achieve the harmonious balance of aesthetics, utility, and news value, which is rarely achieved in general articles due to limited time and manpower. *The New York Times* uses concise visualization design to highlight the functionality of its pieces to readers and users.

3. Reorganization
Although not every media agency can organize a data journalism team of more than a dozen people like *The New York Times*, data journalism has undoubtedly become a key development area of many media agencies. In 2014, data journalism pioneer *The Guardian* reorganized its editorial team and announced data journalism as one of its three development directions. Newly created media organizations, such as Quartz, Vox, and Buzzfeed, are also building their data journalism teams.

Bloomberg News

Bloomberg's 'World's Billionaires' is a data news application based on network interaction to show the wealth of the world's top 100 billionaires. It combines the daily stock market ups and downs, macroeconomic changes, and Bloomberg's original reports to calculate the personal wealth of these billionaires, whose rankings and changes are constantly updated online. Visualization is presented in four ways: pictures, graphics, scatters, and maps. Full-time data journalists keep the information up-to-date. This application won a number of design and journalism awards, and two trends are very obvious:

1. Data-driven
Background data updating is the vital ingredient of a long-term data journalism project, creating more space for project development and encouraging more users to have their own ideas through the observation of data in news clues. Compared with the Forbes World's Billionaires list, which is updated once a year, Bloomberg's list may have surprising changes every single day, increasing the user retention rate.

2. Interaction
The application provides complete data in many different areas, providing users sufficient space to explore and discover. Readers can browse the information of the billionaires they are interested in through different indexes, such as profession, nationality, sex, age, and source of wealth.

Data Journalism Design

Basic Elements of Data Journalism Design

Different data presentation methods have different interpretative results, and data selection and application can directly influence the audience's understanding of the news. The basic elements of data journalism design are numbers, graphics, and colors.

1. Numbers
Around 1986, renowned psychologists Daniel Kahneman and Amos Tversky conducted a famous series of experiments to illustrate that different data presentation methods would affect the audience's choice behavior. The following are their questions and strategy options:

Imagine that the United States is facing an unusual epidemic, and 600 people are estimated to be dead. At present, there are two strategies, and it is assumed that scientists have precisely evaluated the results of each strategy. If strategy A is taken, 200 people will be saved; if strategy B is taken, it has a one-third chance of saving all the people and has a two-thirds chance of saving no people. The result is that 72% of the 600 people surveyed chose strategy A and 28% chose strategy B.

Another approach proved that if the results were the same but the data was described in different scenarios, participants would tend to choose the option that highlighted the people saved rather than the people who would die. If strategy A is taken, 400 people would die (22% of the participants chose this option); if strategy B is taken, it has a one-third chance of saving all the people and a two-thirds chance of saving no people (78% of the participants chose this option).

Thus, it can be seen that the way numbers are presented can directly affect readers' judgment on the central idea of the article. Data is the

001
Smoking Infographic

002
The Rise of the Silver Surfers

most important element in data journalism, and each step—from data collection to data presentation and finally to data description—may affect readers' understanding of the content.

News media often uses digital strategies to set the media agenda. For example, when reporting the data of the International Monetary Fund (IMF), Peruvian newspaper *El Comercio* pointed out that China's purchasing power would be $17.6 trillion, beating the $16.4 trillion of the United States. This figure was calculated using IMF's latest purchasing power calculation method. However, if calculated by the original method, China still lagged $6.5 trillion behind the United States. This kind of data presentation reveals the framing effect of news media. If the newspaper wants to highlight China's rapid economic growth, they can use the latest IMF data, and if they want to express that China will not overtake the United States within a short period of time, they can use the unadjusted data.

2. Graphs

In addition to the presentation of numbers, the visual presentation of graphs can directly affect the audience's psychological reaction. When making infographics, rational use of geometric elements can increase the appeal of data, enriching the data with emotional color. The infographic in Figure 001 is designed to draw the reader's attention to the fact that smoking is harmful to health. Graphic symbols associated with death, such as 'skulls' and 'chemicals', were used to illustrate the statistics surrounding the health hazards caused by smoking. These graphic elements were adopted to encourage more vigilant behavior from readers when looking after their own health.

The graphs of data journalism often need other graphic elements to beautify pages and often use symbols rather than text to make the presentation more attractive. Figure 002 depicts the evolution of media used at different times by older people of 50 years old and above. In this graph, simple symbols are used instead of text classification to make the content clear at a glance and to make the news more attractive.

001

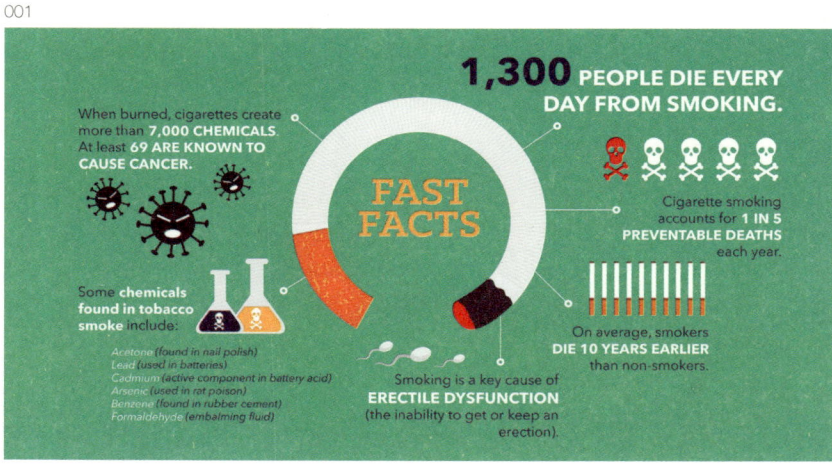

3. Color
Color selection for data journalism is also very important. Media around the world will turn their websites into black and white after catastrophes to express sympathy. During the National Day of China, major news websites adopt a red theme for celebration. The environmental protection theme is reflected in infographics by the use of green as the base color.

Though color has the least amount of impact among the three influencing factors on data presentation, its role should not be discounted. Different cultures associate different meanings to colors. For example, gray white can be used to represent funeral ceremonies in China, but represents purity and relates to marriage in Christian countries. Meanwhile, rainbow color is a symbol of homosexuality in the United States and other western countries. Today, the world is closely connected through the Internet, and news reports are no longer confined to domestic audiences. Therefore, there's a need for careful color selection in news reports involving international issues (particularly when dealing with topics such as race and gender).

4. Other Related Concepts
Before we discuss the design and production of data journalism, it is necessary to clarify some concepts that are commonly used in statistics and scientific research methods, and are in line with international norms.

Data: Data is the information carrier—the numbers and characters describing the properties of things and a set of all the symbols that can be used for statistical analysis.

Index / variable: An index is a concept that explains overall quantitative features. An index can define the scope of a set of data. For example, Figure 003 shows the 'area' distribution of sugarcane yield, and the 'area' is an index that can be used to determine the interval of total amount of data. An index is also called variable in the data with mathematical significance.

002

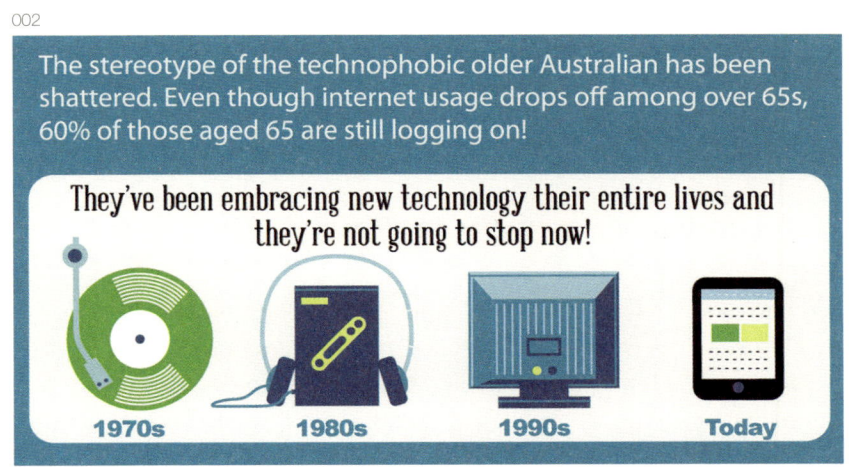

003

Sugarland Distress

Project Description /
The graphic shows the quantity and growth of the sugar industry in India. Uttar Pradesh is India's largest state involved in the production of sugarcane, but it was in crisis at the time of publication. Santosh Kushwaha explored and illustrated the data by using physical pictures and some graphic elements to make it easily understood.

Client / *Business Today*, *India Today* Group
Design Agency / Visual Best
Designer / Santosh Kushwaha
Completion / 2013

004

Space Shuttle Missions Timeline

Project Description /
This interactive timeline is about NASA's space shuttle missions from 1977 to 2010. All the content is very clear and easy to navigate in this innovative visualization.

Client / lainformacion.com
Designer / Carlos Gámez Kindelán
Completion / 2014

Sample / total sample: The sample is a subset of observations taken from a parent population according to a random principle, and the size of the sample is the total sample. For example, India has 16 states and one capital district. If five main sugarcane production areas are taken to represent India's overall sugarcane yield, the sugarcane yield of these five areas is the statistical sample, and the sample size is five.

Case: Each of the individuals making up the sample is called a case.

Data value: Data value describes the sample data in numbers.

For example, Figure 003 shows the sugarcane yield all over India, and 'sugarcane yield' can be a set of data composed of the sugarcane yield of five areas in India. In this set of data, the total sample is the sugarcane sample of these five areas, the sugarcane yield of each area is one 'case', the area is one 'index', and the yield is 'data value' rather than 'data'.

Traditional Design Methods

Descriptive data is the most fundamental type of data journalism. Descriptive statistics is describing and summarizing the overall distribution of data using a variety of design methods, such as a line graph, radar chart, histogram, bar chart, pie chart, and scatter plot.

Figure 003 describes the development and current crisis of the sugar industry in India. This is a piece of descriptive-style news and it adopts a variety of design methods, including a line graph, pie chart, histogram, and bar chart.

Before working on the graphic design of the descriptive data, the first thing to consider is the integrity of the data. Data integrity means that the data can represent a complete concept within a certain range. For example, Figure 003 presents a picture of India's sugarcane economy and so depicts the sugarcane yield data of the whole country. In addition to the yield data of four main sugarcane-producing states—Bihar, Uttar Pradesh, Tamil Nadu, and Karnataka—the author included information on states with smaller sugarcane yields, but used 'Others' to present the overall yield situation, so that the data is complete.

Similarly, in order to analyze China's rice production, the data will not be complete if it only uses data of major rice-producing regions in the South and ignores the statistical data of rice production in the Northeast, North China and other small areas.

If all data is not available—say, for example, because the government has not disclosed it—the designer will need to change the report strategy by narrowing the coverage. In the case of rice production in China, if it is difficult to obtain the rice yield data of the northern provinces, the designer can change the subject to 'Statistics on the development of China's major rice-producing areas.'

1. Line Graphs
In the above example, a line graph is used to describe the price trend of sugarcane in India from 2007 to 2013, with a green line representing the government-controlled prices and an orange line representing the prevailing market prices. The graph clearly shows the price fluctuation over the seven years (highest price, lowest price).

In addition to describing different data for different years, a line graph can illustrate trends over time. Figure 004 shows NASA's aircraft missions from 1977 to 2010. Due to the 33-year time span, it is appropriate to use a line graph to show specific flight missions and trends relating to the annual amount of missions over time.

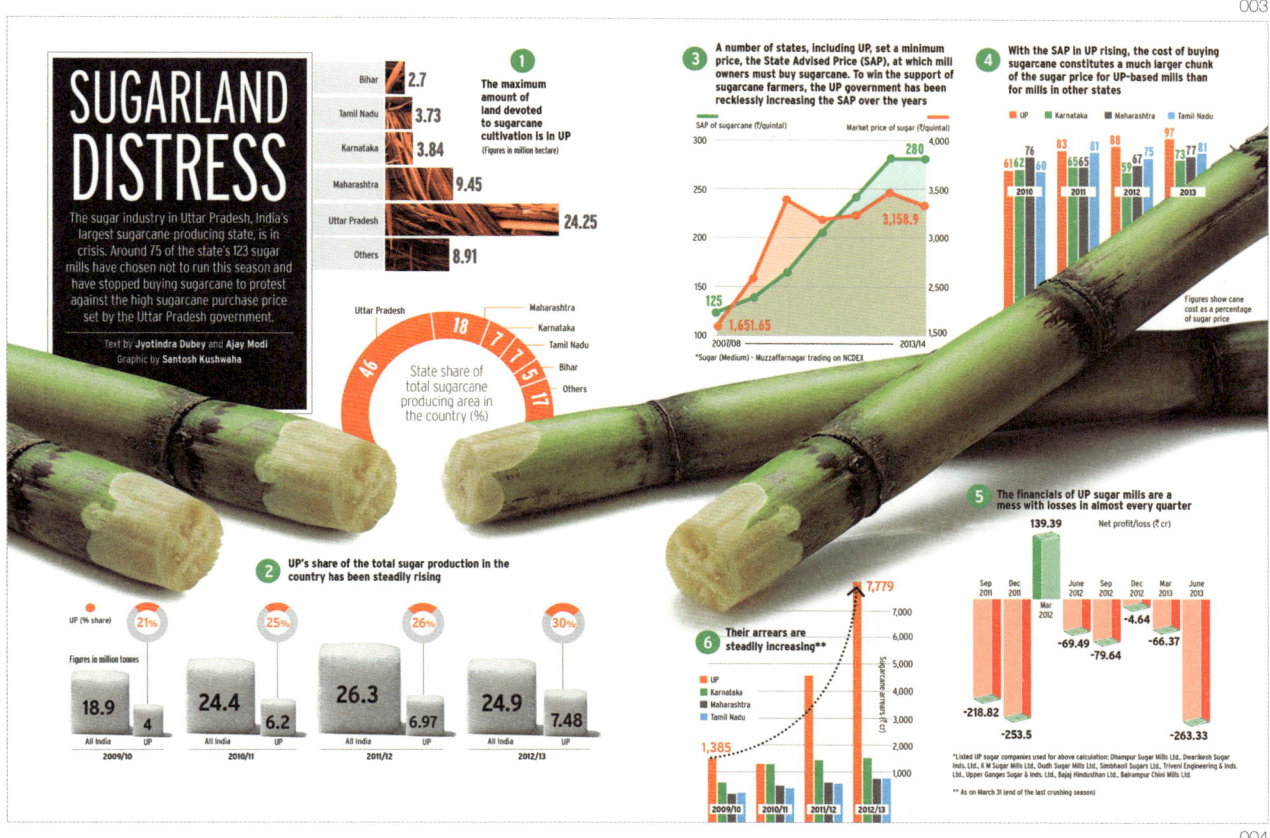

005

Discomfort Food

Project Description /
The story is about increasing food inflation over several months. The reasons for the persistent high food inflation of the last few years have been much debated. There is a great need to improve supply chains and reduce wastage. Designer Santosh Kushwaha's popular graphic style uses real images. He thought it would get more traffic if he created something eye-catching using real images, rather than vector graphics. He used major food elements to create a human story. The story is serious, so he tried to express that in his visual representation.

Client / *Business Today, India Today* Group
Design Agency / Visual Best
Designer / Santosh Kushwaha
Completion / 2012

Line graphs are suitable for periodic data, such as an analysis of social media users, in which the graph can show the age distribution trends of social media users.

The following is a list of data types best illustrated by line graphs:
- Data with time features—for example, weather trends over long periods, monthly oil price fluctuations, and quarterly per capita consumption.
- Data that ranks numbers—for example, the age distribution of radio listeners or the salary distribution of various jobs.
- Data showing regularity—for example, temperature distribution from south to north, or the distribution of soil fertility according to altitude change.

Line graphs have the advantage of clearly illustrating trends. Figure 005, made up of bar charts and line graphs, shows the rising trend of food prices. Large fluctuation trends are best presented in bar charts or line graphs; small fluctuations are best illustrated using line graphs.

How to make a line graph:
- Determine the horizontal and vertical coordinates. Generally, variables such as data, age, and altitude are used as the horizontal coordinate. The vertical coordinate is the value of the data to be described, and the range of those values is determined by the maximum and minimum values of the data.

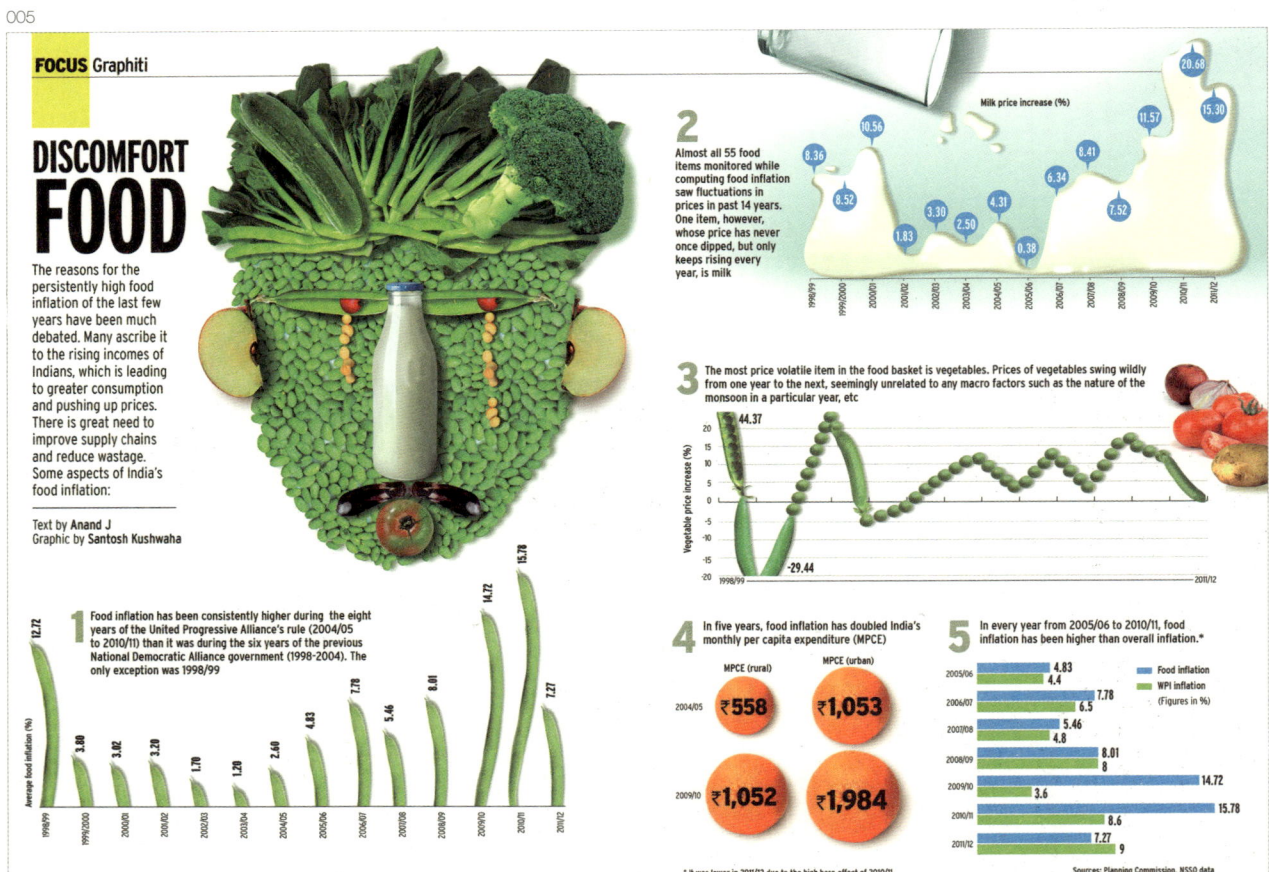

- Mark the data. Determine the position of the data in the coordinates according to the data values on the horizontal and vertical coordinates. In line graphs, one data value corresponds to one coordinate point.
- Connect the coordinate points. The amount of coordinate points directly reflects the size of the data sample.

2. Pie Charts

In the case of Figure 003, the pie chart is used to reflect the sugarcane yield of different areas in India, and Utta Pradesh is the largest sugarcane-producing area, accounting for 46% and occupying nearly half of the diagram. To make it more attractive, the pie is designed as a sector diagram, rather than a circle. Both pie charts and sector diagrams use area to represent the proportion of different data types and can directly reflect information, such as areas, regions, and percentages.

Pie charts are most useful for complete data sets. When the data set is incomplete, use the designation 'other' to label the segment that makes up the percentage shortfall.

Two features of pie charts:
- Integrity
- Parallel relationship between subset data

Figure 006 describes the four main causes of deforestation: agriculture, timber (the logging industry), pasture (cattle ranches), and fuel. These relate to the four main uses for trees—agriculture, industry, animal husbandry, and energy—which have a parallel relationship with each other and no overlapping relationship. When combined, they constitute a complete set.

But when relating to other data, such as the Purchase Management Index (PMI), pie charts or sector diagrams may not be suitable because of the sheer number of indexes the infographic needs to cover. The PMI is known as the 'health checklist' for measuring a country's manufacturing industry, and has a number of indexes: production, new orders, commodity prices, inventory, employees, order delivery, new export orders, and import. Though these indexes cannot all be listed, the designation 'others' can be used to label the segment that makes up the percentage shortfall.

Pie charts can be made into flat round cakes, solid round cakes, single-layer circular cakes, multi-layer circular cakes, and sector diagrams. Whether a circular or sector type is used, the total area of the graph represents a complete set of data (which must total 100%), with each segment representing a percentage of the whole data set.

3. Bar Charts and Histograms

Bar charts and histograms look similar but they are not the same thing.

Bar charts use the height or length of bars or columns to represent data values. They generally contain data relating to different entities, with at

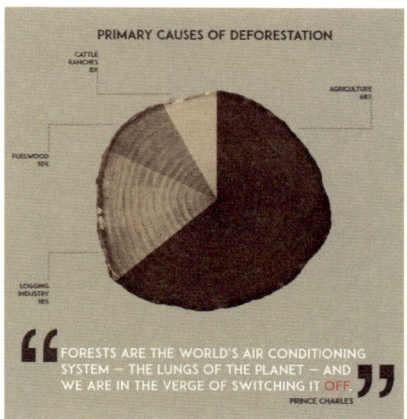

006

Deforestation

Project Description /
Unfortunately, deforestation is a rapidly increasing problem that negatively impacts the human race, as well as other forms of life in our environment. This poster summarizes the causes of deforestation, as well as the effects on the ecosystem. Also, it invites the viewer to take action to create awareness and to minimize the problem by doing simple things like taking care of trees and spreading the message of environmental protection. One of the main design elements of the poster is the tree trunk used as a pie chart. This imagery directly relates to the issue; it has been used to make a stronger impression on the reader, to give the piece an emotional impact rather than just showing numbers and graphics.

Designer / Regina Torres
Completion / 2014

007
The Portrait of
American Travelers Study

009

2015 Oscar Series: the Best Foreign Films

Project Description /
The infographic charts how many entries there were at the Academy Awards in 2015—from 83 countries to the nine short-listed films to the eventual five nominees. It also shows how many awards these films have won at other film competitions.

Client / *Times of Oman*
Designer / Adonis Durado
Completion / 2015

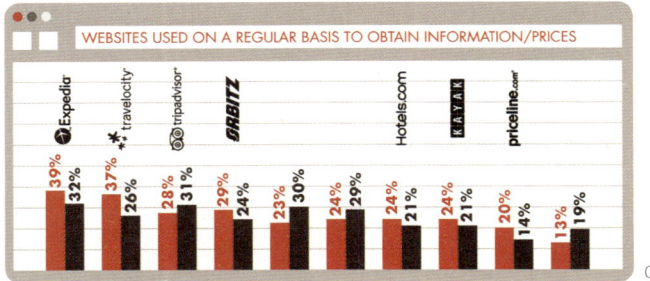

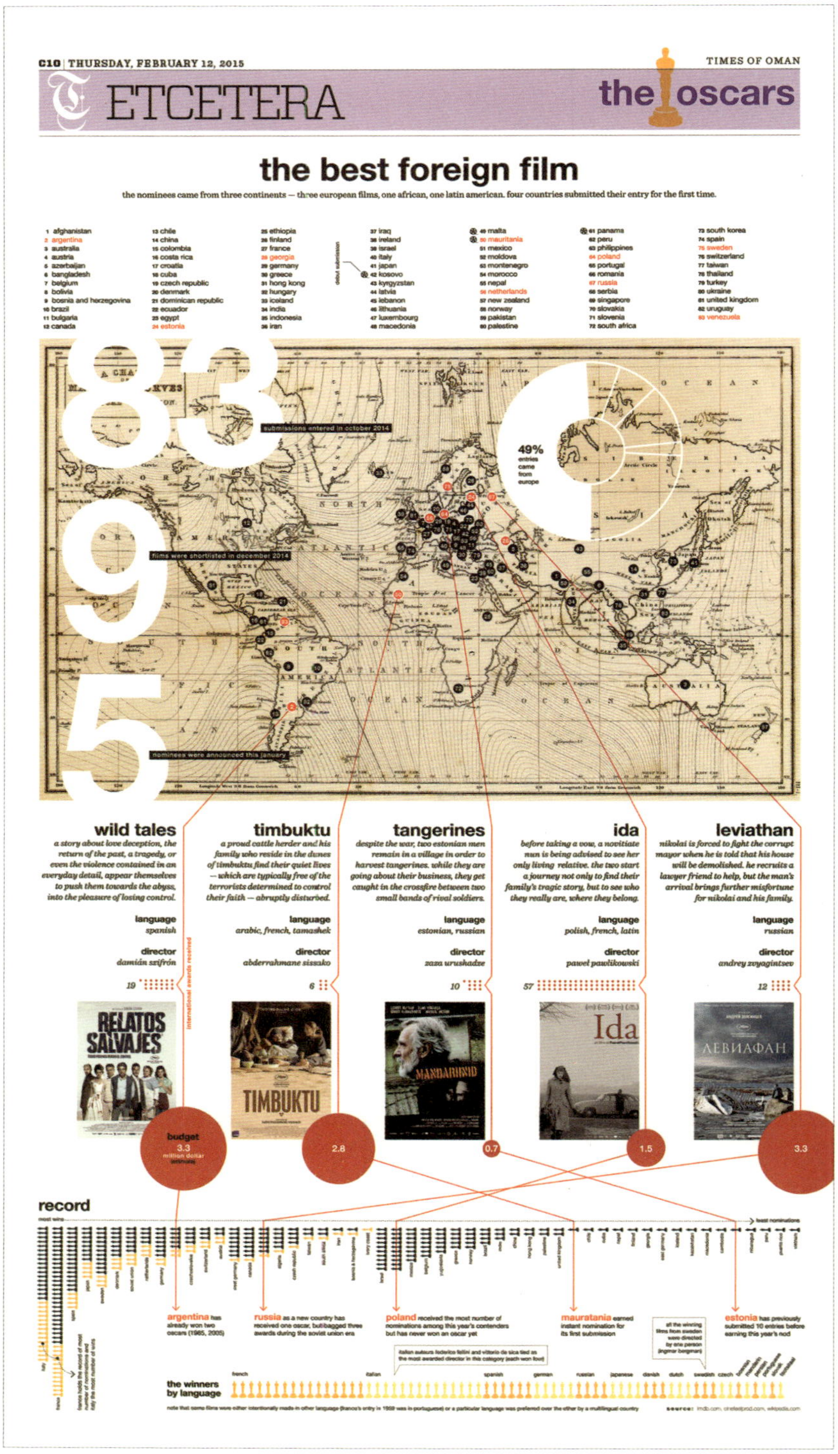

least two types of data for comparison. A gap is used between bars to indicate that they are separate entities, and different types of data should be different colors.

In Figure 003, five types of bar charts are used. The first chart describes the proportion of land growing sugarcane in the local agricultural area, with the length of bars representing the data value so that comparisons can be made between different sets of data. In the case of fewer groups and large data values, bars and columns can be distributed horizontally rather than vertically.

The data used in bar charts does not need to be a complete set because they are designed to compare different groups or entities. For example, Figure 007 shows the proportion of online visitors from the USA who search for travel information and prices, and the websites they visit. However, it only lists 10 popular websites, those that account for the highest numbers of people searching for travel information and prices rather than listing all the websites. This is the advantage of bar charts over pie charts and line graphs, which require complete sets of data.

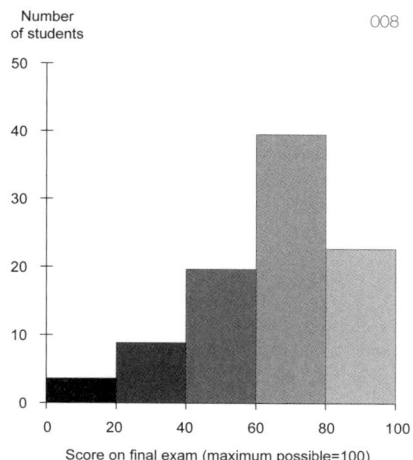

008

Histograms differ from bar charts by using area rather than height to indicate quantity. The variables of the histogram must be continuous and can be divided into a number of equal sections, with each section's value determined by the following formula:
(Maximum value − minimum value) / group number = section value

In a histogram, there is no space between adjacent blocks, and the total area of the blocks—their height multiplied by their width—must add up to 100% of the total data set. Histograms not only enable the reader to conveniently observe the proportions of each element, they indicate the proportion of the whole that each block represents.

Figure 008, for example, shows the distribution of student numbers according to their scores. The horizontal axis has been divided into five equal parts, each representing a score range of 20 marks, with the size of each block also representing the proportion of students of the whole who received marks within that range.

4. Scatter Plot

Scatter plots can show the distribution and properties of all cases. Figure 009 lists all 83 films entered into the Academy Award competition for Best Foreign Language Film, with nine films screened as candidates and five chosen as the final nominations. All 83 countries are marked on the map, and the five nominated films are described in more detail. The biggest feature of scatter plots is giving prominence to individual cases.

Scatter charts present the data in the form of a set of points whose values are represented by their positions on the chart. The position is controlled by two variables. Scatter plots are often applicable to cross-category aggregated data—that is, the variables of horizontal and longitudinal coordinates belong to different categories. A benefit of

010

The London Olympic Games—Game Over

Project Description /
This overview features the strangest and most ancient games of the Olympics, which are no longer included in the modern games. The designer made use of a scatter plot to clearly explain the information.

Client / *Sportweek—La Gazzetta Dello Sport*
Designer / Gianluca Seta
Completion / 2012

scatter plots is that they can show simple correlation, making it easy to see the scattered distribution or aggregation of the variables in two-dimensional space.

Making a scatter plot is similar to making a line graph. The difference is that data points of line graphs may not be detailed cases and the longitudinal coordinates represent the data values of individual cases, while scatter plot is still one of the variables of the data. There are only two steps for making a scatter plot: First, determine the two variables of the case, namely the abscissa and ordinate (there should be at least two variables like the latitude and longitude on a map); then, determine the positions of each case according to their coordinates. In Figure 010, the coordinates of each target are determined by two variables, which are 'ancient sport' and 'year'. The scatter plot reveals the gradual disappearance of the most ancient and competitive Olympic sports; from 1936 only two ancient sports were retained.

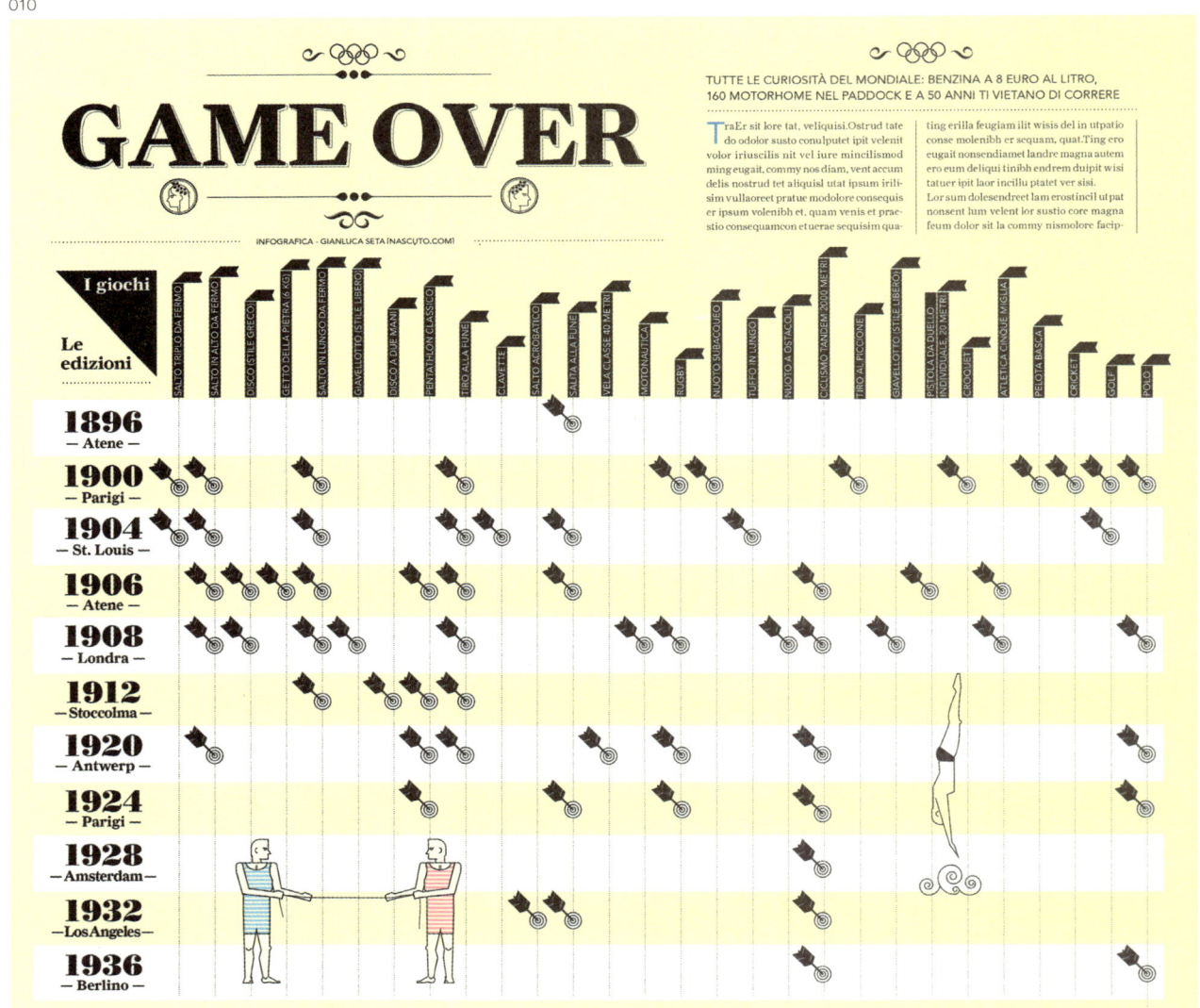

010

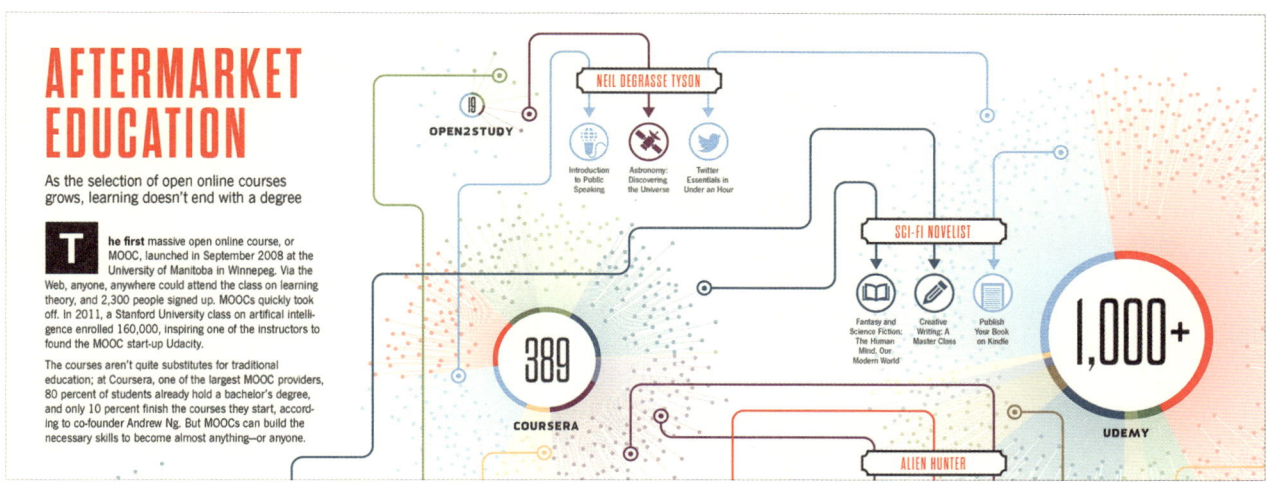

5. Radar Chart

A radar chart is also known as a web star, star chart, spider chart or irregular polygon. It is mainly used to compare data of relatively independent categories. Several equiangular spokes start from the same point, with each spoke representing an independent variable. Each spoke has a data point, from which the length to the center point is determined according to the proportion of the variable to the total amount. Connect these data points and a radar chart can be drawn.

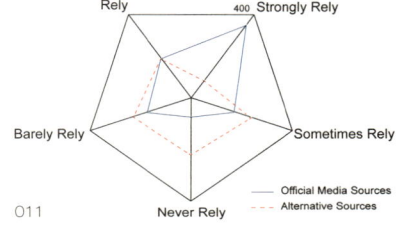

For comparing the progress and qualities of each subproject, a radar chart is very direct and effective, using positions to describe distribution trends. Figure 011, for example, represents the statistics of news sources on which Chinese social media users rely. The blue star protrudes towards the northeast, meaning users strongly rely on official media sources. But the red star for 'alternative sources' does not show a clear tendency, as the star only shows a concave in the northeast but it's uniform in other directions.

There are two key steps for making a radar / star chart:
- Determine the number of spokes according to the requirements of data indicators. For example, in Figure 012 in 'Online Courses', the numbers and categories of free online courses are presented in a graph combining pie charts and star charts, in which pie charts show a rough category of all online courses, dots in pie charts represent the courses in each category, and the number of spokes represent the number of courses.
- Determine the positions of data points. Each spoke of radar / star charts represents sampled data and has a data point on the spoke whose length is in proportion to the size of data value. In the 'Online Courses', the lengths of spokes represent the course's popularity—the longer the course, the more popular it is.

Radar / star charts can be made with the aid of Origin, Visio, AI, and other software.

012
Aftermarket Education: the MOOC Landscape

Other Descriptive Methods

Descriptive data can use a variety of graphics, individually or jointly, to help interpret the data. With rapid development of the technology, the presentation methods of descriptive data are becoming more diverse, interesting, vivid, and lively.

1. Word Cloud / Tag Cloud
Word Cloud / Tag Cloud is a type of visual graph that uses Internet technologies to extract and randomly arrange some keywords from the text. It determines the fonts and colors of these keywords according to their frequencies. Word cloud technology can aid the reader to quickly grasp the core words and their frequencies, highlighting the central topics and related framework of the text.

Figure 013 is a BBC word cloud analysis of Indian leader Narendra Modi's Independence Day speech in August 2014. The graph shows that the most frequent words are 'India', 'one' and 'country', which are marked in brown. Other key words include 'government' and 'want'. Based on this analysis, the BBC discerned that India's leader was very eager to announce his ideas for the government and future of India.

The following websites provide word cloud automatic generation technology services:
- www.jasondavies.com
- www.wordle.net
- http://worditout.com

Word cloud technology is mostly used for analysis of text with a lot of opinion and a large number of words, especially when the central idea of the text is not immediately clear. Word cloud analysis can help confirm whether specific words appear frequently. It is often used for analyzing political leaders' speeches, refining the themes of websites, and illustrating government reports.

2. Mixed Graphs
In order to visualize some data news, it's sometimes necessary to use mixed graphs, which are suitable for presenting complex data that have a variety of indicators, variables and categories. Figure 014 shows Brazil's irrigation conditions from various standpoints through a combination

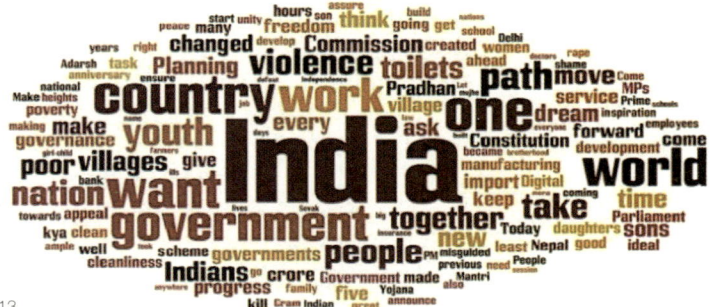

013

of scatter plots, line graphs, pie charts, maps, and other charts. In this infographic, the line graphs show a downward trend year by year, the pie charts highlight the proportion occupied by each economic sector, and the scatter plots clearly show the significant effect of water shortage on the whole country of Brazil.

Data journalism uses data as the main information carrier, giving priority to data presentation rather than text content. Sometimes one type of graph cannot cover all aspects of a story, so mixed graphs are used to capture all components.

Hydroelectrics in Brazil

Project Description /
Hydroelectrics are Brazil's biggest source of power. However, climate changes make it rain less than usual in some regions, causing blackouts in some states. This infographic shows how Brazil's integrated power source works. The lack of rain in one region affects the whole country. Despite the southeast region producing more than 70% of the hydroelectricity, it's still deficient.

Client / *O Estado de São Paulo*
Designers / Carol Cavaleiro, Rubens Paiva, Edmilson Silva
Completion / 2013

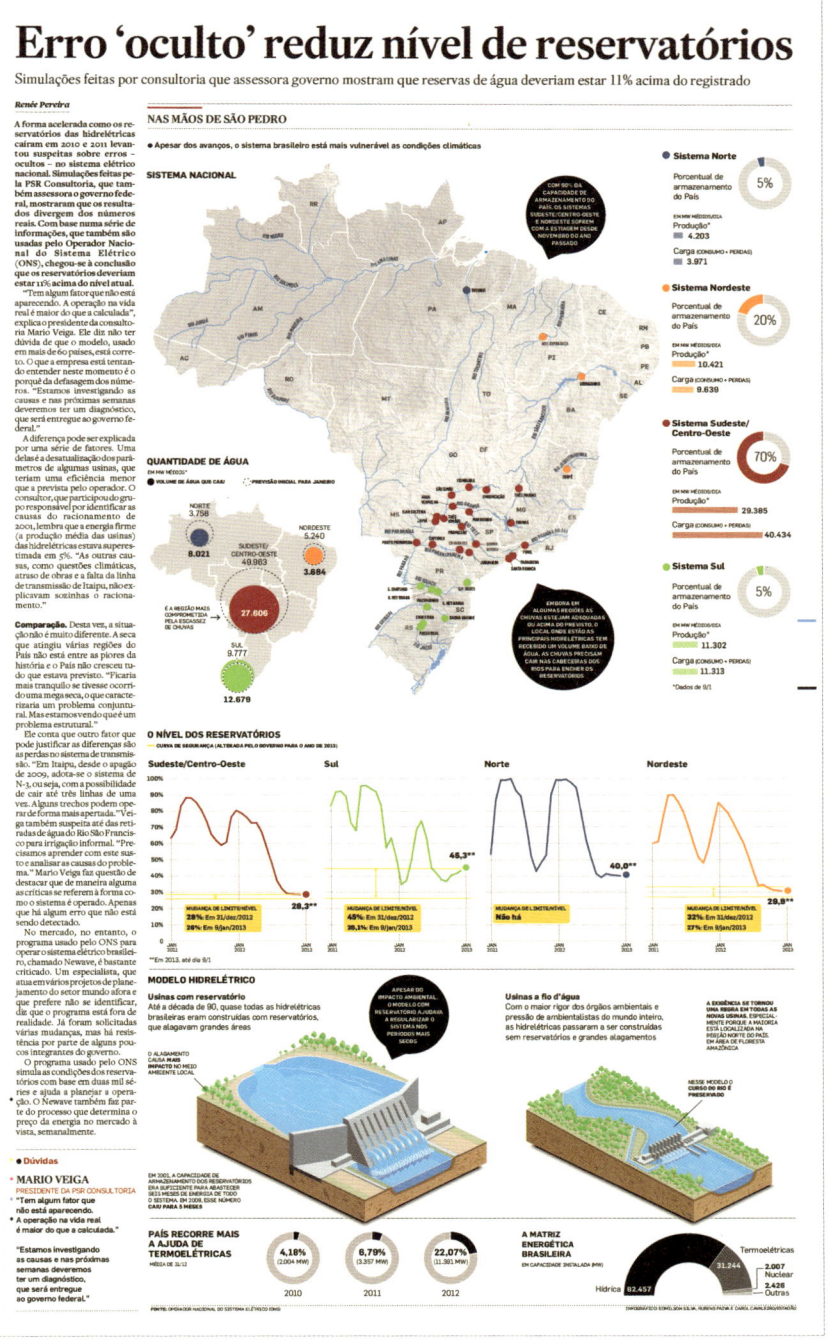

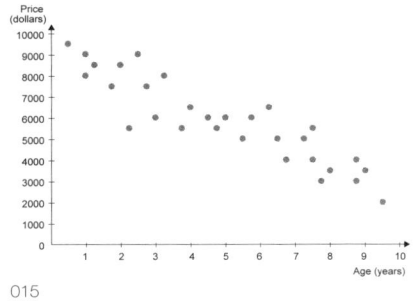

015

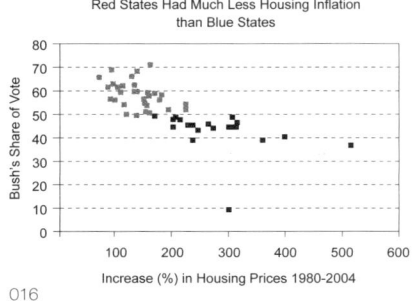

016

This kind of work can be carried out with Microsoft Excel. Several types of graphs can be combined to make the data readable, visible, and clearly identifiable. Creating a data journalism graph is different from making a statistical chart, because the latter is used for scientific research and needs to explain the data in an accurate, rigorous way by using neutral, objective words. For example, '48%' cannot be interpreted as 'nearly half'. Data journalism charts, on the other hand, aim to report accurate data, but also contain some subjective opinions of the journalists. This type of chart promotes mass communication, enables more people to understand the hidden meanings in the data, and increases the practical significance of the data. Related pictures are often inserted into the graphs to make them more visual and direct.

Multidimensional Data Journalism Design

Correlation is the uncertain quantitative relationship between variables. With correlation data, if one variable changes, the other variable will change accordingly. News has an important function as a social watchtower, which not only describes what happens in brief words, but also explores the hidden factors, causes and effects of the event. It can also make predictions about the future. Data journalism can effectively work as a social watchtower, because the fundamental objective of correlation analysis and multidimensional multilevel analysis of the data is explaining and predicting the relationships and trends between variables.

1. Simple Correlation
If the data has a simple linear correlation, one variable increases/decreases in line with the other variable. Drawing a scatter plot can simply verify the correlation of two variables.

Scatter plots can not only present single cases, but also show the correlation between two variables, and if a correlation exists, the point distribution will be aggregated or scattered according to certain rules. Linear aggregation is linear correlation. For example, Figure 015 shows the points distribution of data in linear correlation; it surveyed 30 vehicles that were in service over different time periods, and marked a point for each vehicle according to their service lives and market prices. The graph shows that the market prices of vehicles decline along with the increase in service lives, which is a negative correlation.

If scattered points are marked in different colors, individual cases can be compared. For example, Figure 016 represents the presidential electoral result of the former US President George Bush, with red color points representing the Republican vote and blue representing votes for the Democratic Party. The chart shows that Republican voters are mostly located in areas with lower house price inflation. Therefore, it can be said that the inflation rate of house prices is related to the votes for Bush.

2. Side-by-side Comparison
Data news often compares two data sets to highlight their differences, which can be used to create charts with strong visual impact. This kind

of data should be presented with the following principles in mind:
- The same indicators should be used for comparison. For example, you cannot compare the variable of age in one data set with the variable of gender in another data set.
- The data sets should be comparable. Otherwise, the comparison will be meaningless.
- The difference between data sets should have social significance. For example, although the populations of China and the United States vary widely, comparing their consumption habits or per capita income levels has more social significance than simply comparing the two country's populations. That is to say, journalists should select some meaningful indicators for data comparison.

Here is an example. Figure 017 shows a comparison of the numbers of married and divorced households in Portugal in 1985 and in 2012. The graphic reflects a sharp rise in the divorce rate as well as a fall in the marriage rate, reflecting a main problem of the current society in Portugal. This chart is concise and to the point, with obvious comparisons and profound social significance.

017
Families of Tomorrow

Project Description /
   This comprehensive study of typical Portuguese families over 50 years shows how the average number in a household is gradually decreasing, as marriages decrease and divorces increase over the decades. Based on this study, two years in particular are compared (1985 and 2012). The results are startling. They almost seem like an exaggeration, causing us to reflect on the problems surrounding marriage and the formation of families.

Designer / Marta Sofia Ribeiro Freitas
Completion / 2013

Our Changing House Market

Project Description /
The client wanted to show data of 40 years of sale prices and stepped growth. Such data can be very dry, so Rahadyo Widyastomo needed to present the data visually in an interesting way to engage customers. The data is blended with the graphic of a house.

Client / mitchellhomes.com
Designer / Rahadyo Widyastomo
Completion / 2013

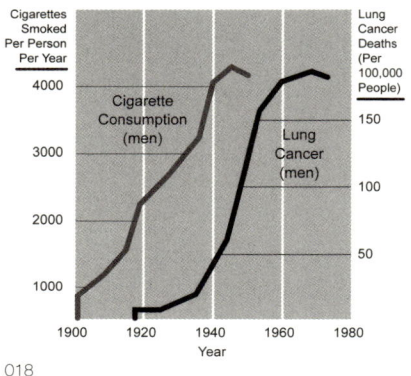
018

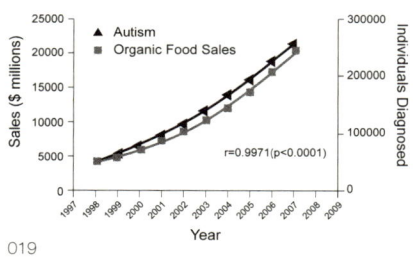
019

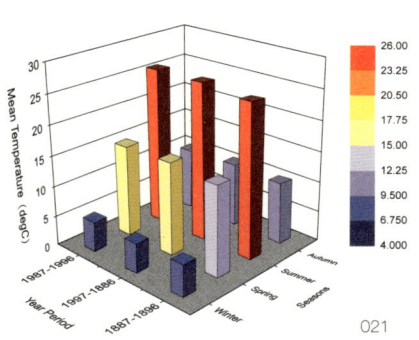
021

3. Causation

As news needs to explain social phenomena, data is more convincing than expert opinions in the exploration of causation, because data carries objective, unchanging facts, while expert opinions are often subjective and open to external influences. As a result, audiences and journalists tend to rely on data to present neutral and objective explanations.

The data with following conditions can be assumed to have a causal relationship:
- Variables of the data can be divided into two or more sets. One of these sets is the independent variable, which is assumed to be the causal variable; and the other set is the dependent variable.
- Dependent and independent variables have a sequential order in time.
- Independent variables cause changes in the dependent variables.

For example, Figure 018 shows a famous study arguing that tobacco causes lung cancer. From the chart we can observe that tobacco consumption is an independent variable in terms of time, and it was the sharp rise of tobacco consumption in 1900 that resulted in the increase of lung cancer deaths 20 years later.

However, correlations are not necessarily causal in nature. For example, Figure 019 shows a case of the identification of a causal relationship that did not, in fact, exist. By chance, some researchers found a positive correlation between the prevalence of organic food and the amount of autistic patients. They then drew a conclusion that organic food increased the possibility of autism. This was later discounted, because the researchers neither show a clear sequential order in time of two variables nor exclude other causes of autism.

4. Three-dimensional Graph

In some cases, 3D graphs are used only for aesthetic reasons and have no special statistical meaning. For example, the 3D house images are used in Figure 020 to illustrate the subject (housing prices) and the chart is essentially a line graph.

The 3D data with statistical meaning should use at least three variables to determine data values. For example, Figure 021 uses four variables—quarter, year, mean value, and temperature—to determine the locations, colors, and heights of columns.

The 3D graphs can be made not only using satellite maps but also with drawing software, such as 3ds Max, Maya, and Cineme4d.

5. Multilevel & Multidimensional Data

To fully explain the central idea of a piece of news, sometimes multidimensional multilevel data is used to support the original theme in greater depth.

For example, Figure 022 is a National Day special edition published in *The Times of Oman*, showing the history of Nizwa Fort, which is the

OUR CHANGING HOUSING MARKET:
THE UPS AND DOWNS IN SALE PRICE AND HOME SIZE OVER THE LAST 40 YEARS

AVERAGE HOME SALE PRICE GROWTH since **1970-2012**

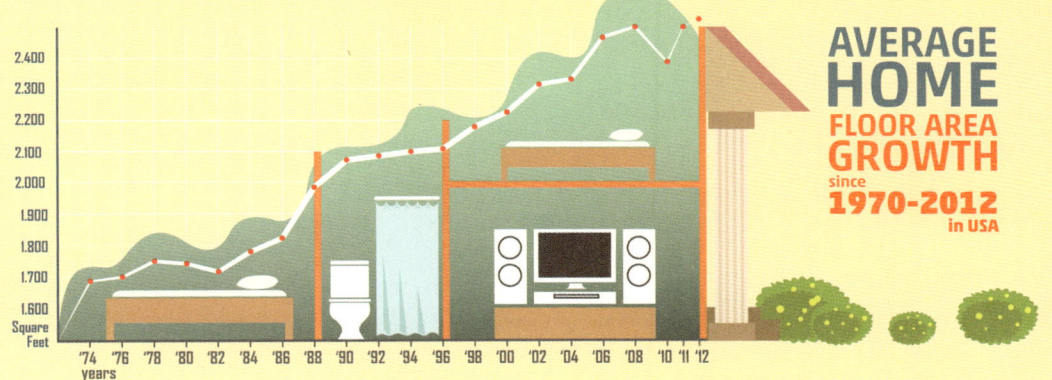

AVERAGE HOME FLOOR AREA GROWTH since **1970-2012** in USA

 **FACTS!**

Did You Know?

- The average home in 1950 was only 1,000 sq/ft and had only 1 bathroom.
- There were 37.2 million homes counted in the first housing census in 1940. There were 131.7 counted in 2010.
- In 2012 the average new single-family home sold was built on a lot of 15,634 square feet.

REFERENCES:
http://www.census.gov/const/uspriceann.pdf
http://www.census.gov/const/C25Ann/sftotalmedavgsqft.pdf

www.mitchellhomesinc.com

The Great Fort of Nizwa

Project Description /
Antonio Farach was commissioned to produce an infographic about the forts in Oman, to be published in the newspapers *Times of Oman* and *Al Shabiba* as a double page for Oman's National Day celebrations. He decided to focus on Nizwa Fort because it is one of the most majestic among the more than 500 forts that still exist in Oman, and because of its unique zig-zag trap-stairs system.

Client / *Times of Oman*
Designer / Antonio Farach

oldest and most representative castle in Oman. The 3D sectional view shows the reader the inner structure of the castle, including the unique Z-shaped stairs. The functionality of each part of the castle is vividly described in text and strong images, giving the final work great collection value.

Interactive Data News Design

Interactive news uses software to analyze and interpret large volumes of constantly changing data. Common interactive graphs include real-time maps, process flowcharts, and heat maps that show intensity.

1. Real-time Maps

The most common type of interactive data news is the weather forecast, which achieves real-time broadcasting with the aid of satellite technology, showing the flowing states of clouds and cyclones. In addition to weather and geographical conditions, major international events and news stories involving a large amount of statistic data may be presented in the form of real-time maps. For war reports, for example, TV news often show the satellite maps of war zones, accompanied by descriptive data.

From a technical point of view, it's very difficult to create a real-time map that needs to monitor a vast amount of constantly changing data and requires the assistance of data mining technology. This creates fresh challenges for journalists, because the work on deep data mining and big data analysis requires computer science knowledge.

2. Process Flowcharts

Real-time dynamic graphs are often used to illustrate the ups and downs of the stock market. They show data changes and developments in a real-time manner, similar to live TV broadcasting.

The UK-based *Financial Times* often launches interactive data news in its Interactive news column, in which it often features graphs about stocks and bonds. These graphs will show additional data analysis and relevant news when the readers move their cursor to certain time points.

The process flowchart is static in the print media. Figure 023, for example, uses text, numbers, patterns, charts, and other elements to present the migration of the monarch butterfly from Canada to Mexico as well as its evolutionary history and hatching process.

These graphs help journalists explain a subject's dynamic features over a specific time period, so they can present a good overview and further explain their findings.

3. Heat Maps

Heat maps highlight data density or data size with color brightness or geometric symbols, and are often used for news about diseases, disasters, and temperature. Dynamic heat maps can monitor the distributions and trends of information in a real-time manner.

023
Monarch Butterfly from Canada to Mexico

Project Description /
This infographic forms part of a special project '40 years of the monarch butterfly in Estado de México'. It focuses on the monarch butterfly's travels from Canada to Mexico, and the evolution from a caterpillar to a beautiful butterfly. The infographic also presents the characteristic of the two sexes, and the food and nutrients needed to support the long journey.

Design Agency / Diario La Razón de México
Designer / Diana Estefanía Rubio

Dilma Won

Project Description /
The results of the presidential elections in Brazil won by Dilma Roussef are illustrated here in a simple day-by-day format. This type of work usually does not reflect the reality of the vote in each part of the country, but the designer believes this map is the best way to effectively interpret and display the election results, as it shows who had the most votes in each municipality according to its size.

Client / *Diário Económico*
Designer / Mário Malhão
Completion / 2014

Heat maps are often used to present meteorological data, such as temperature, air pressure, and humidity. Graphs that combine heat maps and real-time maps have a larger visual impact. Taking Figure 024 as an example, the votes for Brazil's presidential election are shown in the heat map, which does not directly present the actual numbers of votes but effectively predicts the voting results of each state. As the heat map predicts, Dilma Roussef won the final election.

Data is the most precious resource of interactive news. A piece of interactive data is a small database, which is open to the reader in the graphs drawn. The reader can get the data by simply moving his/her mouse and keyboard. For example, Figure 025 is a piece of data news launched by *The Los Angeles Times*, whose data source is teachers' assessment data from 11,970 elementary schools in Los Angeles. From here, the readers can search for assessments of their primary school's teachers.

The simplicity of this kind of data presentation method is that readers can easily obtain the data they're after, and journalists do not have to analyze and classify the vast amount of data piece by piece.

4. Others
With the help of the Internet, dynamic data is presented in a variety of ways in social news and science news. Common data types suitable for

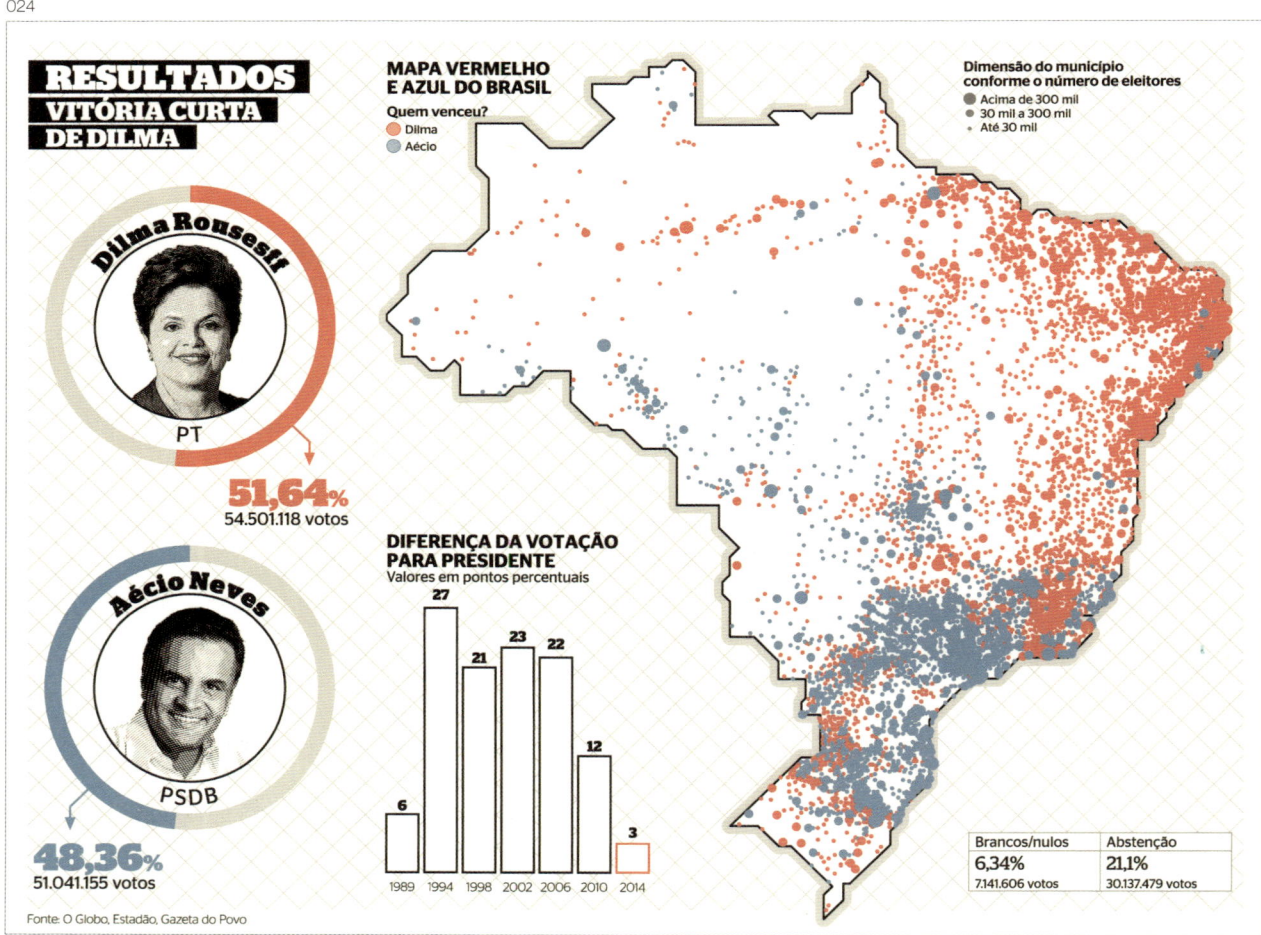

dynamic graphs are crime rates, traffic conditions, disaster casualties, and regional distribution of disease outbreaks.

Dynamic data is usually presented in multilevel and multidimensional dynamic graphs, based on descriptive diagrams and using a variety of presentation methods. One of the common methods is maps. For example, Figure 026 is the dynamic graph of the bicycle accident distribution in San Francisco, from which the readers can learn about the total bicycle accident numbers in some hot spots by clicking these spots. This data graph is a combination of multiple presentation methods such as a map, a scatter diagram, and a heat map.

When making data charts, news agencies and journalists inevitably set some frameworks and impose some subjective intentions to the objective data. For example, Figures 027 and 028 show the percentage of American families subscribing to daily and Sunday newspapers in the past 12 years, and the inevitable drop due to the emergence of the Internet. In Figure 027, the drop in subscriptions does not look significant. But when the vertical scale is narrowed to 30%–60% in Figure 028, the changes are made to appear much more dramatic. A journalist who wants to emphasize the changing media landscape might choose to use Figure 028.

The work of data journalists is scientific work to some extent, and the processing of the data has to follow some basic principles:

(1) Truthfulness
Journalists should ensure that data collection has been rigorous and authentic, and data sources should be formal and reliable.

(2) Integrity
In the process of presentation, description, and explanation, the integrity of the data should be maintained without overgeneralization.

(3) Rationality
The explanation of data correlation and causation should be scientific and rational, without misusing data correlations.

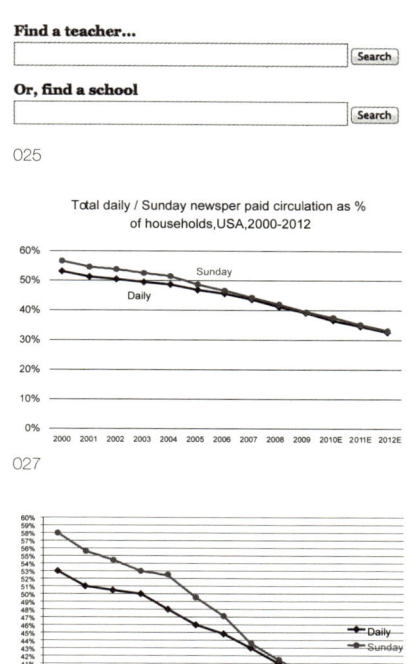

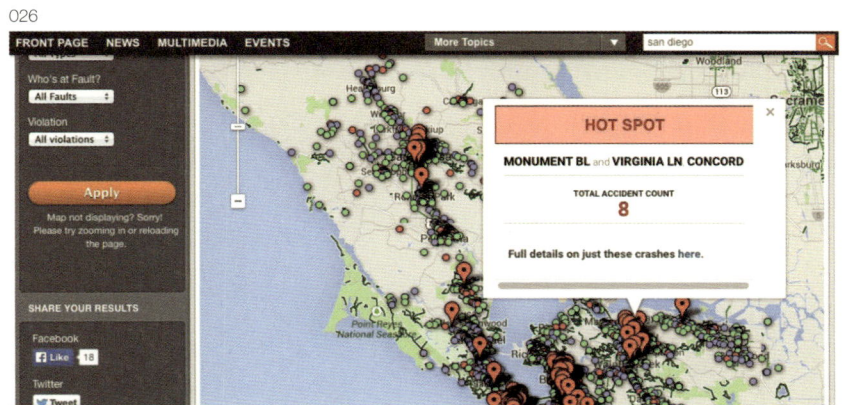

Case Studies

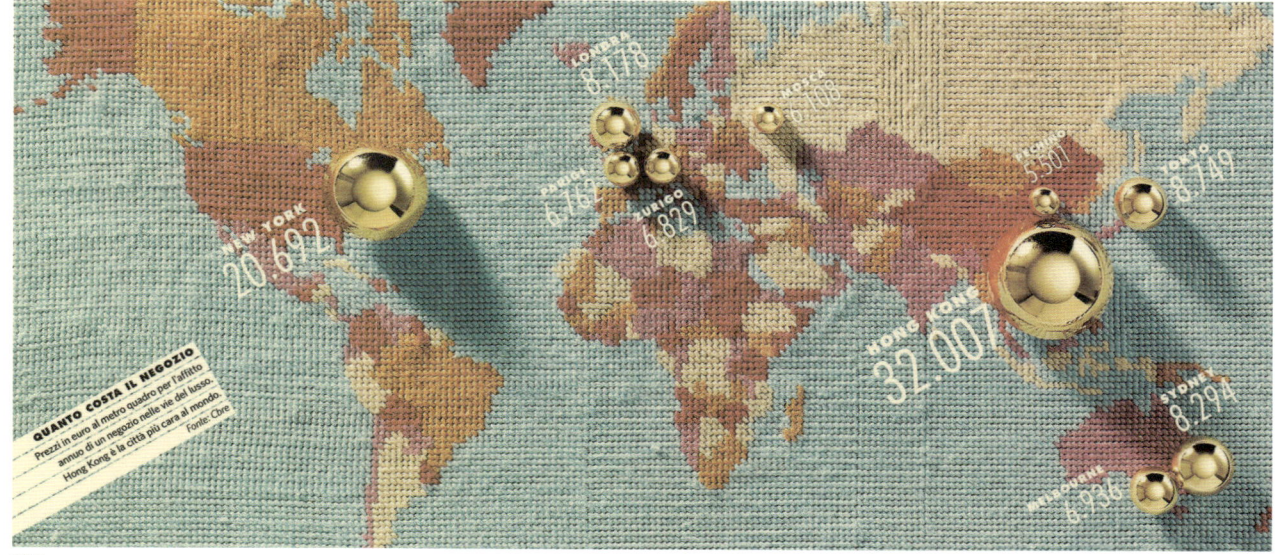

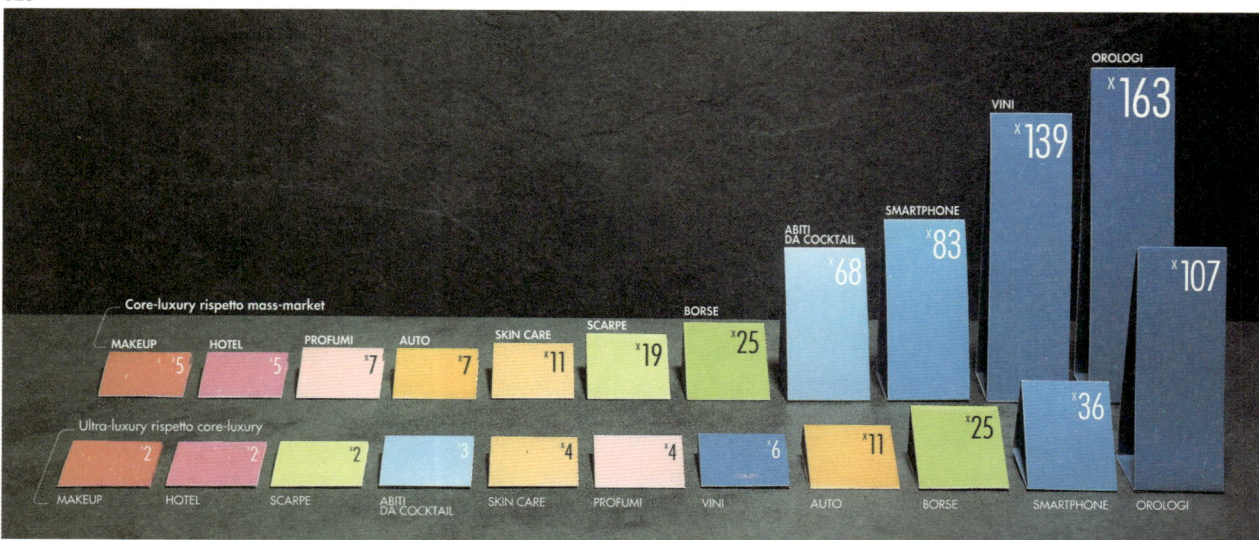

[029 – 037]
Client / *Moda24 – Il Sole 24 Ore*
Designers / Adriano Attus, Luca Pitoni,
Luisa Milanese, Federico Miletto
Completion / 2013

029

Rent Prices

Project Description /
The picture shows the prices in euros per square meter of renting a store in the luxury streets of the main cities. Hong Kong is the most expensive in the world. The map is entirely embroidered by hand.

030

Price Stretching

Project Description /
Prices are different for the same product category in three different segments: mass market, core luxury, and ultra luxury. On the first row, the designers use cards to show the price increases between core luxury and mass market, and the second row shows the price increases between ultra luxury and core luxury.

031

Italy—France

Project Description /
This project is a comparison of the total turnover and exports between the fashion industry systems in Italy and France. Those of Italy are three times the size of France. The composition of fabric ribbons, buttons, and wool balls gives a visual representation of the differences between the two countries.

032

Export

Project Description /
The graphic shows the top 12 export countries of Italian men's fashion (outerwear, knitwear, shirts, and so on) in the first six months of 2012. Europe remains stable, the United States shows a strong increase, and China begins to gain significance.

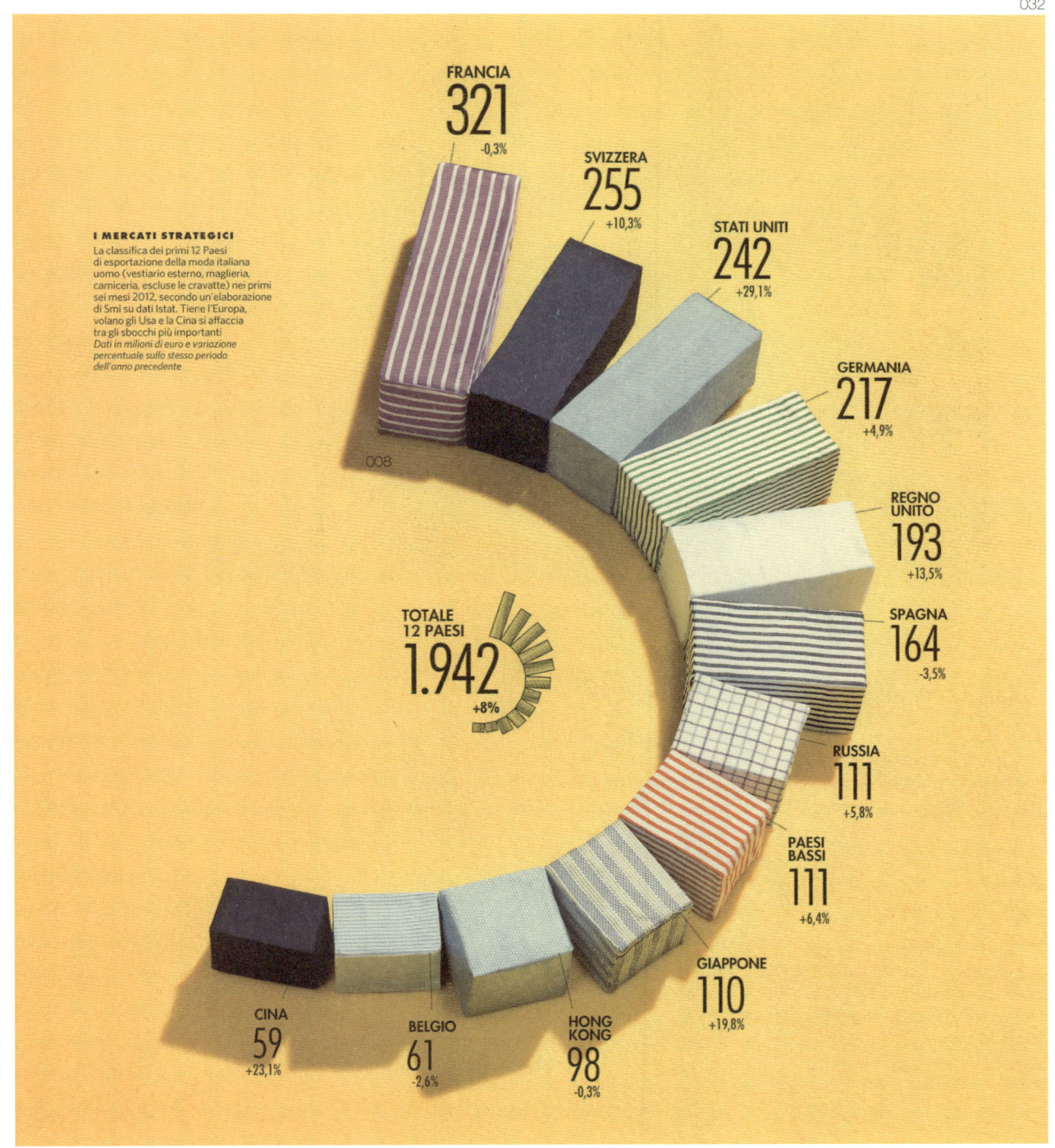

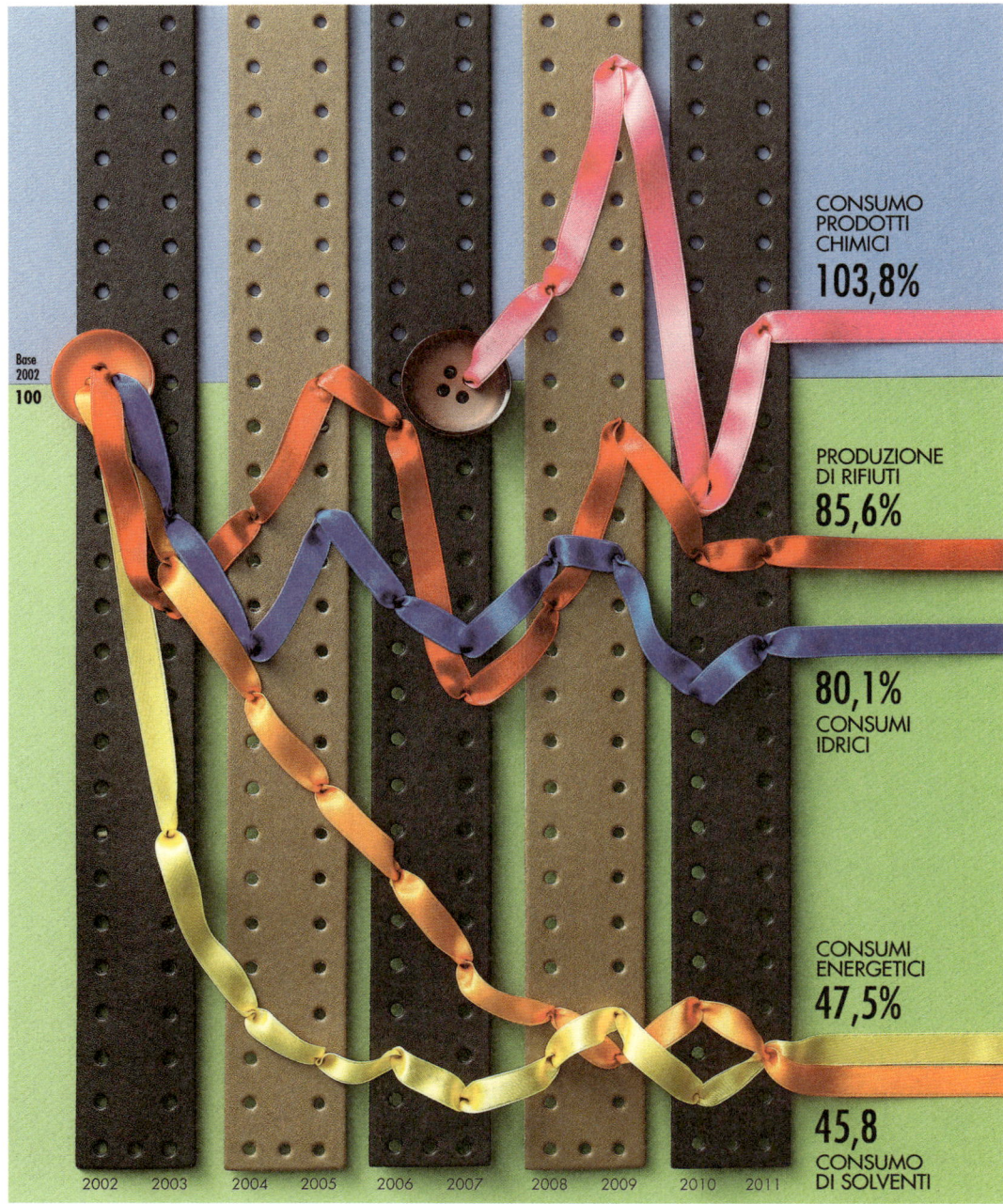

033

033
Tanning Industry

Project Description /
The graphic shows the changes in consumption and emissions of the Italian tanning industry from 2002 to 2011.

034
Leather goods

Project Description /
The designers use leather belts to demonstrate which countries have the greatest increases in imports of leather goods in the first 11 months of 2011. China is on the top of the list.

035
Shoes

Project Description /
The designers use shoelaces to show the countries that have the highest increases in imports of Italian shoes in the first 11 months of 2011. China is on the top of the list.

036
Jeanswear

Project Description /
The global sales of jeanswear equal €2 billion. Italy is the top exporter in the luxury field, but where does Italy export to? The pie chart (entirely made of actual denim) shows in detail the different foreign markets that import Italian jeanswear.

I MAGNIFICI SETTE DELLA PELLETTERIA
I paesi che hanno registrato i maggiori incrementi nell'export italiano nei primi 11 mesi del 2011
(Fonte: Aimpes)

CINA +98%
SINGAPORE +72%
OLANDA +71%
HONG KONG +61%
EMIRATI ARABI +51%
TURCHIA +50%
COREA +42%

CINA +85%
HONG KONG +47%
CANADA +31%
UCRAINA +27%
EMIRATI ARABI +27%
SVEZIA +24%
POLONIA +21%

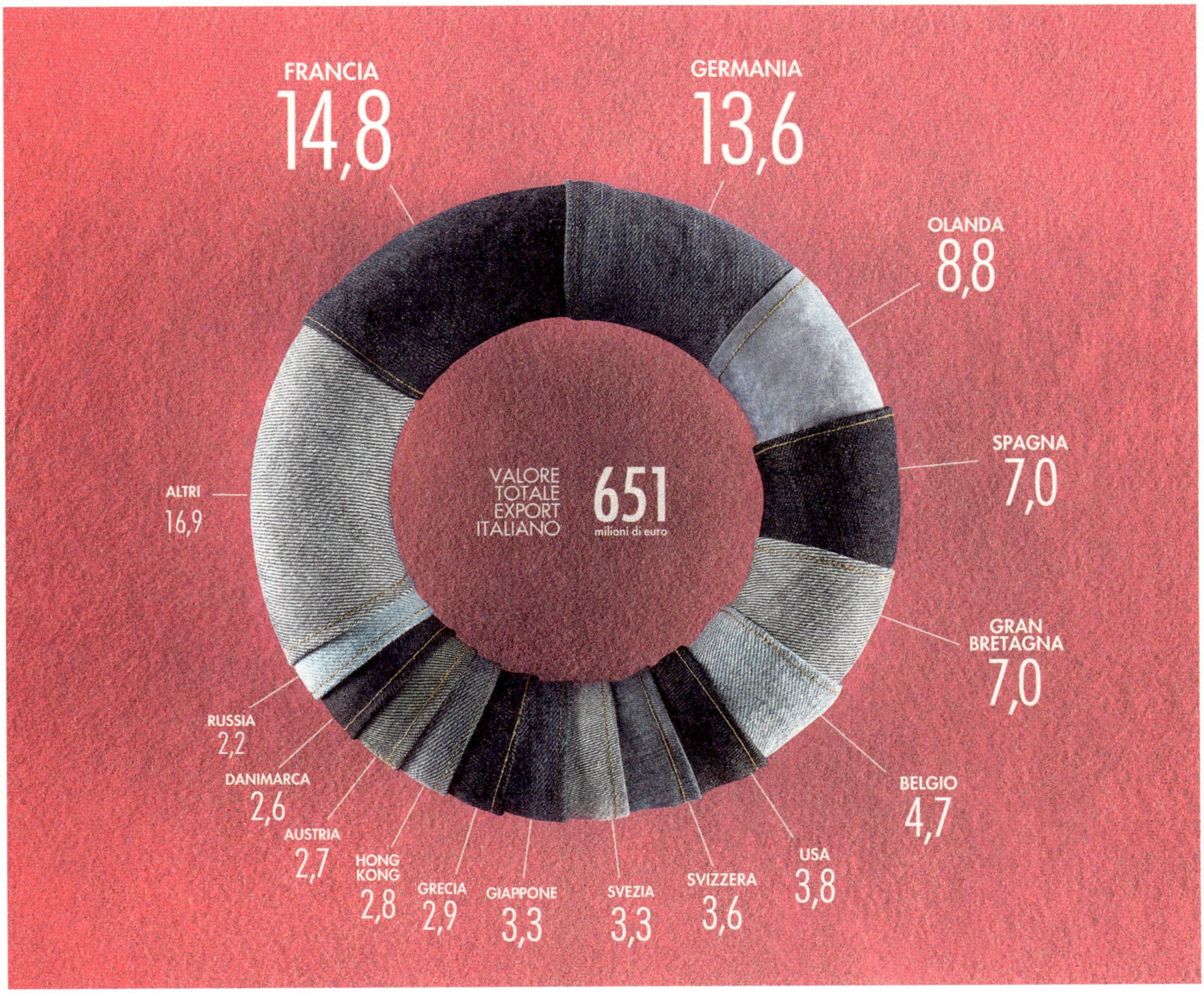

FRANCIA 14,8
GERMANIA 13,6
OLANDA 8,8
SPAGNA 7,0
GRAN BRETAGNA 7,0
BELGIO 4,7
USA 3,8
SVIZZERA 3,6
SVEZIA 3,3
GIAPPONE 3,3
GRECIA 2,9
HONG KONG 2,8
AUSTRIA 2,7
DANIMARCA 2,6
RUSSIA 2,2
ALTRI 16,9

VALORE TOTALE EXPORT ITALIANO
651 milioni di euro

Prices

Project Description /
The graphic shows 10 iconic fashion products and their prices in Europe, Hong Kong, and Shanghai. It can be seen from the price differential that the 'old continent' is the place for luxury shopping, in terms of prices.

Lenwood Volatility Control Index™

Project Description /
The volatility control index is a financial investment index designed to perform in various economic climates. The methodologies themselves were quite abstract and hard to explain easily. Likening the ideas and scenarios to horse tracks and horse racing was seen as a good analogy, using a more familiar and easily understood situation to explain the concepts. The illustrations are deliberately simplistic and blocky, so as not to distract the reader away from the text.

Client / Index Methodologies
Design Agency / RussellTate.Com
Designer / Russell Tate
Completion / 2014

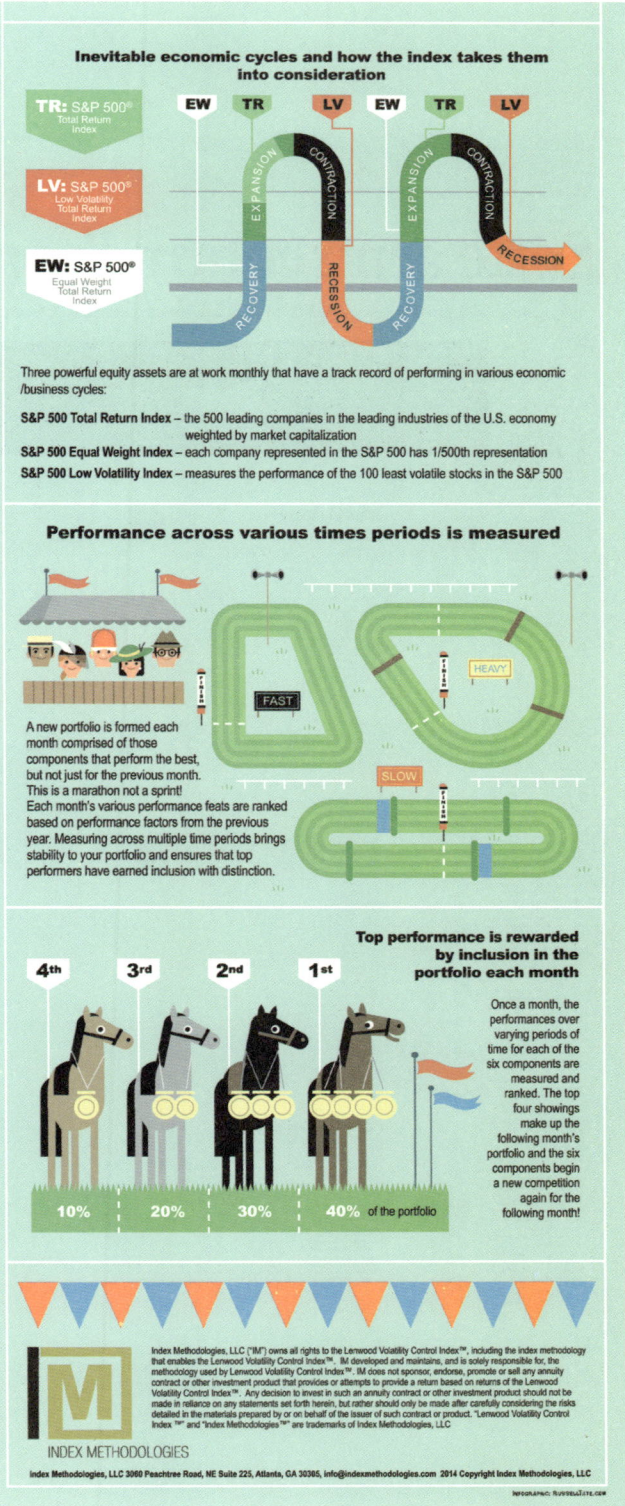

Seven Tools to Fight Tax Evasion

Project Description /
The 'Revenue radar' includes and describes seven tools that the government can use to check for tax evaders. Changes, working principles, and expected revenue are highlighted for each tool, showing the different levels of the same subjects and the same professional categories.

The Calendar of Italian New House Property Taxation

Project Description /
The path shows the increase of house taxation for homeowners in Italy. Deadlines and tax rates are defined along the route, using six different colors for different types of property to guide the reader through the tax information.

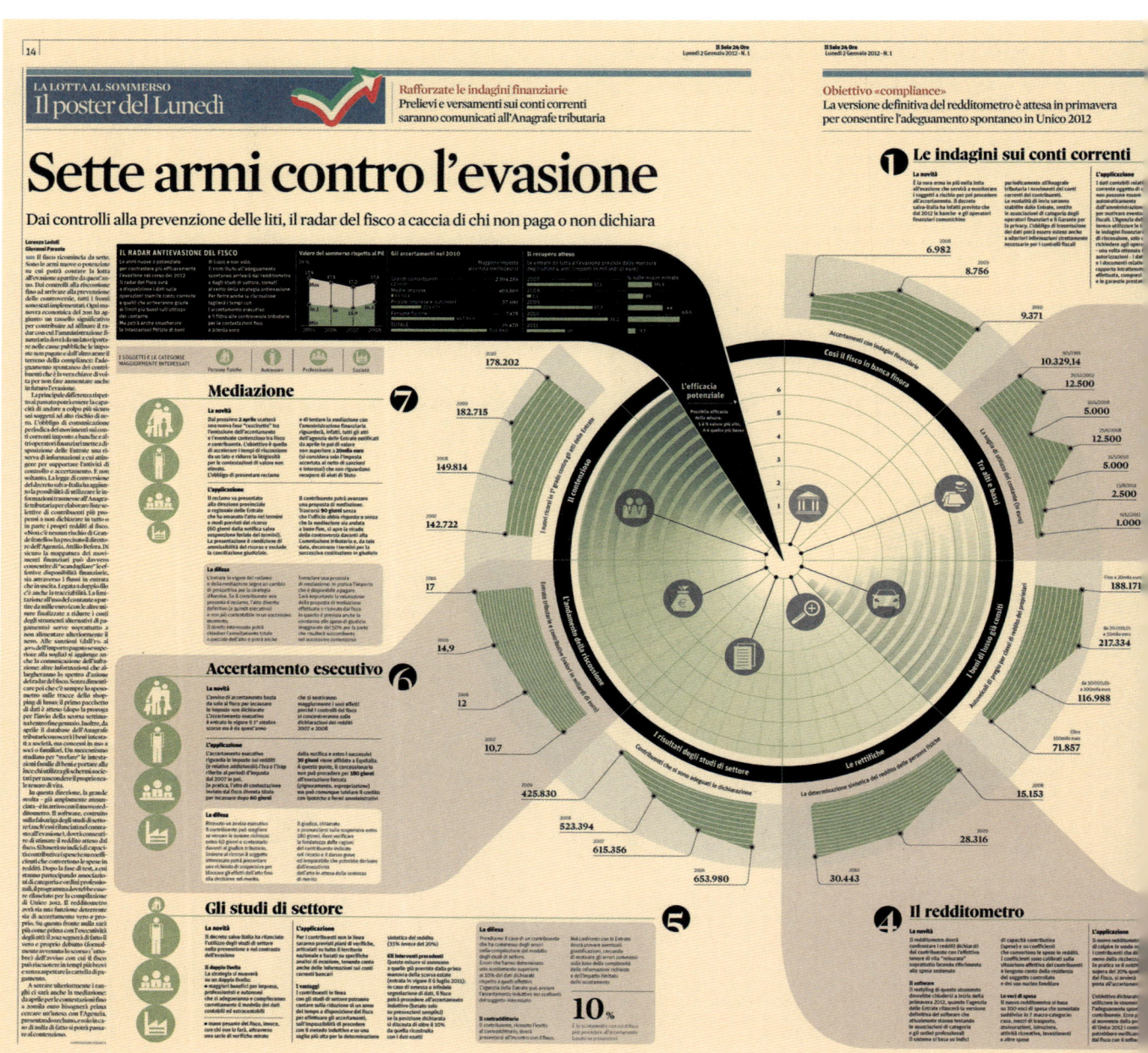

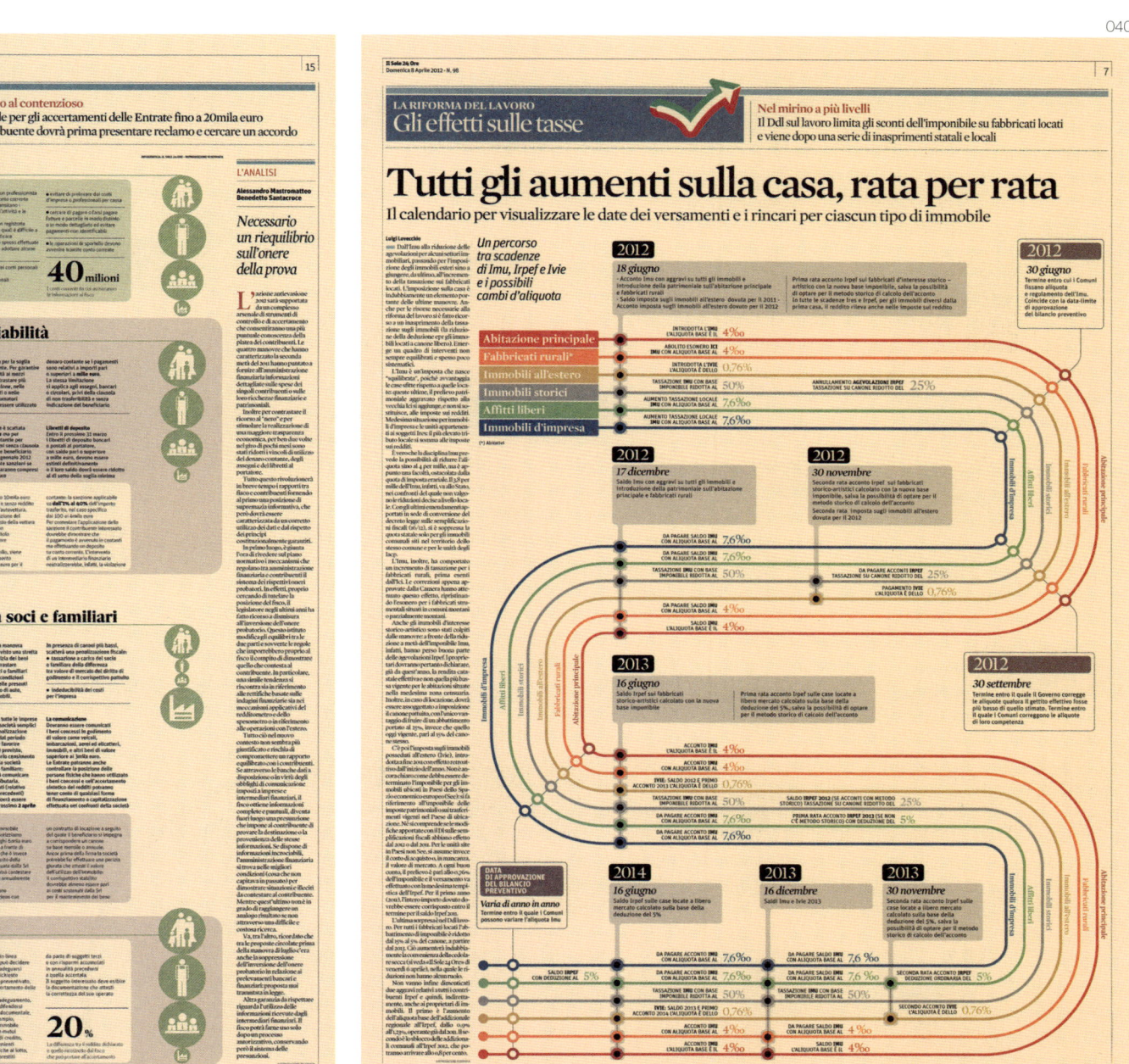

[039 — 040]

Client / *Lunedì – Il Sole 24 Ore*
Designers / Adriano Attus, Federico Barbara, Fulvio D'Angelo, Renato Nonno
Completion / 2012

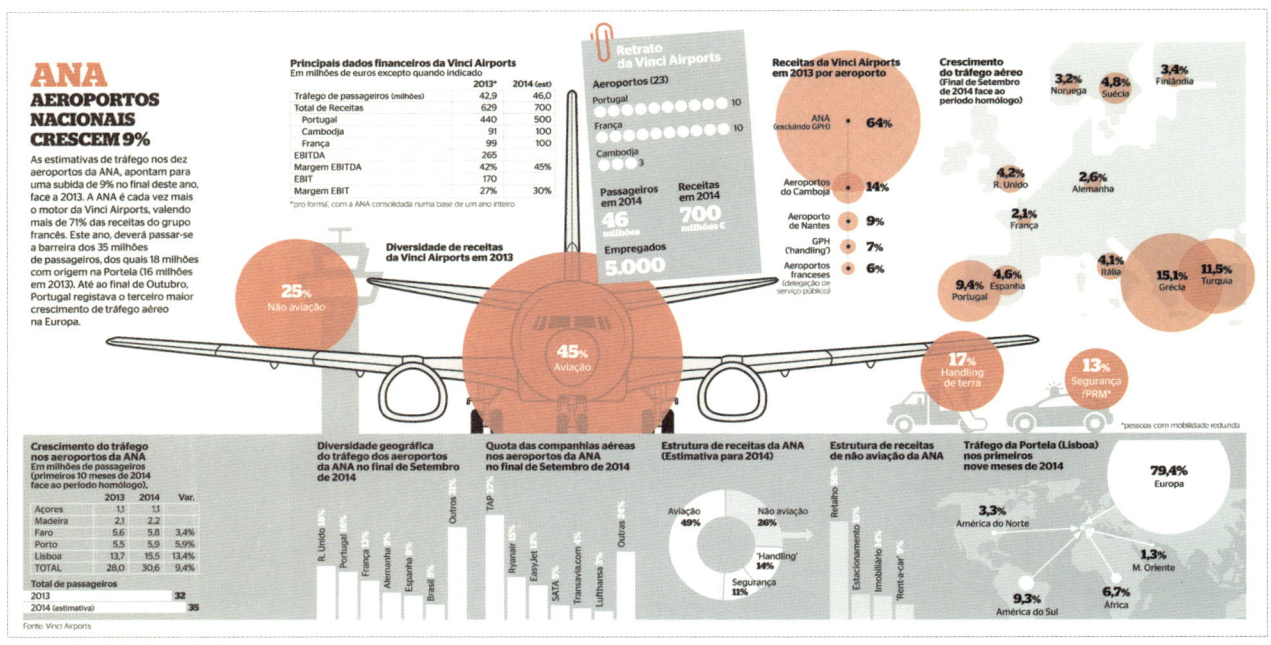
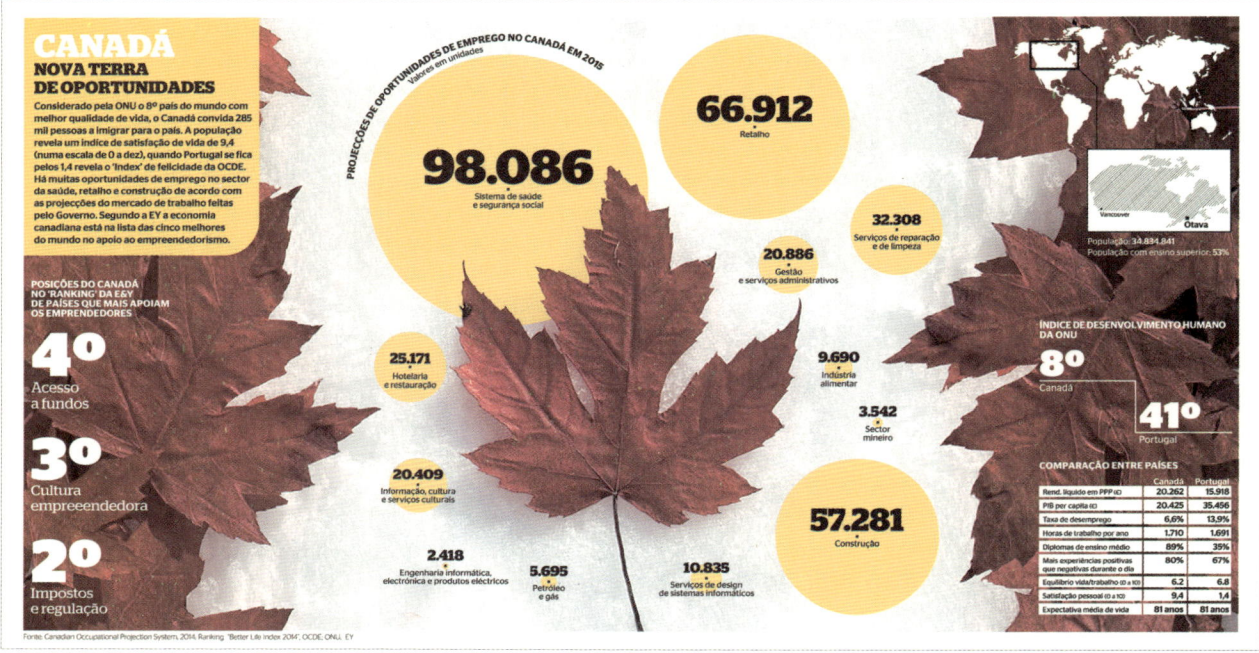
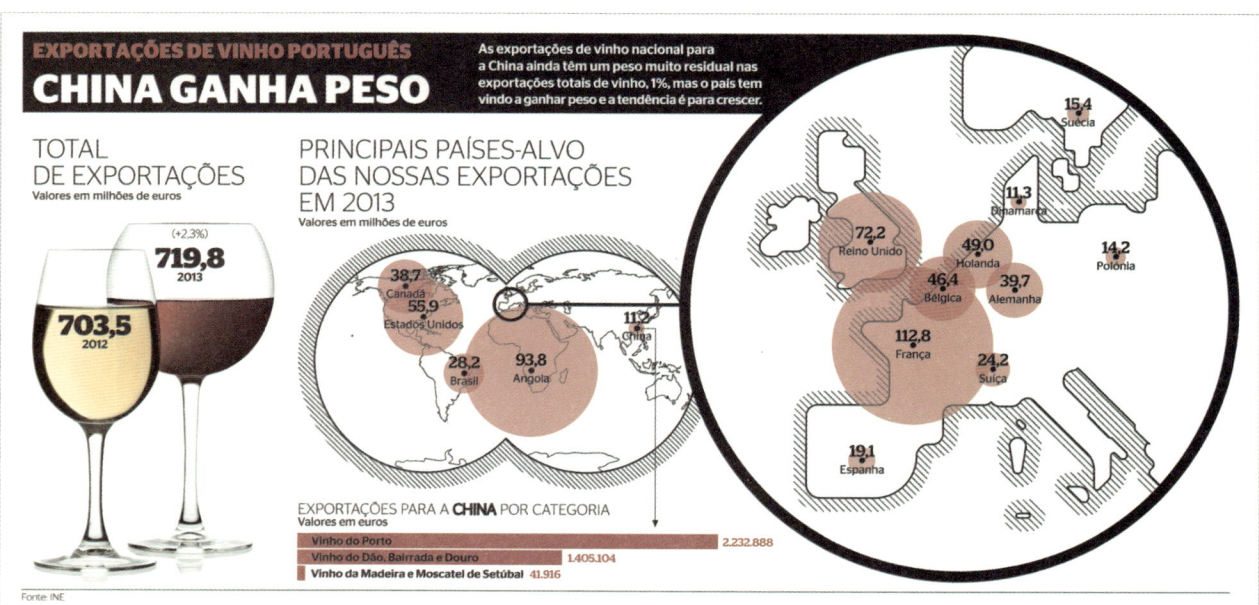

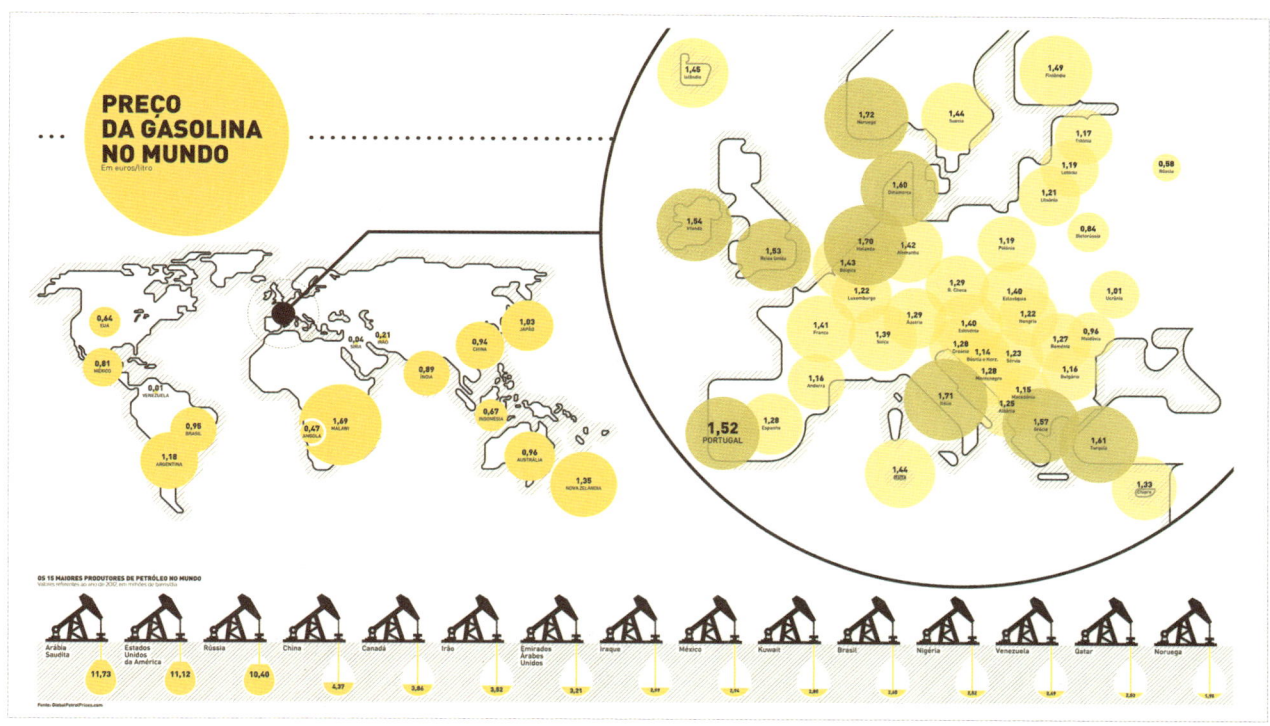

041
ANA—National Airports Grows 9%

Project Description /
This infographic, published the day after the figures were presented, uses a two-color scheme. It is about the aviation business and airports in Portugal. The amount of information included is so great that a simplistic style was used so that the reader would not lose interest. The gray and red create a good contrast effect between the background and the information requiring more prominence. A very simple vector plane shows key information, and a horizontal bar differentiates the information.

042
Canada: New Land of Opportunity

Project Description /
This infographic uses an elaborate graphic concept for the background with beautiful maple leaves (the symbol on the Canadian flag). The main information, the number of employment opportunities provided in 2015 in Canada, is shown in the center of the infographic. The margins of the 'flag' show some secondary information: rankings, comparison between countries, and a simple locator map. Once again, there are one or two colors in the whole infographic.

043
Exports of Portuguese Wine

Project Description /
This infographic shows the enormous range of prices of gasoline in many countries around the world, with a focus on Europe. The ranking of the world's biggest oil producers is shown as secondary information. The design concept is very minimalistic, trying to convey the information rapidly to the reader. The work was published at a time when the prices of the raw materials were very low, and this was not reflected in the price to consumers of gasoline in Portugal.

044
Gasoline Prices in the World

Project Description /
In this infographic, the designer tried to show the enormous range of prices of gasoline in a large number of countries around the world, with a focus on Europe. He also used the rankings of the world's biggest oil producers as secondary information. The design concept used is very minimalistic, intended to pass the information rapidly to the reader. The work was published at a time that the prices of the raw materials were very low, but this was not reflected in the prices of gasoline for consumers in Portugal.

[041 – 044]
Client / *Diário Económico*
Designer / Mário Malhão
Completion / 2014

045

Emanuel—Story About Fair Trade Coffee

Project Description /
This infographic presents data on coffee drinking habits. Designer Kata Kerekes wanted to make the design more personal, so she used real data and presented it from the perspective of a coffee-bean picker.

Client / Kulturgorilla
Design Agency / CYKLOPS
Designer / Kata Kerekes
Completion / 2013

046

World Currency

Project Description /
The infographic shows the total economy of the world and the total amount of money (in US dollars) and gold in the world as of March 2013. There are almost 182 currencies officially used in the world. The graphic shows the top 10 most valuable currencies in terms of US dollars, starting from the Kuwaiti dinar to the Cayman Island dollar. It also shows the least valuable currencies of the world, from the Iranian rial to the Zambian kwacha. The infographic gives detailed information on the 10 most commonly used currencies in the world, and compares exchange rates in dollars and Indian rupees.

047

Indian Television

Project Description /
With 176 million analogue and digital television broadcast subscribers, India is the second-largest market in the world, after China. The infographic gives detailed information of Indian television history, consumer numbers and the production of Bollywood movies. All the figures given are accurate as of March 2013.

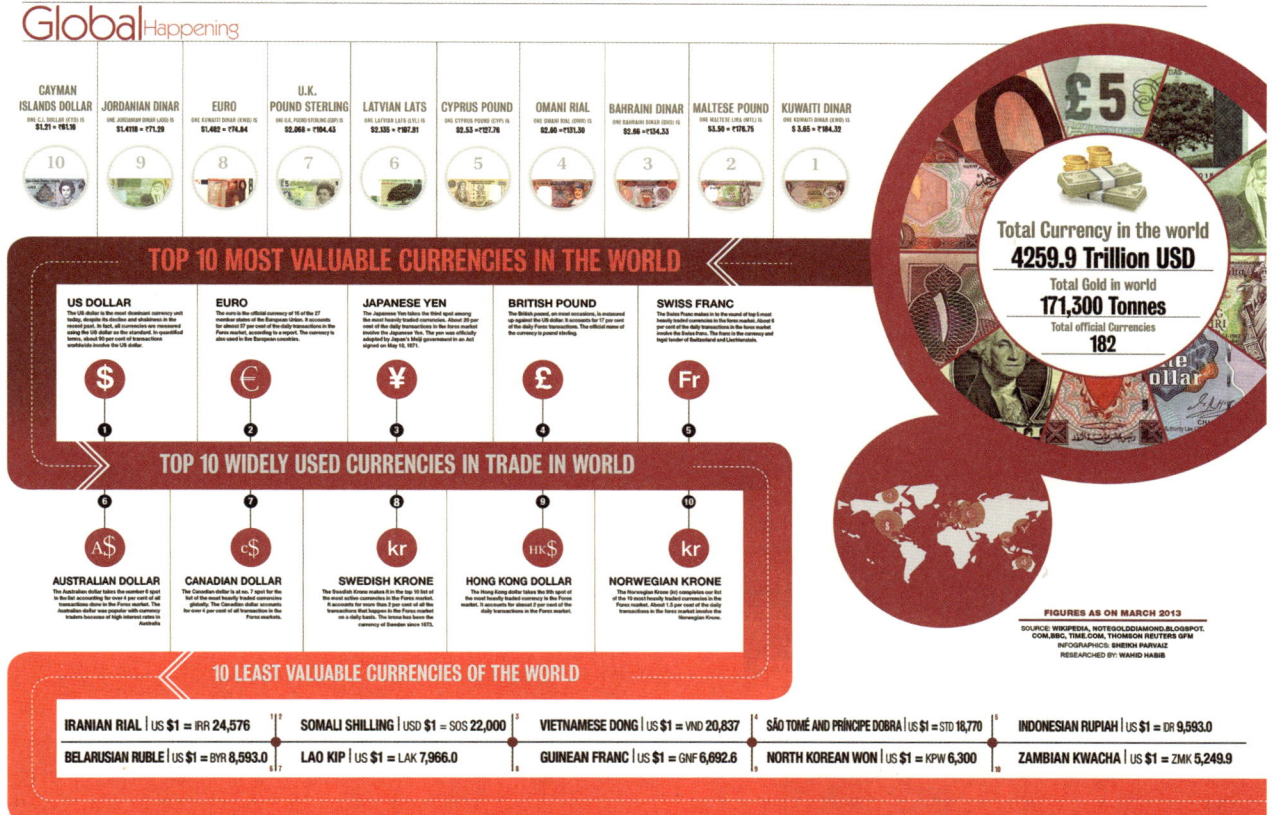

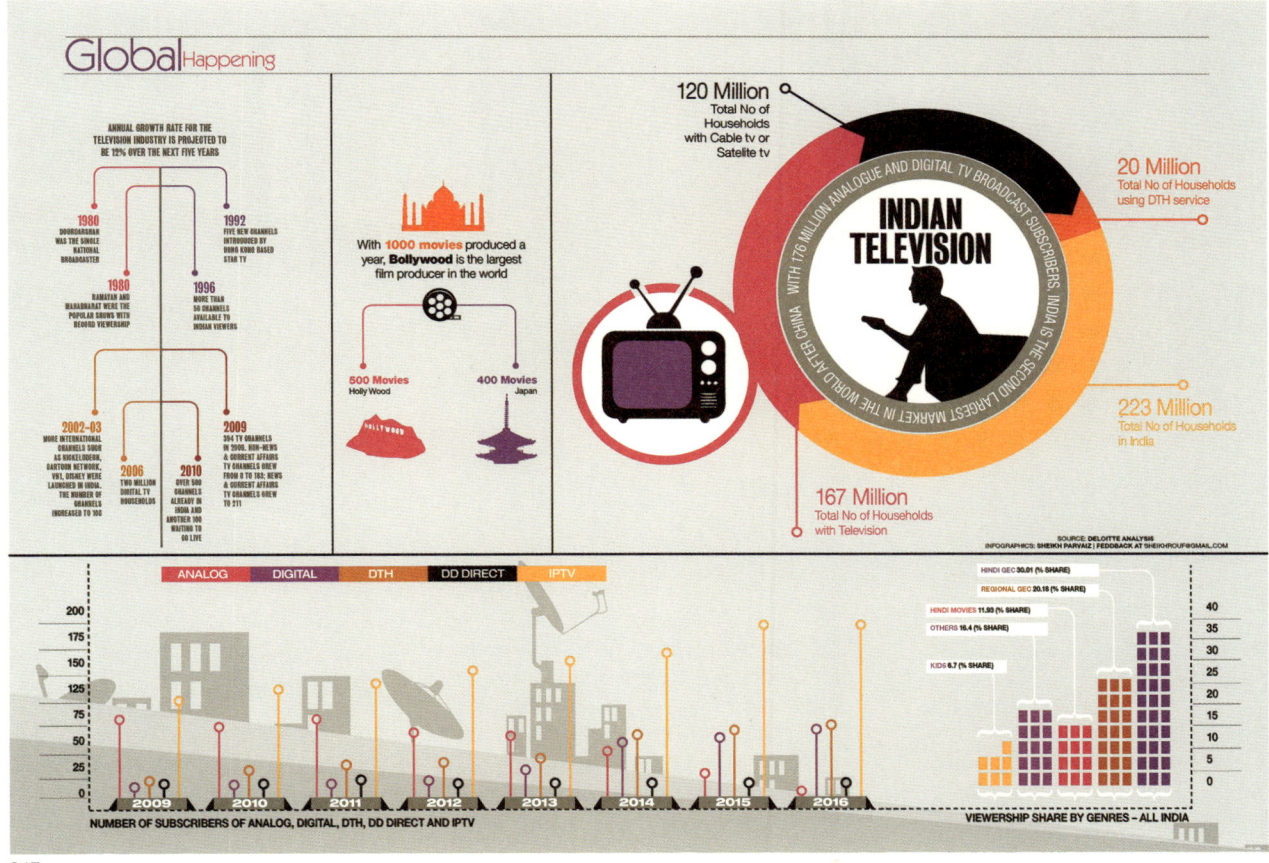

[046 – 047]

Client / *The Counsellor* magazine
Designer / Sheikh Parvaiz Ahmad
Completion / 2013

[048 — 050]

Client / *Business Today*, *India Today* Group
Design Agency / Visual Best
Designer / Santosh Kushwaha
Completion / 2012—2013

048

Less Taxing

Project Description /

Santosh Kushwaha composed the data using tax-related graphic elements, creating an attractive, easy-to-understand infographic.

049

The Golden Goose

Project Description /

The project is all about the demand for gold, its high prices, and how prices declined over the months. In emerging economies, including India and China, the slowdown has hurt consumer demand for gold. The title of the project was very interesting, and was incorporated into the visual representation. The initial plan was to create all graphics using gold elements, but it did not turn out looking as expected. Instead, the simple vector graphic is used with gold elements, so it doesn't look cluttered. The designer always tries to make the graphic look clean and easy to understand.

050

Eating Up Funds

Project Description /

The graphic is all about the National Food Security Bill and how it affects the final prices to the consumer. Considering the serious nature of the subject, designer Santosh Kushwaha uses strong graphics along with grain pictures, creating unique visuals.

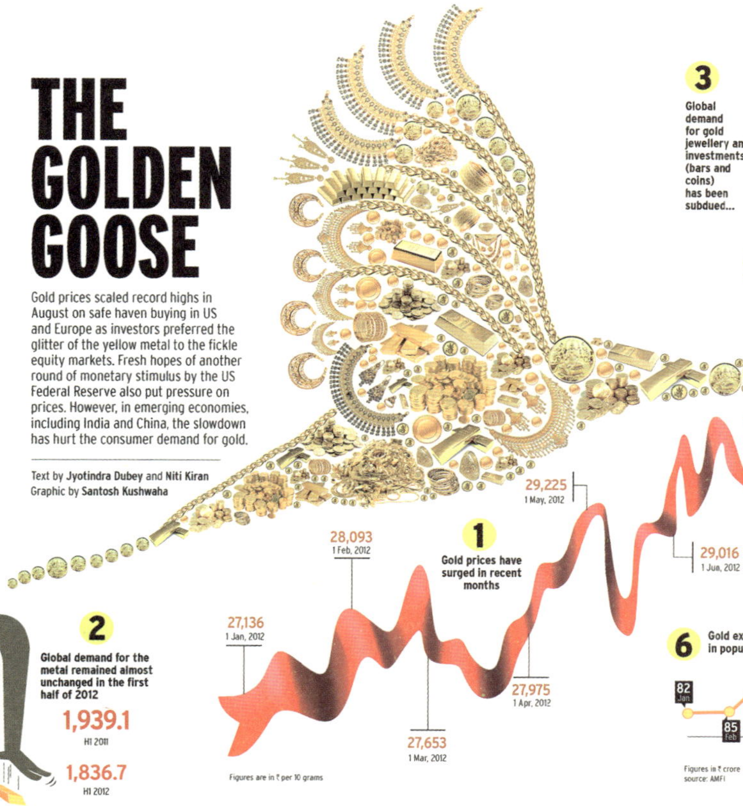

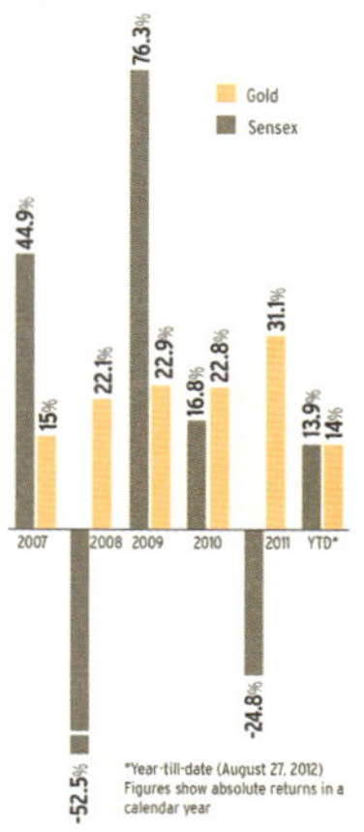

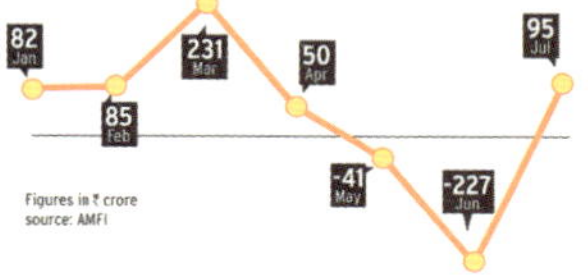

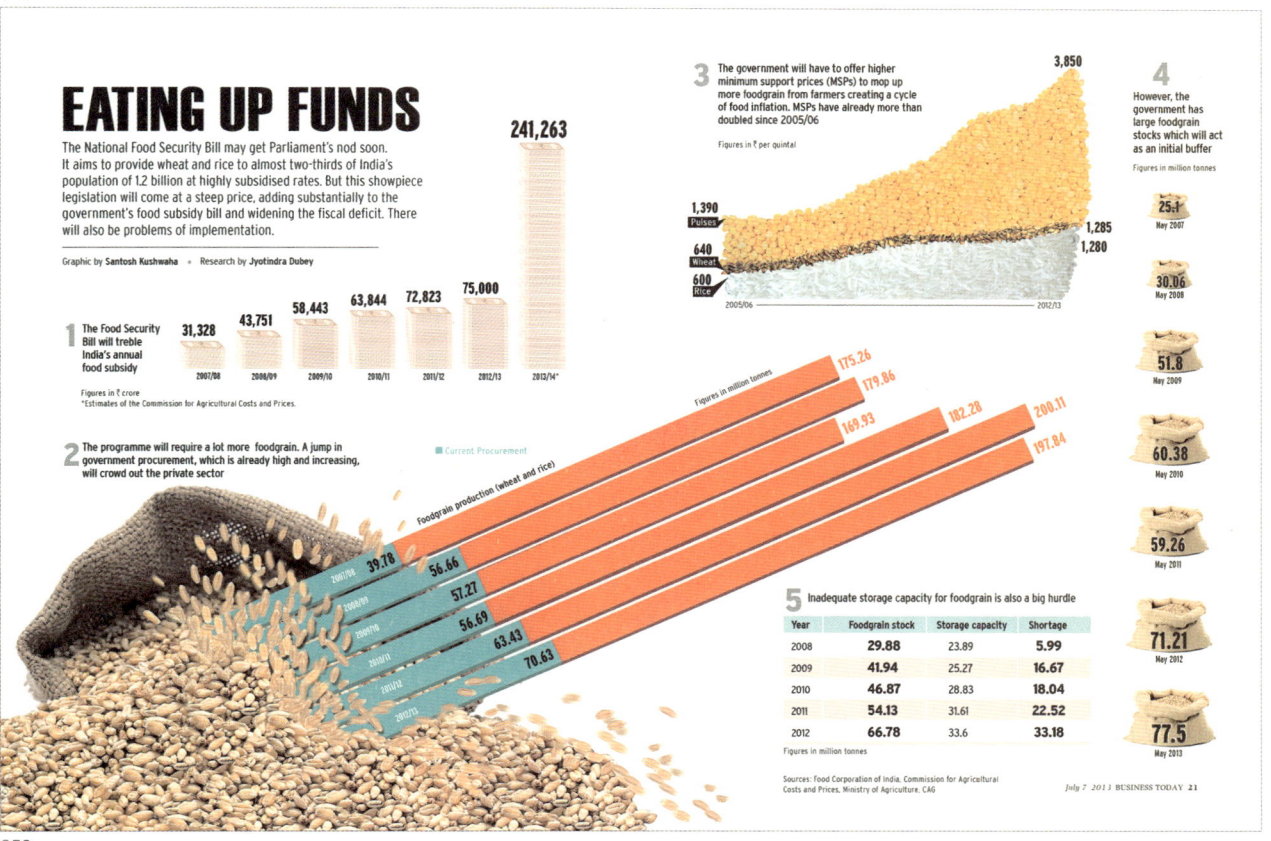

051

Gas Tariffs

Project Description /
The infographic displays the scheme of extraction, import, transportation, trade, and delivery of natural gas in Ukraine. The complex graph is supported with the exact gross and net prices of gas (extraction, trade, consumption by different consumers). The infographic aims to inform readers that current gas tariffs for the public are very low, and need to be increased to help pull Ukraine out of debt.

Client / *Vox Ukraine*
Designer / Oleksandr Guzenko
Completion / 2015

052

Top Mortgages in the Spanish Market

Project Description /
The infographic lists the most advantageous mortgages in the Spanish market at the time of the first economic improvements after the last financial crisis. It displays the names of the financial products and the names of the financial institutions offering them. It shows the different conditions of each loan, such as interest rates and terms. It also shows particular requirements, such as the need to acquire other products along with the loan.

This kind of information could have been displayed in a simple table. In order to make it more attractive for the reader, the graphic representation of a house was used. The advantage is that it used a grid to arrange the content in an organized manner, while including ornamental details, such as furniture, the bird, the tree, the chimney smoke, the flower or the family's car and bike in the garage, without interfering with the content.

Client / Spanish financial newspaper *Cinco Dias*
Designer / Alejandro Meraviglia-Crivelli Roche
Completion / 2014

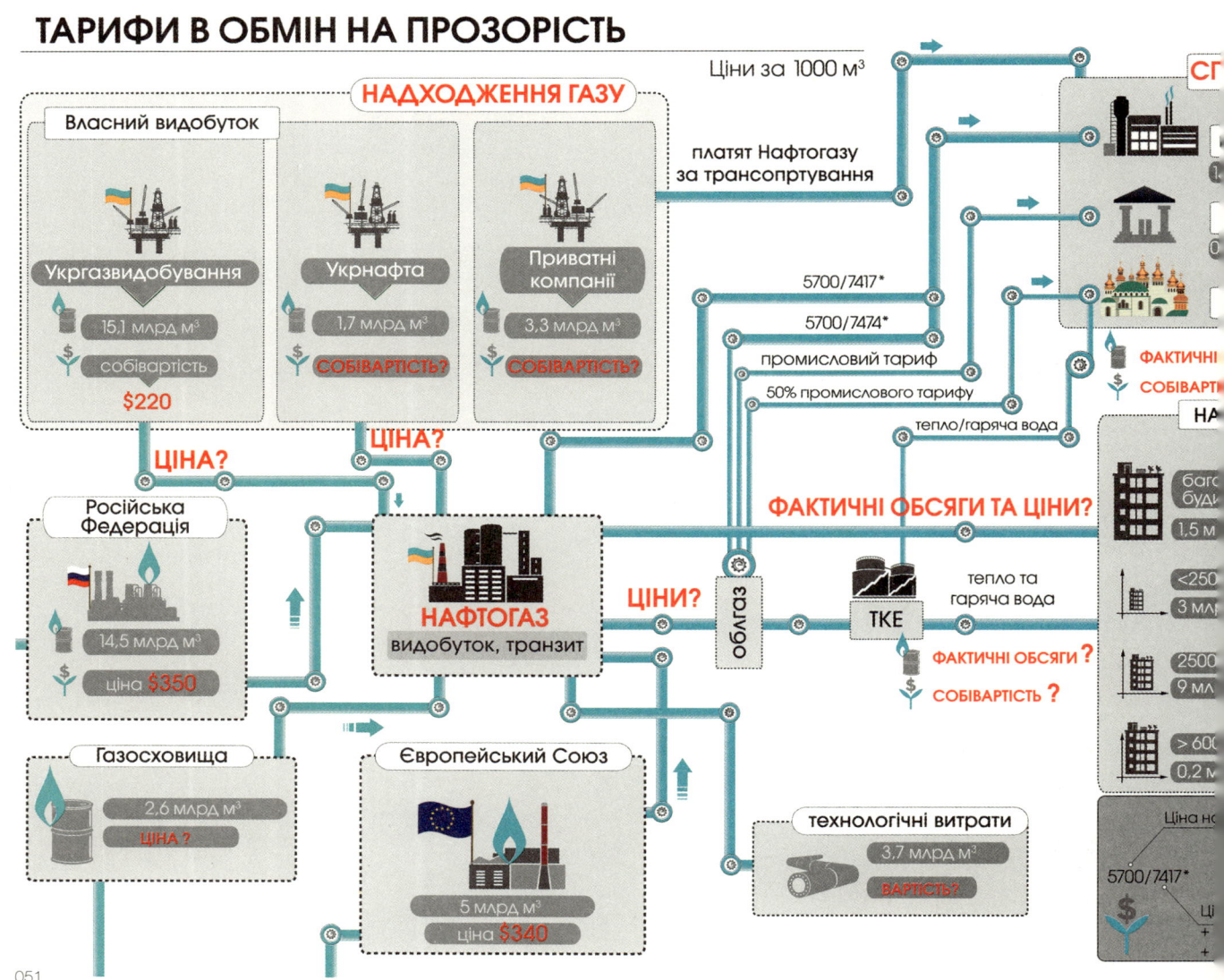

051

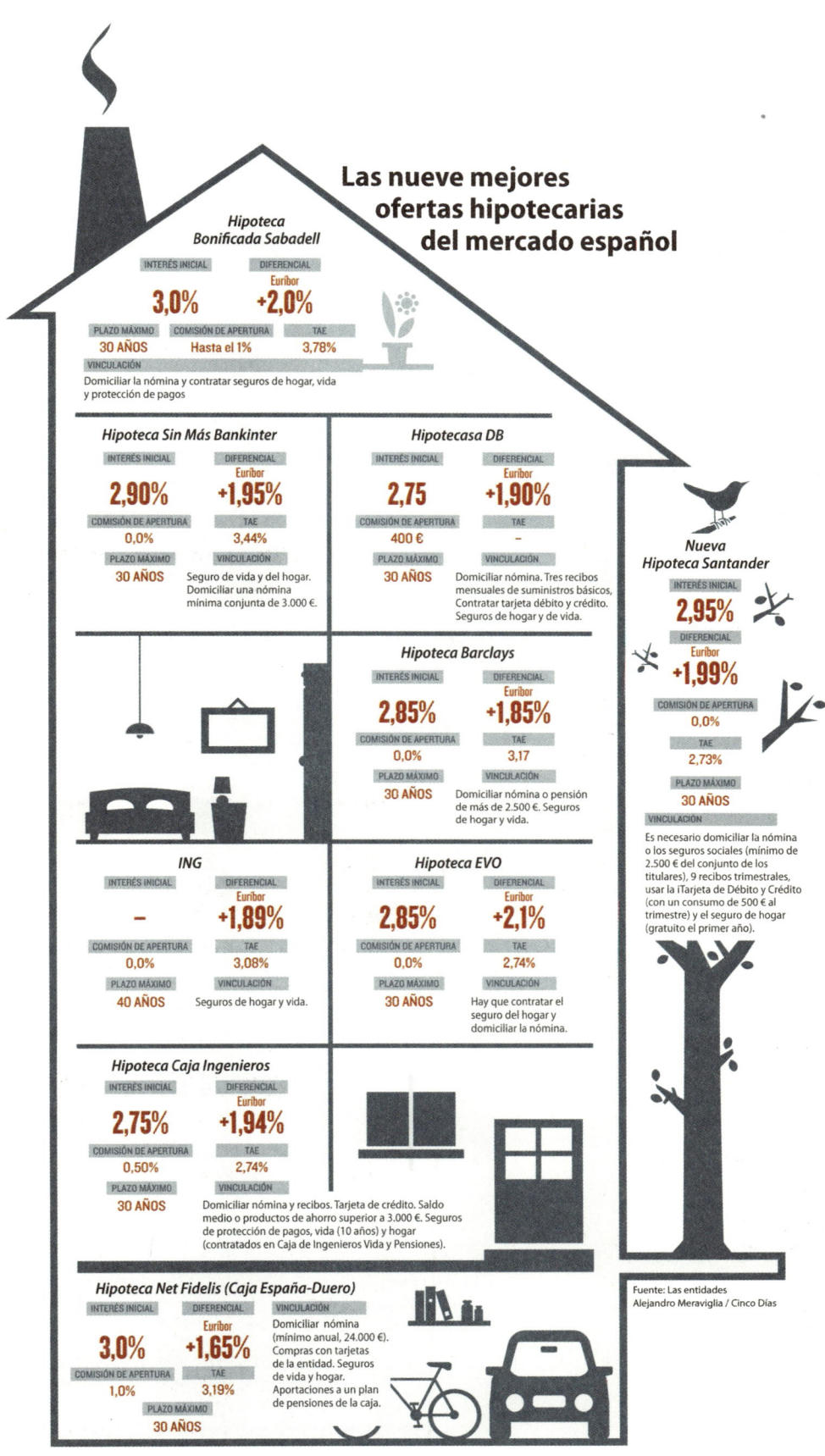

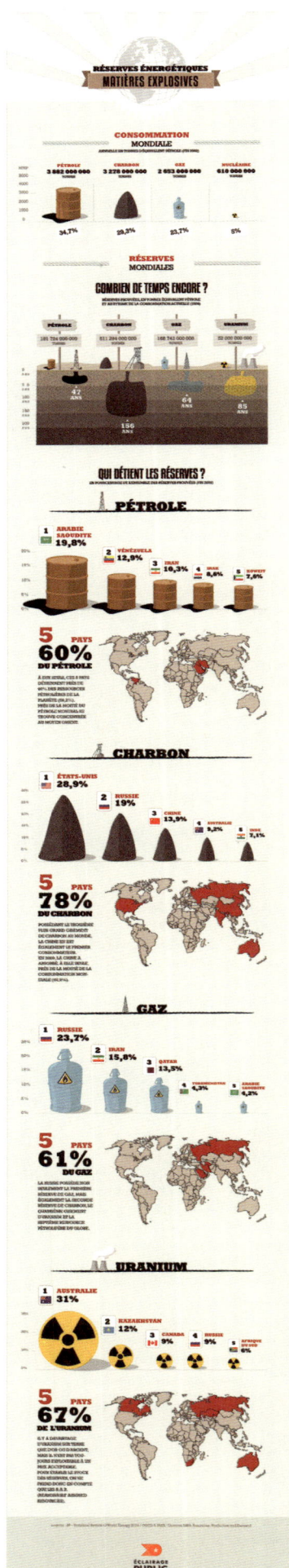

053-1

053
Global Energy Reserves

Project Description /
How much oil, coal, gas, and uranium does the world consume per year? What are our reserves? Where are they located? Who owns them? How long can we hold out with these stocks? In this infographic, ÉCLAIRAGE PUBLIC undertook to enlighten readers on a very important but sensitive subject.

Design Agency / ÉCLAIRAGE PUBLIC
Designer / Nicolas Verrier

054
Palm Oil

Project Description /
Palm oil is a hot topic. It is accused, among other things, of increasing cardiovascular risk. Yet it is found hidden in many preparations of the food industry. Where is palm oil produced? Where does it come from? In what products is it used? What is the key to its success? And what problems does it really pose? Everything you need to know about palm oil is in a single image.

Design Agency / ÉCLAIRAGE PUBLIC
Designer / Nicolas Verrier
Completion / 2012

053-2

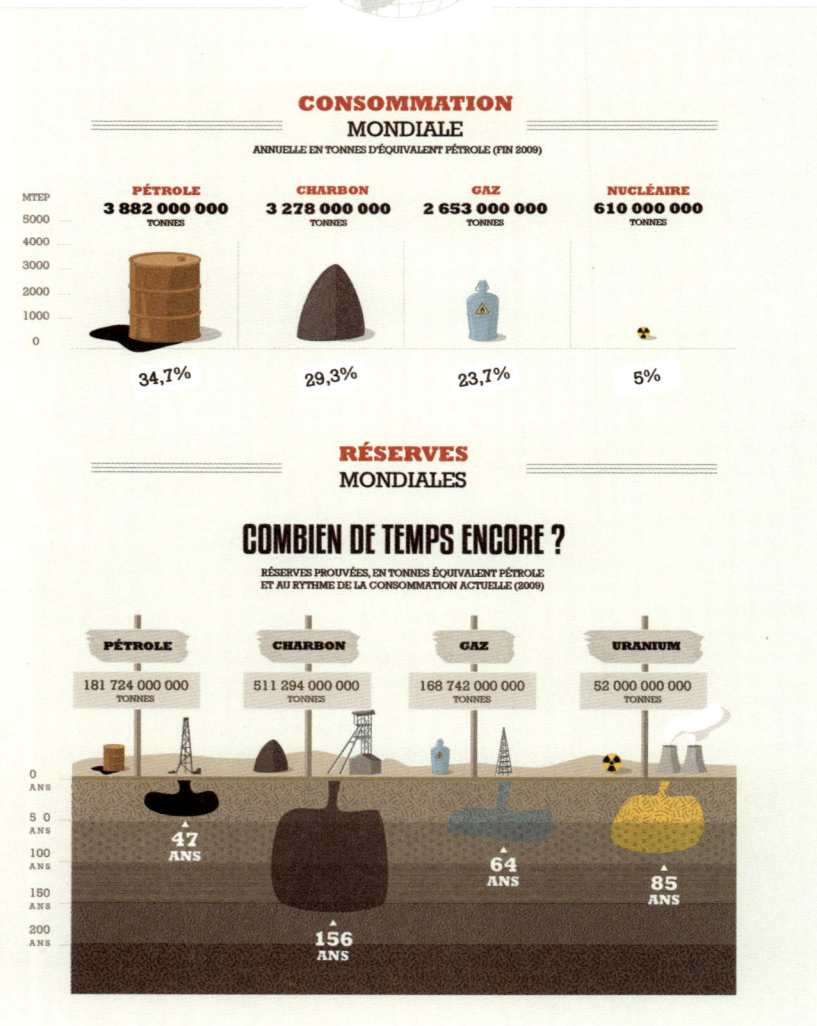

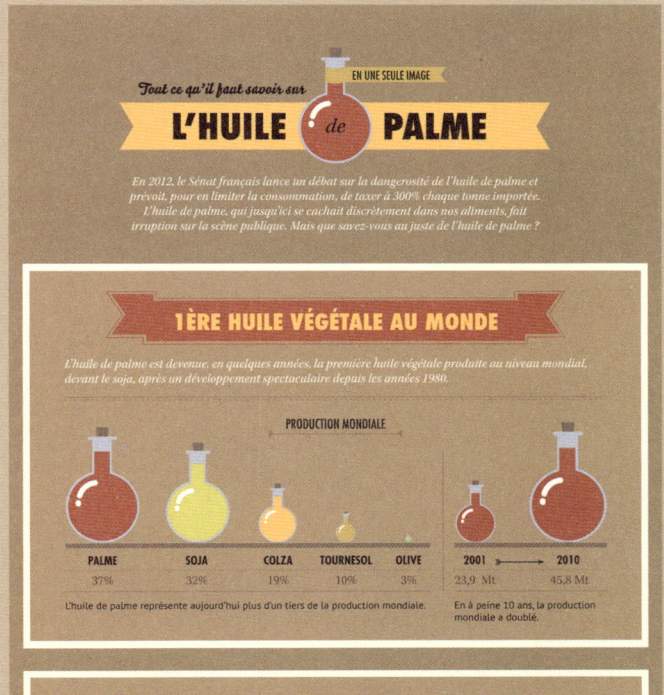
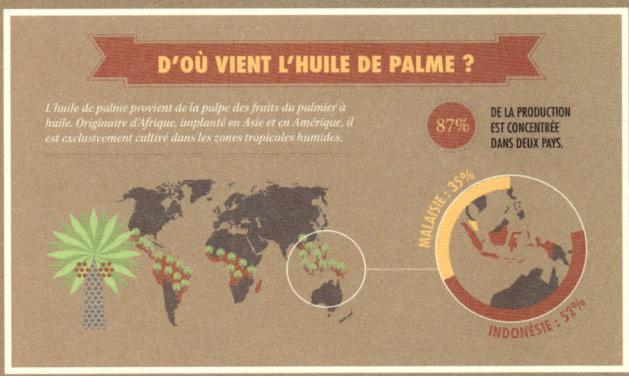

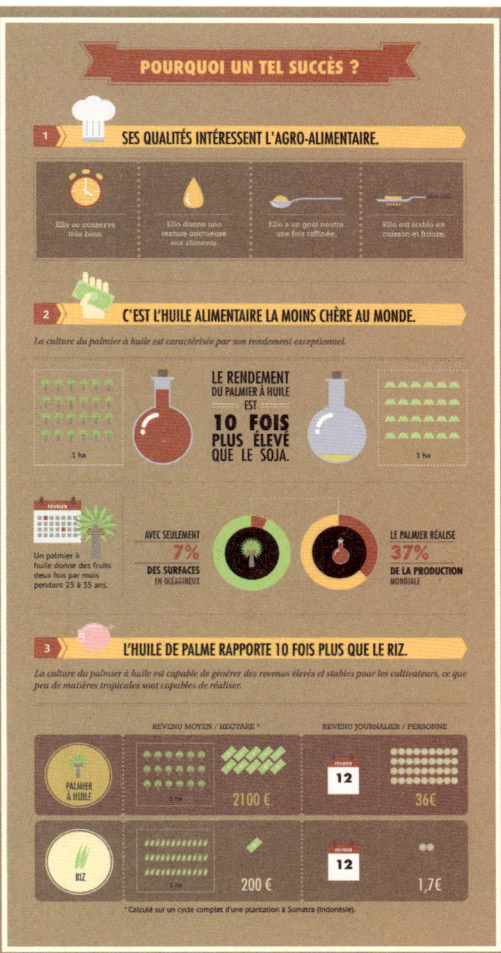
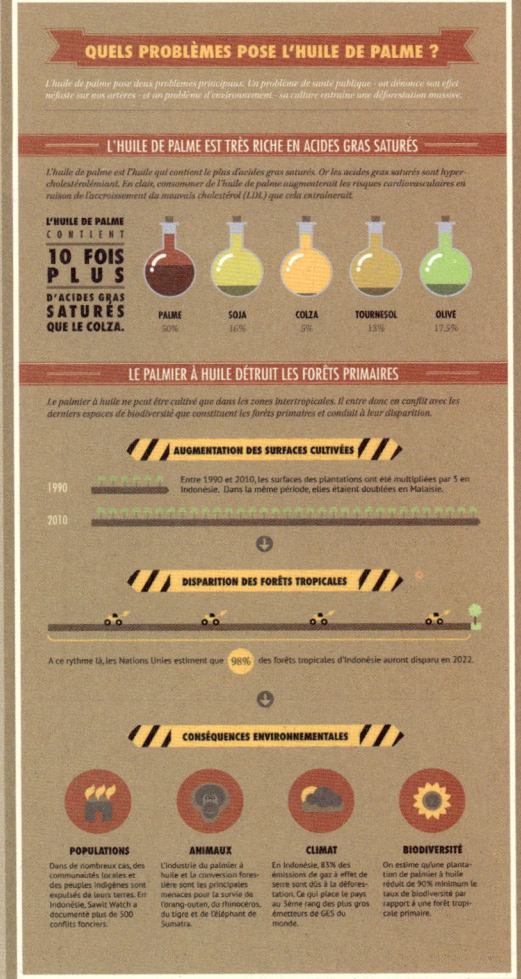

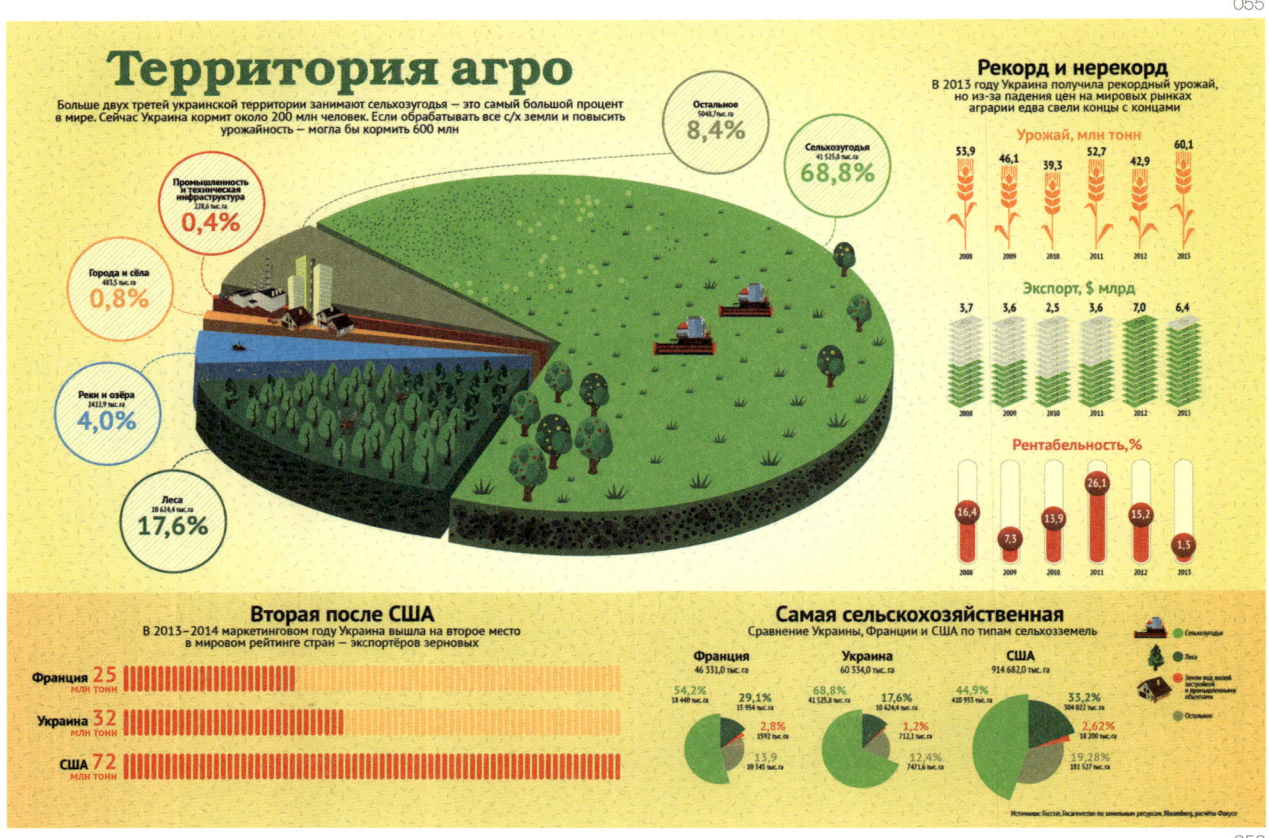

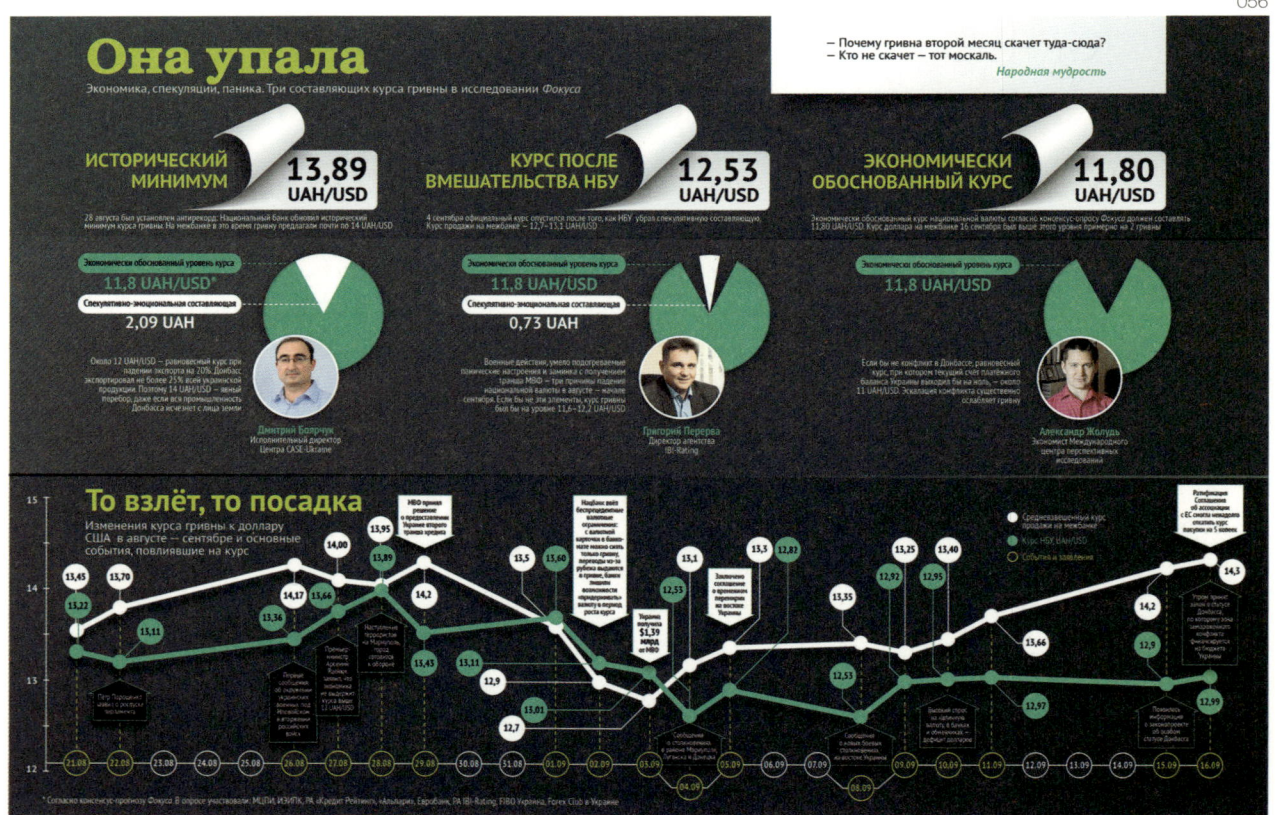

[055 – 056]

Client / *Focus* magazine
Design Agency / Focus Media LLC
Designer / Lizaveta Bukreeva
Completion / 2014

055
Agrarian Sector

Project Description /
    The project demonstrates how the territory of Ukraine is divided into several land types: agricultural lands, forests, rivers and lakes, cities and villages, industrial buildings, and so on. It shows a comparison of three countries—Ukraine, the United States and France—and represents the types of farmlands and the quantities of exported grain for each nation.

056
Course

Project Description /
The project shows the Ukrainian national currency (Hryvnya), its exchange rate to the US dollar in August and September 2014, and the main events that influenced its course.

057
Agribusiness is Rising in Angola

Project Description /
    Agricultural output is of major importance to the Angolan economy, and its ongoing development is represented in this infographic. The data shows that the demand for domestic production has increased, and new investors, businesses and industries have played an important role in the country's development.

Client / *Expansão* magazine
Design Agency / M Infographics, Illustration & Design
Designer / Marta Carvalho
Completion / 2014

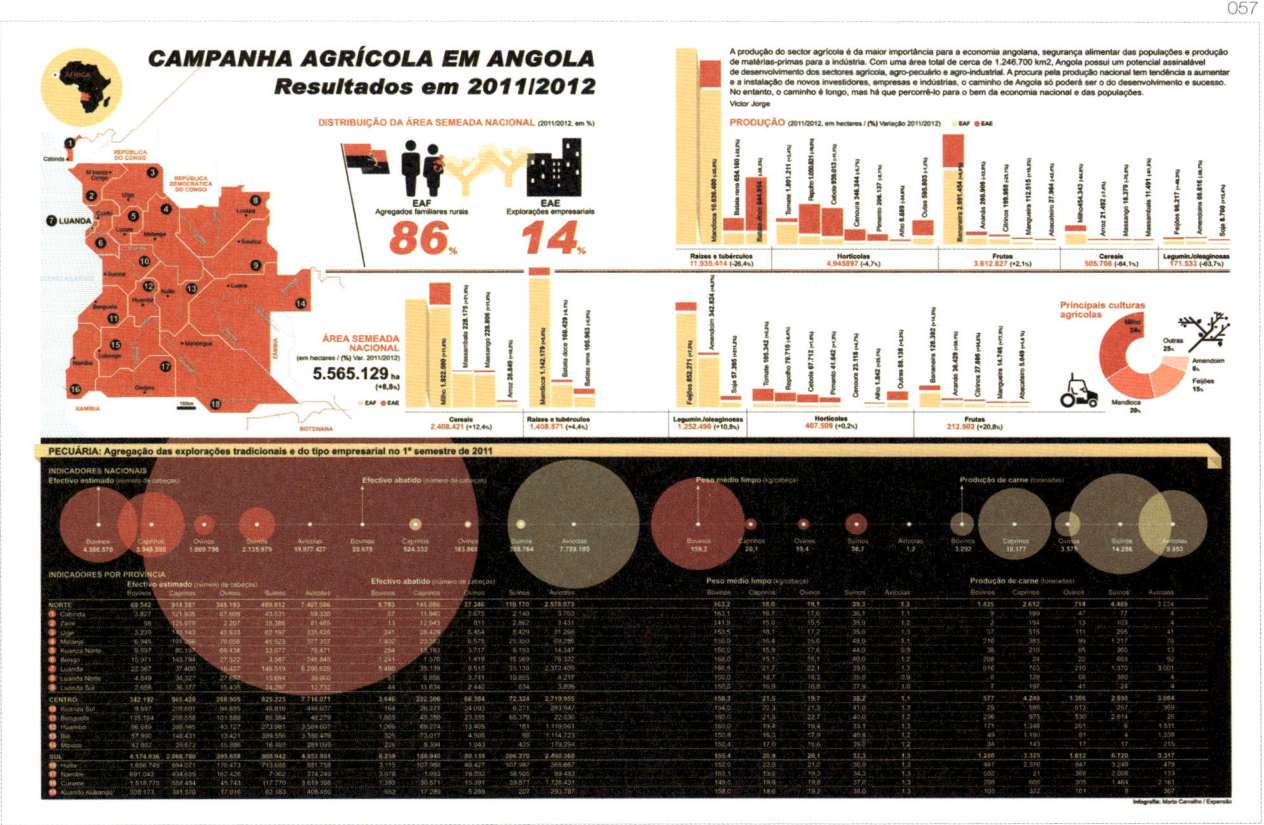

Investment Climate in Kaluga Region

Project Description /

This infographic, about the investment climate in Russia's Kaluga region, shows the average wage, investment in production, and the number of people in the region, as well as priority areas of investment and infrastructure. It details investor support from the state and features a success story of one of the companies in the region. Designer Vitaliy Turov structured the text with visual images to make the information clearer and more interesting.

Client / crosdigital.ru
Designer / Vitaliy Turov
Completion / 2014

Поддержка инвестора

Предоставление государственных гарантий

Возмещение процентов по ставкам за пользование кредитами банков

Субсидии малому и среднему бизнесу на лизинг оборудования

Льготы по налогу на прибыль организаций и налогу на имущество организаций

Таможенные льготы

Возмещение затрат на подключение к электросетями и участие в выставках

Инвестиции в инновационные предприятия (объём венчурного фонда – 280 млн рублей)

Концессионные соглашения в рамках государственно-частного партнерства

Гранты начинающим предпринимателям

История успеха

Samsung Electronics Co.

2007 г.
Начало проекта

2 000 чел
Количество сотрудников

$290 млн
Объём инвестиций

Производство
 Телевизоры
 Мониторы
 Домашние кинотеатры

Россия, Белоруссия, Украина, Казахстан
География поставок

7 млн. единиц
Годовой объём продукции

53 000 м²
Крупнейший в Европе логистический центр

40 600 м²
Площадь помещений

 Все телевизоры и мониторы Samsung, продающиеся в России, произведены на этом заводе

© Агентство стратегических инициатив, 2014

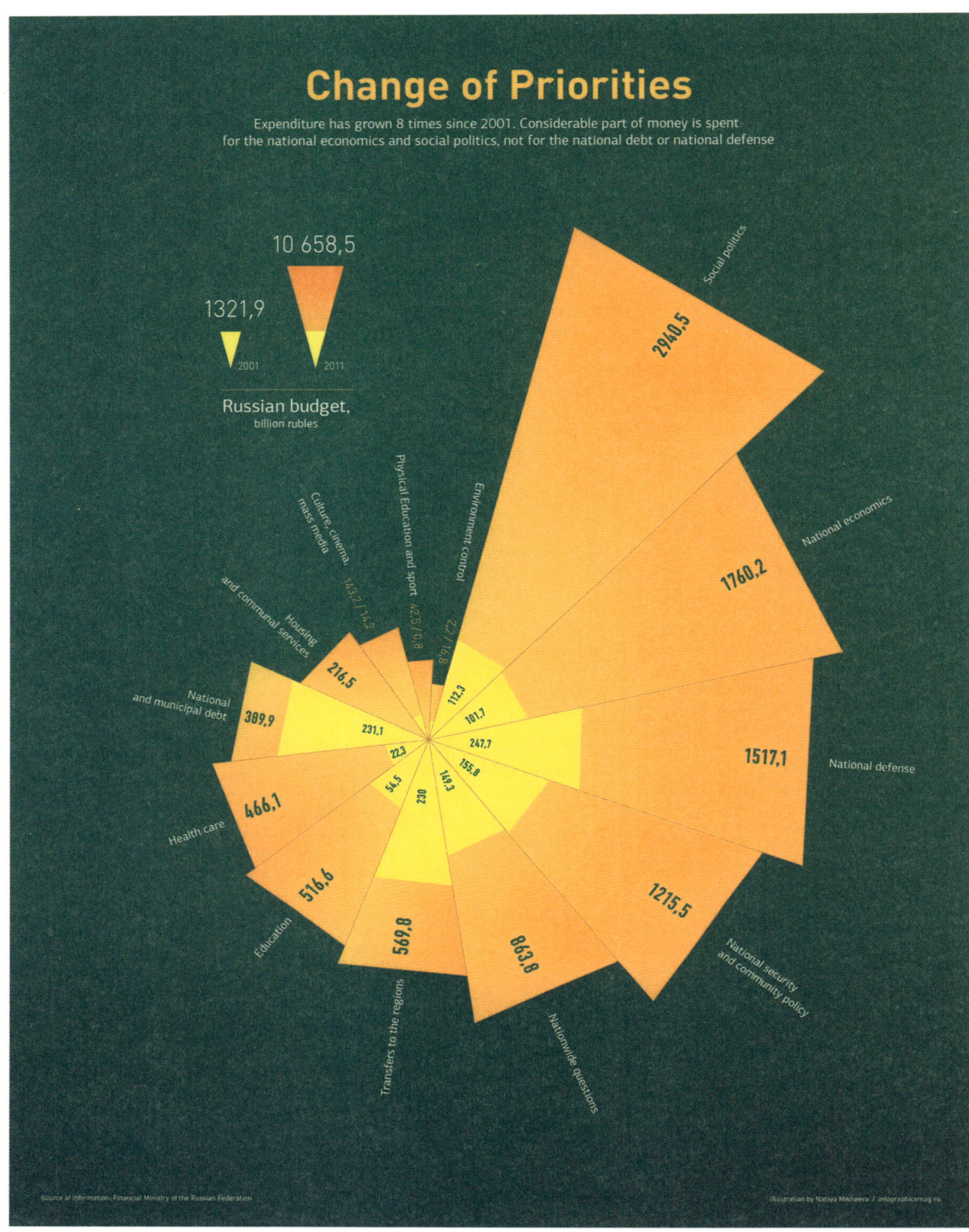

Change of Priorities

Project Description /

Many people love to quote numbers from the Russian budget without knowing their true context or meaning. At one point there was much discussion about the incredible sixfold increase of expenses for national security. Naturally, this affected the rest of the budget. In this infographic, the designers compared all budget items of government expenses from 2001 to 2011. It contrasted Russia's government debt to GDP ratio with that of different European countries. It summarized that national security expenses in Russia are, indeed, in the top three, but they follow expenses for the country's education system and public health service.

Client / *Infografika*
Design Agency / Infografika Magazine
Designer / Nastya Mikheeva
Completion / 2012

060

Shavers Five Years Long

Project Description /
   The idea for this design was to show typical stock market information in a beautiful way. To make the article more interesting, the designers used stock numbers of famous companies from the Moscow Central Stock Exchange: Gazprom, MTS, Lukoil, and so on. The design work on this infographic was very challenging, and the most difficult part was the 3D modeling element.

Client / *Infografika*
Design Agency / Infografika Magazine
Designer / Artem Kuzovkin
Completion / 2013

Shavers five years long

If you swirl the graphics of the stock-exchange quotations around their axis, they will look like pencil shavers. Russian stock market was turned pretty much in the last five years

23.05.2008 — 23.05.2013

MOSCOW STOCK MARKET ▼ -24,6%

MTS ▼ -12,5%

LUKOIL OIL COMPANY ▼ -19,4%

GAZPROM ▼ -65,8%

SBERBANK ▲ +22,9%

▼ -74,3%

Information Source: Moscow Central Stock Exchange

Illustration by Artyom Kuzovkin / infographicsmag.ru

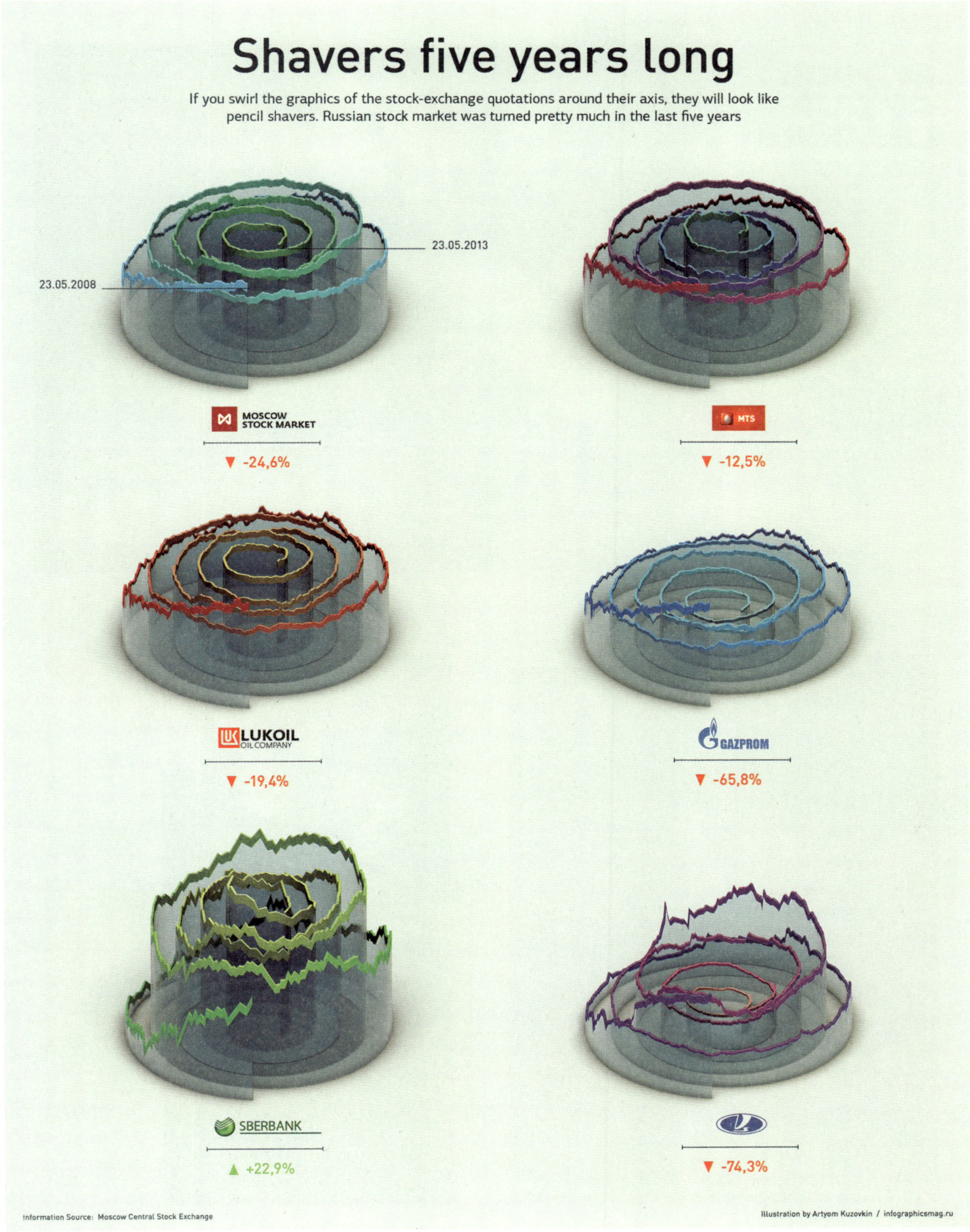

IN DOUBT OF OUR LEADERS

Europeans struggle to understand public finances and distrust governments to manage resources effectively, research by ICAEW and PwC shows. So what can be done to educate them and to restore it?

European populations have little understanding of public finances, do not trust their governments to handle them and believe there is a need for better planning and management of public spending, according to research carried out by ICAEW and PwC in late 2014.

The research, entitled *Trust in public finances: A survey of citizens in 10 European countries*, is part of the two organisations' joint *Sustainable public finances - EU perspectives* initiative. Its aim is to promote discussion among policymakers and stakeholders on how to improve public sector accounting and financial management in Europe.

The survey profiled people in countries across Europe, including a wide geographic spread and drew on countries both within and outside the eurozone. ▶

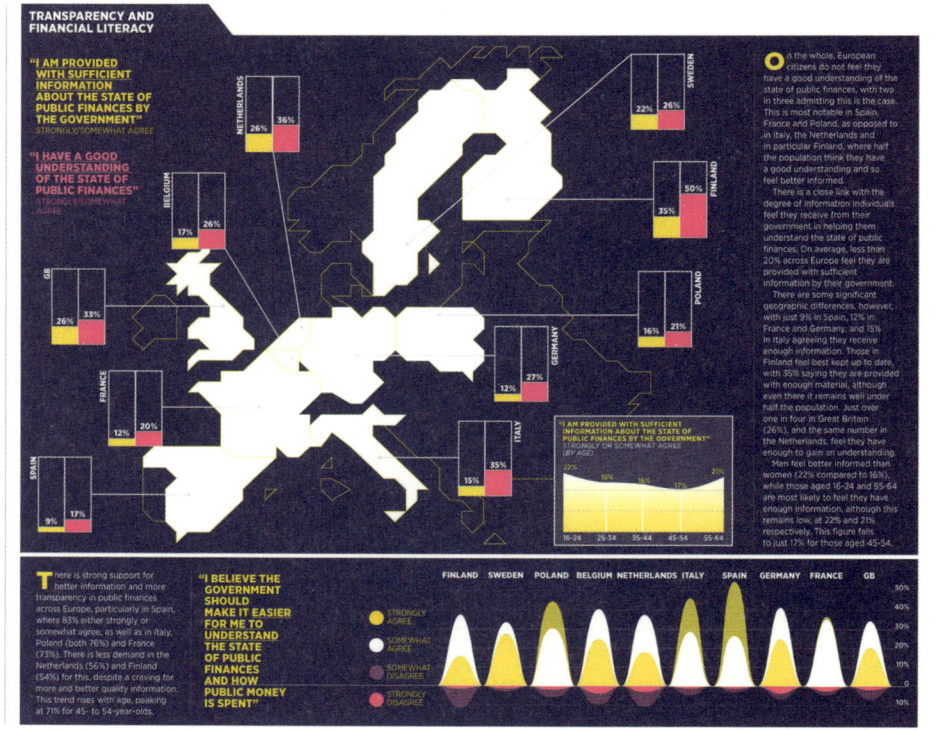

TRANSPARENCY AND FINANCIAL LITERACY

"I AM PROVIDED WITH SUFFICIENT INFORMATION ABOUT THE STATE OF PUBLIC FINANCES BY THE GOVERNMENT"
STRONGLY/SOMEWHAT AGREE

"I HAVE A GOOD UNDERSTANDING OF THE STATE OF PUBLIC FINANCES"
STRONGLY/SOMEWHAT AGREE

On the whole, European citizens do not feel they have a good understanding of the state of public finances, with two in three admitting this is the case. This is most notable in Spain, France and Poland, as opposed to in Italy, the Netherlands and in particular Finland, where half the population think they have a good understanding and so feel better informed.

There is a close link with the degree of information individuals feel they receive from their government in helping them understand the state of public finances. On average, less than 20% across Europe feel they are provided with sufficient information by their government.

There are some significant geographic differences, however, with just 9% in Spain, 12% in France and Germany, and 15% in Italy agreeing they receive enough information. Those in Finland feel best kept up to date, with 35% saying they are provided with enough material, although even there it remains well under half the population. Just over one in four in Great Britain (26%), and the same number in the Netherlands, feel they have enough to gain an understanding.

Men feel better informed than women (22% compared to 16%), while those aged 16-24 and 55-64 are most likely to feel they have enough information, although this remains low, at 22% and 21% respectively. This figure falls to just 17% for those aged 45-54.

There is strong support for better information and more transparency in public finances across Europe, particularly in Spain, where 83% either strongly or somewhat agree, as well as in Italy, Poland (both 76%) and France (73%). There is less demand in the Netherlands (56%) and Finland (54%) for this, despite a craving for more and better quality information. This trend rises with age, peaking at 71% for 45- to 54-year-olds.

"I BELIEVE THE GOVERNMENT SHOULD MAKE IT EASIER FOR ME TO UNDERSTAND THE STATE OF PUBLIC FINANCES AND HOW PUBLIC MONEY IS SPENT"

TRUST AND CONFIDENCE

"I AM CONFIDENT THAT THE CURRENT GOVERNMENT WILL BE ABLE TO FINANCE CORE PUBLIC SERVICES IN THE FUTURE"
STRONGLY/SOMEWHAT AGREE

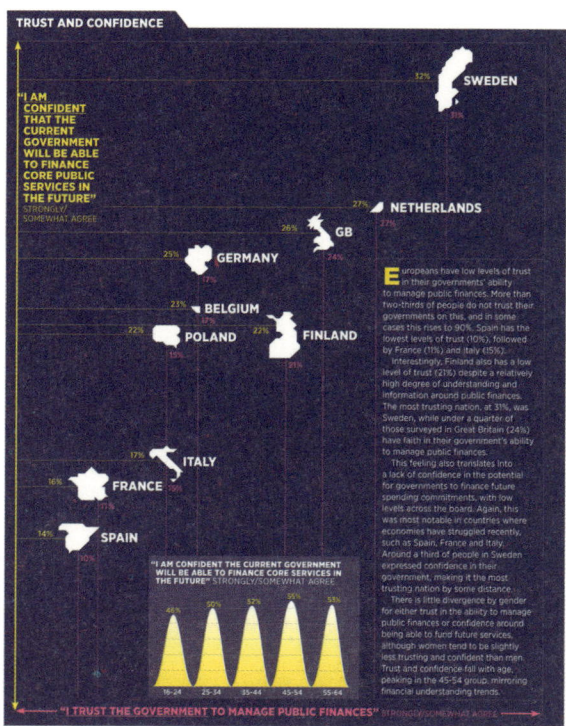

Europeans have low levels of trust in their governments' ability to manage public finances. More than two-thirds of people do not trust their governments on this, and in some cases this rises to 90%. Spain has the lowest levels of trust (10%), followed by France (11%) and Italy (15%).

Interestingly, Finland also has a low level of trust (23%) despite a relatively high degree of understanding and information around public finances. The most trusting nation, at 31%, was Sweden, while under a quarter of those surveyed in Great Britain (24%) have faith in their government's ability to manage public finances.

This feeling also translates into a lack of confidence in the potential for governments to finance future spending commitments, with low levels across the board. Again, this was most notable in countries where economies have struggled recently, such as Spain, France and Italy. Around a third of people in Sweden expressed confidence in their government, making it the most trusting nation by some distance.

There is little divergence by gender for either trust in the ability to manage public finances or confidence around being able to fund future services, although women tend to be slightly less trusting and confident than men. Trust and confidence fall with age, peaking in the 45-54 group, mirroring financial understanding trends.

PUBLIC FINANCES

"I BELIEVE THE GOVERNMENT SHOULD REDUCE PUBLIC DEBT"
STRONGLY/SOMEWHAT AGREE

Across Europe, there is strong backing for government action to reduce debt, with seven in 10 Europeans agreeing this should be a priority. Again, there are regional variations; this feeling is – perhaps understandably – highest in those countries where the economies have suffered most, particularly Italy (81%), Spain (77%) and France (75%).

The feeling is strongest in Poland, however, at (82%), where the economy has performed better. Sweden (49%) and Belgium (57%) are least concerned about reducing debt, while 63% in Great Britain believe this needs to be reduced.

There is also a clear demand for better financial planning and management, and to spend money more efficiently in the future. More than three-quarters of Europeans regard this as important, with Italy, Poland, Spain and Finland feeling most strongly, while those in Great Britain, the Netherlands and Sweden appear to be less concerned.

ACTION POINTS

▶ Martin Manuzi, ICAEW regional director, Europe, describes the results as a "strong call by citizens across Europe for greater transparency, democratic accountability as well as more effective and efficient public expenditure".

He adds: "The accountancy profession has an important role to play, helping to promote greater transparency of financial information for a more informed public debate, encouraging robust financial leadership in the public sector and improving interaction with financial markets."

Patrice Schumesch, global public finance and accounting partner at PwC, believes the public sector should adhere to the same kind of reporting requirements as those applied to the private sector. "In private companies you have fixed reporting requirements and those that are listed have to use international standards," he says. "It's only by having those that you have the foundations for good reporting."

It's a view echoed by Michael Theurer, a German member of the European Parliament and the Economic and Monetary Affairs Committee, who welcomes the ICAEW and PwC Sustainable Public Finances initiative. "The crisis revealed worrying episodes of inaccurate reporting of deficits and debts, be it public or private entities," he says.

"One of the main lessons to draw from this is for efficient and effective public audit and political oversight and, therefore, we need efficient and effective management and control. Now that we have got the ball rolling, we should be pushing for answers and more debate on public finances."

061

EU Public Finances Survey

Project Description /
The *Economia* magazine, for the Institute of Chartered Accountants in England and Wales (ICAEW) membership, examined the results of a survey about public finances in the European Union. The aim of the design is to highlight the general public's lack of understanding and trust in their governments' handling of public finances. It also reveals the big difference in how the European countries emerged and recovered from the financial crisis.

Client / *Economia* magazine, ICAEW
Design Agency / Progressive Customer Publishing
Designer / Henrik Pettersson
Completion / 2015

062

Economic Stagflation Infographic

Project Description /
This graph was designed to accompany a *New York Times* business section article and shows economic trends from the year 1970 to the beginning of 2008. The aim was to highlight periods of stagflation and to flag possible indicators of stagflation happening again in 2008. The design strategy utilizes three colors: orange (inflation), blue (GDP), and gray (where inflation and GDP overlap). By neutralizing the overlap areas with a light gray, the graph highlights significant difference with strong color, where we can locate stagflation (lots of orange) or a robust economy (lots of blue). The graph takes the shape of a circular histogram, not only to reflect the nature of economic cycles, but also to support the article's assertion that stagflation might be happening again.

Designer / Chotiga Chotisorayuth
Completion / 2015

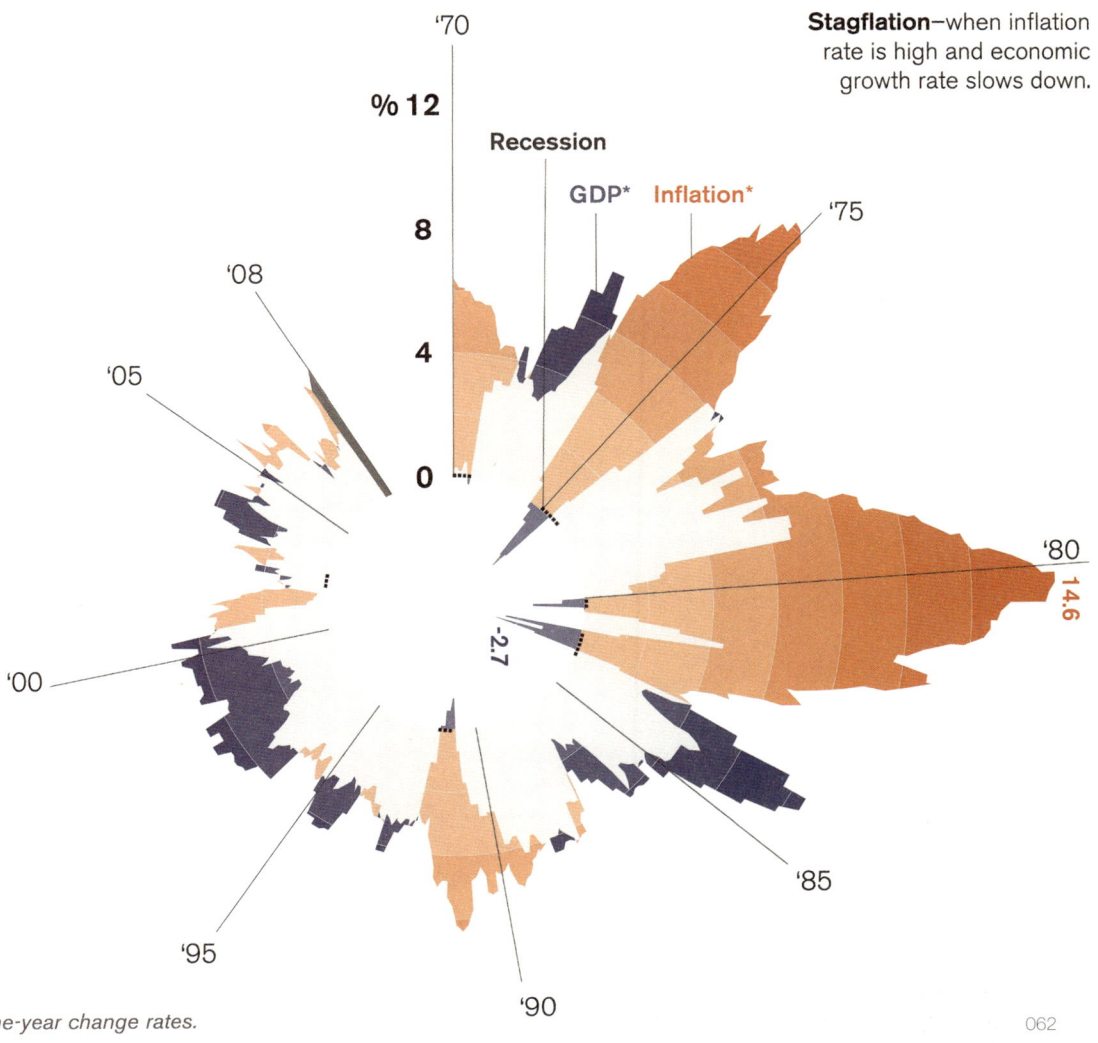

*over-the-year change rates.

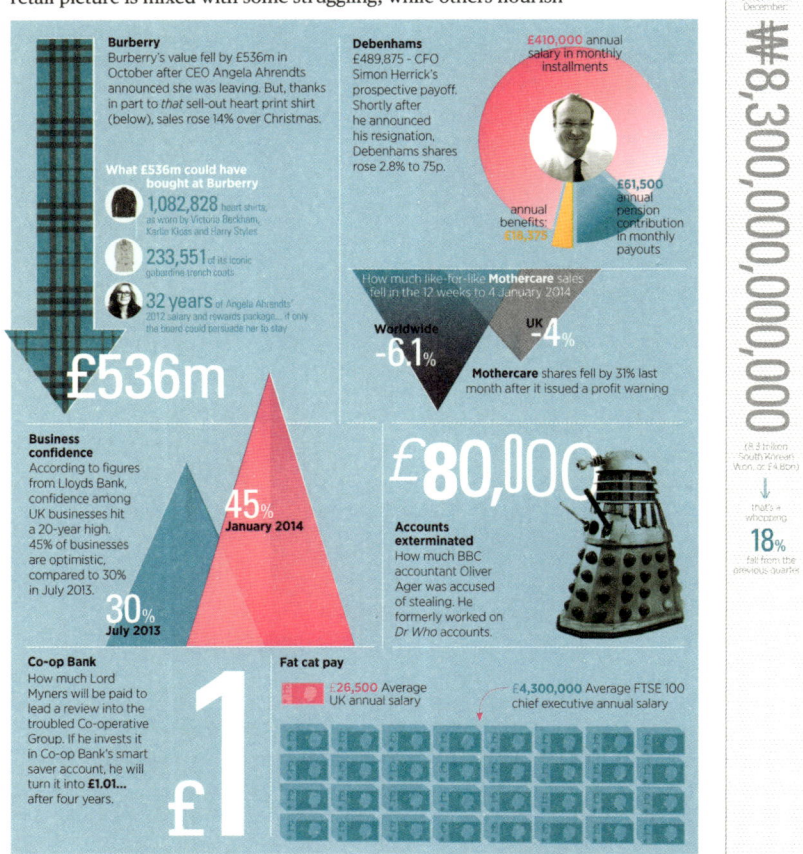

The Graph

Project Description /
The content within this infographic covers a range of different subjects, from fashion to finance, and film to food—anything that could be of interest to the accountancy audience of the Institute of Chartered Accountants in England and Wales (ICAEW). The design aims to be varied and light within quite strict style guidelines.

Client / *Economia* magazine, ICAEW
Design Agency / Progressive Customer Publishing
Designer / Henrik Pettersson
Completion / 2014 – 2015

In our statistical portrait of the last month, Deloitte and Sainsbury's are soaring but the UK outlook is less sunny thanks to those floods

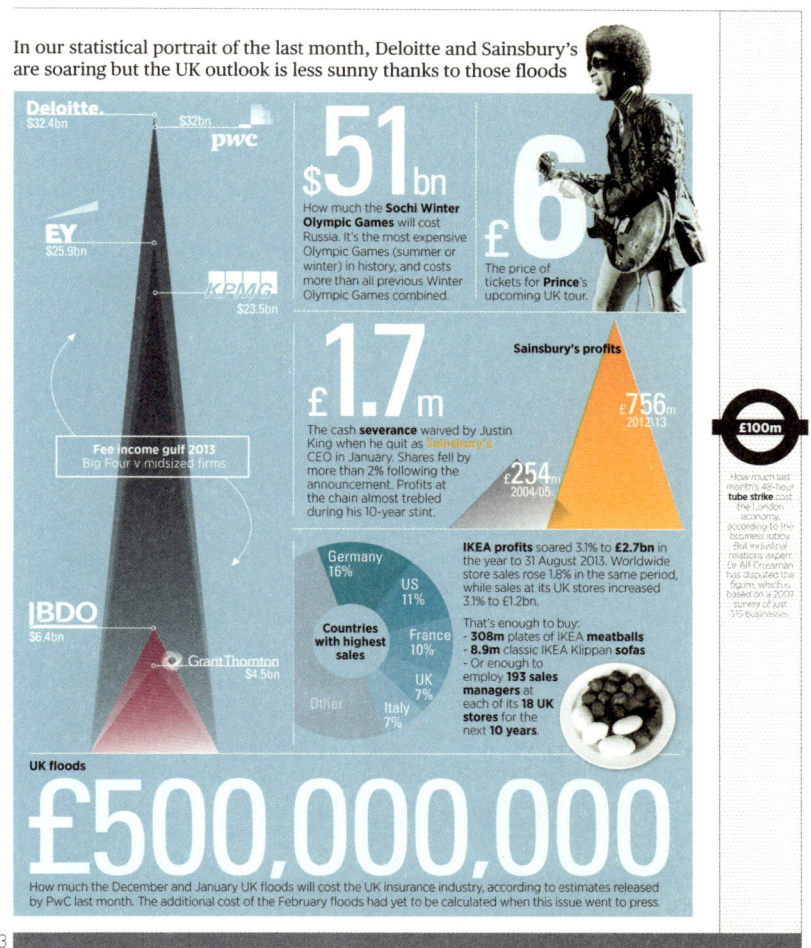

Britain by numbers, a statistical portrait of the month just gone:

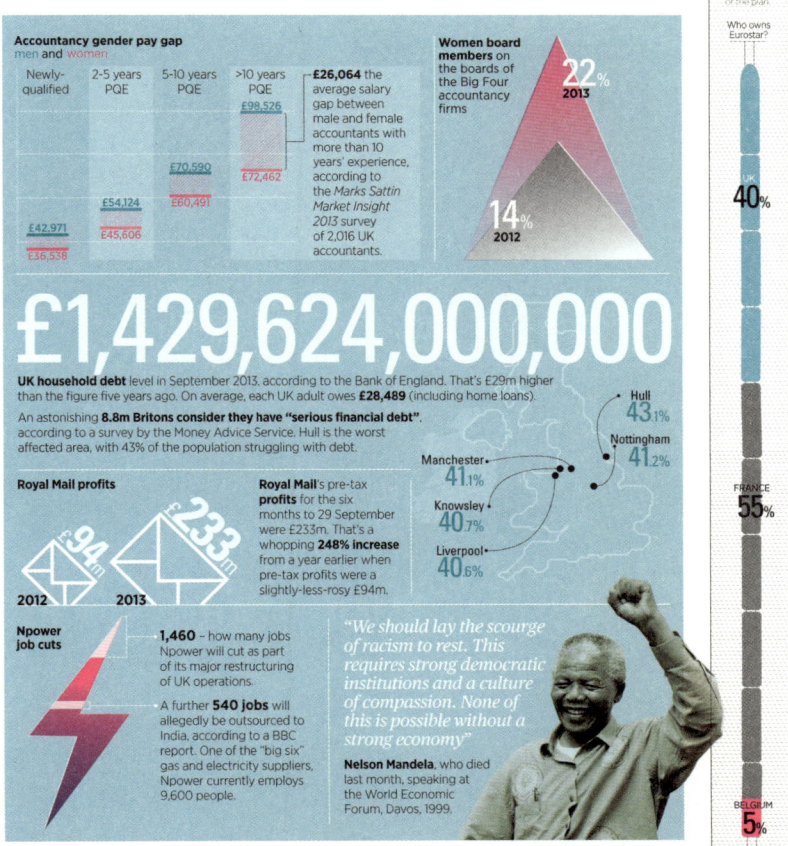

Agriculture in Italy

Project Description /

The agricultural industry is one of the most important sectors of the Italian economy, recognized and appreciated not just in Italy but all over the world. The 'Made in Italy' brand in alimentary products is synonymous with quality, research and specialization, all values that represent the high standards that the agricultural industry tries to follow. This infographic aims to illustrate the structure and characteristics of the agricultural industry in Italy. The graphic in the upper part highlights one of the strengths of the system, namely the diversification of the agricultural sector. In the infographic's center, Italy's total agricultural surface is represented as a field divided by type of use. Also visualized are the number of companies working on the land and a breakdown of their land use. The lower part shows the main agricultural associations in the country.

Design Agency / Corriere Della Sera Infographic Newsroom
Designer / Sabina Castagnaviz
Completion / 2015

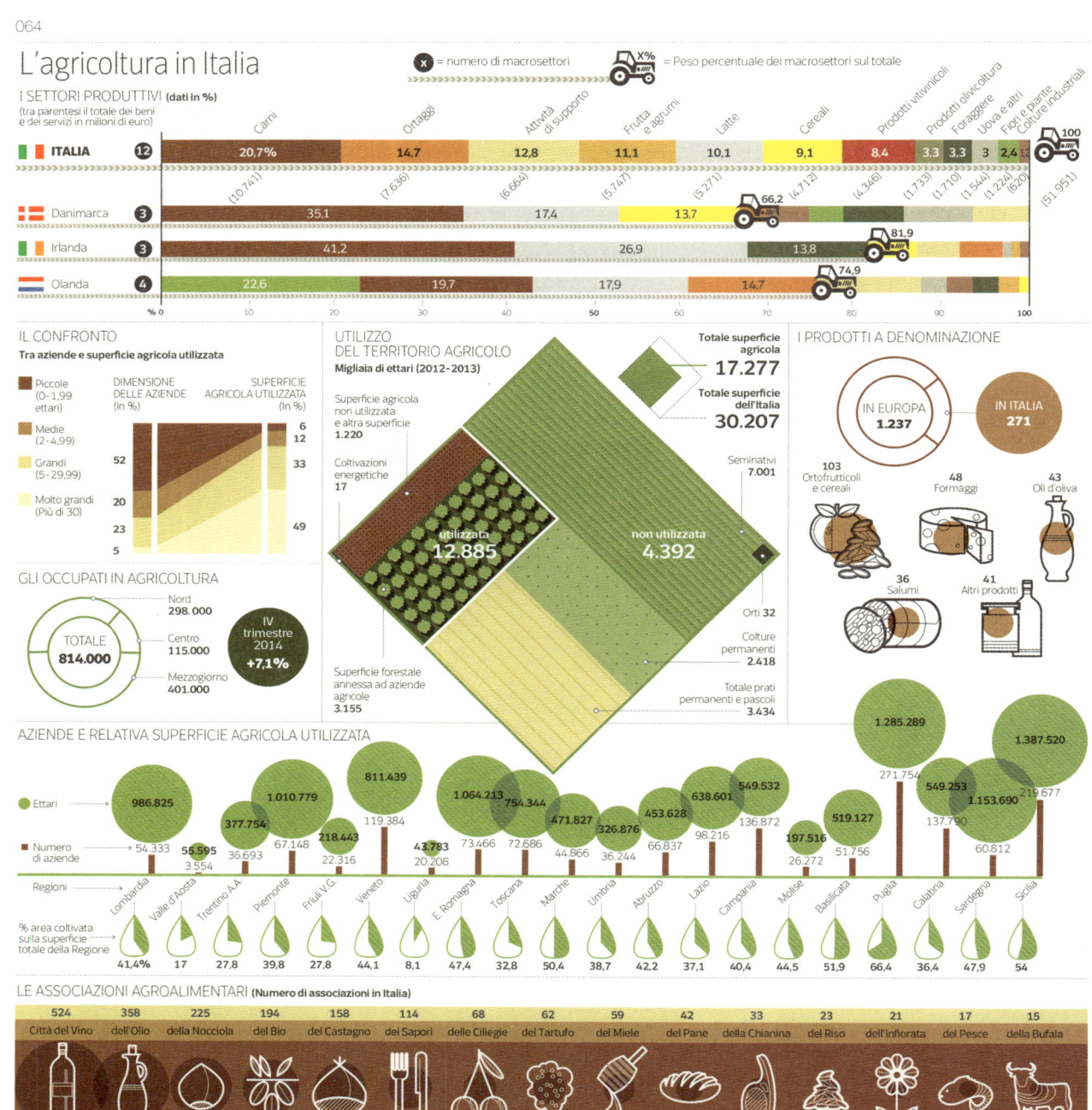

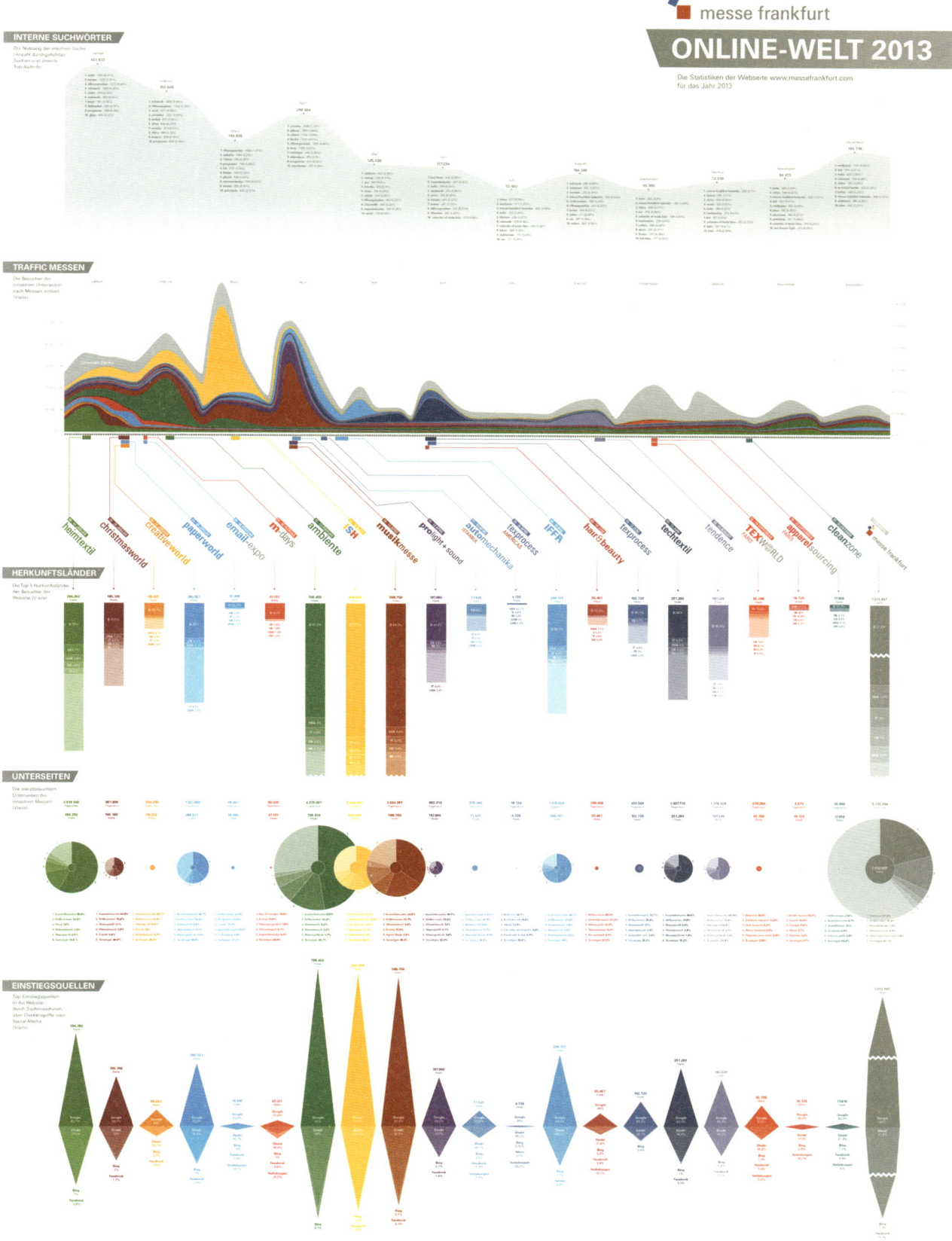

Statistics of Messe Frankfurt

Project Description /
The project explores the statistics of the Messe Frankfurt website 2013. It provides an overview of the entire traffic for each exhibition, the visitors and their countries of origin, the most visited sub-pages, entry sources and keywords of the internal search.

Client / Messe Frankfurt
Designer / Lana Bragina
Completion / 2014

066

Will Investors be Back?

Project Description /
This graphic illustrates the findings of a global survey by Franklin Templeton that shows Indians are optimistic about stocks, but will be conservative in their investments in 2013.

Client / *Economic Times*
Designer / Raj Kamal
Completion / 2013

067

Snack Sales

Project Description /
This diagram illustrated an article about current and past snack consumption. With no pictures other than images of snacks accompanying the article, the infographic was the primary image. This meant that the infographic needed to be more than a simple pie chart. The designer chose to design the diagram using photographs, which created a strong physical impact.

Client / Sydsvenska Dagbladet
Designer / Erik Nylund
Completion / 2013

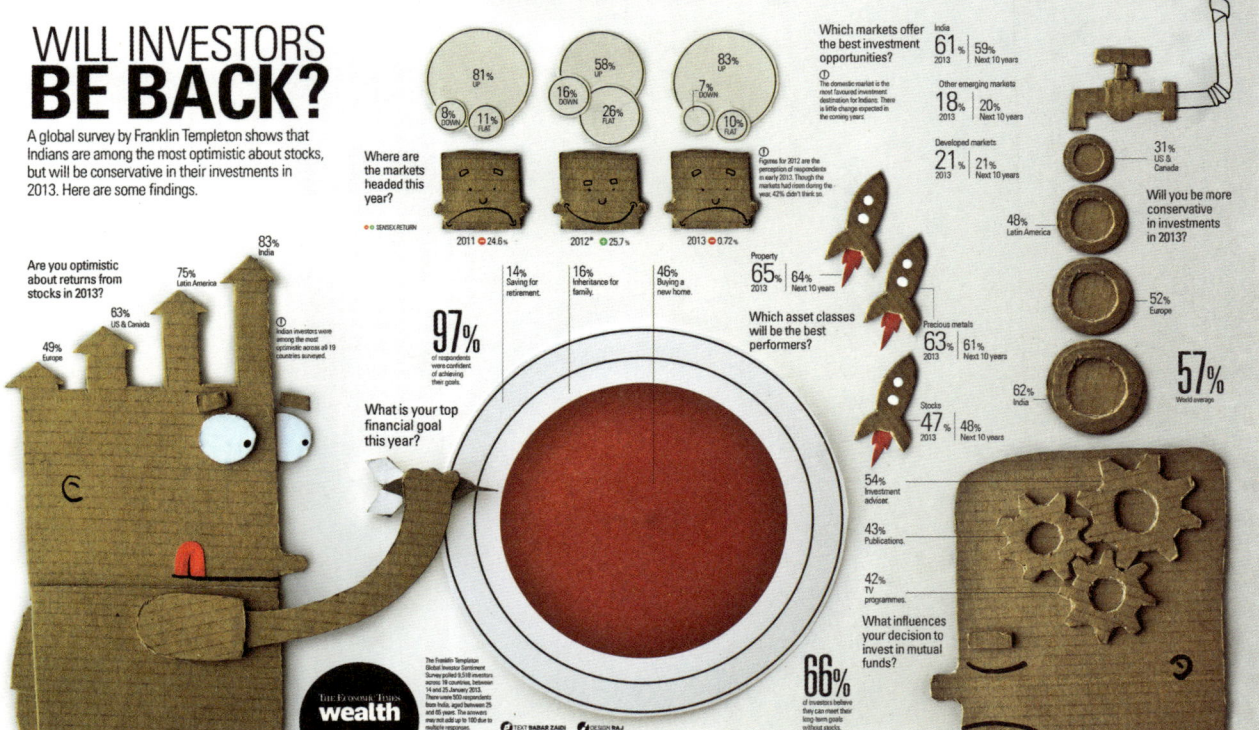

066

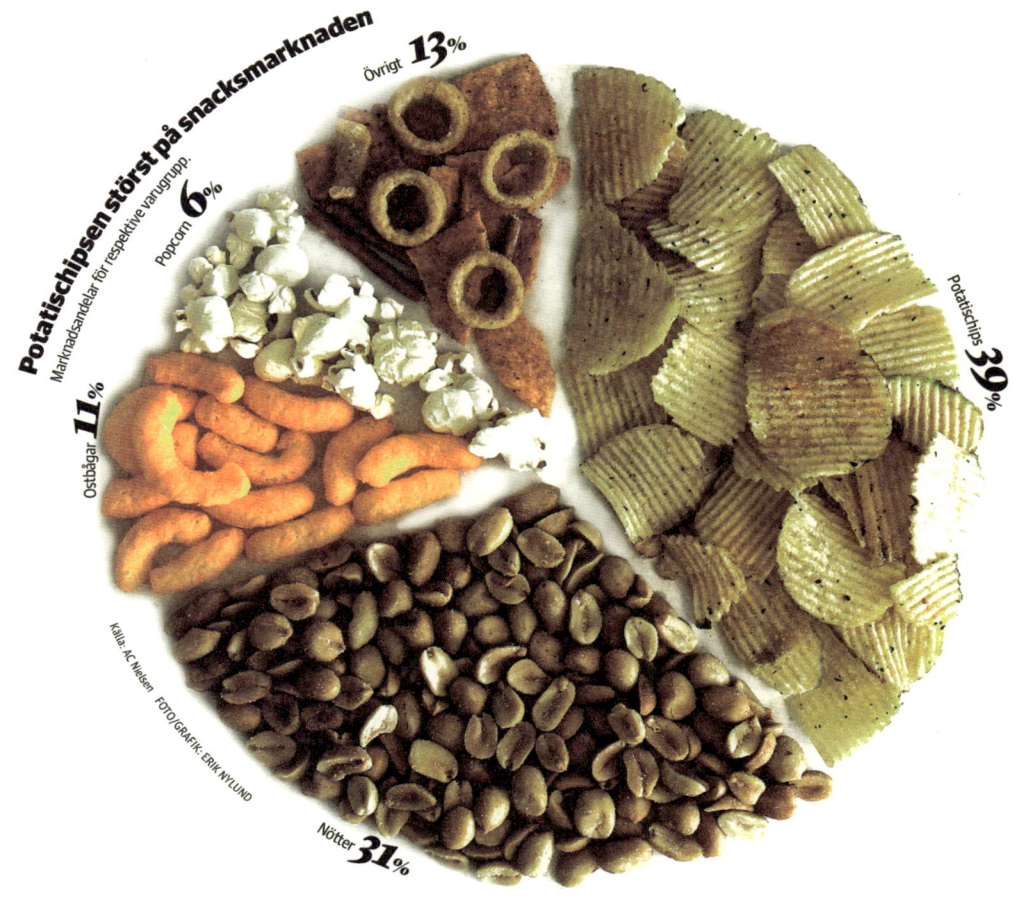

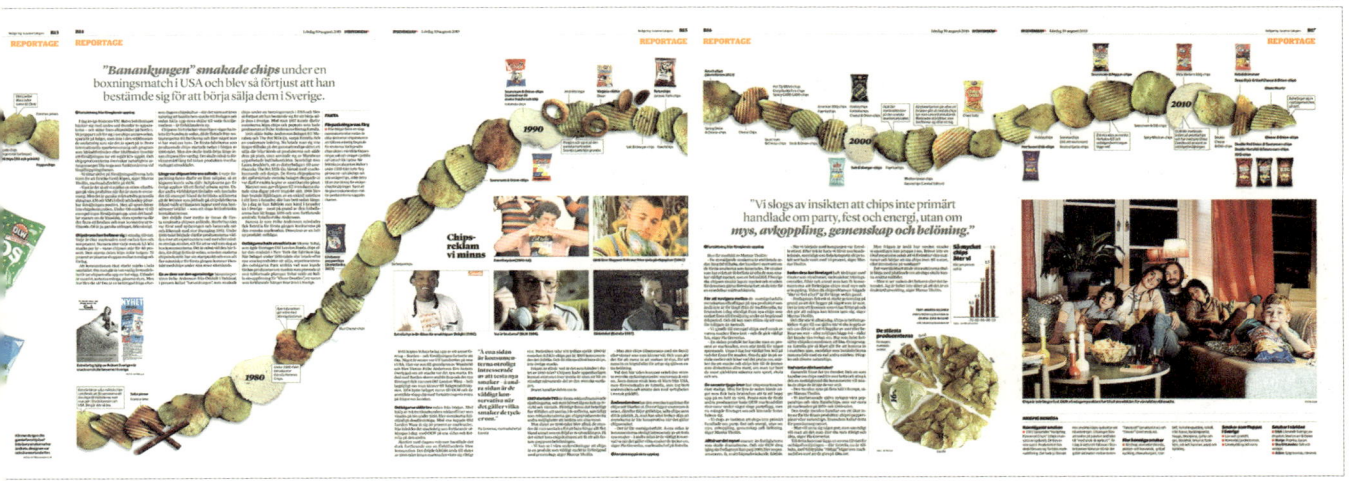

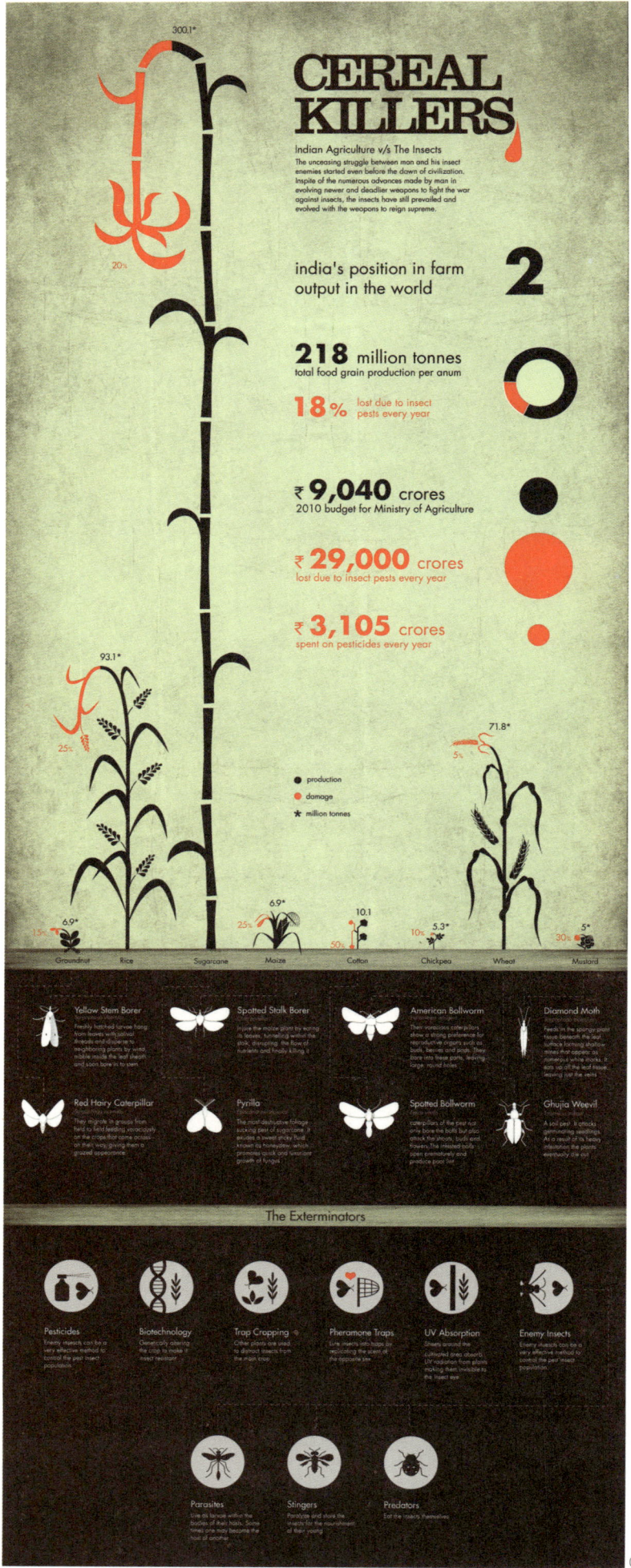

Cereal Killers

Project Description /
Insects cause massive losses to agricultural production and revenue every year. Despite significant scientific advances—such as newer and deadlier chemical weapons to fight the insect destroyers—they still prevail by evolving to produce resistance to pesticides. This infographic shows the impact of insects on India's eight main crops. It also gives details of the insects involved and the measures taken to combat them.

Designer / Pratyush Gupta

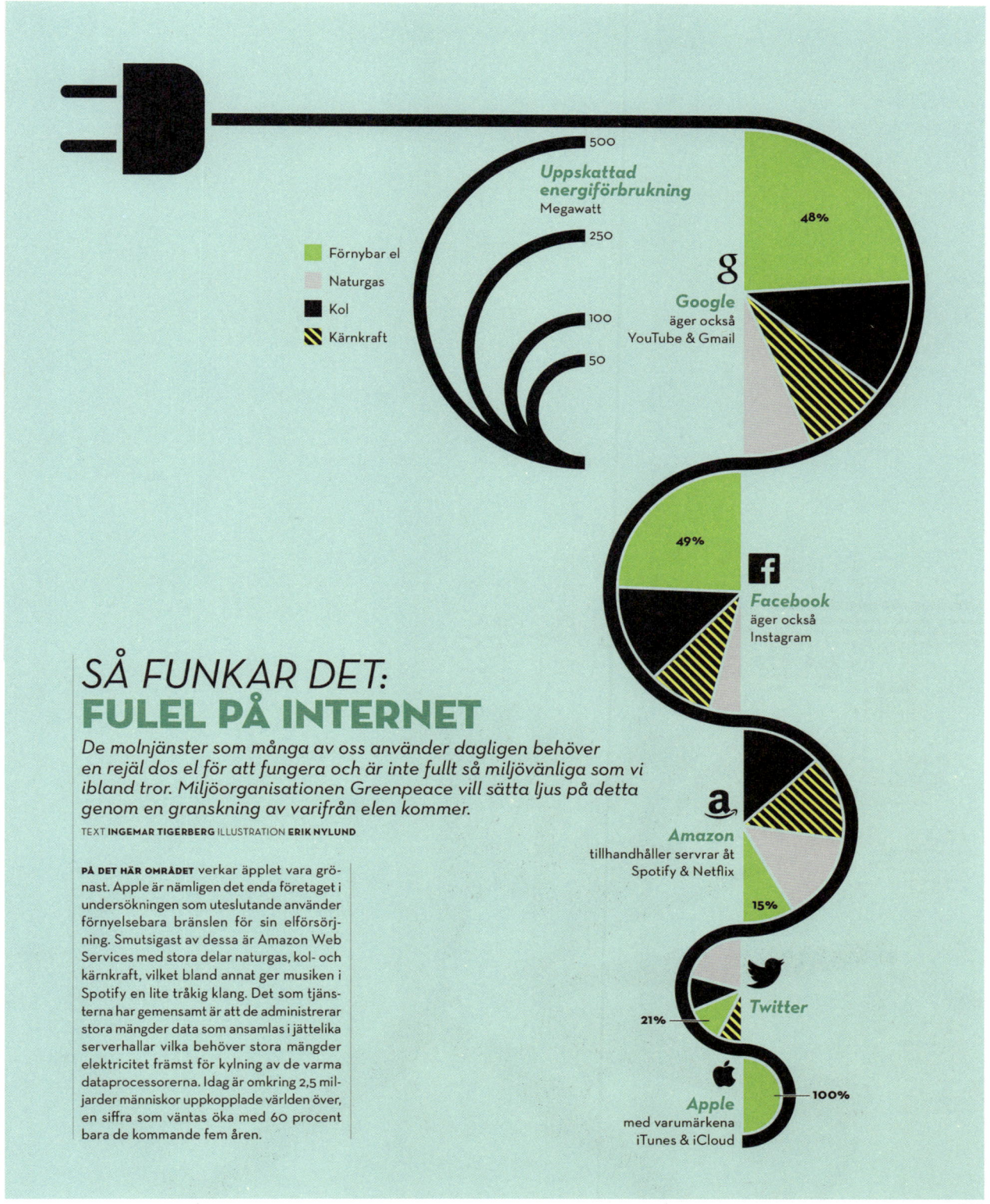

The Amount of Clean Energy

Project Description /

This infographic illustrates the energy usage of cloud service companies, such as Google, Facebook, Amazon, Twitter, and Apple. It focuses on energy usage but also the sources of energy and how clean it is. The graphic was the only image on the page so the designer had to make it an illustrative element as well as an information provider. He did this by visualizing the data around an electrical cord.

Client / Camino
Designer / Erik Nylund
Completion / 2014

How the Municipality Budget is Distributed

Project Description /
Infographics showing the municipality budget are common. The subject itself tends to get quite boring for news consumers, which requires a pedagogical but also cosmetic visualization. The idea of using a real cake in this infographic is quite simple and is based on a Swedish metaphor—'getting a piece of the cake'.

Client / Helsingborgs Dagblad
Designer / Erik Nylund

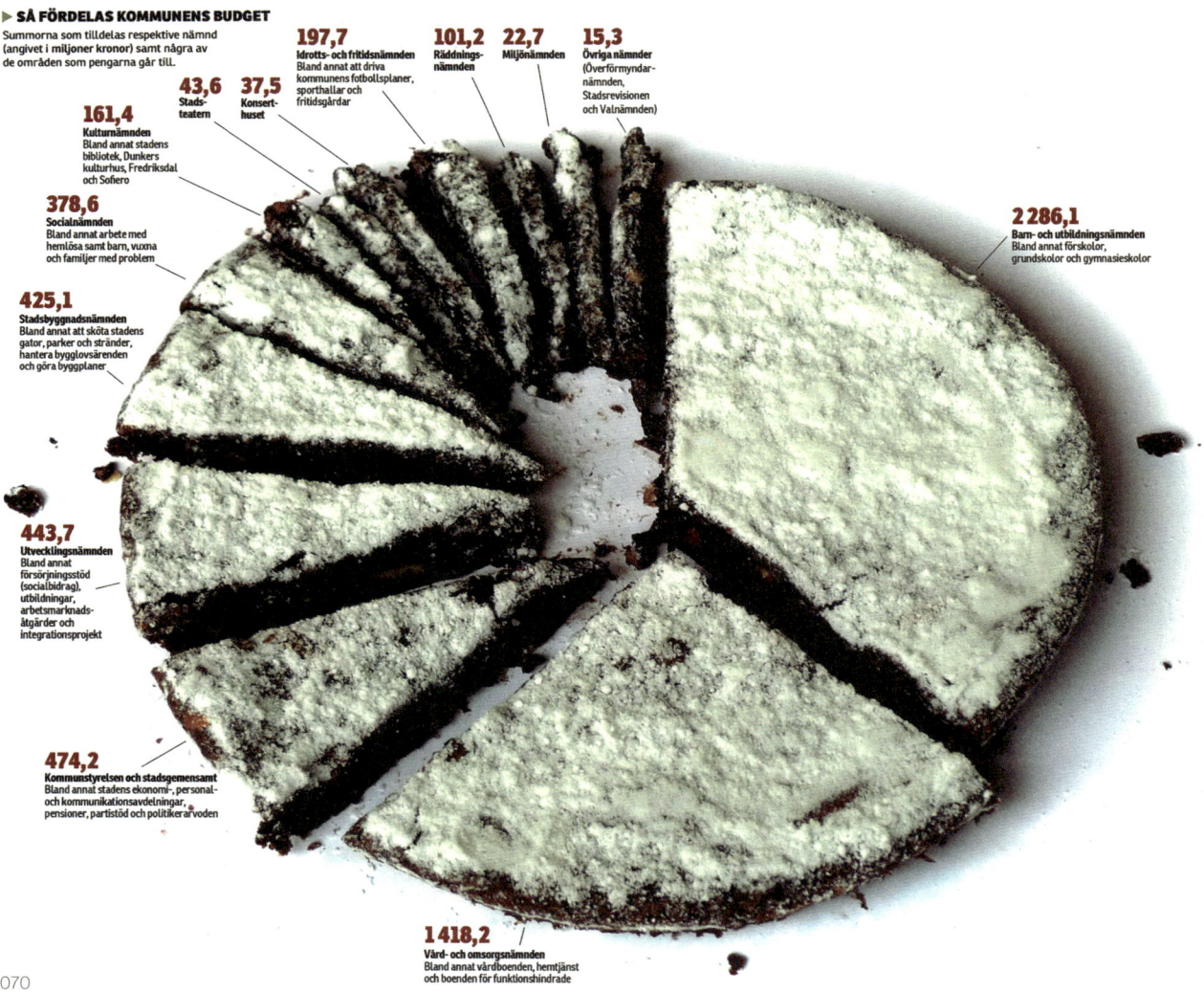

[071 – 075]
Client / *Diário Económico*
Designer / Mário Malhão
Completion / 2013—2015

071

The 101st Tour de France

Project Description /
 Malhão created this infographic to mark the 101st Tour de France. The focus of the work is an image of champion Portuguese cyclist Rui Costa. Malhão used a simple and direct graphic language, with a digitally altered image of the rider and all information around it. The main graph shows the level of difficulty of the stages of the race.

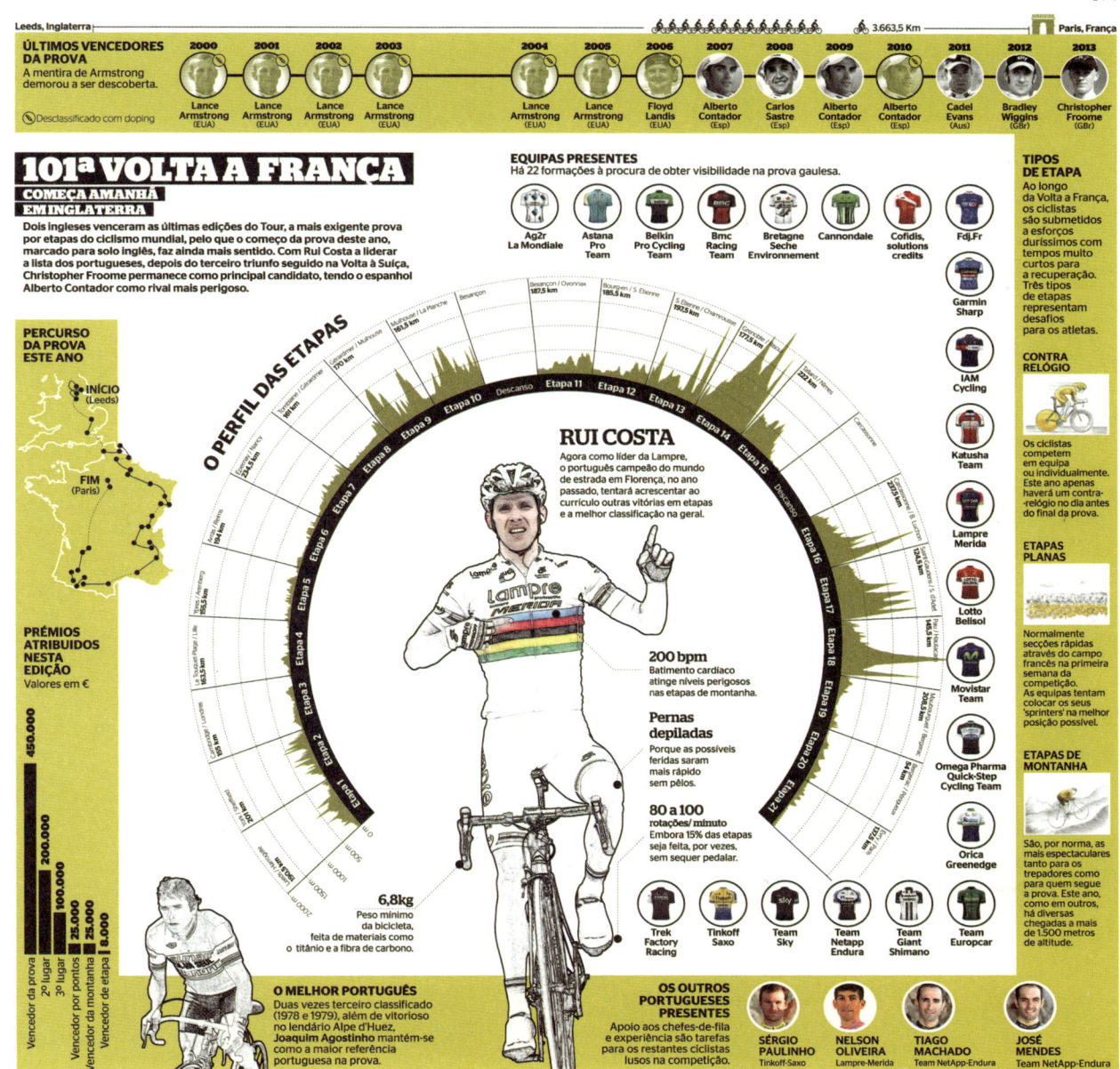

Formula 1: World Title is Decided This Weekend

Project Description /

This infographic was published days before the last race of the world championship. As always in his works, Malhão used few colors. The main graphic is circular, and includes the results of the two contenders in all their previous races of the championship. Around that main graphic are secondary graphics, such as earnings, previous winners of the last race in other years, a championship points table, and the track itself.

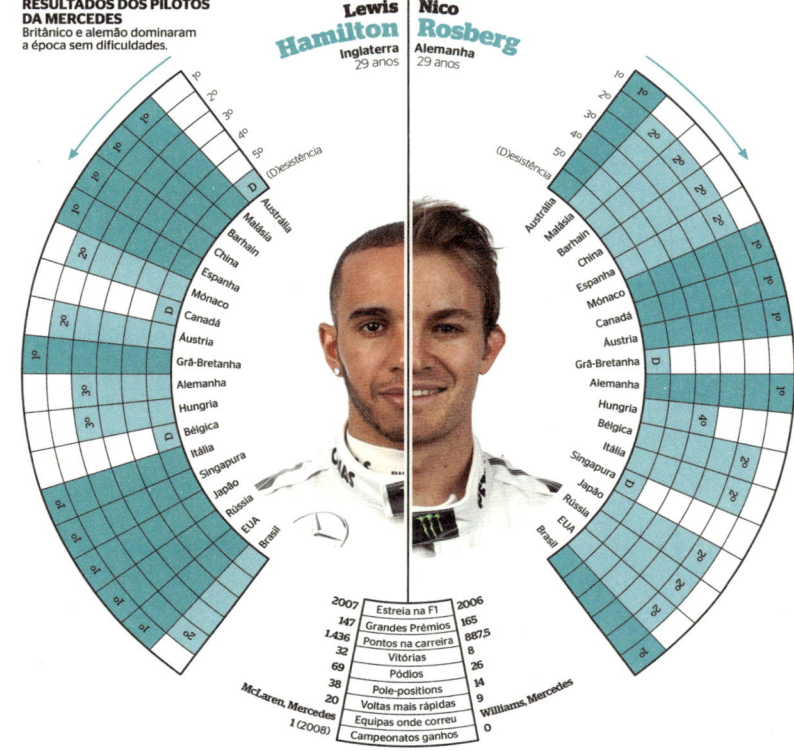

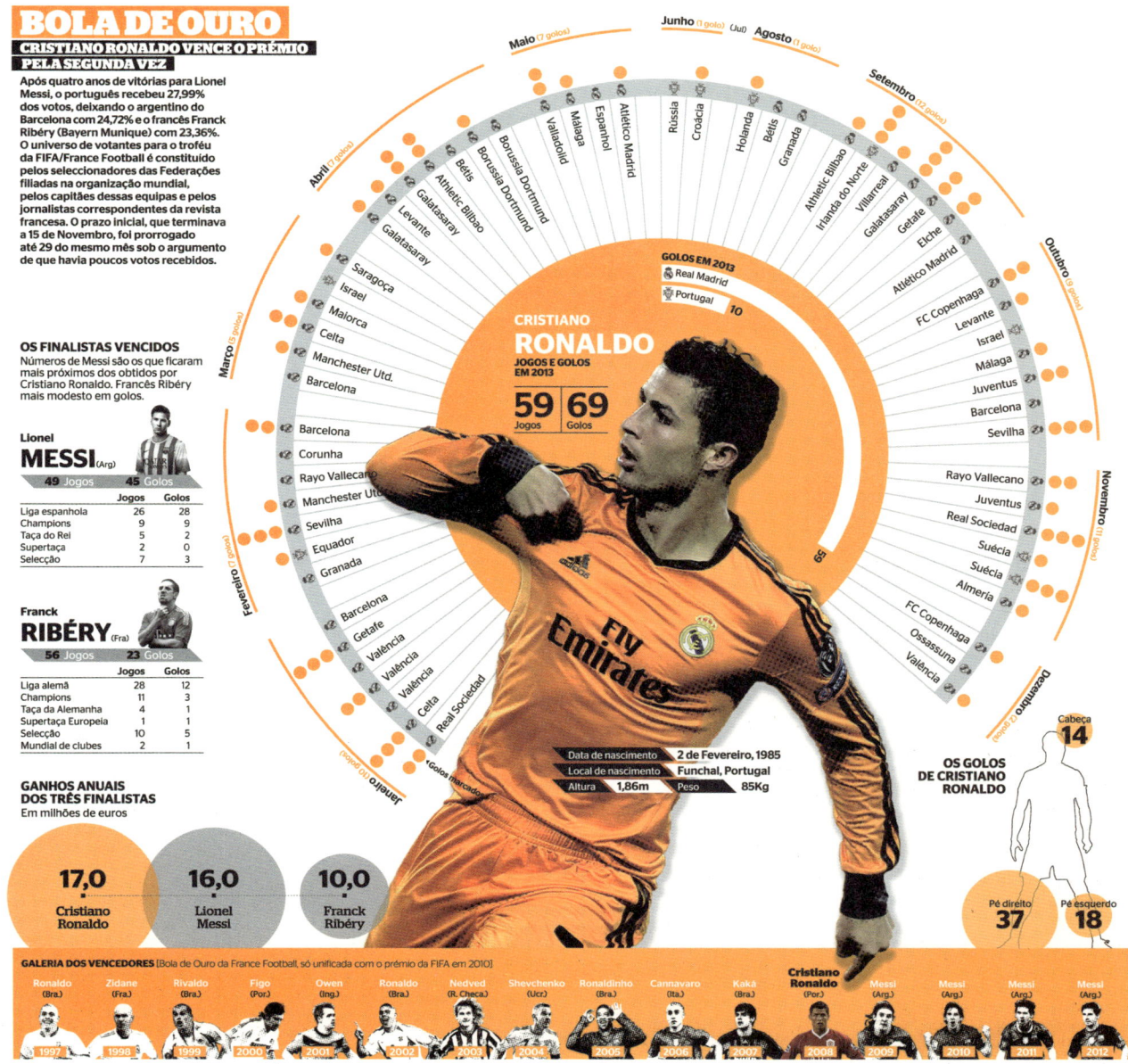

Ronaldo Gold Ball 2013

Project Description /

This graphic refers to the trophy for best player in the world. Malhão used an illustration of Cristiano Ronaldo as the central image of the work and made a circular chart around it showing all the goals scored by the Portuguese soccer star in 2013.

074

MotoGP Losail Race

Project Description /
This project was done for each of the MotoGP world championships. The infographic shows the performance of each driver in each lap in all the rounds in every race of the championship. Clarity and simplicity are its defining features. As the work was only published online, the designer chose to use a black background, something he never did for work published in the print edition of the newspaper.

075

Zero Cost

Project Description /
For this work, Malhão was inspired by a football table game. Using a range of colors, he shows one team from Portugal against another team of overseas players, with each team on opposing sides, introducing the basic information of every footballer.

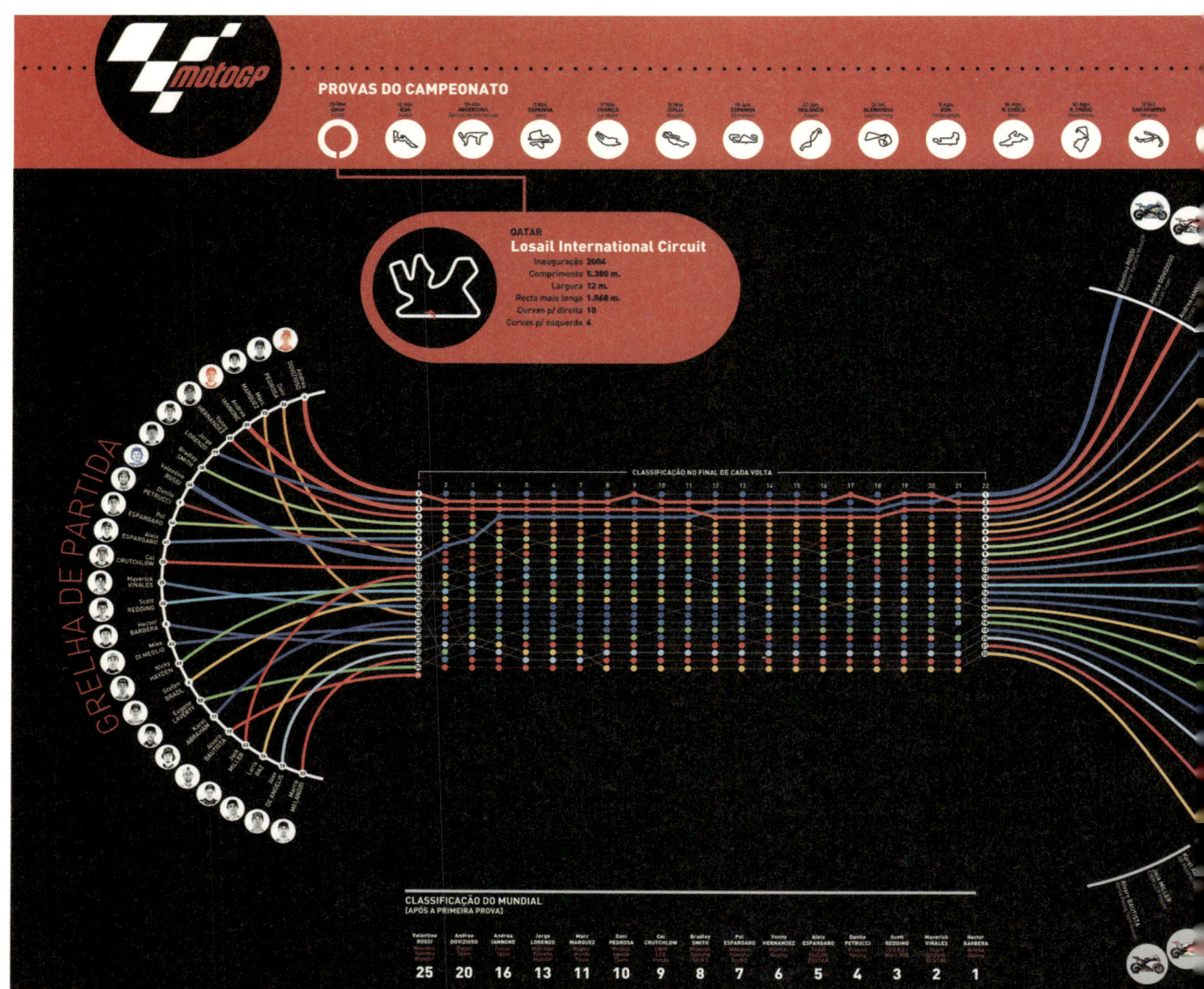

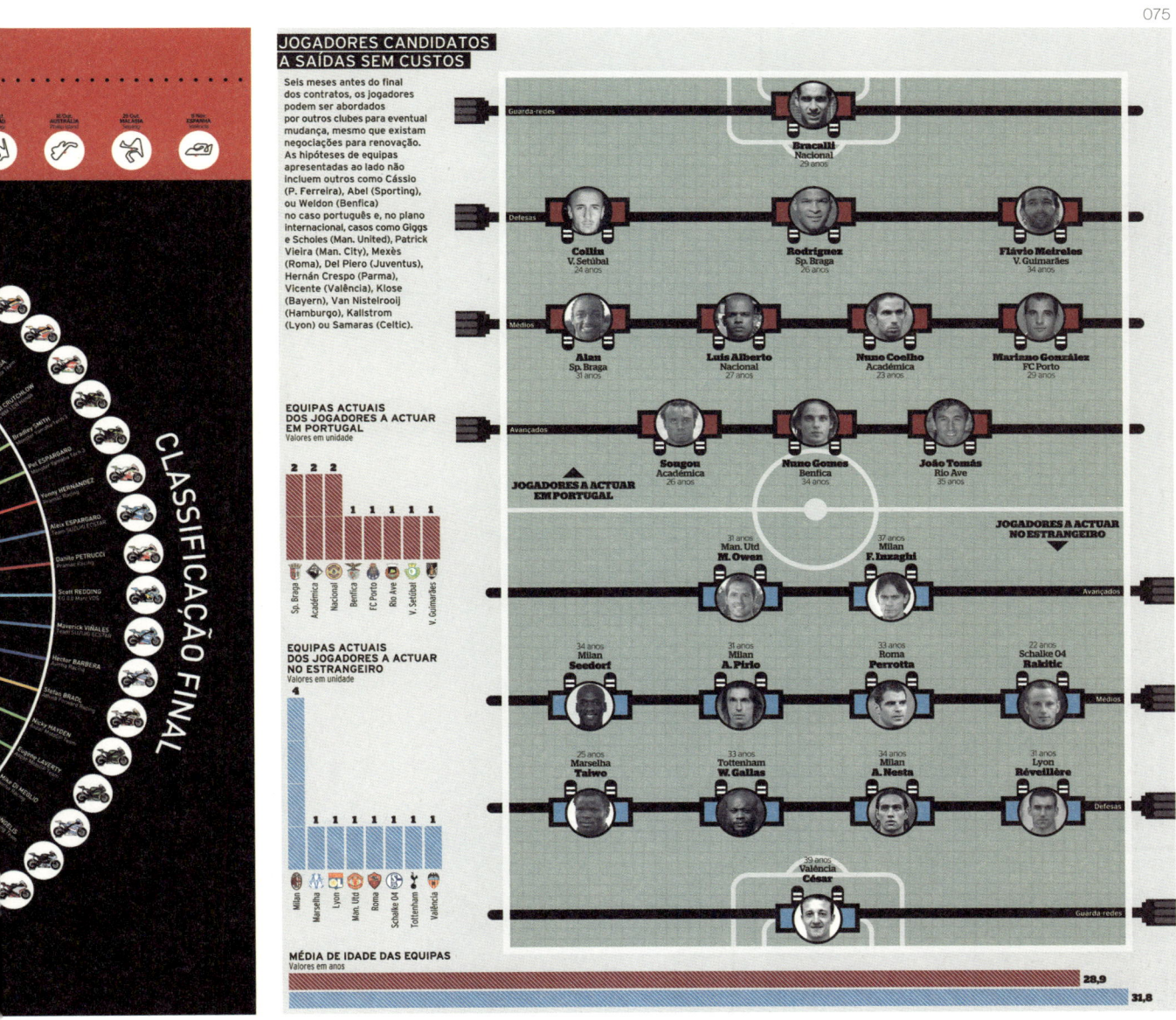

Ball Story Infographic

Project Description /

The evolution of the ball is a natural topic to print every four years in the lead-up to the FIFA World Cup. Many infographic designers do the same before the tournament starts. The interesting thing is the different ways they tell the same story, and how readers can find historic facts to collect.

In this case, the big plus is that there are established facts about the different stages of the development of footballs. There is also a part that explains the record of Ronaldo Luís Nazário de Lima as top scorer in the history of the World Cup, and which footballs were used to achieve it. There is information about footballs before the World Cup tournament began, and the contribution by Richard Lindon, the English leather worker who developed

A distribuição das 32 seleções nos grupos

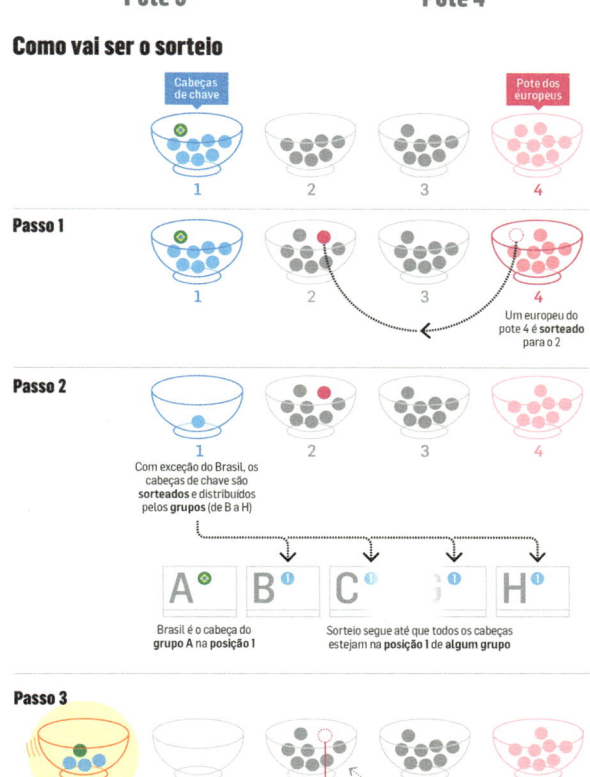

Pontapé inicial do Mundial será hoje na Bahia

Sorteio dividirá as 32 seleções em oito chaves. E existe a possibilidade de três campeões do mundo se enfrentarem já na primeira fase

Almir Leite
Raphael Ramos
ENVIADOS ESPECIAIS
COSTA DO SAUIPE

A seleção brasileira conhecerá hoje os seus três primeiros adversários na Copa do Mundo. A Fifa faz, a partir das 14h, o sorteio dos grupos do Mundial em evento na Costa do Sauipe, litoral norte da Bahia. Por enquanto, sabe-se apenas que o Brasil, como país-sede do torneio, ocupará a posição 1 do Grupo A. Com as mudanças nas regras do sorteio anunciadas terça-feira pela Fifa, é possível a formação de um grupo da morte, com três campeões mundiais. Essa combinação até saiu no ensaio geral realizado na quarta-feira. Na simulação feita pela Fifa, o Grupo A era formado por Brasil, França, Austrália e Itália.

Esse cenário, no entanto, não agrada à Fifa. Para a entidade, o ideal é que as oito seleções campeãs do mundo avancem às oitavas de final. A entidade, então, resolveu adotar uma nova regra para o sorteio a fim de tentar proteger a França. Em outubro, mês utilizado como referência para a Fifa definir os parâmetros do sorteio, os campeões do mundo de 1998 eram a pior seleção europeia do ranking da entidade, apenas no 21.º lugar.

Como o continente possui nove times no Mundial, além das quatro cabeças de chave, a tendência era que a pior equipe, no caso a França, fosse deslocada para o Pote 2 com os africanos e mais Chile e Equador.

Mas a Fifa preferiu adotar uma maneira de tentar preservar os franceses. "Surgiram algumas ideias e elas chegaram a sair em alguns jornais. Uma delas era colocar a seleção com a pior colocação do ranking no Pote 2. A outra era mudar automaticamente uma seleção e a terceira, aquela que acabou sendo adotada, foi o sorteio. Assim, o sorteio começará com a retirada de uma seleção do Pote 4 para o 2", disse ontem o secretário-geral da Fifa, Jerôme Valcke.

A opção não impede que a França vá para o Pote 2, apenas coloca os franceses nas mesmas condições das outras oito seleções europeias mais bem posicionadas no ranking.

Para evitar que essa equipe fique no grupo de um cabeça de chave europeu, a Fifa criou o Pote X. Nele serão colocados Brasil, Argentina, Colômbia e Uruguai, de onde será escolhido o país que receberá em sua chave a seleção europeia proveniente do Pote 2.

Outra mudança feita pela Fifa é que a posição das equipes nas chaves também será decidida por sorteio. Antes, o sorteado do Pote 2 que iria para o Grupo A era "A2". Agora, depois que for direcionado para um grupo, o time dependerá das bolinhas para saber se ocupará a posição 2, 3 ou 4. Isso influi na ordem dos jogos.

O sorteio será comandado por Valcke, que contará com a ajuda de oito ex-jogadores representando cada país campeão do mundo: Cafu (Brasil), Hierro (Espanha), Zinedine Zidane (França), Cannavaro (Itália), Lothar Matthäus (Alemanha), Ghiggia (Uruguai), Geoff Hurst (Inglaterra) e Mario Kempes (Argentina).

Eles participaram de um longo treino durante a semana para que se familiarizassem com o sistema do sorteio. A intenção da Fifa é evitar contratempos num evento que será transmitido para 193 países.

Os dirigentes da entidade ainda não se esqueceram do incidente proporcionado pelo chef Alex Atala um ano atrás, durante o sorteio da Copa das Confederações, que teve como consequência a alteração de posicionamento das equipes e prejuízo para Belo Horizonte. A cidade deixou de receber seleções fortes na primeira fase.

Pelé foi chamado para ajudar a retirar as bolinhas dos potes, mas abriu mão do convite. Mesmo assim, o Rei terá papel de destaque na cerimônia de acordo com a organização.

O **Estado** apurou que o ex-jogador Bebeto, membro do COL (Comitê Organizador Local), também vai ser chamado ao palco. Ele deve contracenar com Fuleco, mascote do Mundial, e repetir com o boneco a comemoração que fez na vitória sobre a Holanda na Copa de 1994, quando simulou embalar o recém-nascido filho Matheus.

Show. O sorteio dos grupos é o maior evento pré-Copa e terá 90 minutos. A audiência estimada do evento é de 500 milhões de pessoas. A apresentação ficará por conta do casal Rodrigo Hilbert e Fernanda Lima.

As apresentações musicais começarão com Alcione e Emicida. Depois virão Vanessa da Mata e Alexandre Pires, a coreógrafa Deborah Colker e Margareth Menezes com o Olodum.

COLABOROU J.F. DIÓRIO

AUDIÊNCIA

500 milhões de pessoas deverão assistir ao sorteio da Copa pela tevê. O evento será transmitido para 193 países.

NA WEB

Ao vivo. Confira tudo do sorteio a partir das 11h
estadao.com.br/e/sorteio

The Olympic Medallion

Project Description /

This infographic was published during the 2012 London Olympic Games. It presents the London 2012 gold medal, which will be the biggest and heaviest medal ever, measuring 85 millimeters (3.35 inches) in diameter and 400 grams (14 ounces) in weight, and it also shows other Olympic medallions from 1896 to 2008. Antonio Farach used three colors to represent gold, silver and bronze medals, and made all the medals circular, so that readers can understand all the information much more quickly.

Designer / Antonio Farach
Completion / 2012

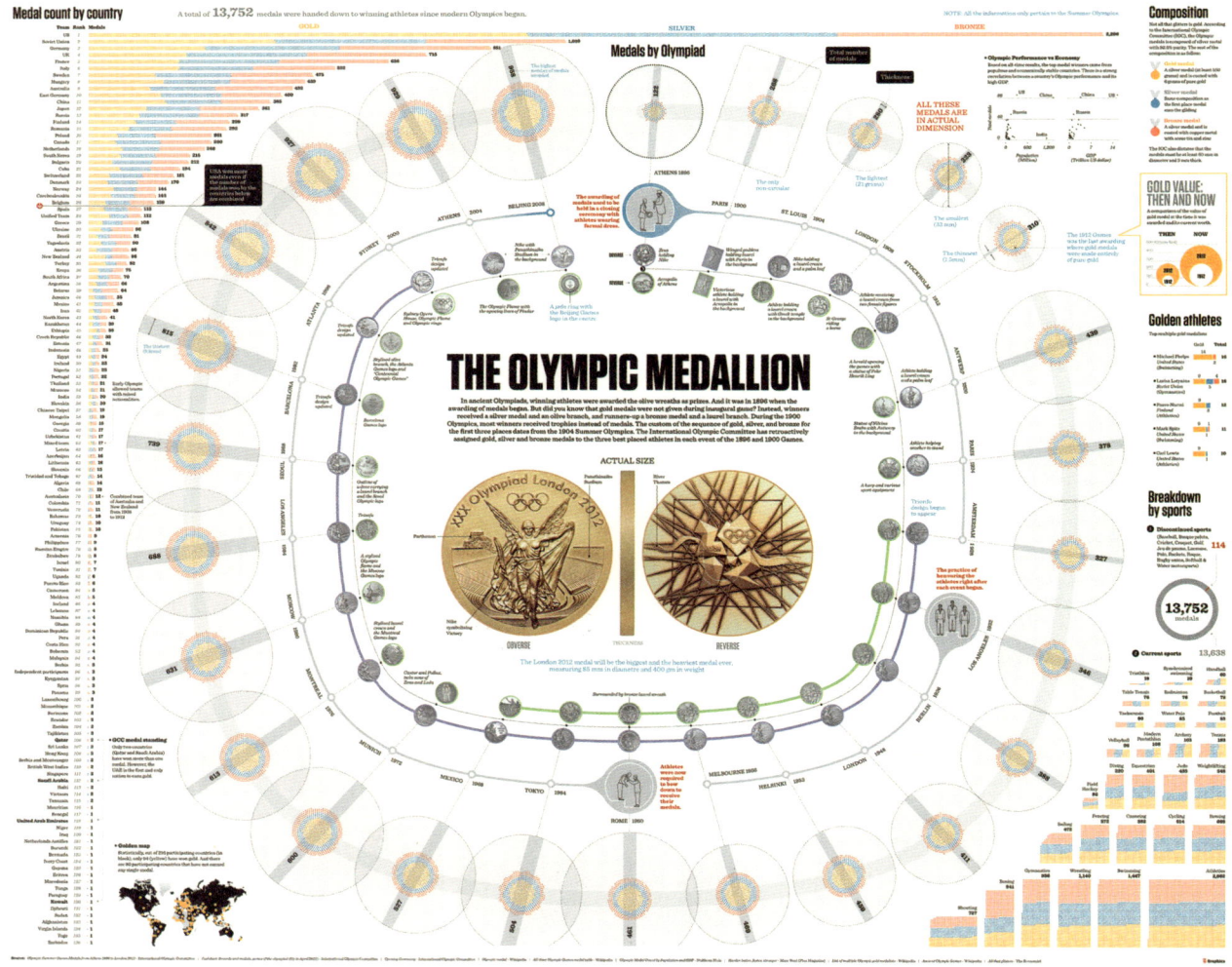

Summer Sports

Project Description /

This visualization was one of a series that Antonio Farach created about the London 2012 Olympic Games, which was published in the *Times of Oman*.

One sport, by Olympic definition, may be divided into several disciplines, which are then often regarded as separate sports. Each Olympic sport is represented by an international governing body. The infographic describes the basic structure, sport selection, history of current events, and changes in the sports of the Olympic Games. Antonio Farach used dots in different colors to show every event, and the timeline presents all the information clearly.

Client / *Times of Oman*
Designers / Antonio Farach, Sreemanikandan Satheendranathan, Isidore Vic Carloman
Completion / 2012

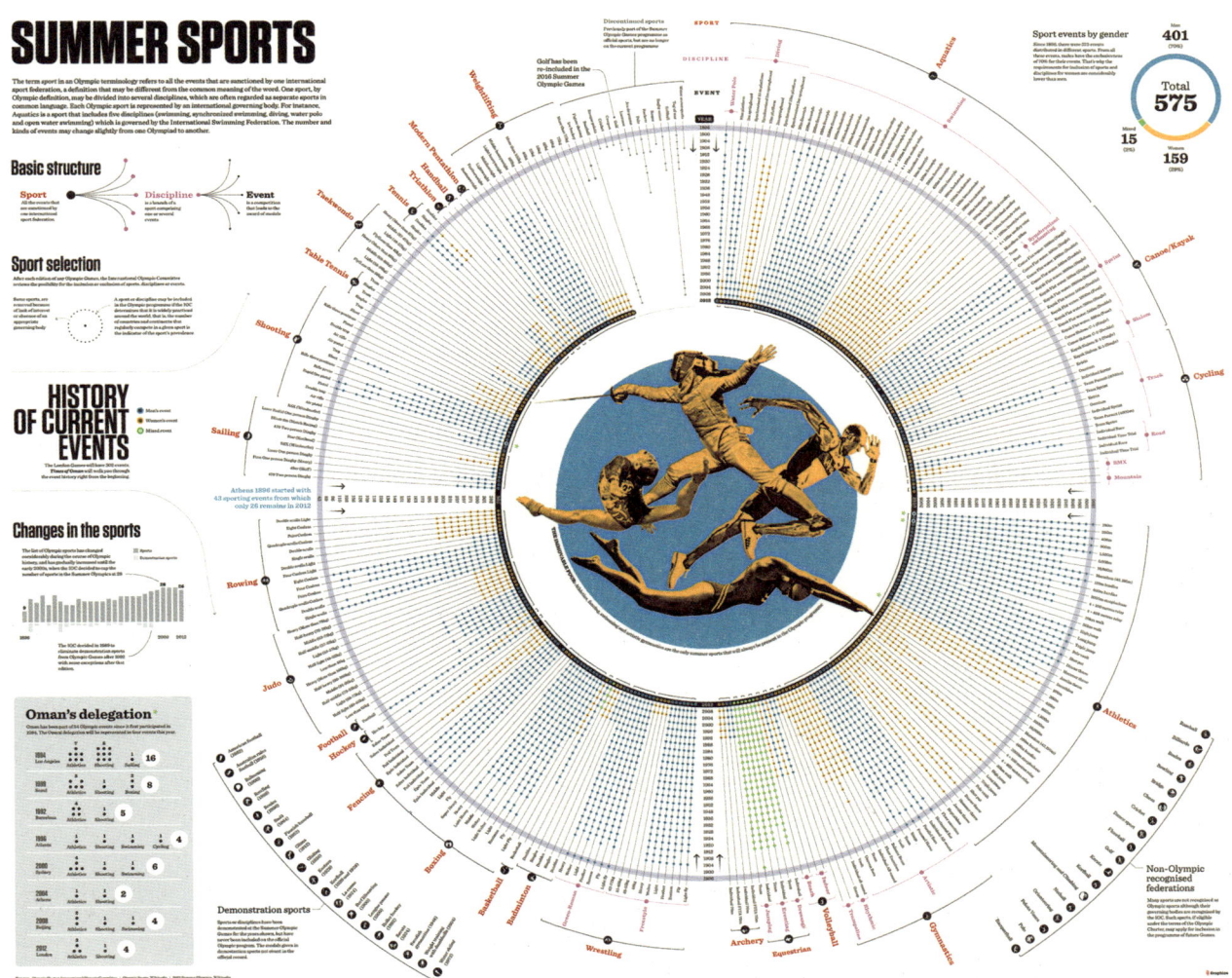

[080 – 082]
Client / *Diario La Prensa*
Designer / Alejandro Colmenárez
Completion / 2013

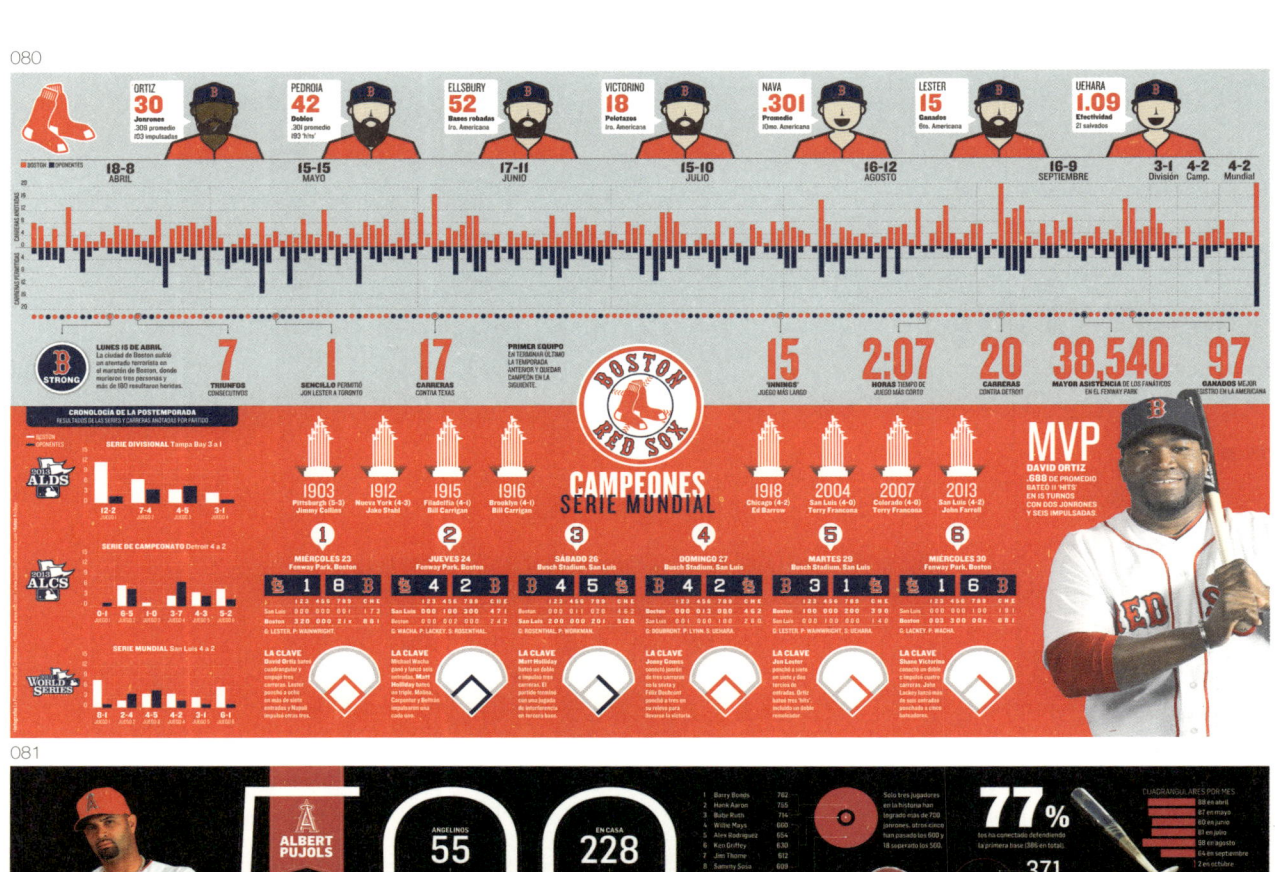

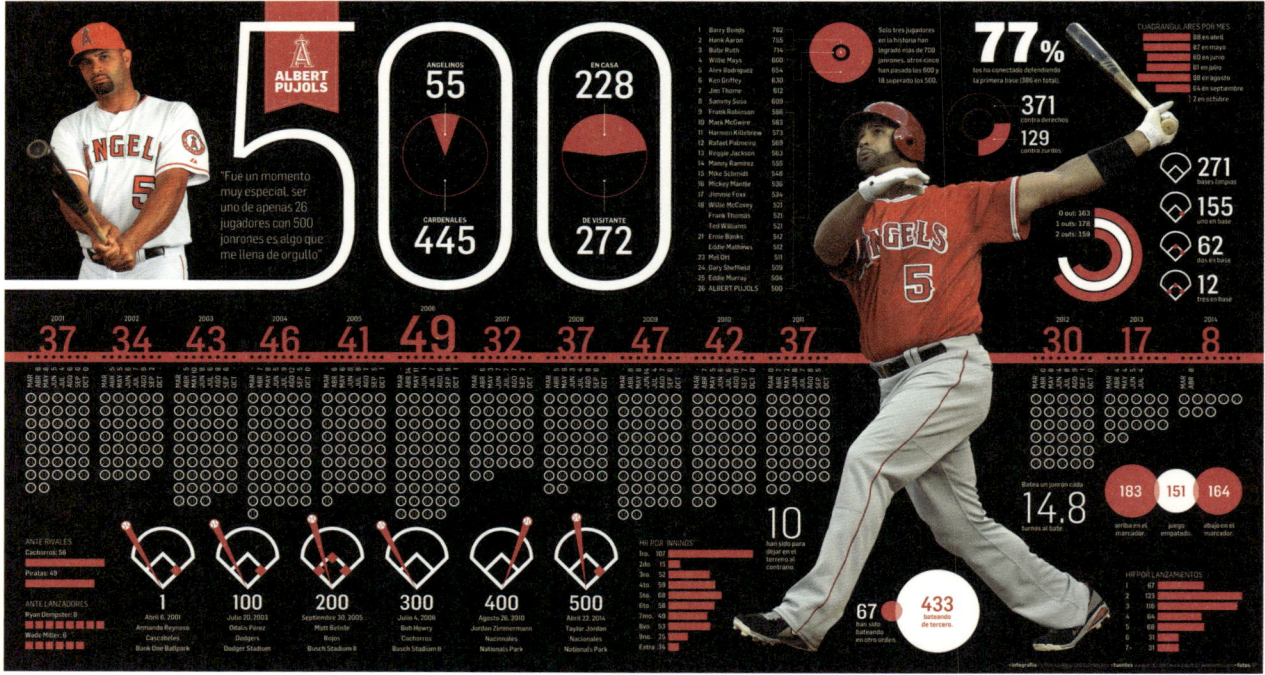

080

MLB 2013 World Series

Project Description /
The infographic is dedicated to the Boston Red Sox winning the 2013 World Series. The tribute to the 2013 champion team in the Major League Baseball shows that they played 162 games during the season and postseason. Inspired by their leader David Ortiz, the Red Sox beat the Cardinals in six games in a season that was affected by the tragedy of the Boston marathon. The designer likes using icons and other graphic elements in his infographics. He offers something a little different, and presents statistics to the public in an entertaining way.

081

Albert Pujols 500HR

Project Description /
The infographic is dedicated to Albert Pujols. The Angels first baseman became the first major-league player to hit his 499th and 500th home runs in the same game. Being one of the most respected players in baseball, he has always worked appropriately for achieving some particular brand. Alejandro always liked to illustrate homers in months, weeks, against which pitchers, seasonally, and from 100 to 100.

082

Alex Rodriguez Ties Lou Gehrig

Project Description /
Alejandro Colmenárez has designed an infographic about baseball, where readers can see the detail about each home run. Information includes the stadium, rival pitcher, opposing team, score, inning, outs, count, launch, and batting order. The designer used two figures and the colors of the Yankees to create something different and entertaining.

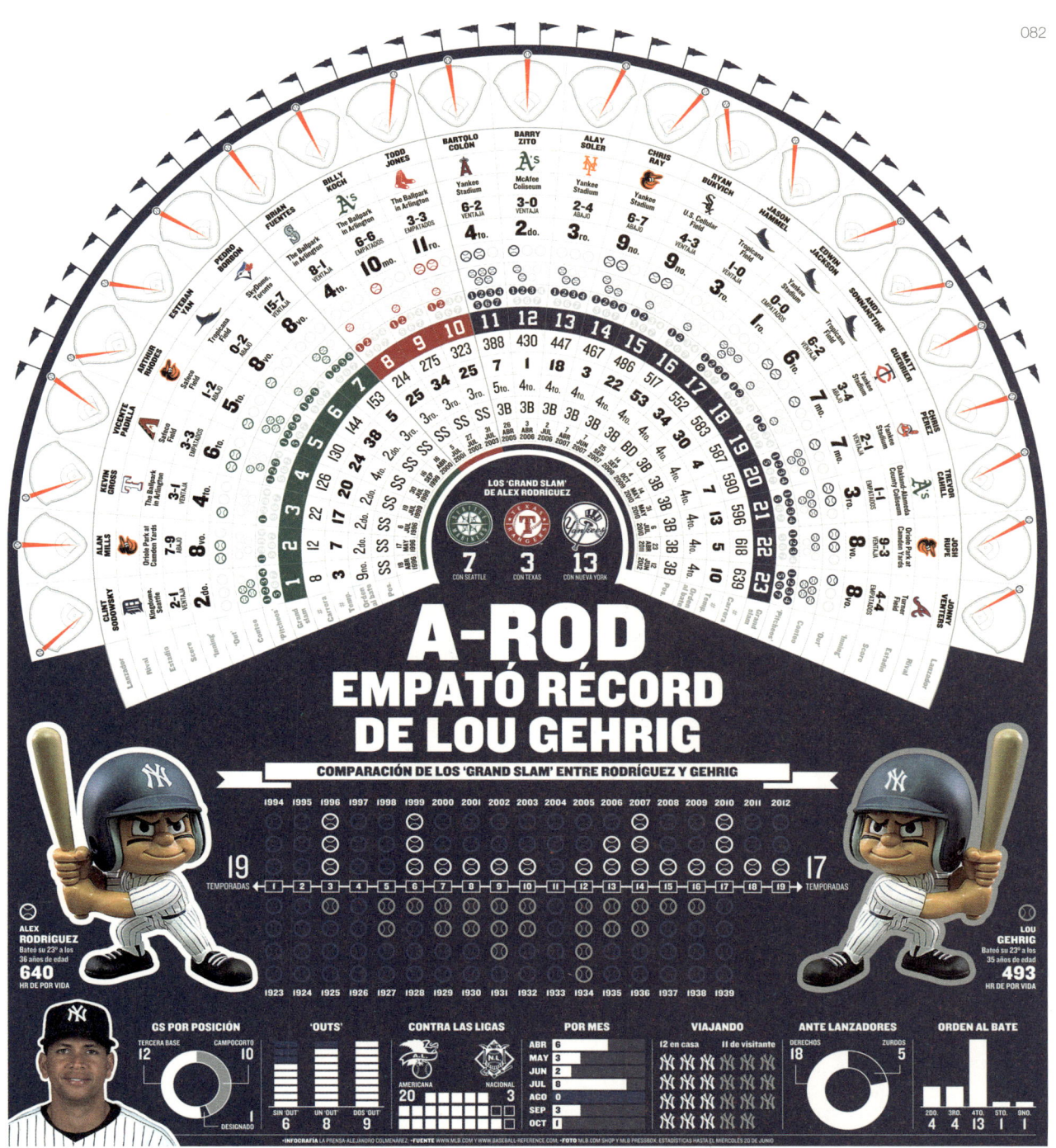

2014 Australian Open: the New Champions

Project Description /

Following the finals for the Australian Open 2014, tennis has a new set of champions—Li Na from China for women's singles, and Stanislas Wawrinka from Switzerland for men's. This was the 102nd Australian Open tournament, and the first Grand Slam of 2014. Li Na defeated Dominika Cibulkova, while Stanislas defeated Rafael Nadal.

It's a straightforward data visualization of the two players' road to success (inverted tree chart), and to give it a more fitting and relevant design, the data is shaped like a tennis racket. The data (lines) shows the beginning of the tournament and follows all of the match winners right up to the final tournament champions. The profile features of the champions is also an added design element. Colors are kept minimal: pink for women's, blue for men's. And, of course, to wrap things together in this page, they chose to make caricatures of the players, and use monochrome colors to keep the consistency of the obvious color choices.

Client / *Times of Oman*
Designers / Lucille Umali, Antonio Farach
Completion / 2014

The Instability of Sport in Cucuta

Project Description /

The Sport Cucuta has been participating in different campaigns, but with no good results. John Velasco wanted to show the different campaigns this year, so he used different photos, and statistical data represented as poker cards to make people guess what was going to be the next technical direction of the team.

Client / *La Opinion* newspaper
Designer / John Velasco
Completion / 2013

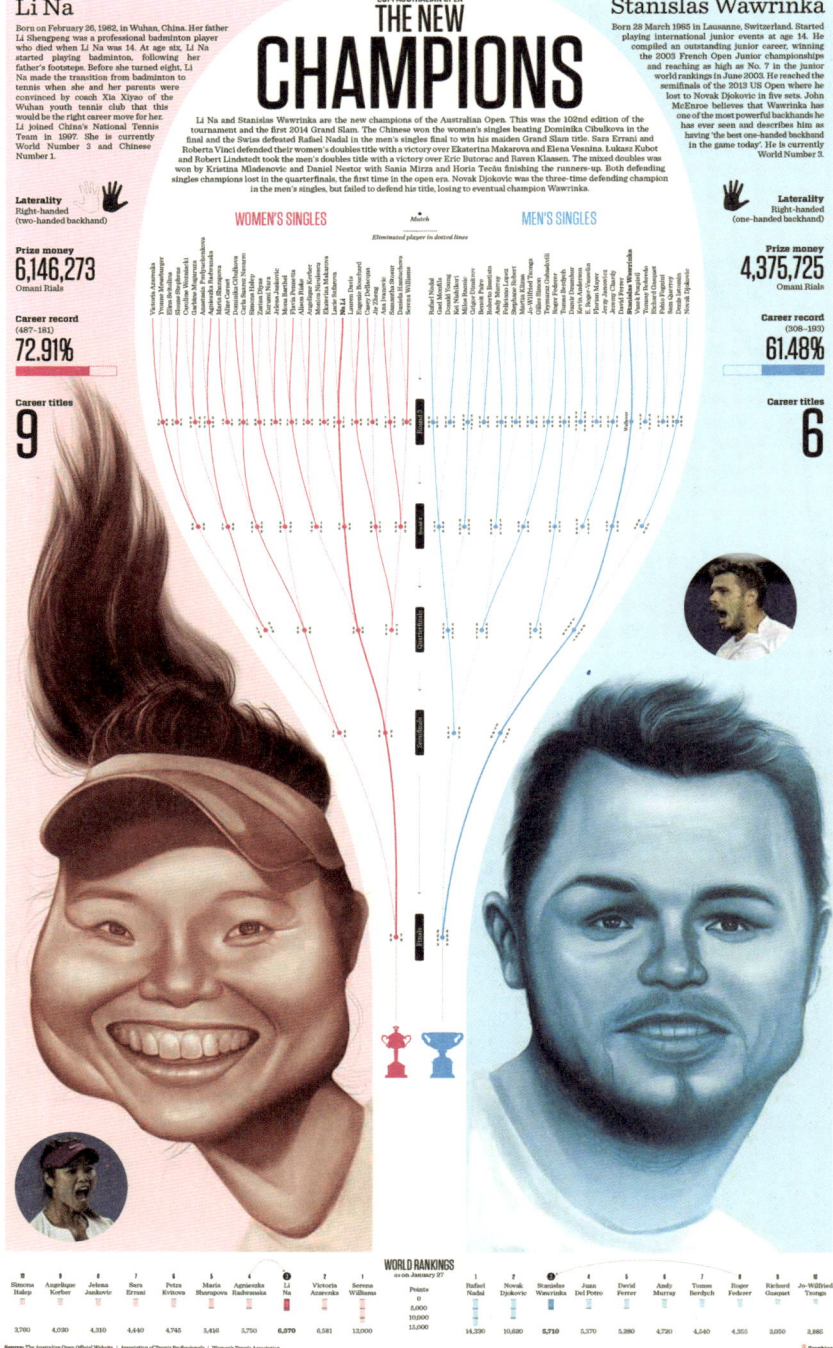

Infografía

13 TÉCNICOS EN OCHO AÑOS

2006 — 1 JORGE LUIS PINTO
Pinto llegó en el mejor momento del Cúcuta Deportivo tras su regreso a primera categoría. Formó una base de jugadores que fueron claves para conseguir el primer campeonato de la institución.

Total 50 — Ganados 27 · Empatados 11 · Perdidos 12

LOGROS
- Título en 2006 torneo finalización.
- Clasificación a Copa Libertadores
- Cuadrangulares torneo apertura 2009

2009 — 5 JORGE LUIS PINTO
Luego de su salida de la Selección Colombia, el técnico santandereano regresó al equipo con el que logró el campeonato en el 2006. Pinto traía nuevos ideales para la reorganización de la institución que no pudo concretar.

Total 42 — Ganados 13 · Empatados 13 · Perdidos 16

2007 — 2 JORGE LUIS BERNAL
Con la salida de Jorge Luis Pinto, el máximo accionista del equipo en aquel entonces, Ramiro Suárez buscó a uno de los mejores técnicos que tenía el fútbol colombiano. Jorge Luis Bernal paradójicamente se convirtió en técnico del equipo con el que había perdido la final en el 2006.

Copa Libertadores

Total 60 — Ganados 22 · Empatados 13 · Perdidos 13

LOGROS
- Semifinal Copa Libertadores
- Cuadrangulares Torneo Apertura
- Cuadrangulares Torneo Clausura

2008 — 3 PEDRO SARMIENTO
Llegó al Cúcuta como reemplazo de Jorge Luis Bernal, con la responsabilidad de jugar el torneo local y hacer una presentación en la Copa Libertadores mejor que la del año anterior.

Total 32 — Ganados 8 · Empatados 5 · Perdidos 11

2008 — 4 ANÍBAL RUIZ
Exjugador y entrenador uruguayo, su llegada al Cúcuta Deportivo se da ante los malos resultados de Pedro Sarmiento, venía con un palmarés importante, en el 2006 había dirigido a la selección de Paraguay.

Total 12 — Ganados 3 · Empatados 2 · Perdidos 7

2010 — 6 NÉSTOR OTERO
En su palmarés estaban dos subcampeonatos en el fútbol colombiano antes de llegar al Cúcuta Deportivo. El 'Matemático' fue criticado por un sector del periodismo y la hinchada rojinegra.

Total 11 — Ganados 2 · Empatados 4 · Perdidos 5

2010 — 7 JUAN CARLOS DÍAZ
El 'Nene' asumió como técnico del Cúcuta como solución a las constantes derrotas que venía sufriendo el equipo motilón. Era escuchado y querido por la hinchada cucuteña por su paso como jugador con la camiseta roja y negra.

Total 51 — Ganados 19 · Empatados 17 · Perdidos 15

2012 — 9 JUAN CARLOS DÍAZ
Regresó en el 2012, el argentino ha sido uno de los técnicos más queridos por la afición, pero en su segunda parte sólo logró 7 puntos que catapultaron su salida.

Total 8 — Ganados 2 · Empatados 1 · Perdidos 5

2011 — 8 JAIME DE LA PAVA
Llegó en julio de 2011. Con la renuncia del argentino Juan Carlos Díaz, asumió como técnico del Cúcuta Deportivo, llegó a un equipo en crisis económica y deportiva y renunció al finalizar el año tras recibir propuestas del fútbol venezolano.

Total 18 — Ganados 2 · Empatados 9 · Perdidos 7

2012 — 10 HÉCTOR QUINTABANI
Tres títulos en el fútbol colombiano fue la principal razón por la que los directivos del Cúcuta Deportivo contrataron al técnico argentino. Salió por la puerta de atrás, inclusive agredió al presidente del Cúcuta Deportivo cuando decidió marcharse de la ciudad.

Total 16 — Ganados 3 · Empatados 1 · Perdidos 12

2013 — 11 GUILLERMO SANGUINETTI
Su principal objetivo tras su llegada al Cúcuta Deportivo era salvar al equipo del descenso. Ganó la promoción en dos juegos frente al América de Cali. Su salida se dio con la crisis económica que atraviesa el Cúcuta Deportivo.

LOGROS
- Ganó la promoción frente al América.

Total 20 — Ganados 7 · Empatados 5 · Perdidos 8

2013 — 12 ÁLVARO APONTE
Luego de la renuncia de Guillermo Sanguinetti, los directivos eligieron al vallecaucano, asegurando que conocía la ciudad y el equipo por su paso por el Cúcuta en los 90s. Su estadía fue corta, ya que a la cuarta fecha Aponte renunció.

Total 4 — Ganados 1 · Empatados 0 · Perdidos 3

La inestabilidad del Cúcuta Deportivo

TEXTO: MAURICIO JARAMILLO MUTIS
mauricio.jaramillo@laopinion.com.co
Estadísticas: Johan Manuel García
johan.garcia@laopinion.com.co

En los últimos ocho años, el equipo rojinegro ha cambiado 13 veces de entrenador. Eso refleja la falta de un proyecto serio, pensado y estructurado a largo plazo. Incluso, más de la mitad de los técnicos no dirigieron un torneo completo.

Si se miran las estadísticas (infografía) es posible determinar que el equipo motilón ha probado todas las opciones. Colombianos, extranjeros, con títulos, sin títulos, con experiencia, sin experiencia, jóvenes, viejos, etc. Lo único que en realidad no se ha intentado es contratar a un técnico para armar un proceso sólido para que se obtengan resultados a largo plazo.

Los números hablan por sí solos y demuestran que el Cúcuta ha cometido infinitos errores a la hora de buscar directores técnicos y de planificar un proyecto deportivo.

De los estrategas que tuvo el equipo, solo Jorge Luis Pinto, Jorge Luis Bernal y Juan Carlos Díaz completaron más de dos torneos al frente del cuadro fronterizo, lo que habla de una inmediatez de resultados que no permite un trabajo planificado. El club deja entrever, tal como ocurre con un castillo de naipes, la fragilidad e inestabilidad para sostener un plan específico de trabajo.

Ejemplos de esta misma situación hay muchos en el fútbol nacional. Santa Fe, por nombrar un caso, demostró en Colombia que los procesos si traen buenos resultados. El equipo capitalino duró 37 años sin obtener un título y durante décadas probó con diferentes entrenadores, sin obtener los mejores resultados. Después de que muchas directivas fracasaran, año tras año, el club decidió llamar a un hombre de la casa (Wilson Gutiérrez) y sostener un proyecto a pesar de lo negativo que fueron los números del equipo en un principio. Un semestre pasó y el equipo levantó cabeza y con ese técnico que pocos querían, consiguió la octava estrella de su historia futbolística.

En manos de los directivos estará recomponer la situación y empezar a construir un futuro sólido para el 'Doblemente Glorioso'. Lo único que queda claro con los números del once motilón en los últimos años es que las cosas no se están haciendo bien y que, cada vez más, es necesario un cambio radical. Ojalá cuando llegue, si es que llega, no sea demasiado tarde.

Julio González, entrenador uruguayo, llegó al equipo luego de la derrota 5-1, en la quinta fecha de la Liga Postobón, frente al Júnior de Barranquilla.

Cúcuta Deportivo: 1. Diego Martínez, 2. Darío Bustos, 3. Luis Payares, 4. Walter Moreno, 5. Mauricio Duarte, 6. Javier Flórez, 7. Jaime Córdoba, 8. Rubén Bustos, 9. Javier Araújo, 10. Rodrigo Soria, 11. Víctor Uribe. DT. ¿?.

085

Tragic Deaths in Sport

Project Description /
This infographic focuses on the most shocking deaths in sport, emphasizing cases of Mexican athletes, as well as foreigners who played in Mexico, such as Ecuadorian footballer Christian Benitez. The black strip in this design represents respect for each athlete mentioned.

Client / Synthesis Newspaper Association
Designers / Ivón Guzmán Pérez, Omar Guerrero Pérez, Evelyn Romero Cárdenas, Jorge Balderas Velasco, Alfredo González, Joaquín Sánchez
Completion / 2013

086

Ora Pedala

Project Description /
This is a visual representation of the 2012 Tour de France, the popular bicycle race held annually in France. The charts flowing along the spread show, at a glance, information for the 99 times the event has been held, which took place from 1900 to 2012. The story takes the readers through each event, listing key facts such as the length of the race, the number of participants, the name of the winner, and the value of the prize. The design combines statistical representations and illustrations, giving a quick overview of the subject matter, as well as a chance to explore related interesting facts.

Client / IL—Il Sole 24 ORE
Designers / Francesco Franchi, Laura Cantadori, Andrea Manzati
Completion / 2012

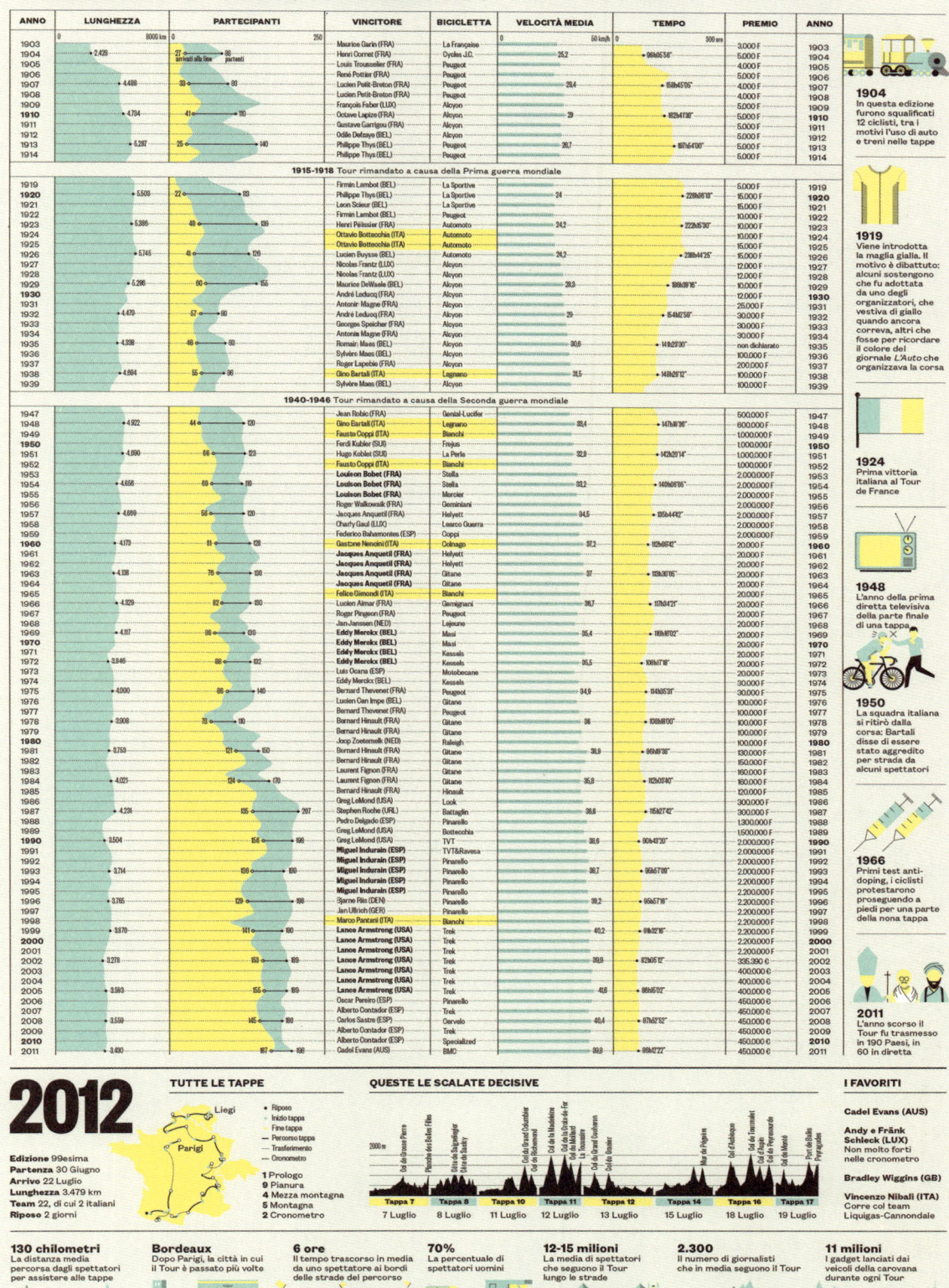

087

Evolution of Football

Project Description /

In anticipation of the World Cup football championship, designer Anton Osipov decided to make an infographic focusing on the evolution of football, based on examples of previous World Cups. In this work, Osipov doesn't provide a narrative; instead, he simply provides the facts to his readers, allowing each reader to find something of interest to them. The aim was to compress as much data as he could in a readable, good-looking format. It was challenging to show so much diverse data simultaneously. The designer used four different types of graphs and a variety of information differentiation methods: place, color, and geometric form.

Client / championat.com
Design Agency / Rambler Infographics
Designer / Anton Osipov
Completion / 2014

088

Horse Racing Infographic

Project Description /

Every year the Dubai World Cup is one of the most important events in Dubai. The first time the designer saw a telecast, he was shocked at the amount of prize money involved. He wondered: Where does the money all go? How many people are involved in training a racehorse? How do the owners manage those costs?

Money in horse racing, or any other sport, is interesting to a wide range of readers, not just sporting enthusiasts. The next step was to find research, then sketch and write and pour everything onto the page through Adobe Illustrator and InDesign software. Finally, horse-racing specialist Leslie Wilson checked and endorsed all the facts to be printed.

The facts, statistics and figures are explained using icons and simple vignettes to tell the story. Also a simple color palette was composed, using black and red as the main colors, and beige as a supporting color in the background.

Client / *Gulf News* newspaper
Designer / José Luis Barros Chaparro
Completion / 2014

Gulf News | Saturday, March 29, 2014 | gulfnews.com

DUBAI WORLD CUP C17

Slicing the cake
(How the prize money filters down)

EVERYONE, FROM JOCKEY TO TRAINER TO GROOMS AND STABLE STAFF, WILL RECEIVE A SHARE

By **Leslie Wilson Jr.**
Racing & Special Features Writer
Jose Luis Barros
Senior Designer

Imagine for a while that you are a prominent racehorse owner, and suddenly your horse has won the Dubai World Cup, the world's richest race with prize money of $10 million. What happens to the $6million prize money you will receive and how do you distribute it among your team and all the people involved?

Here is an explanation as to how the prize money is shared.

World record achieved for racehorse sales
October 9, 2013: A new world record on sales was reached at Tattersalls auction, the main sales event for racehorses in the UK. The cumulative figure reached was 70.34 million guineas (that is the currency used on the racehorse market), equivalent to 431.44 million AED, which arose from 339 horses sold over three days.

The highest price paid for a horse was for Galileo, a yearling filly, whose price was five million guineas (30.85 million AED) and was paid by Qatar's Shaikh Joaan Al Thani.

Of course, you can buy a racehorse for Dh107,000, which sounds more affordable.

But you'll need a fat wallet for that as some owners have warned that to maintain a racehorse, it will cost you around Dh 120,000 AED a year, unless you get lucky and choose a winner.

$10,000,000
The total prize money on offer in the world's richest race today

The breakdown
- 1st: $6million
- 2nd: $2million
- 3rd: $1million
- 4th: $500,000
- 5th: $300,000
- 6th: $100,000

✈ Flying abroad
Horses also need passports to prove their identity during a journey. A 15-digit number, linked to a micro-chip, is inserted into the crest of the horse's neck at birth.

Dh50
Is the approx cost of an ID passport.

Applications for equine passports can only be accepted for microchipped animals according to the British Horse Racing Authority.

Choosing a class

Freight stalls for an aircraft can hold three horses for economy class travel, two for business class and one for first class.

Dh 25,000
Cost of flying a horse in economy class from the UK to Dubai.

Dh 45,000
from South America to Dubai.

75%
To the owner

Dh 120
Is the return for every Dh600 spent on average*
*A warning from the Racehorse Owners' Association.

The payment of the prize is directly deposited to the owner's bank account

10% To the trainer
10% To the jockey
5% To the stable

Others expenses and issues to consider

Around 50%
is the overall strike rate of a trainer at the top of the sport.

Trainers also might be
- Owners
- Employers
- Jockeys

He shares his reward among:
- **One or two grooms**, depending on the trainer
- **And also his exercise riders**

To the jockey
He will receive a standard share of the prize money, which is mandatory under most racing jurisdictions and is controlled by the local racing board.

FEE The riding fee paid in the UAE is Dh 462

The jockeys usually have:
- **An agent** He can also manage the PR of several jockeys at the same time
- **A valet** One normally attends to several jockeys

To the stable
Basic costs
- Veterinary
- Nutritionist
- Foreman
- Track fees
- Drainage
- Fencing
- Hay, forage and bedding
- Horse boxes
- Horse rugs
- Saddlery and tack

Dh 3000
Approx monthly expenses to stable a horse.

Payouts on a race day
Dh 1500
Approx amount for other jobs, including:
- Mucking out a stall
- Walking a horse
- Exercise rider (per gallop)
- Blacksmith
- Head lads
- Grooms
- Cool-down after race (45min walk)
- Veterinary
- Dentist
- Pull the mane

500dh
Approx cost per race for one set of 4 horseshoes

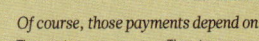

Of course, those payments depend on:
- The country
- The horseracing association
- The race
- The insurance funds
- The prize money
- The taxation
- Administration fees
- Advertising
- Other deductions

Sources: Racehorse Owners' Association | tattersalls.com | britishbloodstock-marketing.com | britishhorseracing.com | weatherbys.co.uk | Horsemen's Benevolent and Protective Association (HBPA) | Gulf News Archives

9 mondiali e 108 gare, tutto l'oro di Valentino

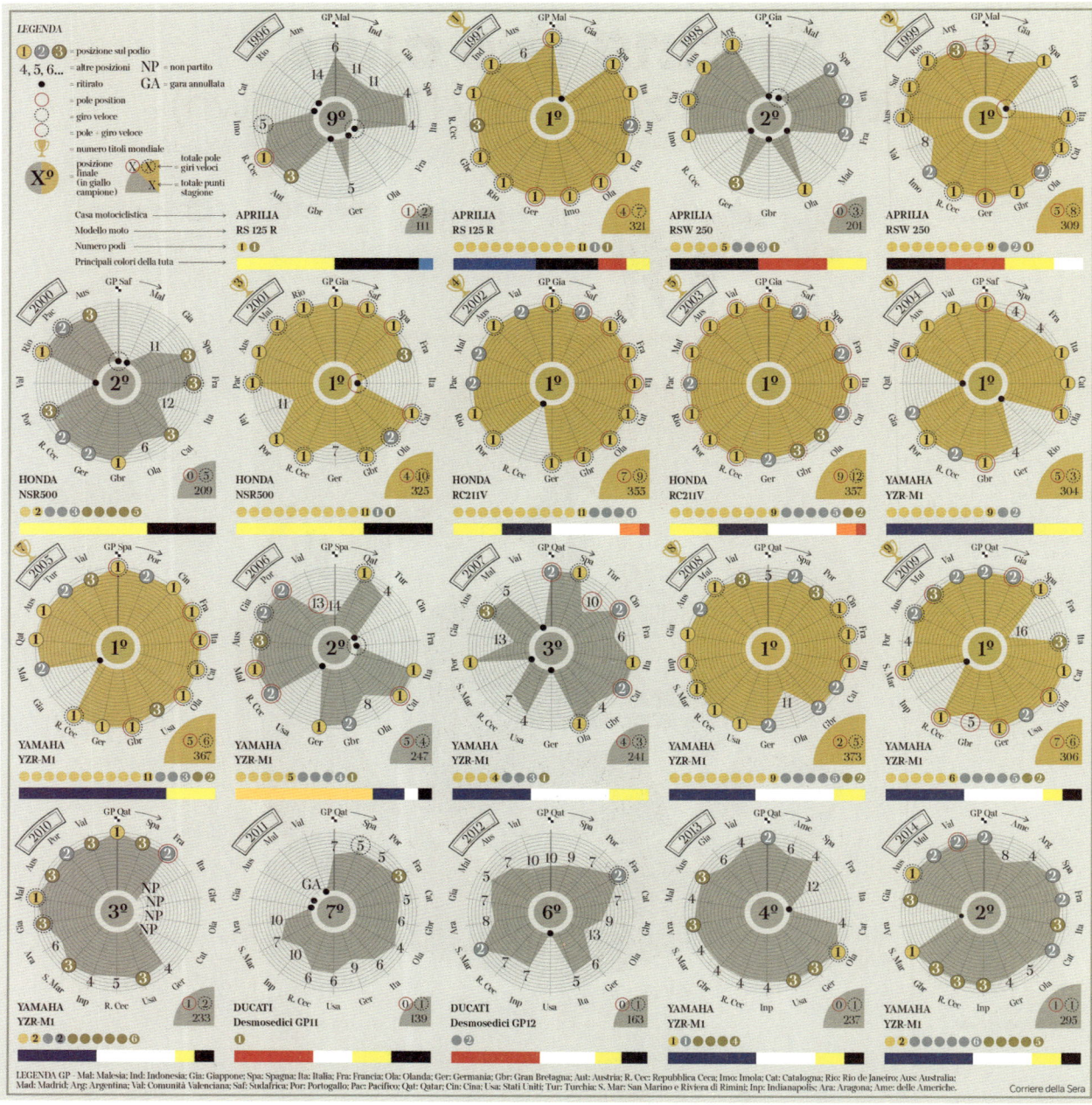

Valentino Rossi

Project Description /

This infographic was developed on the eve of Valentino Rossi's 20th Grand Prix motorcycle race. Rossi had already conquered nine world titles in his long career, and this looked like it could be his 10th title and chance for glory.

The infographic analyzes Rossi's Grand Prix results over the years, indicating his final position in each race, whether he obtained the pole position, and if he made the fastest race lap. The design highlighted the victories as well as the second and third positions, and from the area graphic, it's possible to immediately identify the years in which Valentino Rossi has obtained good results. Since Rossi is very superstitious and carefully chooses his race colors, the infographic also explores the number of times he wore the color yellow as a symbol of good luck.

Design Agency / Corriere Della Sera Infographic Newsroom
Designer / Marcello Valoncini
Completion / 2015

Rise to the Top

Project Description /
Infografika magazine editor Nikolay Romanov is a huge football fan, and his favorite football team is Zenit FC from Saint Petersburg. The idea for this infographic came to mind after Zenit FC lost an important game, and it illustrates how the team played during the whole football season.

Client / *Infografika*
Design Agency / Infografika Magazine
Designer / Sasha Brichkin
Completion / 2013

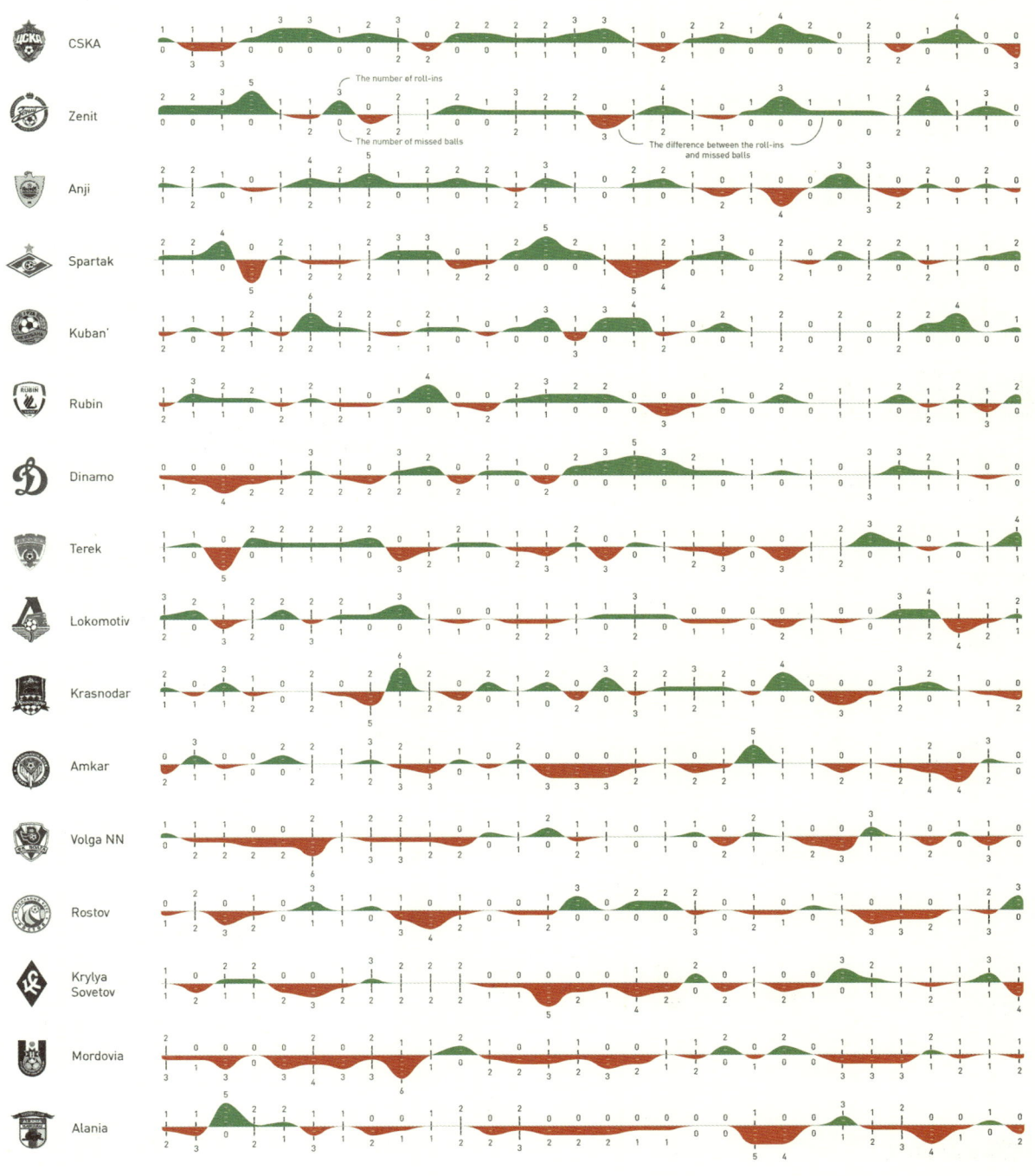

Rise to the top

CSKA deserved to become the champion of Russia in season 2012/2013. They won the most number of games. Most of these victories were very convincing – the difference of more than two roll-ins. But still "Zenit" is the best.

Source of information: Russian Premier League

Illustration by Sasha Brichkin / infographicsmag.ru

091

The Art of Bullfighting

Project Description /

This kind of bullfighting is popular in Oman, as well as in some other Arabic Gulf countries, so Antonio Farach dug deep in his research. The infographic features a description of the fight, how it works, and the mechanism of the 'game'; a location map and a description of the venue so the visitors can choose where to sit, in the safe or in the dangerous zone; explanations on how they prepare the bulls, bull's fighting styles, and the most suitable anatomic features for fighting; a historical timeline on bullfighting; and a cross-section of the venue, showing all the people involved, inside and outside the ring.

Client / *Times of Oman*
Designers / Antonio Farach, Lucille Umali

092

Tale of The Tape

Project Description /

The graphic was part of a preview package in the sports section for a WBA World Heavyweight Championship world title fight. The David vs. Goliath idea was to highlight the huge difference in size between the boxers. Ciaran Hughes wanted to give it the look of a boxing poster, while also designing the graphic so that the 9-centimeter (3.5-inch) advantage in Valuev's reach was actually to scale on the page.

Client / *Daily Telegraph* newspaper
Designer / Ciaran Hughes

093

UFC: World's Fastest Growing Sport

Project Description /

The subject of this infographic is mixed martial arts (MMA), a full knowledge of several different martial arts, such as judo, muay thai, jiu-jitsu and wrestling. Brazil was a pioneer of MMA. In the 1920s, Helio Gracie and his brothers challenged everyone to combat without any rules. In 1993, Rórion, Helio's son, created the Ultimate Fighting Championship (UFC). Since then, the sport has developed, and now has rules, weight divisions and a health insurance for the fighters. The UFC is the main MMA venue in the world. It's broadcast to one billion houses in 150 countries, in 21 languages.

Client / *Época* magazine
Designers / Marco Vergotti, Rodrigo Fortes, Gerson Mora
Completion / 2012

091

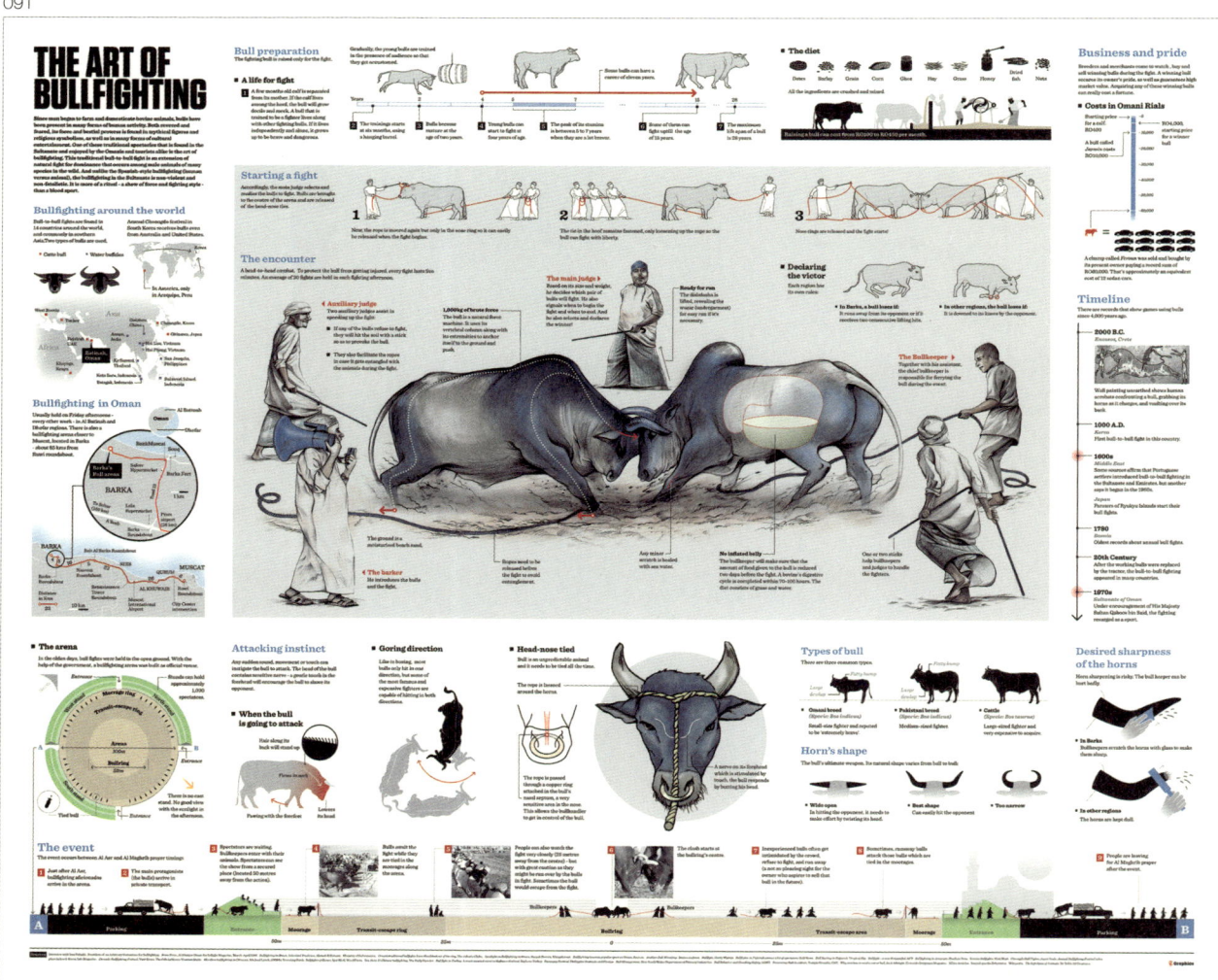

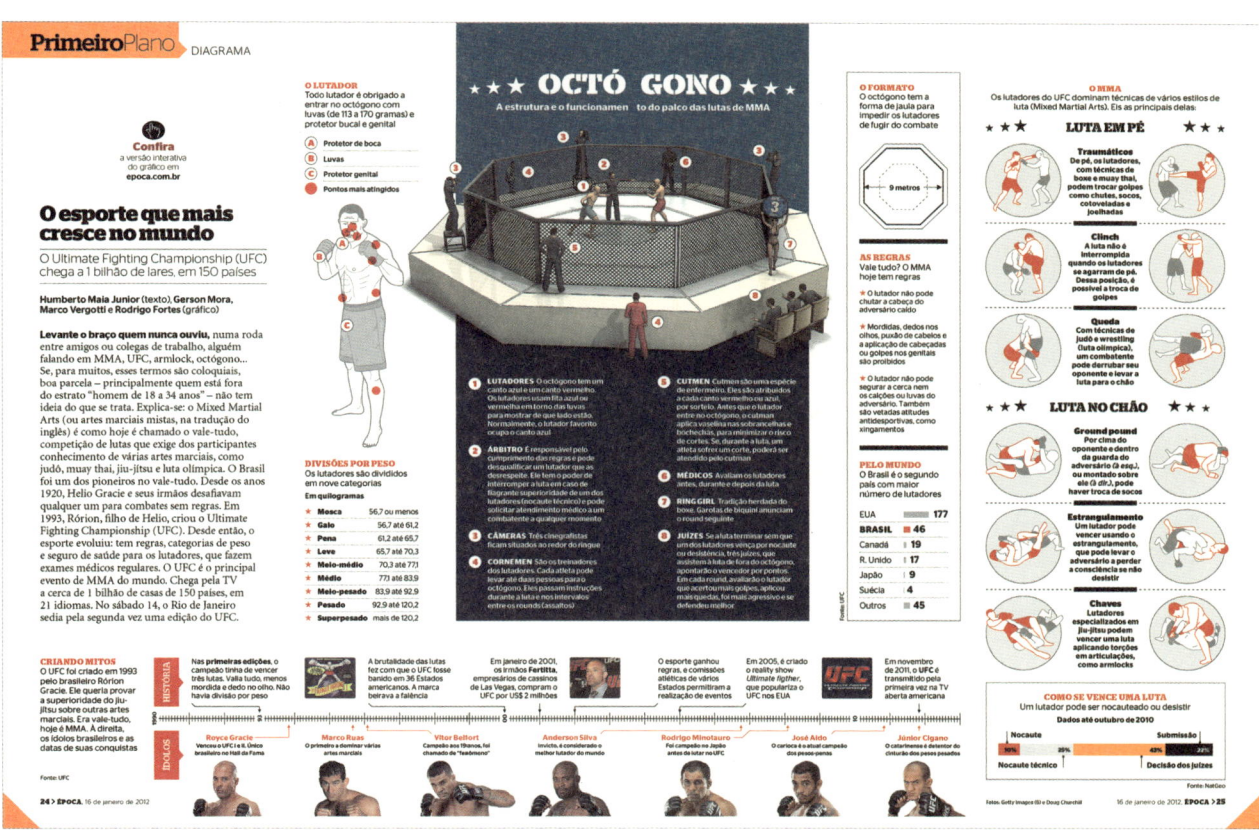

[094 – 096]
Design Agency / La Razón de México
Designer / Miguel Ulloa Maciel
Completion / 2014

094
Brasil 2014 Says Goodbye to 18 Warriors

Project Description /
This special presentation features 18 football stars from the 2014 World Cup, including their countries, ages, positions, and maximum goals. The central colors represent World Cups in which they participated, and the upper graph is divided into three parts representing lost, tied, and won games. At the bottom, the graph is accompanied by three short stories of the World Cup.

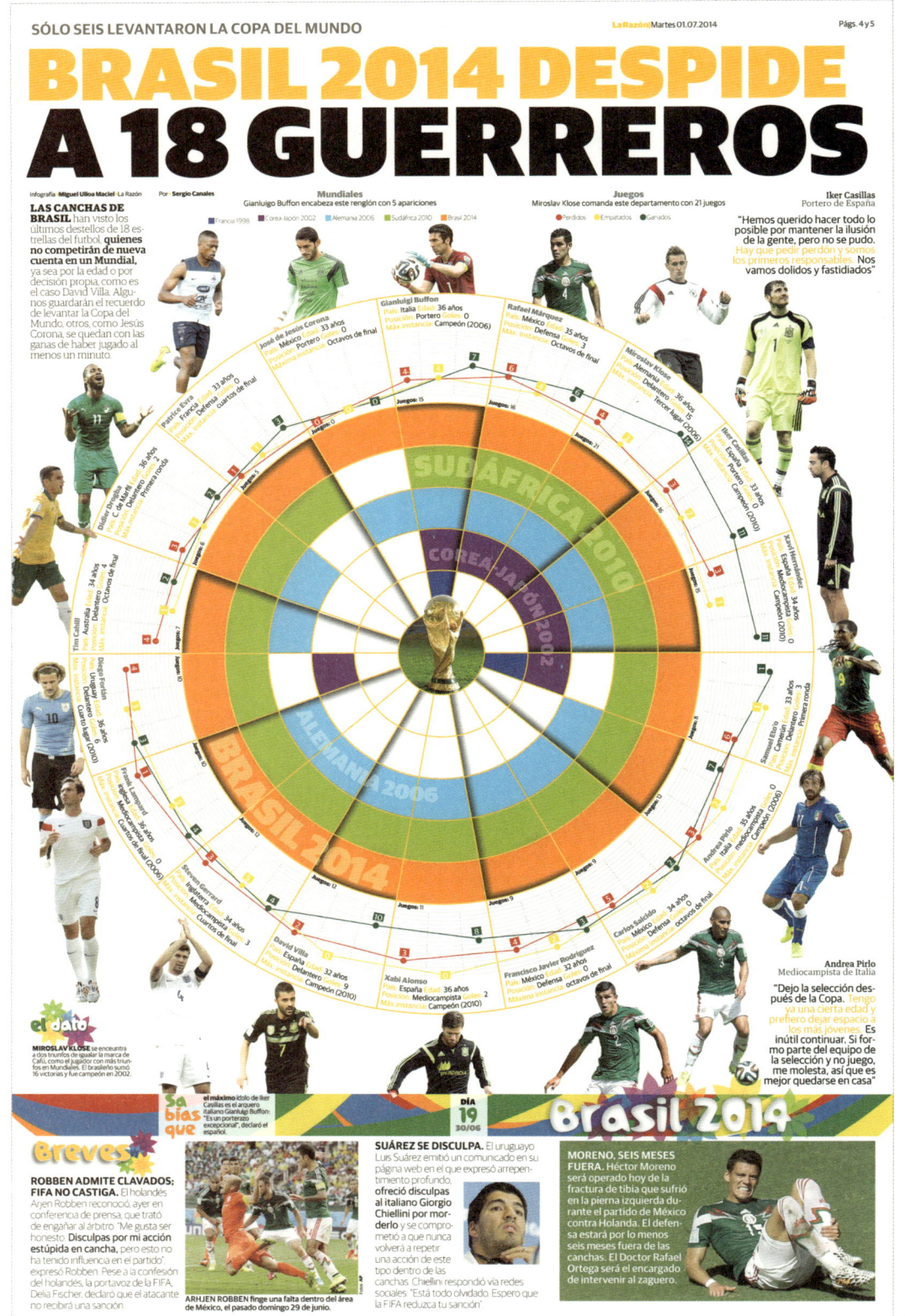

America for Americans in World Cup

Project Description /

In the quarter-final of the 2014 World Cup in Brazil, the Americas teams met the European teams. Brazil, Argentina, Colombia, and Costa Rica were the Americas representatives who believe in the so-called Monroe doctrine and their ideology— 'America for the Americans'. The goal of the Netherlands, Germany, Belgium, and France was to bring the World Cup from the New World to the Old Continent.

Failure of 2,255 M

Project Description /

Spain, England, Italy, and Portugal were four of the most expensive teams in the last World Cup and they were eliminated. This is highlighted in the infographic, which represents the cost of each of the 32 teams of the Cup, and reveals that being expensive does not mean being the best. In addition, it shows four of the most expensive players in the world that were eliminated and their statistics in the World Cup. Information on the right side makes a comparison of the salaries of Mexican players.

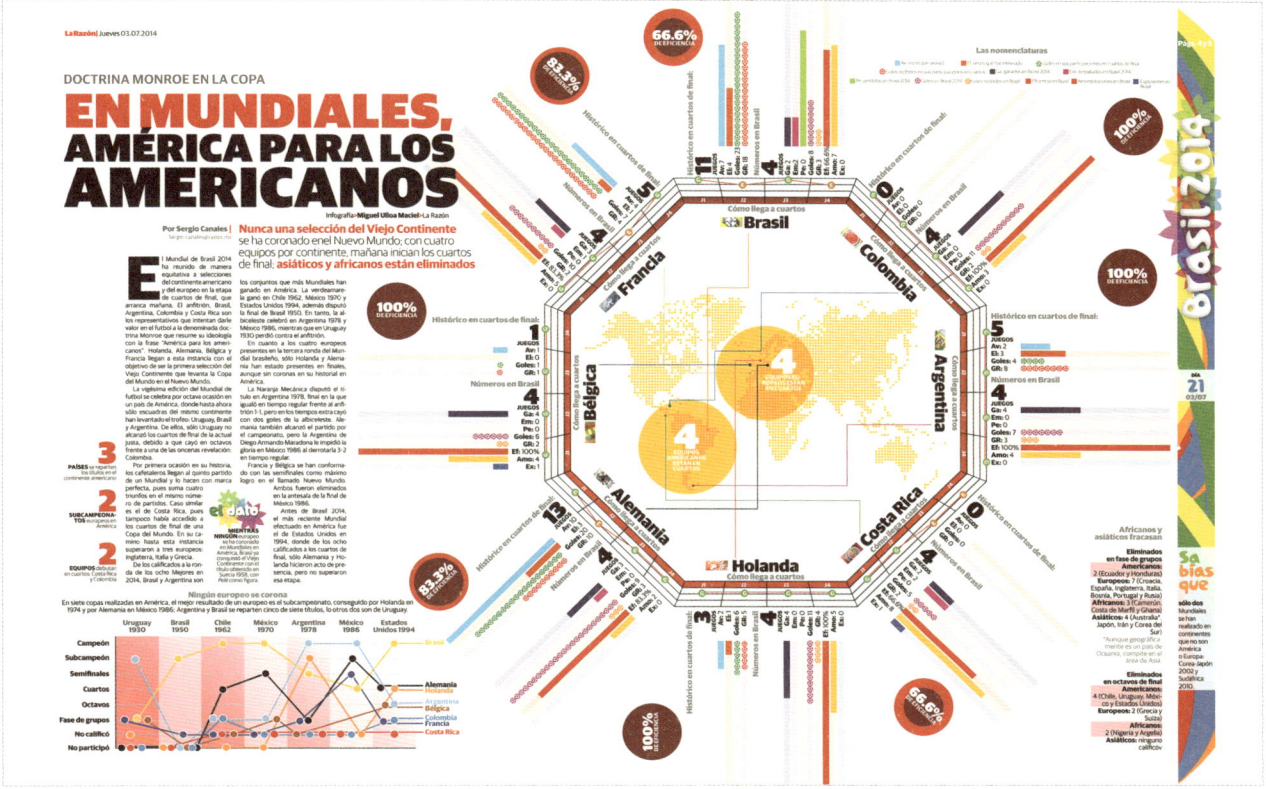

097

Cordobesa Football League

Project Description /
This historical infographic is about the regional soccer league from Córdoba, Argentina. In the middle of the graphic are city maps and the locations of the most important stadiums. The sides highlight the 18 current teams that make up the National League, and the bottom features a chronology about the evolution of the shirts of each team.

Design Agency / La Voz del Interior
Designer / Matías Cipollatti
Completion / 2012

098

Aguerre vs. Cambiaso

Project Description /
This infographic features the history between the best polo players in the world, a comparison of their titles, and a storyline about each team in which they played. Each player image is accompanied by their winning titles in Argentina and the United States. Each color represents a player.

099

Polo Heguy

Project Description /
This infographic features a historical timeline about the Argentine polo-playing Heguy brothers. Each color represents each team where they played. At the bottom stand the four Cup titles that they won in the Abierto Argentino de Palermo.

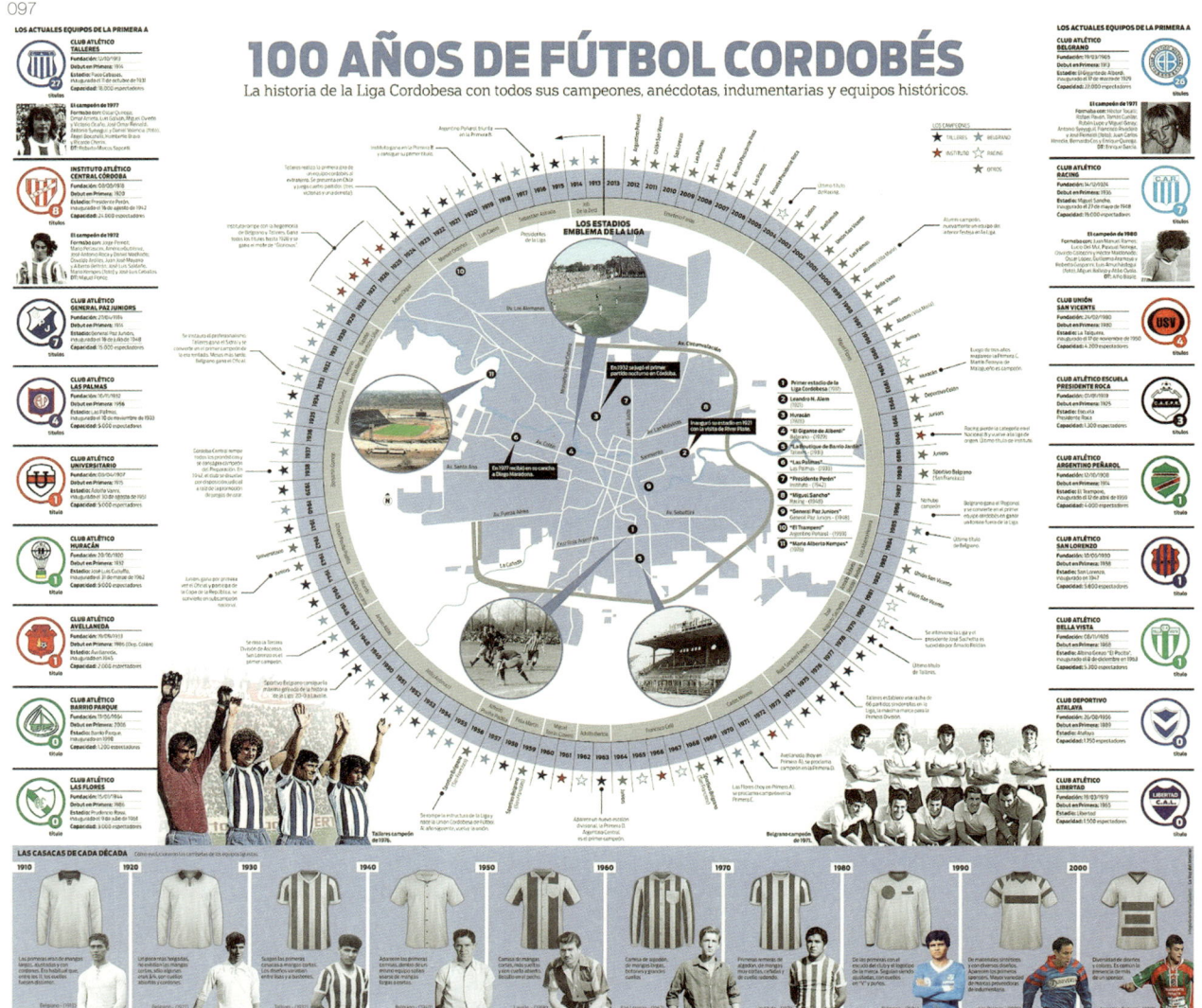

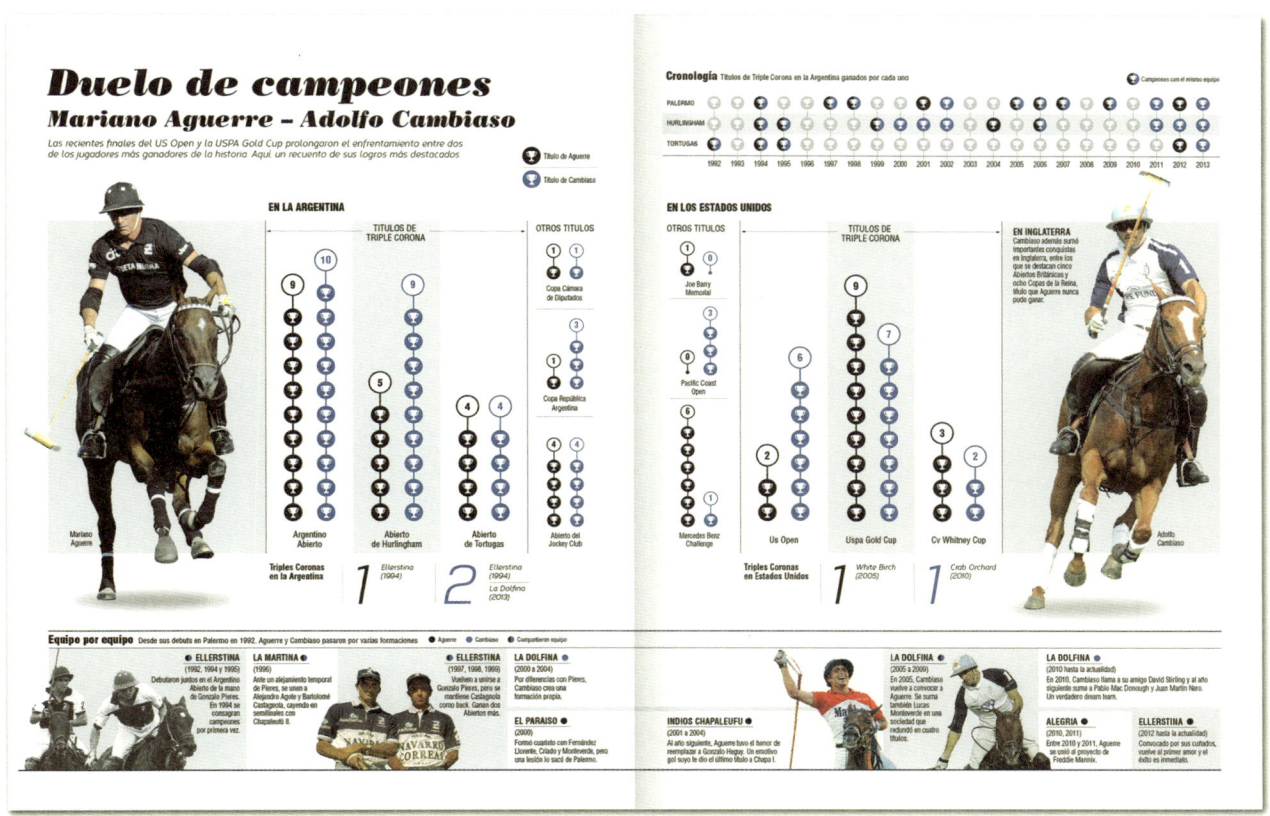

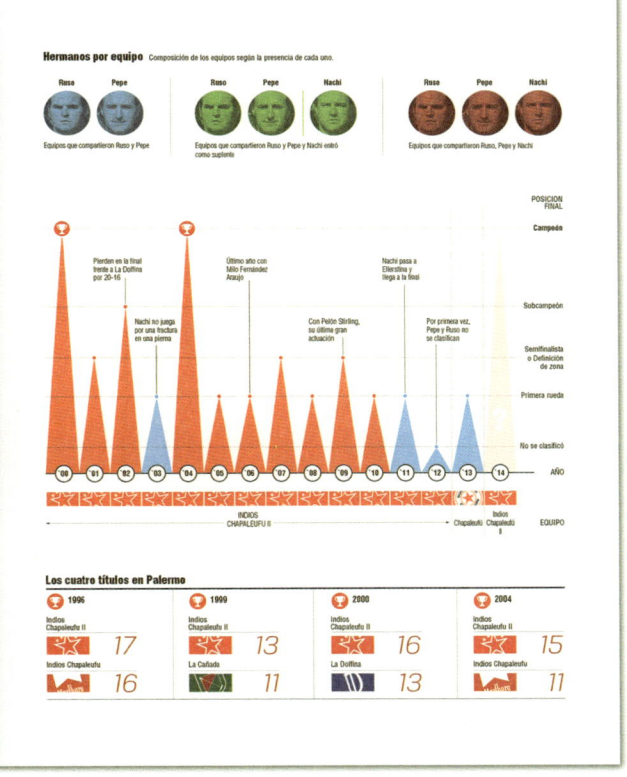

[098 – 101]
Client / *Polo Mundial*
Design Agency / Editorial Mundial
Designer / Matías Cipollatti
Completion / 2014

Cambiaso Years

Project Description /

This circular chronology explores the career highlights of Adolfo Cambiaso, the world's best polo player; the graphic highlights his titles and which of them were 'triple crown' (star). Each color represents a country. At the bottom of the page, there is additional information on his team, 'La Dolfina', with all the triple crowns.

Cambiaso Map

Project Description /
This project is a world map featuring Argentine polo player Adolfo Cambiaso's winning titles. Each color represents a country. At the bottom, there's a chart that shows Cambiaso's number of titles per country.

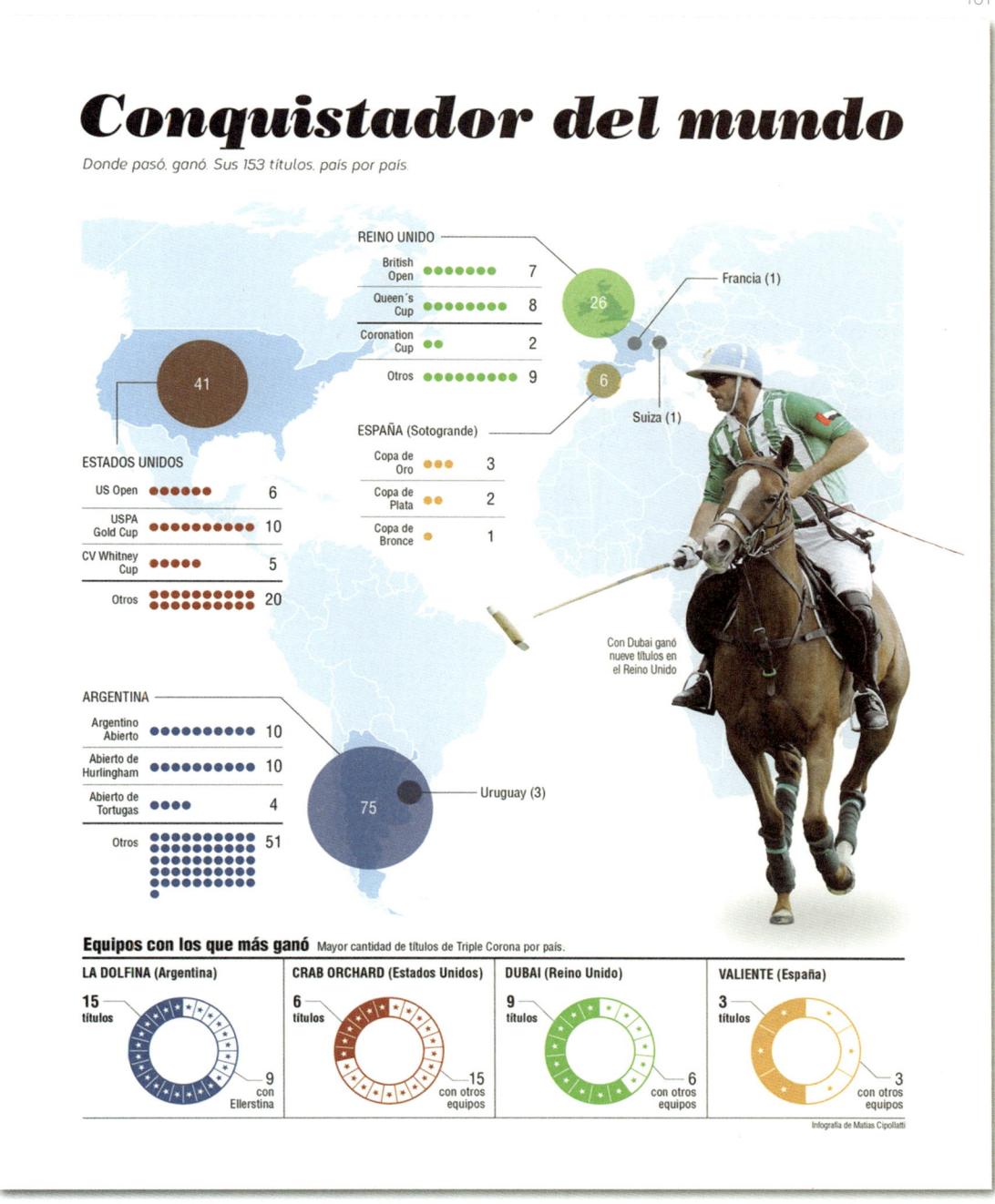

The London Olympic Games—Three Places

Project Description /
This infographic compares the three different Olympic Games that have taken place in the city of London.

The London Olympic Games—Athletics

Project Description /
This infographic compares the number of athletics medals won by the US team with those won by the other participating countries.

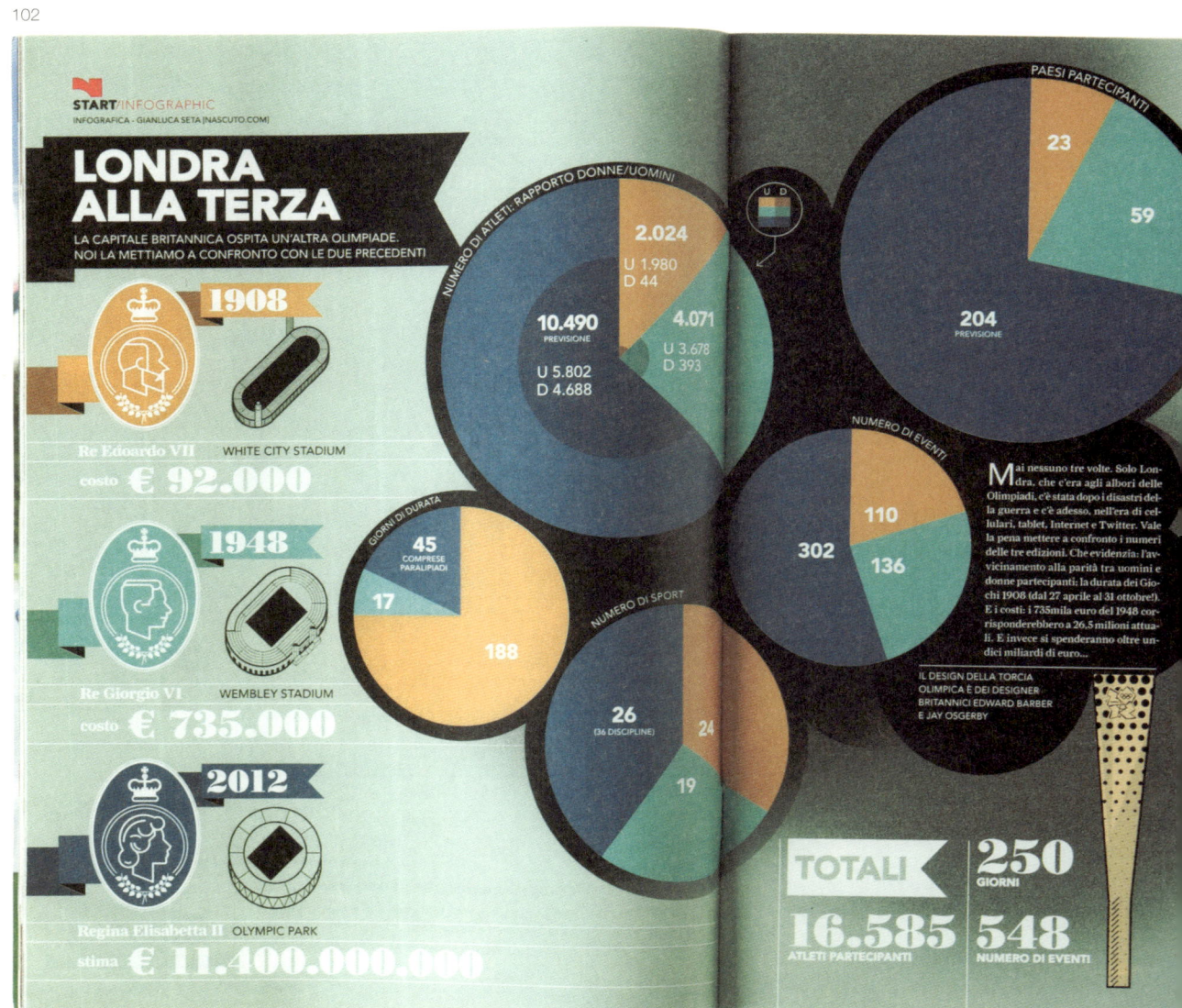

[102 – 106]
Client / *Sportweek—La Gazzetta Dello Sport*
Designer / Gianluca Seta
Completion / 2012

103-1

103-2

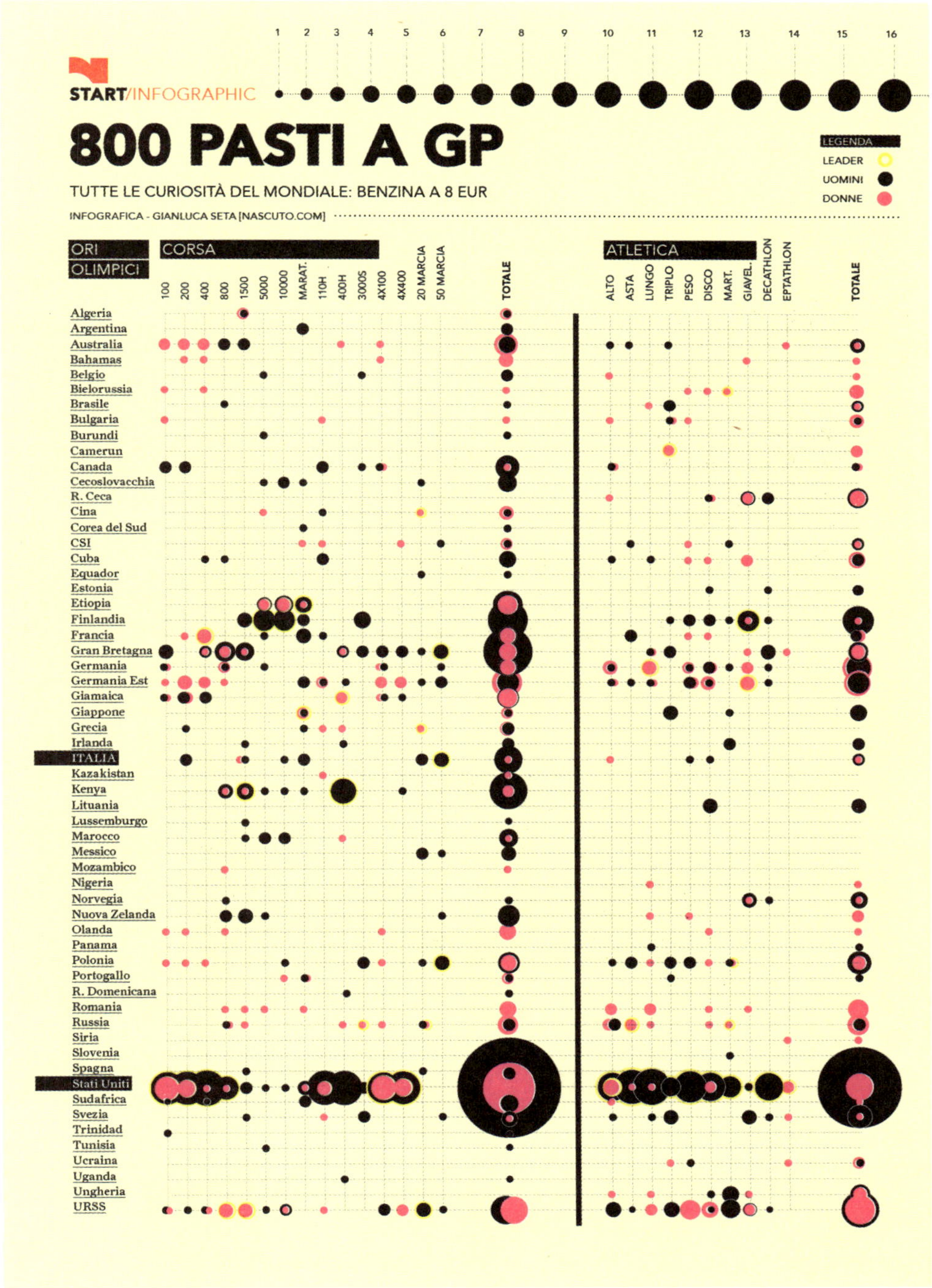

104
The London Olympic Games—Football Uniforms

Project Description /
The palettes chosen for this infographic show the most common colors used in the Olympic uniforms of the Italian football teams, and those of the eight best European leagues. The range of colors used for all European uniforms are represented on these pages.

105
The London Olympic Games—Swimming

Project Description /
This project explores the distribution of gold medals in the London Olympic Games, and compares the success rate of European men and women in the Olympic swimming competition.

106
The London Olympic Games Series—100 Meters

Project Description /
This sporting infographic compares the speeds achieved by all winners of the 100 meters competition, taking the Usain Bolt as a reference.

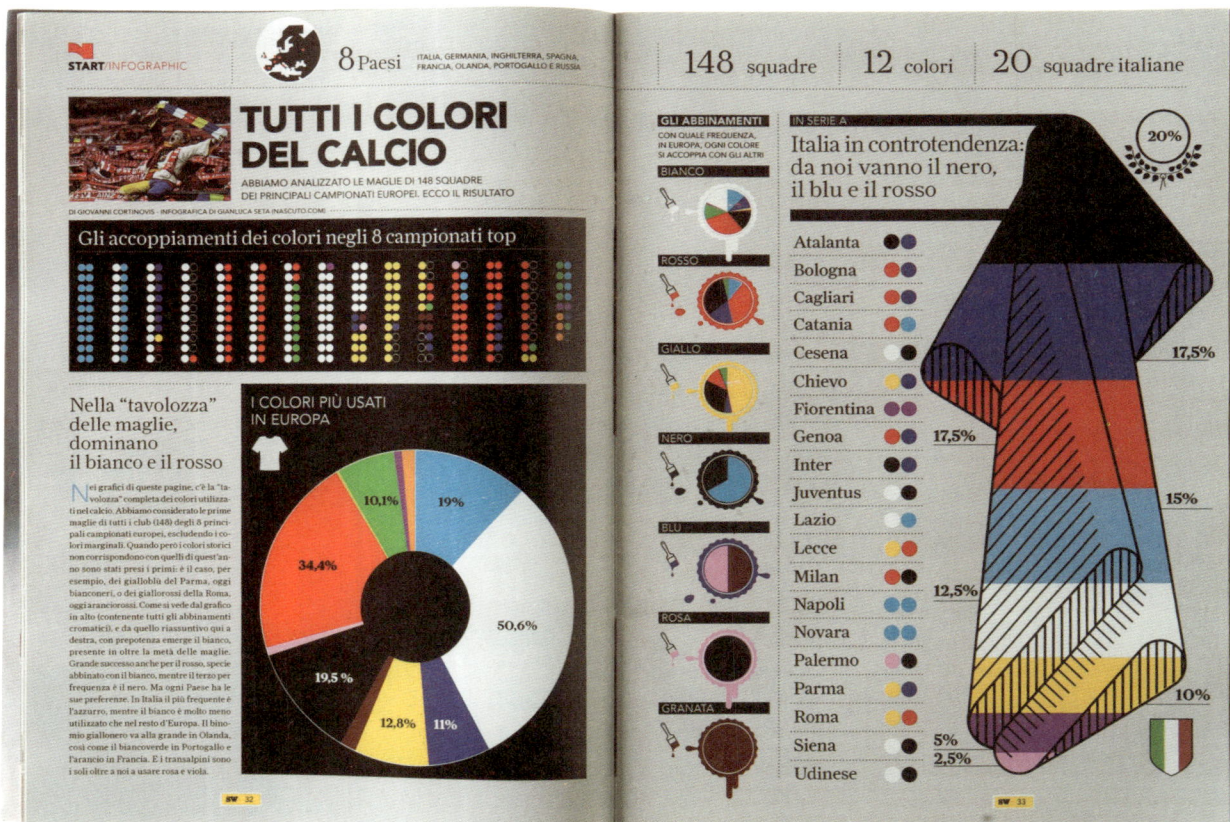

104

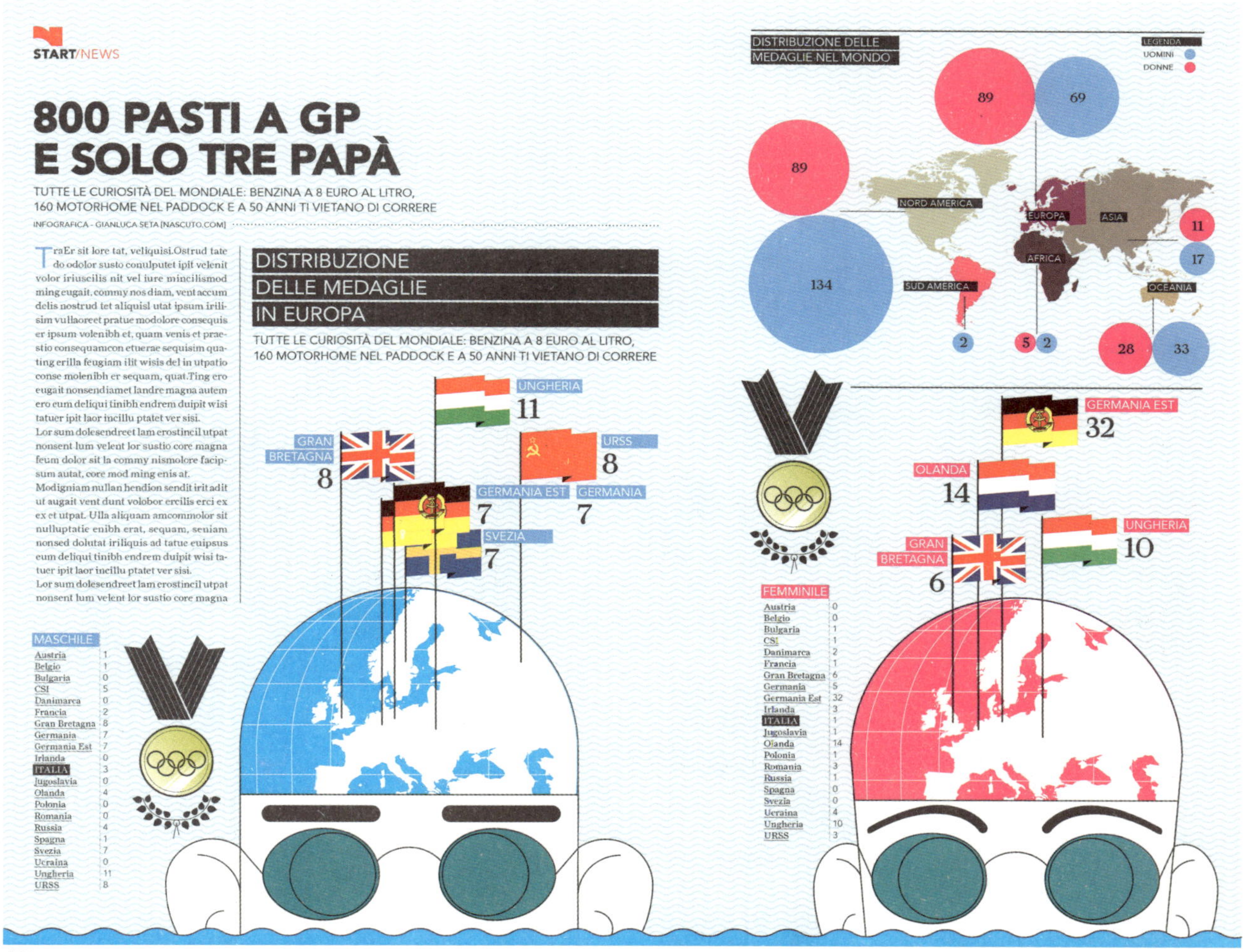

800 PASTI A GP E SOLO TRE PAPÀ

TUTTE LE CURIOSITÀ DEL MONDIALE: BENZINA A 8 EURO AL LITRO, 160 MOTORHOME NEL PADDOCK E A 50 ANNI TI VIETANO DI CORRERE

INFOGRAFICA - GIANLUCA SETA [NASCUTO.COM]

TraEr sit lore tat, veliquisi.Ostrud tate do odolor susto conulputet ipit velenit volor iriuscilis nit vel iure mincilismod ming eugait, commy nos diam, vent accum delis nostrud tet aliquisl utat ipsum irilisim vullaoreet pratue modolore consequis er ipsum volenibh et, quam venis et praestio consequamcon etuerae sequisim quating erilla feugiam ilit wisis del in utpatio conse molenibh er sequam, quat.Ting ero eugait nonsendiamet landre magna autem ero eum deliqui tinibh endrem duipit wisi tatuer ipit laor incillu ptatet ver sisi.

Lor sum dolesendreet lam erostincil utpat nonsent lum velent lor sustio core magna feum dolor sit la commy nismolore facipsum autat, core mod ming enis at. Modigniam nullan hendion sendit irit adit ut augait vent dunt volobor ercilis erci ex ex et utpat. Ulla aliquam amcommolor sit nulluptatie enibh erat, sequam, seniam nonsed dolutat iriliquis ad tatue euipsus eum deliqui tinibh endrem dulpit wisi tatuer ipit laor incillu ptatet ver sisi.

Lor sum dolesincil utpat nonsent lum velent lor sustio core magna

DISTRIBUZIONE DELLE MEDAGLIE IN EUROPA

TUTTE LE CURIOSITÀ DEL MONDIALE: BENZINA A 8 EURO AL LITRO, 160 MOTORHOME NEL PADDOCK E A 50 ANNI TI VIETANO DI CORRERE

MASCHILE

Austria	1
Belgio	1
Bulgaria	0
CSI	0
Danimarca	0
Francia	2
Gran Bretagna	8
Germania	7
Germania Est	7
Irlanda	0
ITALIA	3
Jugoslavia	0
Olanda	4
Polonia	0
Romania	0
Russia	4
Spagna	1
Svezia	7
Ucraina	0
Ungheria	11
URSS	8

- GRAN BRETAGNA 8
- UNGHERIA 11
- URSS 8
- GERMANIA EST 7
- GERMANIA 7
- SVEZIA 7

DISTRIBUZIONE DELLE MEDAGLIE NEL MONDO

LEGENDA: UOMINI / DONNE

- NORD AMERICA: 89 / 89
- EUROPA: 69 / 134
- ASIA: 11 / 17
- AFRICA: 2 / 5
- SUD AMERICA: 2
- OCEANIA: 28 / 33

FEMMINILE

Austria	0
Belgio	0
Bulgaria	1
CSI	1
Danimarca	2
Francia	1
Gran Bretagna	6
Germania	1
Germania Est	32
Irlanda	1
ITALIA	2
Jugoslavia	0
Olanda	14
Polonia	1
Romania	3
Russia	1
Spagna	0
Svezia	0
Ucraina	1
Ungheria	10
URSS	2

- GERMANIA EST 32
- OLANDA 14
- UNGHERIA 10
- GRAN BRETAGNA 6

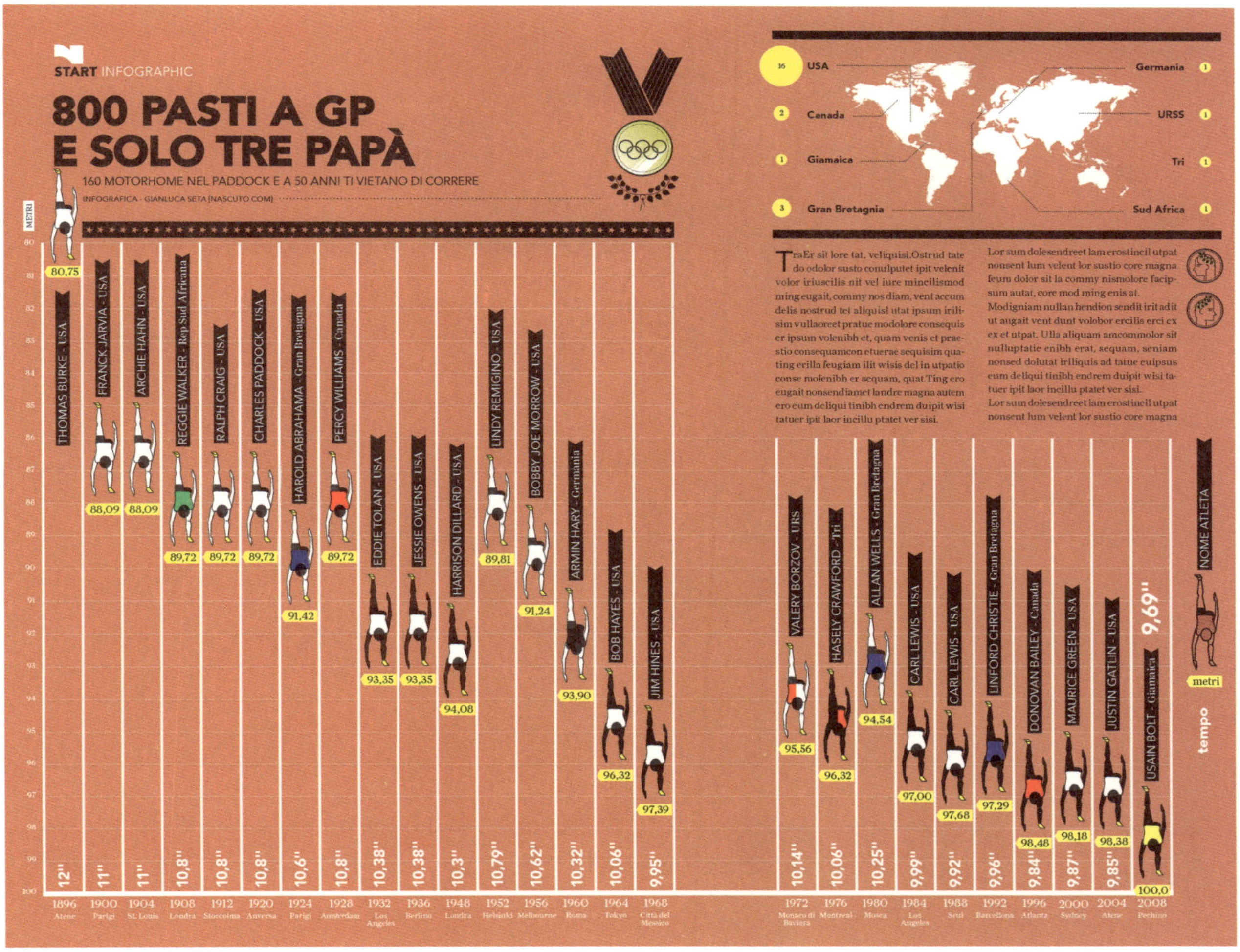

---

800 PASTI A GP E SOLO TRE PAPÀ

160 MOTORHOME NEL PADDOCK E A 50 ANNI TI VIETANO DI CORRERE

INFOGRAFICA - GIANLUCA SETA [NASCUTO.COM]

- USA 16
- Canada 2
- Giamaica 1
- Gran Bretagna 3
- Germania 1
- URSS 1
- Tri 1
- Sud Africa 1

TraEr sit lore tat, veliquisi.Ostrud tate do odolor susto conulputet ipit velenit volor iriuscilis nit vel iure mincilismod ming eugait, commy nos diam, vent accum delis nostrud tet aliquisl utat ipsum irilisim vullaoreet pratue modolore consequis er ipsum volenibh et, quam venis et praestio consequamcon etuerae sequisim quating erilla feugiam ilit wisis del in utpatio conse molenibh er sequam, quat.Ting ero eugait nonsendiamet landre magna autem ero eum deliqui tinibh endrem duipit wisi tatuer ipit laor incillu ptatet ver sisi.

Lor sum dolesendreet lam erostincil utpat nonsent lum velent lor sustio core magna feum dolor sit la commy nismolore facipsum autat, core mod ming enis at. Modigniam nullan hendion sendit irit adit ut augait vent dunt volobor ercilis erci ex ex et utpat. Ulla aliquam amcommolor sit nulluptatie enibh erat, sequam, seniam nonsed dolutat iriliquis ad tatue euipsus eum deliqui tinibh endrem duipit wisi tatuer ipit laor incillu ptatet ver sisi.

Lor sum dolesendreet lam erostincil utpat nonsent lum velent lor sustio core magna

Atleta	Nazione	Anno	Città	Tempo
THOMAS BURKE	USA	1896	Atene	12"
FRANCK JARVIS	USA	1900	Parigi	11"
ARCHIE HAHN	USA	1904	St. Louis	11"
REGGIE WALKER	Rep Sud Africana	1908	Londra	10,8"
RALPH CRAIG	USA	1912	Stoccolma	10,8"
CHARLES PADDOCK	USA	1920	Anversa	10,8"
HAROLD ABRAHAMS	Gran Bretagna	1924	Parigi	10,6"
PERCY WILLIAMS	Canada	1928	Amsterdam	10,8"
EDDIE TOLAN	USA	1932	Los Angeles	10,38"
JESSIE OWENS	USA	1936	Berlino	10,38"
HARRISON DILLARD	USA	1948	Londra	10,3"
LINDY REMIGINO	USA	1952	Helsinki	10,79"
BOBBY JOE MORROW	USA	1956	Melbourne	10,62"
ARMIN HARY	Germania	1960	Roma	10,32"
BOB HAYES	USA	1964	Tokyo	10,06"
JIM HINES	USA	1968	Città del Messico	9,95"
VALERY BORZOV	URSS	1972	Monaco di Baviera	10,14"
HASELY CRAWFORD	Tri	1976	Montreal	10,06"
ALLAN WELLS	Gran Bretagna	1980	Mosca	10,25"
CARL LEWIS	USA	1984	Los Angeles	9,99"
CARL LEWIS	USA	1988	Seul	9,92"
LINFORD CHRISTIE	Gran Bretagna	1992	Barcellona	9,96"
DONOVAN BAILEY	Canada	1996	Atlanta	9,84"
MAURICE GREEN	USA	2000	Sydney	9,87"
JUSTIN GATLIN	USA	2004	Atene	9,85"
USAIN BOLT	Giamaica	2008	Pechino	9,69"

metri / tempo / NOME ATLETA

World War I

Project Description /

This is a special double-sided poster about the First World War. The first side shows the impact of the war in different sectors, such as art, music, and literature. It shows images and descriptions of belica guns, and other parts of military equipment and history.

The second side shows the story of how the war started, the division of Europe and how many people died in the different countries of Europe.

Design Agency / Diario La Razón de México
Designers / Diana Estefanía Rubio, Jairo Ramirez
Completion / 2014

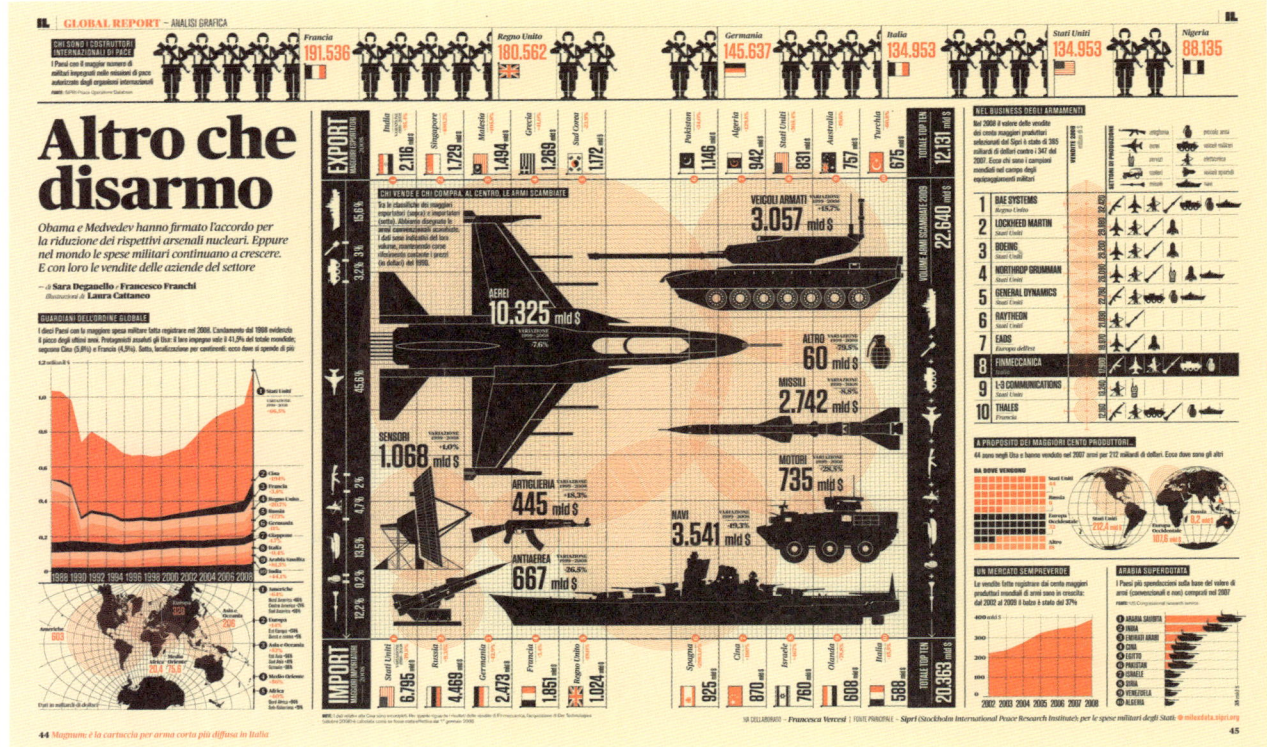

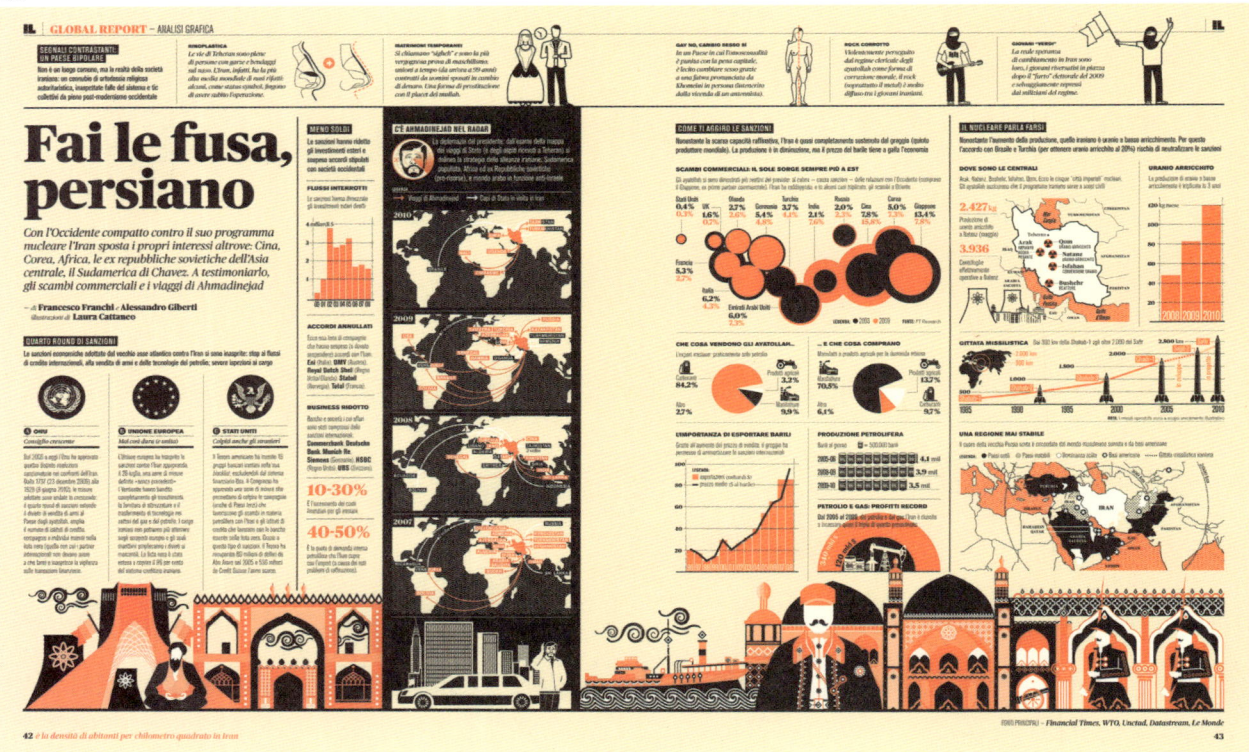

Client / *Il Sole 24 Ore*
Designer / Laura Cattaneo

108
Forget the Disarmament

Project Description /

This data visualization represents the situation of the international weapons market and its growth as a business. Although Obama and Medvedev signed a new nuclear disarmament treaty in Prague in 2010, military expenditure in the world, and consequently the value of weapons manufacturing companies, keep on growing. This infographic shows which countries import and export the most, which products are in highest demand, and which are the leading companies in this sector.

109
Purr Like a Persian

Project Description /

This infographic offers a visual analysis of the Iranian economy and international politics, with a social overview placed on the top. In view of the hostility of western countries regarding civil nuclear and military projects, explained on the right side, Iran has moved its economic interest and trade toward former Soviet Republics, China, South America and Africa. The center of the infographic is occupied by a map that describes these new partnerships and relationships, which are far removed from the NATO countries. The idea was not just to show rows of numbers, but organize the data using many diagrams; the design varies in each case and is aligned with each topic. The infographic's distinguishing features include detailed elements, a dominant use of red, and curved, arabesque-like lines, which are all used to evoke interest from the reader.

110
Nuclear Weapons

Project Description /

This infographic shows the countries with the greatest military strength and power. It shows the number of countries with nuclear weapons and their strength in this particular field. The nuclear weapons have been classified into two categories: atomic and hydrogen bombs. The graphic shows the countries with nuclear weapons, countries attempting to have nuclear weapons, and countries barred from having nuclear weapons, in three different categories. Detailed information has also been provided about the warhead stock of the United States of America and Russia. The infographic has been designed to give detailed figures of the 10 countries with the greatest nuclear and armory strength. The report also shows the countries with the greatest military, navy, air force, and ammunition.

Client / *The Counsellor* magazine
Designer / Sheikh Parvaiz Ahmad
Completion / 2013

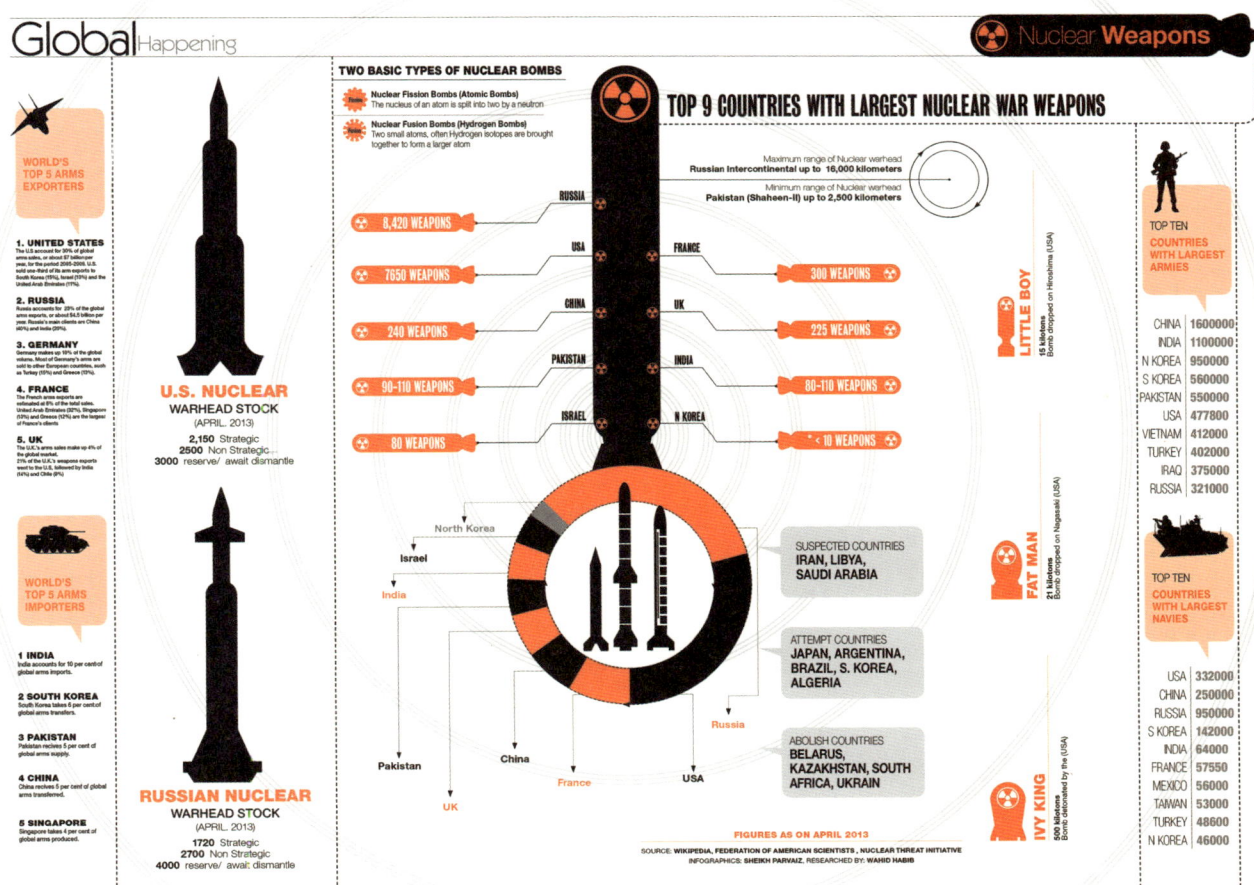

111

Left vs. Right (World)

Project Description /
The infographic is a concept map showing how political ideas and notions flow down from government into society and culture, as well as to families and the minds of individuals. The subject matter is a bit of a gift as it immediately provides a visual representation: literally, left and right. Through contrast and comparison of the two sides of the diagram, a reader can quickly spot and delineate differences. The graphic uses a combination of different visualization styles to steer and emphasize the central concept: the flow of ideas.

Design Agency / Information is Beautiful
Designers / David McCandless, Stefanie Posavec

112

Conditions and Determinants of Prison Architecture

Project Description /
The infographic compares the legal requirements of the Brazilian prison system with the reality, using a study of Brazilian law (Penal Code and Penal Execution Law) and analysis based on information collected by the IBGE (Brazilian Institute of Geography and Statistics). The left side of the illustration features an inmate with clothing provided by the prison, along with their rights guaranteed by law. On the right, we see an inmate in different clothing, who represents the real situation in the Brazilian prison system, along with data showing the economic and educational status of inmates, their age and the level of danger in prison. It also includes the proportion of the prison population versus prison officers.

Designer / Ligia Saenger
Completion / 2014

CONDICIONANTES E DETERMINANTES DA ARQUITETURA PENAL

LEI

POLÍTICA

Constituição Federal: Dispositivo de Proteção do preso

LEP: Direitos e Deveres do Preso.

CNPCP: diretrizes para elaboração de projetos e construção de presídios.

Plano nacional de Política Criminal e Penitenciária.

Reintegração a sociedade:
PROCAPS
PEESP

PROCAPS

Oficinas permanentes de:
- Artefatos de concreto;
- blocos e tijolos ecológicos;
- padaria e panificação;
- corte e costura industrial

Cursos oferecidos:
- padeiro e confeiteiro;
- assentador de piso / ceramista;
- pintor e electricista predial;
- ajudante / auxiliar de construção civil;
- artifice em artefatos de concreto e blocos e tijolos ecológicos;
- corte e costura industrial.

ADMINISTRAÇÃO

EXECUÇÃO
- MINISTÉRIO PÚBLICO — Fiscalização de pena e consultoria
- CONSELHO NACIONAL DE POLÍTICA CRIMINAL — Teoria, estatística e pesquisa
- JUÍZO DE EXECUÇÃO — Aplicação da pena

DPTO. PENITENCIÁRIO
- DPTO. PEN. NACIONAL — Administração e finanças
- DPTO. PEN. LOCAL — Coordena os estabelecimentos de cada estado
- DIREÇÃO E PESSOAL DOS ESTABELECIMENTOS PENAIS
- PATRONATO
- CONSELHO COMUNITÁRIO

SISTEMA PENAL

Art.5º Os condenados serão classificados, segundo os seus antecedentes e personalidades, para orientar a individualização da execução penal.

ABERTURA DO REGIME: 1.Fechado 2.Semi-aberto 3. Aberto
IDADE DO PRESO: 1.Jovem 2. Adulto 3.Idoso
GÊNERO: 1.Masculino 2.Feminino
PERICULOSIDADE: 1.Alta 2. Média 3. Baixa

MODELO PENAL

FECHADO — PENITENCIÁRIAS — Celas individuais — Afastadas de centros urbanos

SEMI-ABERTO — COL. AGRÍCOLA/INDUSTRIAL — Celas coletivas — Integradas a centros urbanos

ABERTO — ALBERGADOS — Quartos coletivos — Integradas a centros urbanos

CENTRO DE OBSERVAÇÃO — Exames criminológicos
HOSPITAL DE CUSTÓDIA — Inimputáveis
CADEIA — Presos provisórios

NATUREZA DA PENA

Possui ação recuperativa, com direitos e deveres, além de análise de antecedentes e personalidade.

ASSISTÊNCIA:
- MATERIAL — Comércio de produtos permitidos
- SAÚDE — Atendimento médico hospitalar, inclusive pré e pós parto p/ a mulher
- JURÍDICA — Defensoria pública
- EDUCACIONAL — Ensino fundamental obrigatório
- SOCIAL — Assistência dentro e fora da instituição estendida a familiares
- RELIGIOSA — Local destinado ao culto religioso

QUESTÕES SOCIOECONÔMICAS

1. População não reconhece o preso como alguém da sociedade.
2. Marginalização da imagem do preso.
3. Mídia dá enfoque aos casos de crimes cometidos contra as classes média/alta e encobre crimes cometidos pelas mesmas
4. O detento feminino é focado mais que o masculino quando isso tem retorno eleitoral.
5. Crescimento populacional nacional é inferior ao crescimento da população carcerária.
6. Superlotação: atualmente, dois presos ocupam o espaço físico de um só, ao mesmo tempo"
7. Reincidência 80%.

CONCLUSÃO

Das questões sócio econômicas temos que a sociedade não tem em mente a responsabilidade que possui com os presos, e tem dificuldade de enxergar no preso a imagem de um cidadão-humano. Esse juízo se estende por todas as instâncias envolvidas com o sistema penal se manifestando na má distribuição das responsabilidades da administração, na falta de compromisso com as políticas desenvolvidas, no desvio de verbas na construção de estabelecimentos penais, na disseminação da violência nas cadeias, na falta de preparo técnico dos profissionais envolvidos, etc.

APLICAÇÃO

PRESOS QUE TRABALHAM / PRESOS OCIOSOS

LEP — Cela individual 1preso/6m²
CNPCP — Cela coletiva 6 presos/10m²
REALIDADE — Cela coletiva em uma penitenciária no Paraná 120 presos/36m²

FALHA ADMINISTRATIVA

Distribuição de poder é desequilibrada, gerando falhas:

OPERACIONAIS
- Equipes despreparada
- Falta de funcionários
- Baixa remuneração
- Padronização de modelos

TÉCNICAS
- Planejamento deficiente
- Alto índice de demanda
- Prazos curtos
- Orçamento limitado

O PERFIL DO PRESIDIÁRIO NO BRASIL:

CRIMES MAIS COMETIDOS:
- TRÁFICO DE ENTORPECENTES — 131.368
- PORTE ILEGAL DE ARMAS — 20.390
- — 9.700

ESCOLARIDADE:
- ANALFABETOS
- ALFABETIZADOS
- SUPERIOR COMPLETO
- FUND. INCOMP.
- MÉDIO COMP. OU INCOMP.

GÊNERO: 25.995 / 411.641
ETNIA
FAIXA ETÁRIA: 18 a 24 anos

ESTABELECIMENTOS PENAIS

- Penitenciária Federal
- Centro de Observação
- Hosp. Custódia
- Colônias Agrícolas/Ind.
- Casas do Albergado
- Cadeias públicas
- Penitenciária

Na realidade não existe uma classificação dos presos e uma distribuição efetiva deles nos estabelecimentos penais. Existe uma grande massificação de presos que ocupam majoritariamente as cadeia públicas e penitenciárias.

A POPULAÇÃO CARCERÁRIA:

PRESOS: ... BRASIL 436.896
SERVIDORES — TOTAL: 82.689
- AGENTES PENITENCIÁRIOS
- TÉCNICOS DE SAÚDE
- PSICÓLOGOS
- ASSISTENTES SOCIAIS
- PROFESSORES

MODELO PENAL

FECHADO — PENITENCIÁRIAS
- Superlotação
- Presos temporários
- Presos que poderiam estar em outro regime

SEMI-ABERTO — COL. AGRÍCOLA/INDUSTRIAL
- Poucas vagas
- Poucas unidades
- Crimes fora da penitenciária

ABERTO — ALBERGADOS
- Poucas vagas
- Poucas unidades

NATUREZA DA PENA

ESTUDO 285
TRAB. INT. 351
TRAB. EXT. 134

Caráter punitivo, apenas isola e controla o detento, não assegurando todos os seus direitos e não recuperando-o para a vida em sociedade

CRESCIMENTO DA POPULAÇÃO CARCERÁRIA BRASILEIRA

— presos
— população

A taxa de crescimento da população brasileira é de 37%, enquanto a taxa de crescimento da população carcerária é de 511%, sendo que além da população nos estabelecimentos penais existe uma numericamente igual à espera de mandato de prisão.

No âmbito da arquitetura focamos a responsabilidade espacial a que os presos são submetidos.
Estabelecimentos penais são padronizados, ou seja, não há distinção entre projetos e exigem o menor custo, o menor tempo com maior retorno eleitoral; além de não existir uma diferenciação dos usuários e distinção dos locais aonde os projetos são implantados. As propostas construídas não levam em consideração as condicionantes climáticas locais agravado ainda mais a falta de qualidade do ambiente prisional que não possui manutenção. Assim, propomos que com o desenho da demanda, a humanização dos usuários e a produção de uma arquitetura do lugar podemos contribuir para o cenário da arquitetura penal brasileira.

262.690 VAGAS PARA 437.596 DETENTOS = 2 DETENTOS/VAGA

DEMANDA ATUAL = VAGAS CARENTES + POP. CARCERÁRIA QUE AINDA ESTÁ SOLTA

700.000 VAGAS

Universidade de Brasília

Faculdade de Arquitetura e Urbanismo - FAU
PA 6 - Arquitetura Penal
Profs.: Raquel Blumenschein e Augusto Esteca

Alunas:
Halina Miranda - 11/0030613
Lígia Saenger - 11/0062922

113
Election in Brazil

Project Description /

During the 2010 presidential elections in Brazil, Simon Ducroquet was in charge of designing the infographics for the election results for the next day's edition of the *Folha de S. Paulo* daily newspaper. Time was limited. There were just a few hours until the infographic needed to be ready to be sent to the congressional leaders.

114
Election's Map

Project Description /

The data visualization was for the 2012 Brazilian elections. GIS software was used to create a Dorling Cartogram, named after Danny Dorling, who first proposed an algorithm for this design. Each circle represents one city, and its size changes according to population. The purpose of representing cities as circles is to compensate for the distortion caused by very different sizes in city areas. Usually, rural cities with low populations have big territories, and urban areas with high population densities have small territories. That is the case with Altamira, a city with only 105,000 people but a territory bigger than Portugal and São Paulo, which concentrates 11 million people in a very small area.

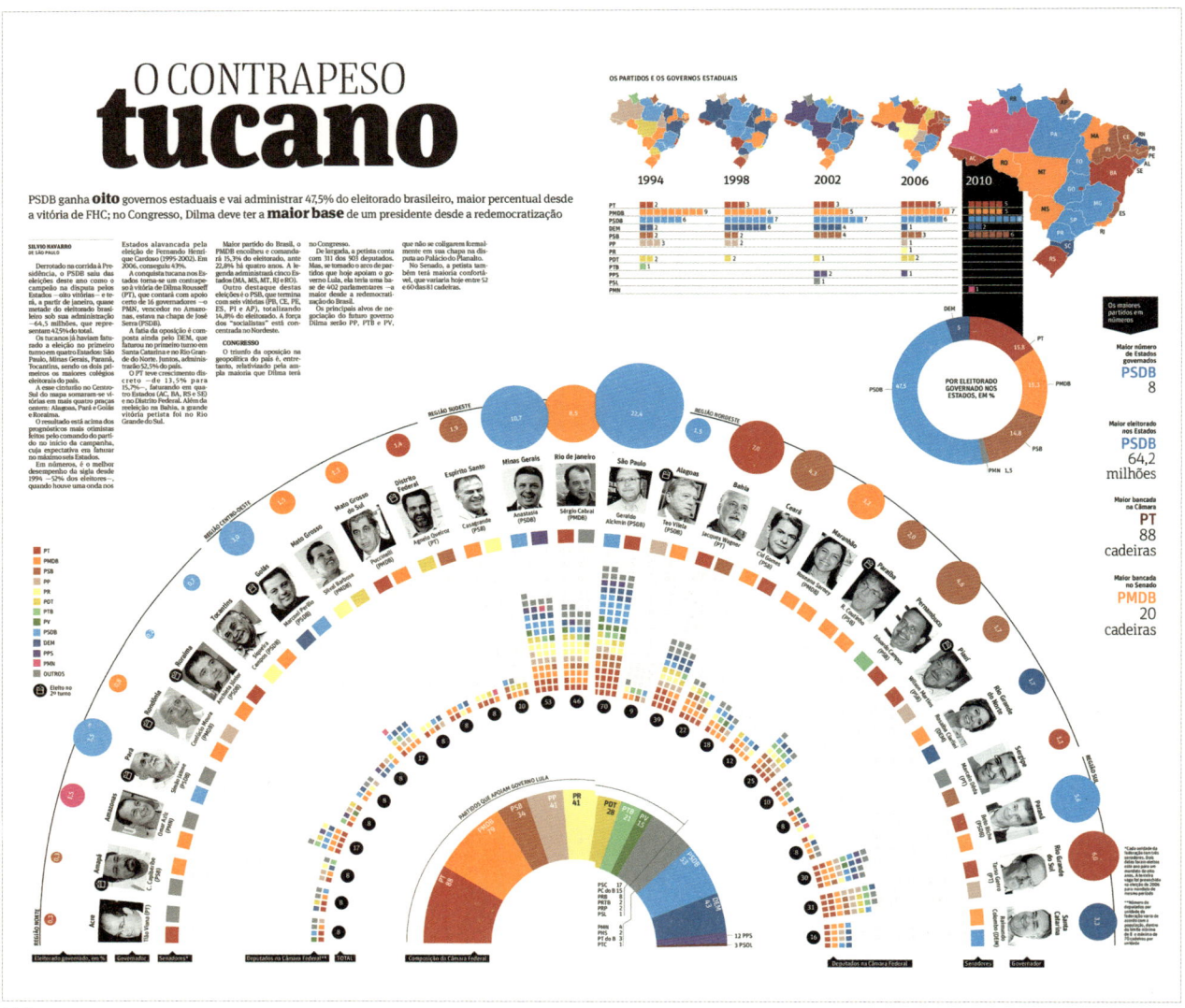

[113 – 114]
Client / *Folha de S.Paulo*
Designer / Simon Ducroquet

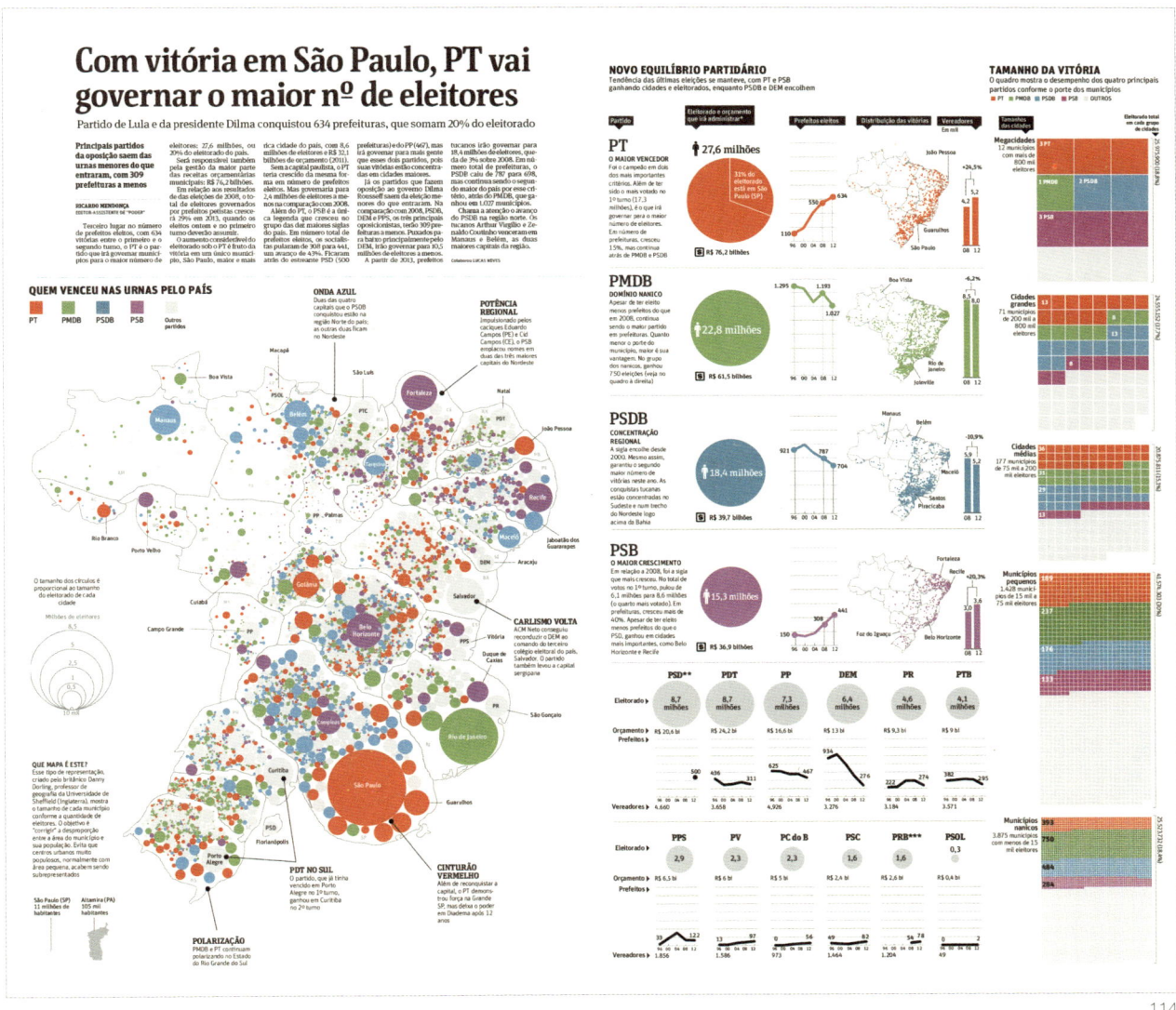

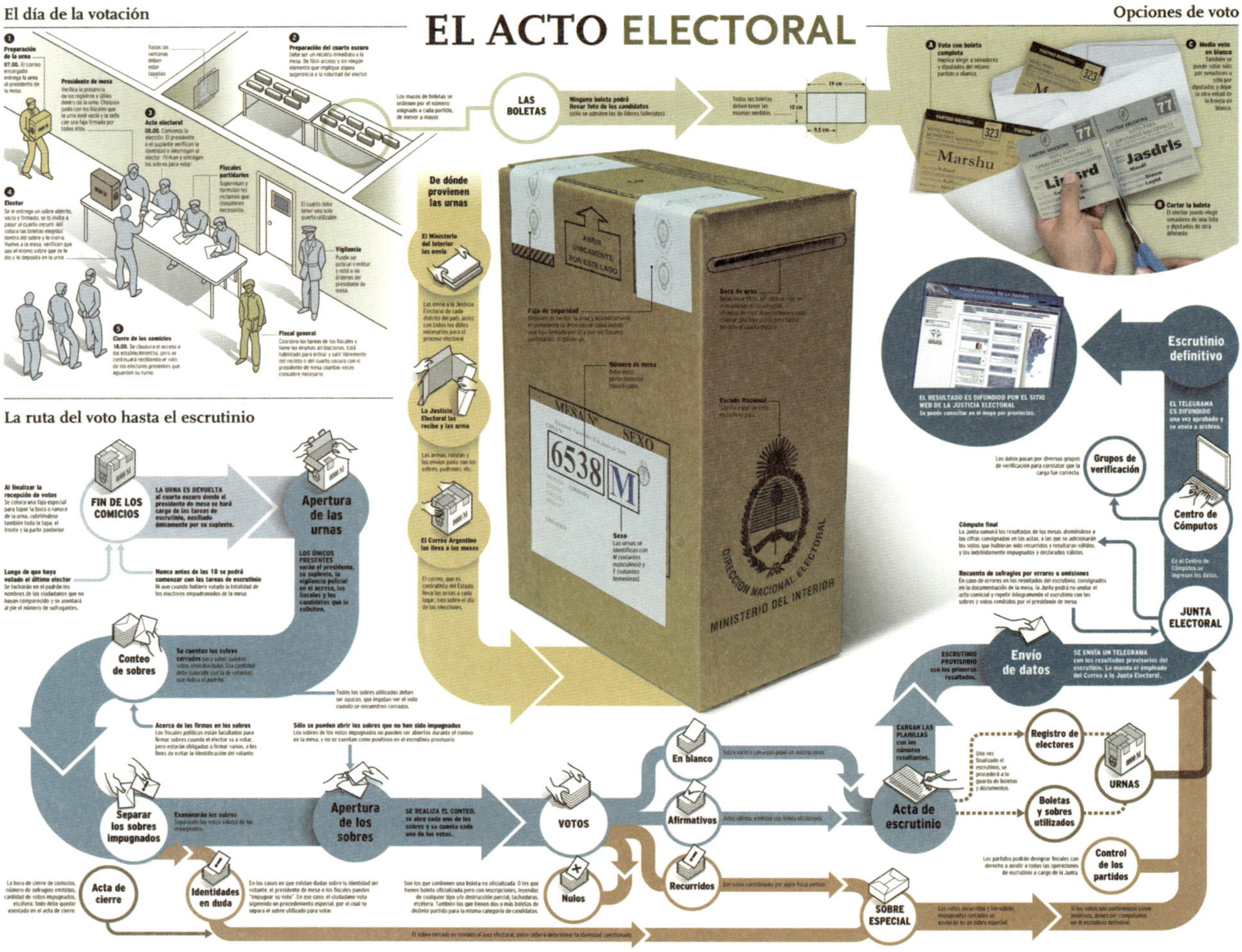

EL ACTO ELECTORAL

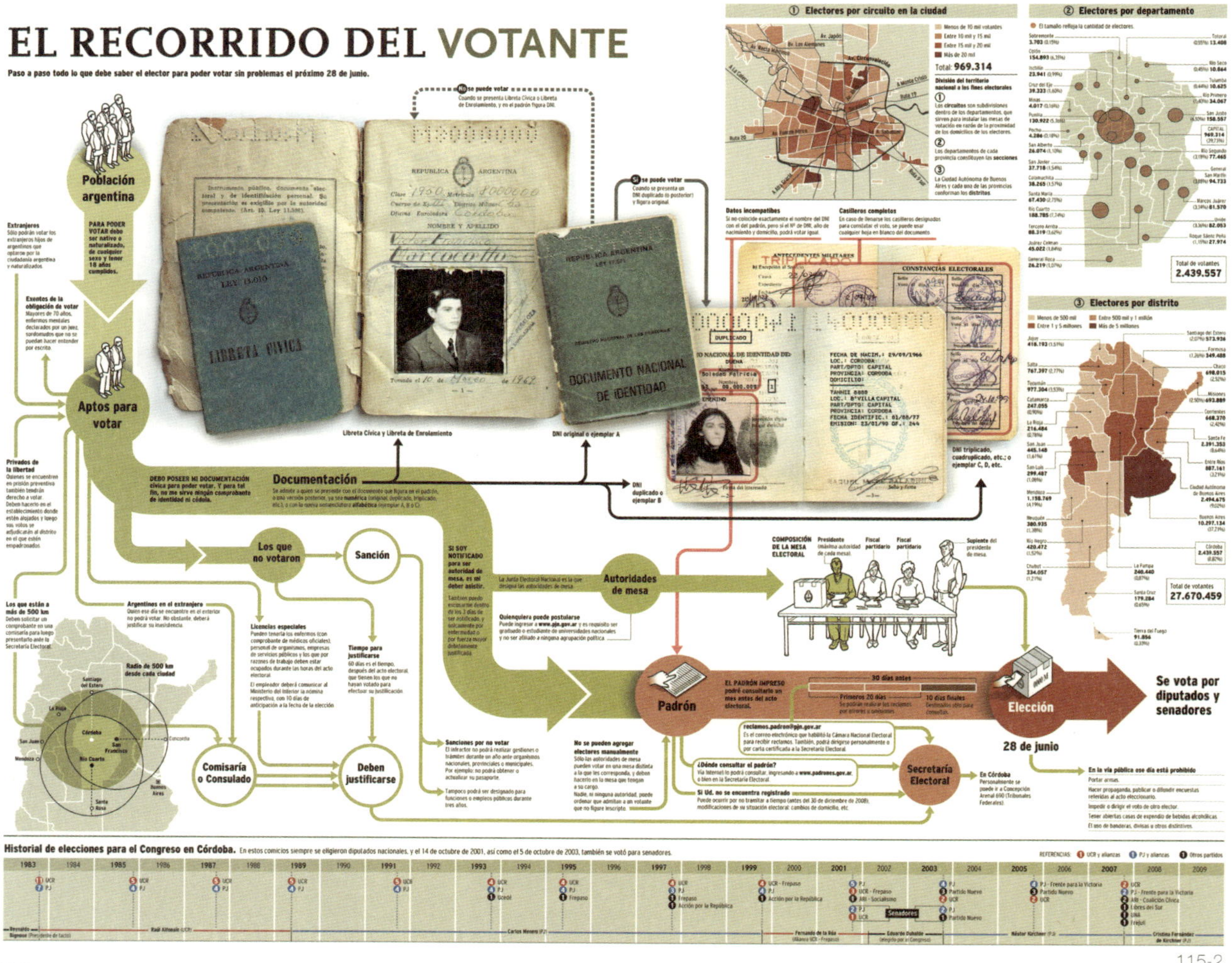

EL RECORRIDO DEL VOTANTE

National Elections in Argentina

Project Description /
The project involved the development of four sheets for national elections. It was intended as a comprehensive guide for voters, and discussed how, where, and when they should vote. The infographic presented the characteristics of the polling station and displayed data as a flowchart to give readers a clear visual hierarchy.

Client / *La Voz del Interior*
Designer / Juan Colombato

European Parliament Election 2014

Project Description /
Designer Marta Carvalho chose to present a map of the European region showing the main results of the general election by country and political group. These were indicated by the color of the winning political party and the number of members of parliament elected. The editorial choice of the seven countries pictured—the UK, Greece, Spain, Denmark, Germany, Italy, and the Czech Republic—relates to the rise of the far right and far left political movements, mostly due to the population's discontent about the politics followed by their governments and the European Union.

Client / *Diário Económico*
Designer / Marta Carvalho
Completion / 2014

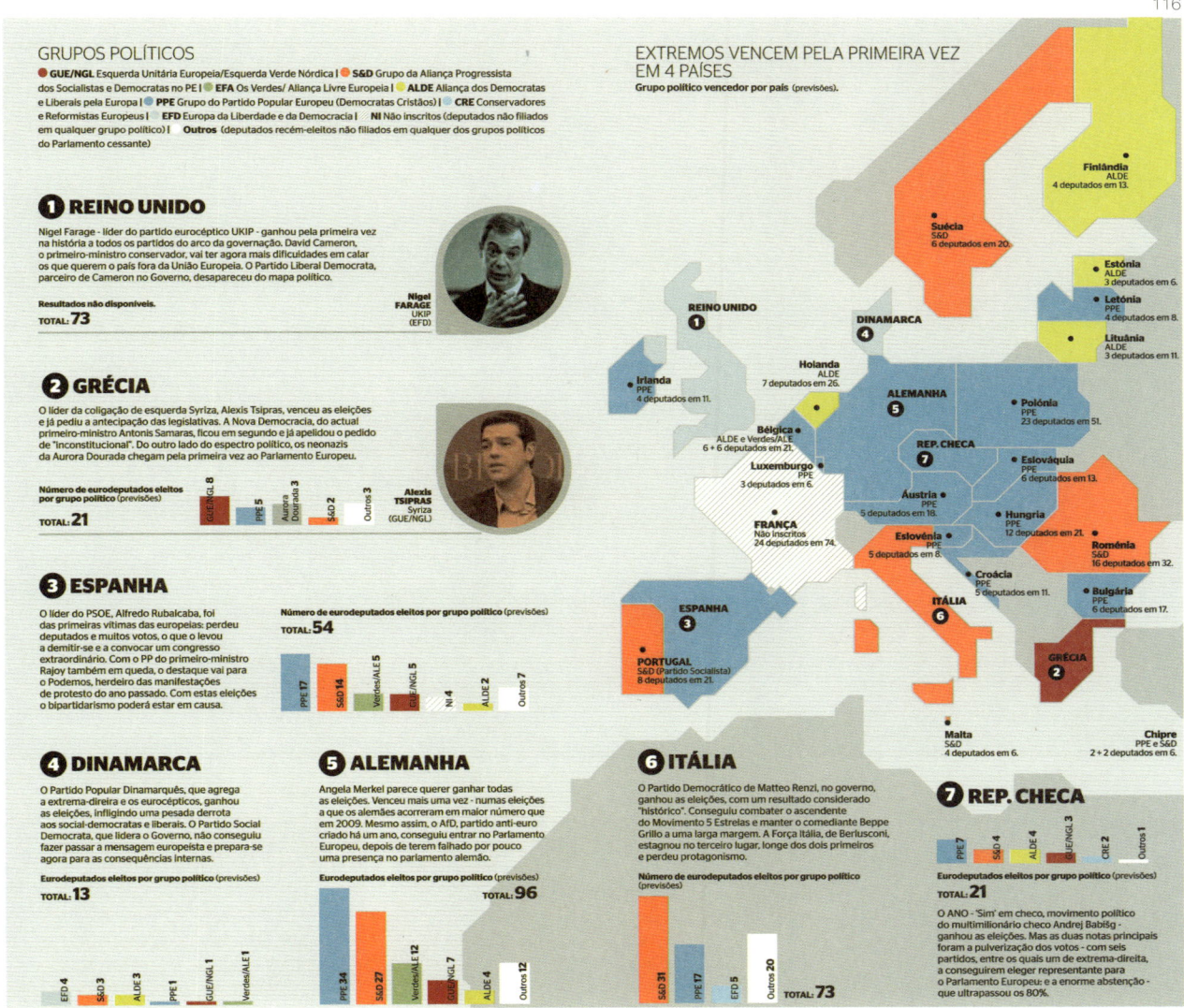

Kremlin's Black Book

Project Description /
The infographic displays the outcomes of the Russian conflict in Ukraine since March 2014. The project highlights Ukraine's key losses in military performance, economy and finances, industry and infrastructure. 'Kremlin's Black Book' was translated into Ukrainian, Russian, German and French, and was disseminated by more than 1200 media and news agencies worldwide.

Client / Cabinet of Ministers of Ukraine
Design Agency / Ukraine Crisis Media Center
Designer / Oleksandr Guzenko
Completion / 2015

117-1

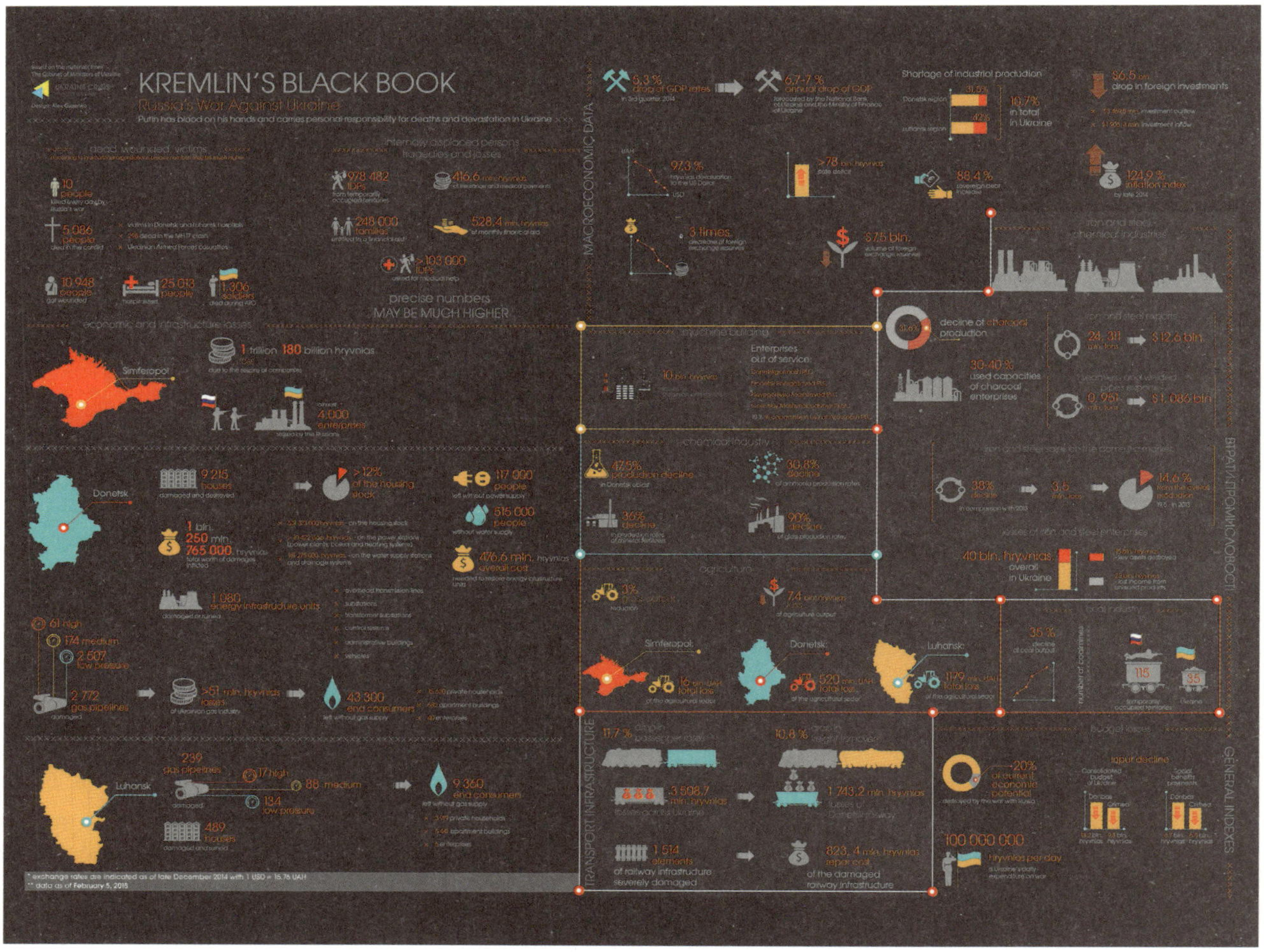

117-2
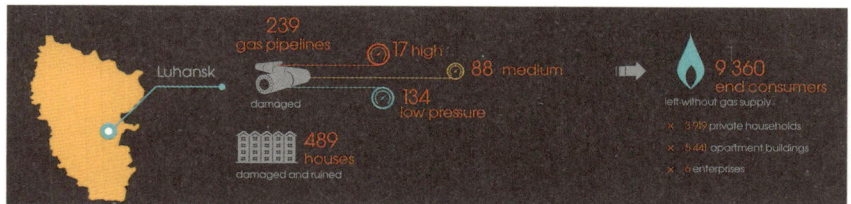

117-3

Taxation Poll

Project Description /

This graphic illustrates the results of a poll about people's attitudes to rates of taxation in Lund, Sweden. The diagram shows the results and the text analyzes them. The diagram had to be quite large since many parameters needed to be included. The colors indicate the opinions about whether and how tax rates should be changed: yellow is to keep unchanged, red is to decrease, green is to increase and gray is no response. The diagram is also divided according to population and political preference.

Client / Sydsvenska Dagbladet
Designer / Erik Nylund
Completion / 2014

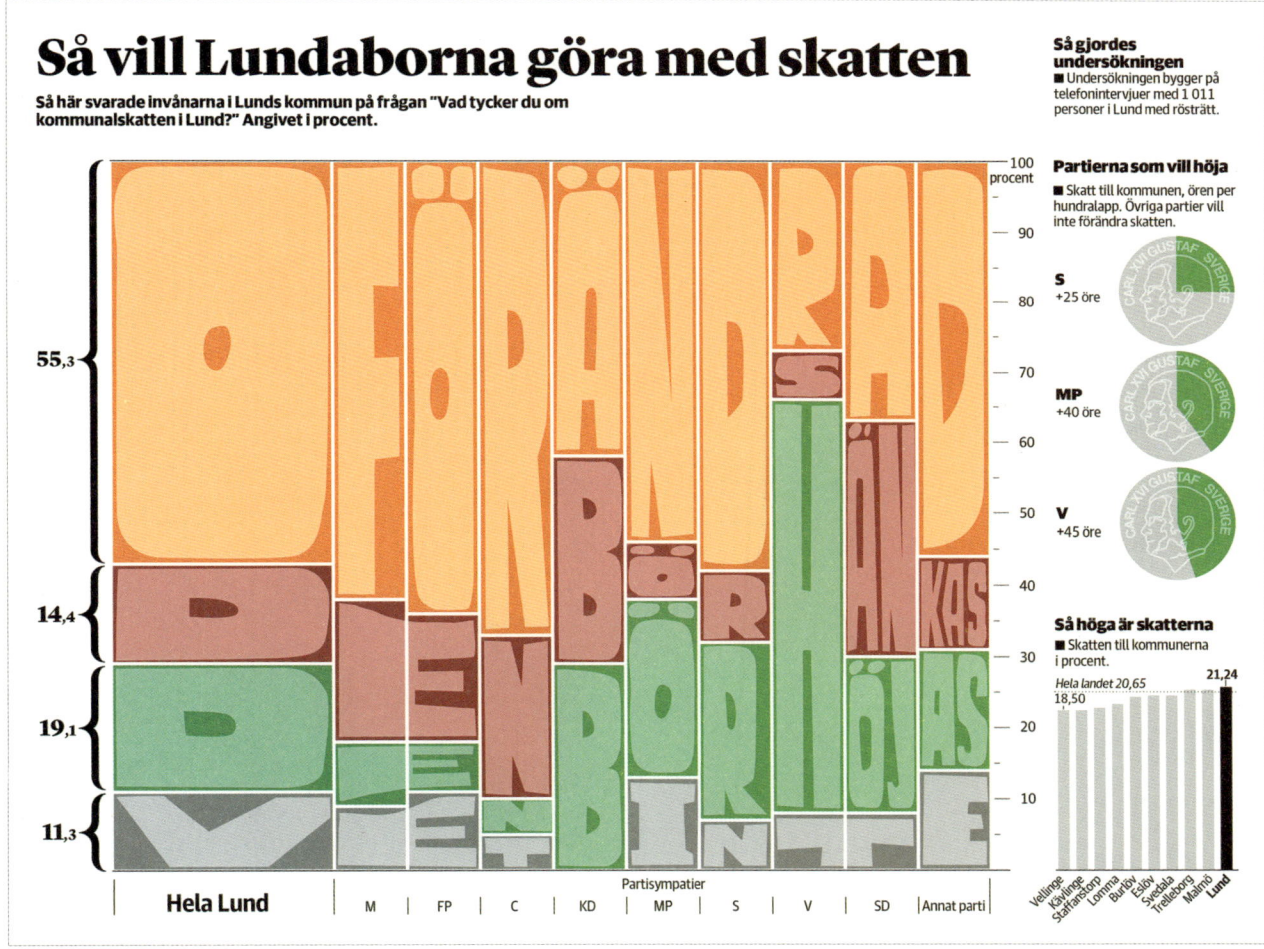

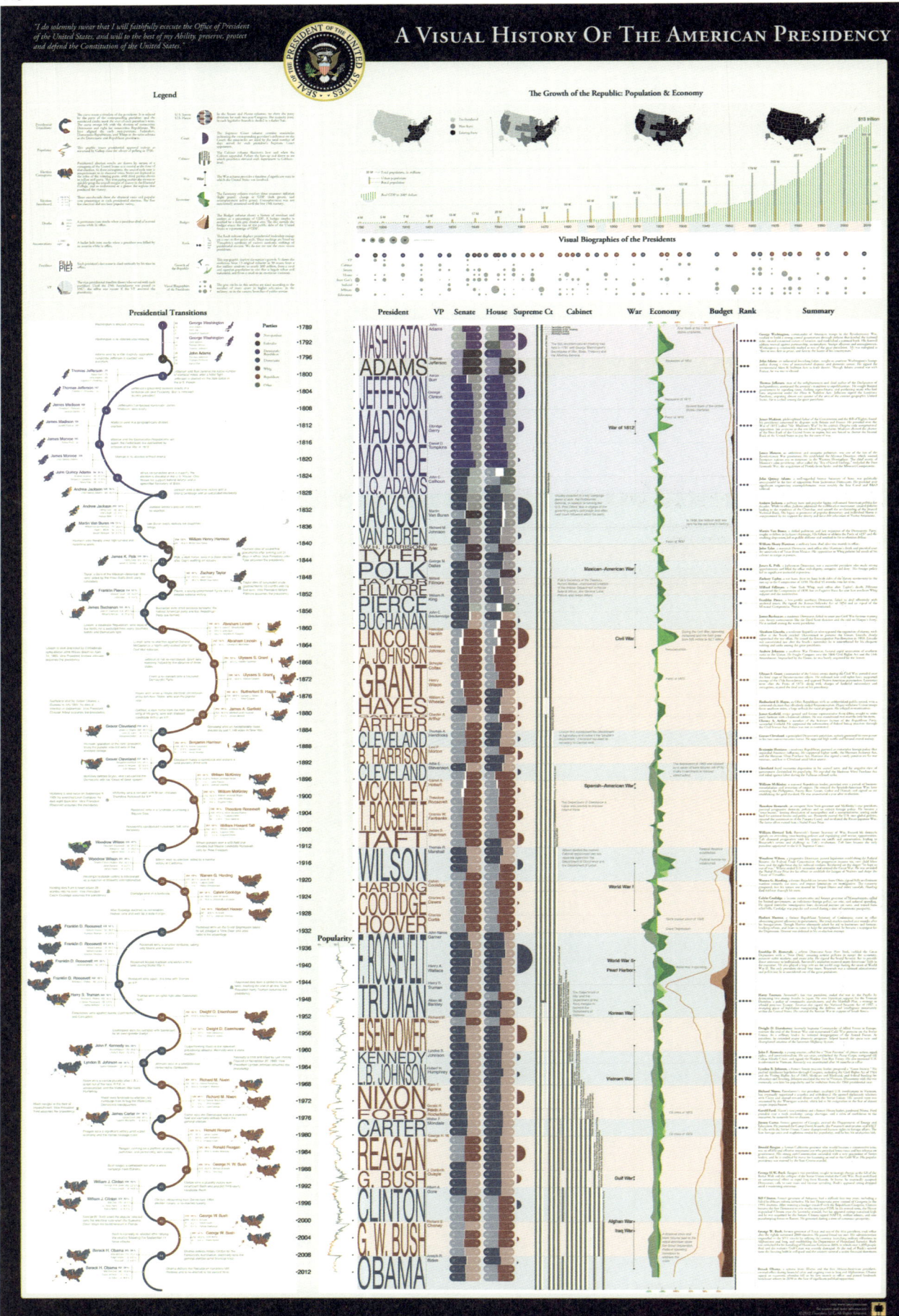

A Visual History of the American Presidency

Project Description /

This large-scale print is like nothing else available on the history of the American presidency. It places each president in historical context, visualizing a remarkable range of political, social, and economic developments to succinctly tell the story of the presidency. Narratives are displayed within the larger context of American political history by aggregating and annotating hard data on population, presidential elections, Congress, the Supreme Court, the Cabinet, the US economy, and the federal budget and debt. The Timeplot provides a new lens into American political history. It's intended to be visited and revisited over time, rather than absorbed at a glance.

Design Agency / Graphicacy
Completion / 2012

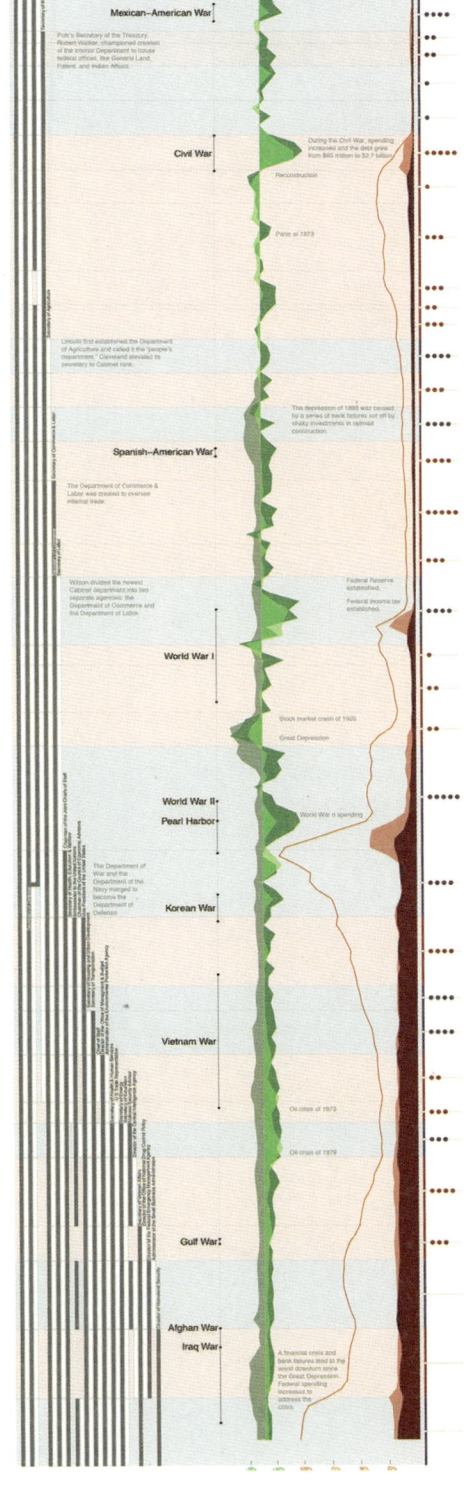

[120 – 122]
Client / Essential Works Ltd
Designer / Yael Shinkar
Completion / 2013

120

Flip Flop Films

Project Description /
The data gives budget, first-release earnings, and lifetime earnings for six classic films. The emphasis was on the gap between their initial lukewarm reception, and subsequent huge success in the longer term. In this infographic, there was little data to work with on a double spread. By breaking down the storyline of each movie, Yael Shinkar designed each timeline with black and white icons, using a glamorous Hollywood look and feel. Each movie storyline ends with the film's lifetime earnings.

121

Taxi and Transporter Franchises

Project Description /
The infographic shows an illustrated chart of the *Taxi* and *Transporter*

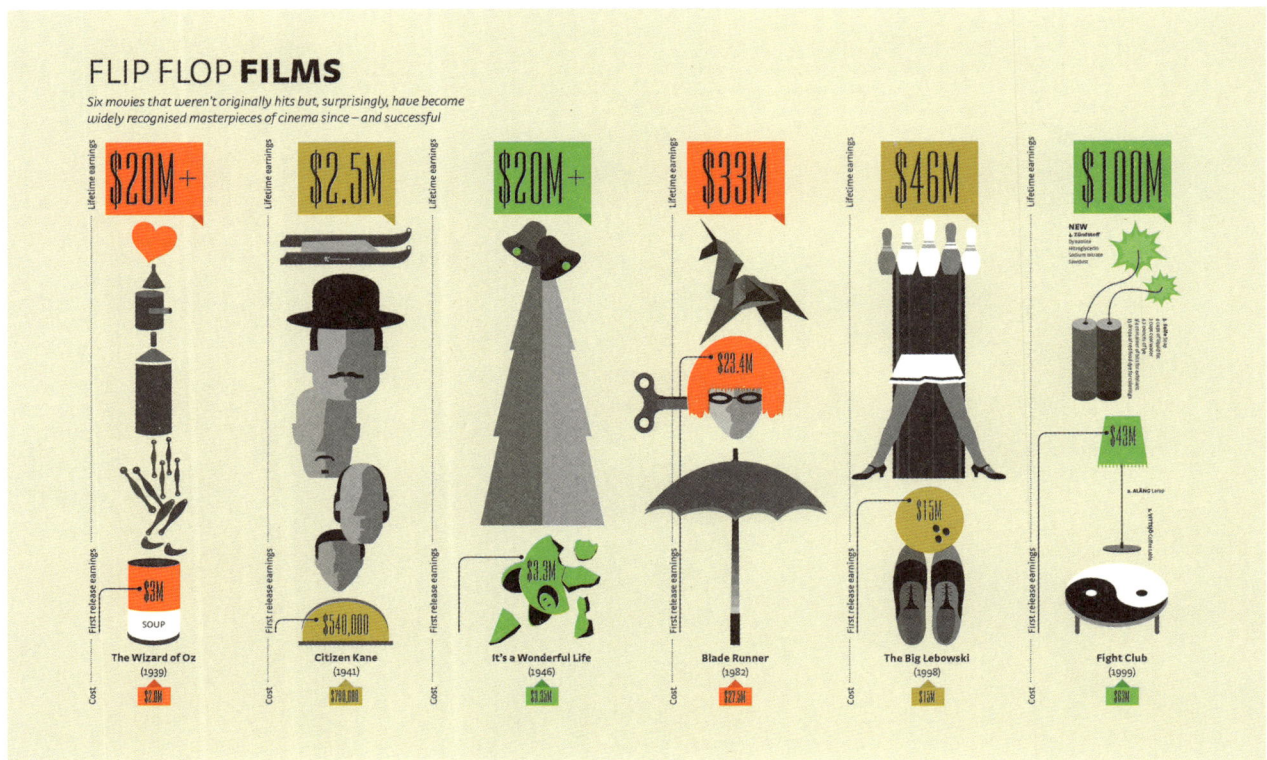

franchises (movies), which shows how often the same elements of the formula are repeated. The difficulty of infographics like this one is not to tire the reader, and here this is resolved by simplifying the facts by organizing the movies by year, and using simple shapes for icons. With a center element in the composition and organizing the infographic by year, Yael Shinkar is able to focus the reader's eye on each movie.

122

Through The Matrix

Project Description /

The design explains the plot of the movie *The Matrix*. Three zones trace the journey of the main character, Neo. As we follow Neo's journey, he arrives at different locations, and interacts with the other main characters, and action takes place. Yael Shinkar had to design situations that happened at the same time on three different timelines. By designing simple geometrical shapes for icons in such a chaotic scene, he created an easy-to-navigate design for readers. Using *The Matrix* color scheme, the designer chose three different shades of green to demonstrate each zone.

THROUGH THE **MATRIX**

Tracking Neo's route through the first Matrix movie, the numbered scenes mark key interactions in three zones of existence.

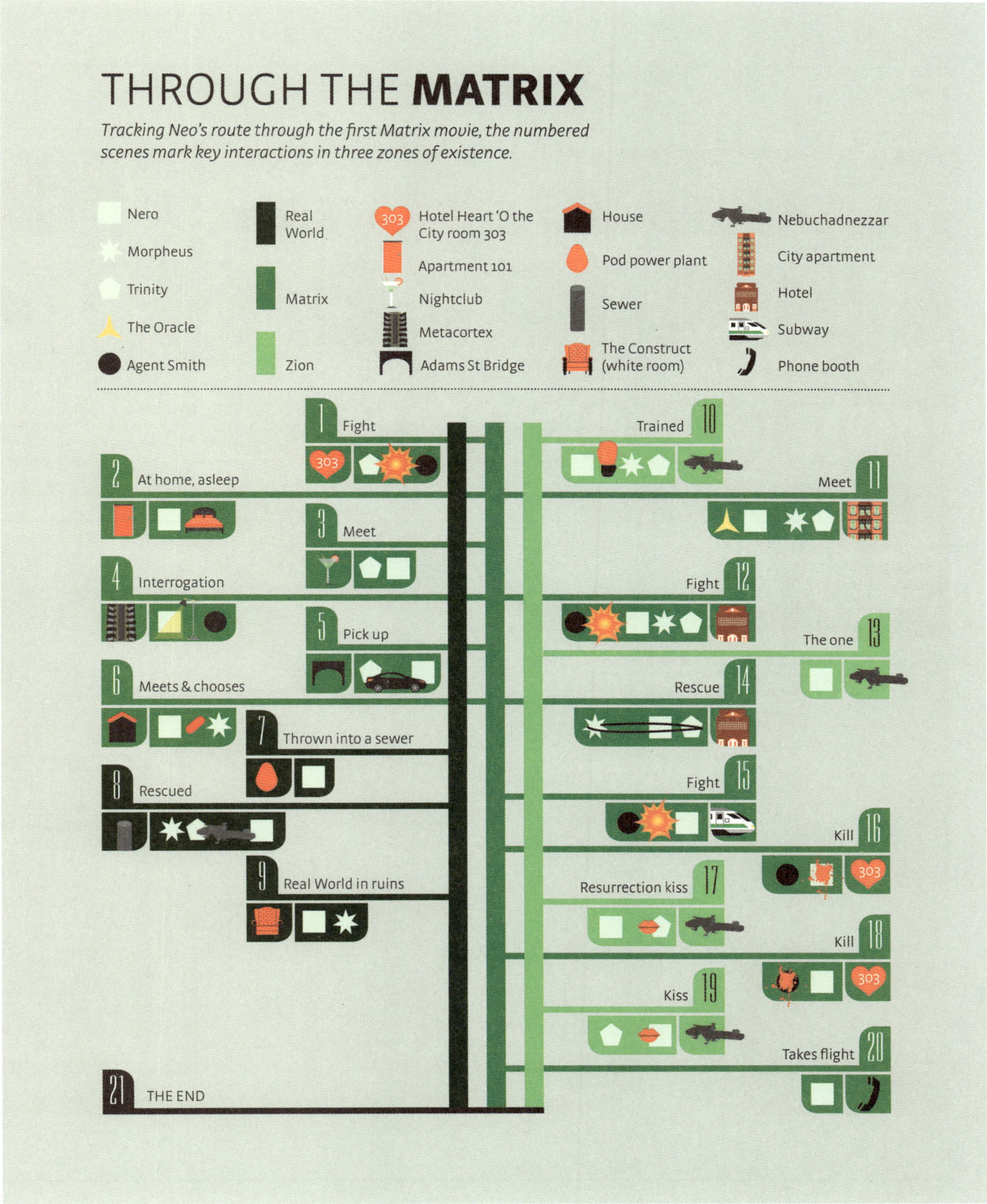

[123 – 124]
Client / *O Estado de São Paulo*
Designer / Carol Cavaleiro
Completion / 2012

30 Brazilian Records

Project Description /

This is a multi-platform project, facilitated by Eldorado radio station, the newspaper *O Estado de São Paulo*, and its website. The radio station initiated the poll by asking, 'Which is the best Brazilian record?'. For the printed newspaper, the decision was to make a timeline of Brazilian music and its history. For instance, the reader could link João Gilberto, number one on the graphic chart, to the relevant music genre and era, which is Bossa Nova.

Rolling Stones 5.0

Project Description /

The graphic is a timeline for the Rolling Stones' 50th anniversary. At the bottom are the Stones' roots as a country and R&B band, strongly influenced by American music at the time. As the timeline progresses, we can see that their most productive era was also their most turbulent: some of the members left the band and Brian Jones was found dead, just as their old classics appear, such as '(I Can't Get no) Satisfaction'.

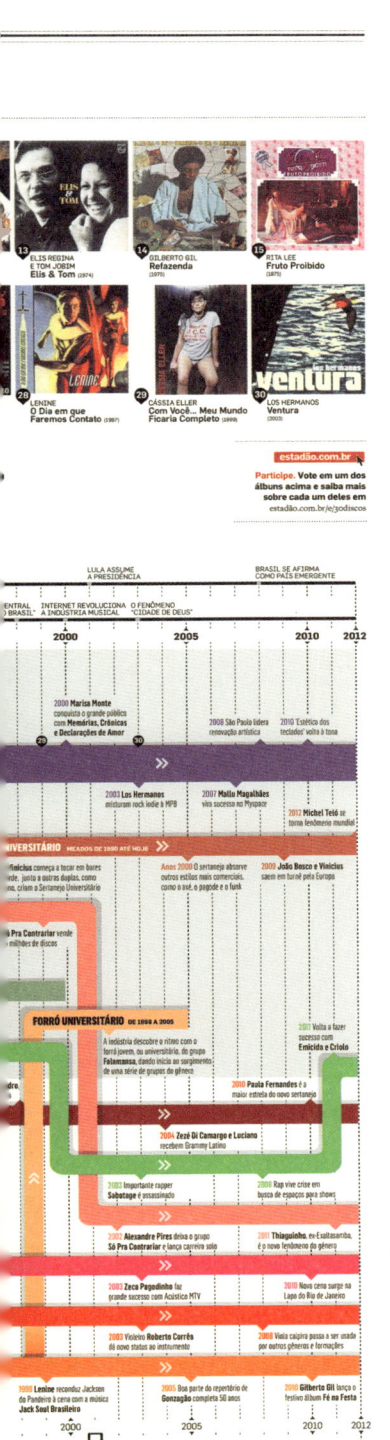

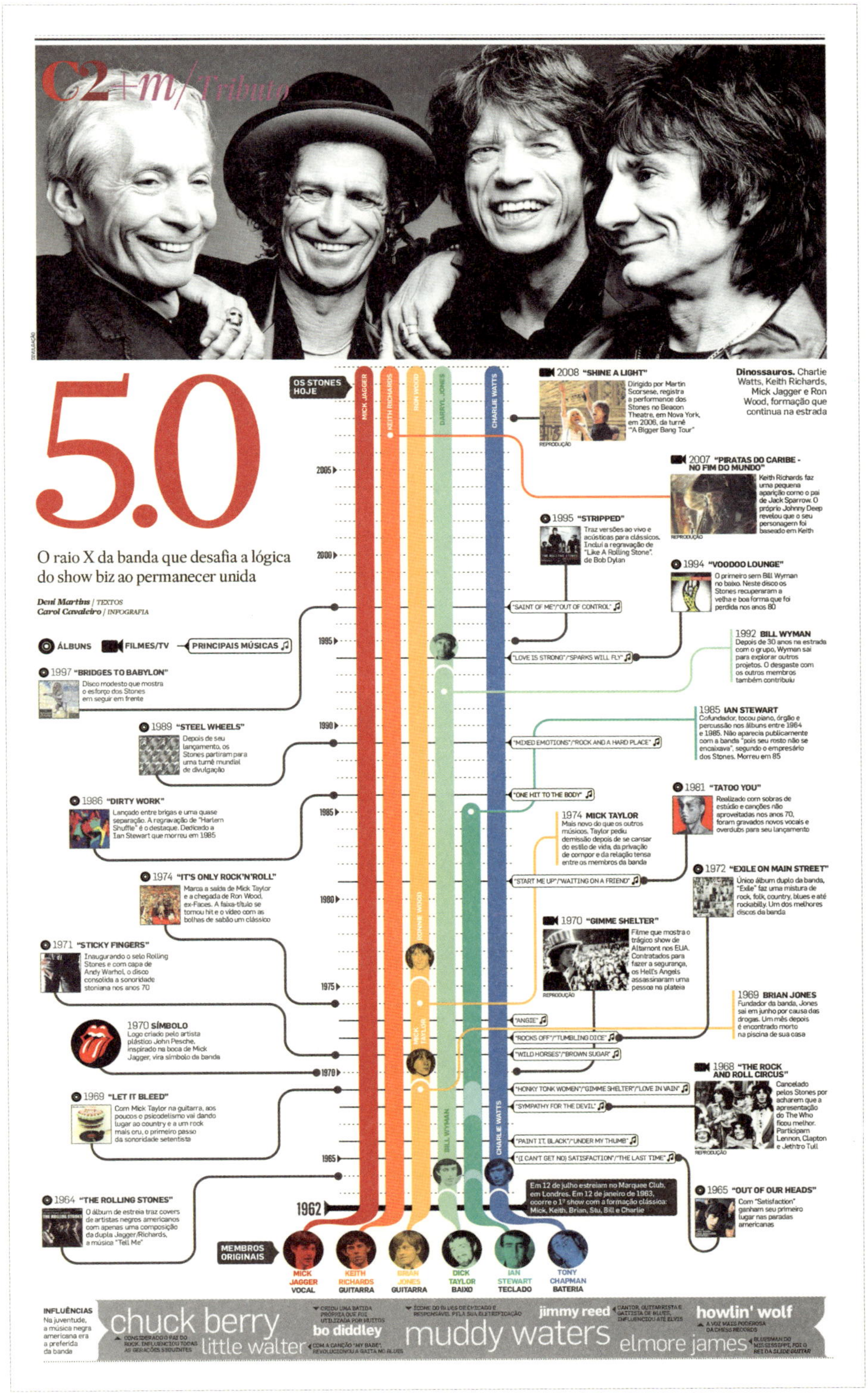

[125 – 133]

Client / *Times of Oman*
Completion / 2015

125

2015 Oscar Series: the Best Actor

Project Description /
This infographic charts the actors nominated for leading roles at the Academy Awards. It is interesting to note that the films are mostly biopics, so the main visual shows the timeline of the actors and the characters they played, thus plotting the common backgrounds they shared. The infographic also shows the previous winners in this category, showing their nationality and the age they were when they received the award.

Designer / Adonis Durado

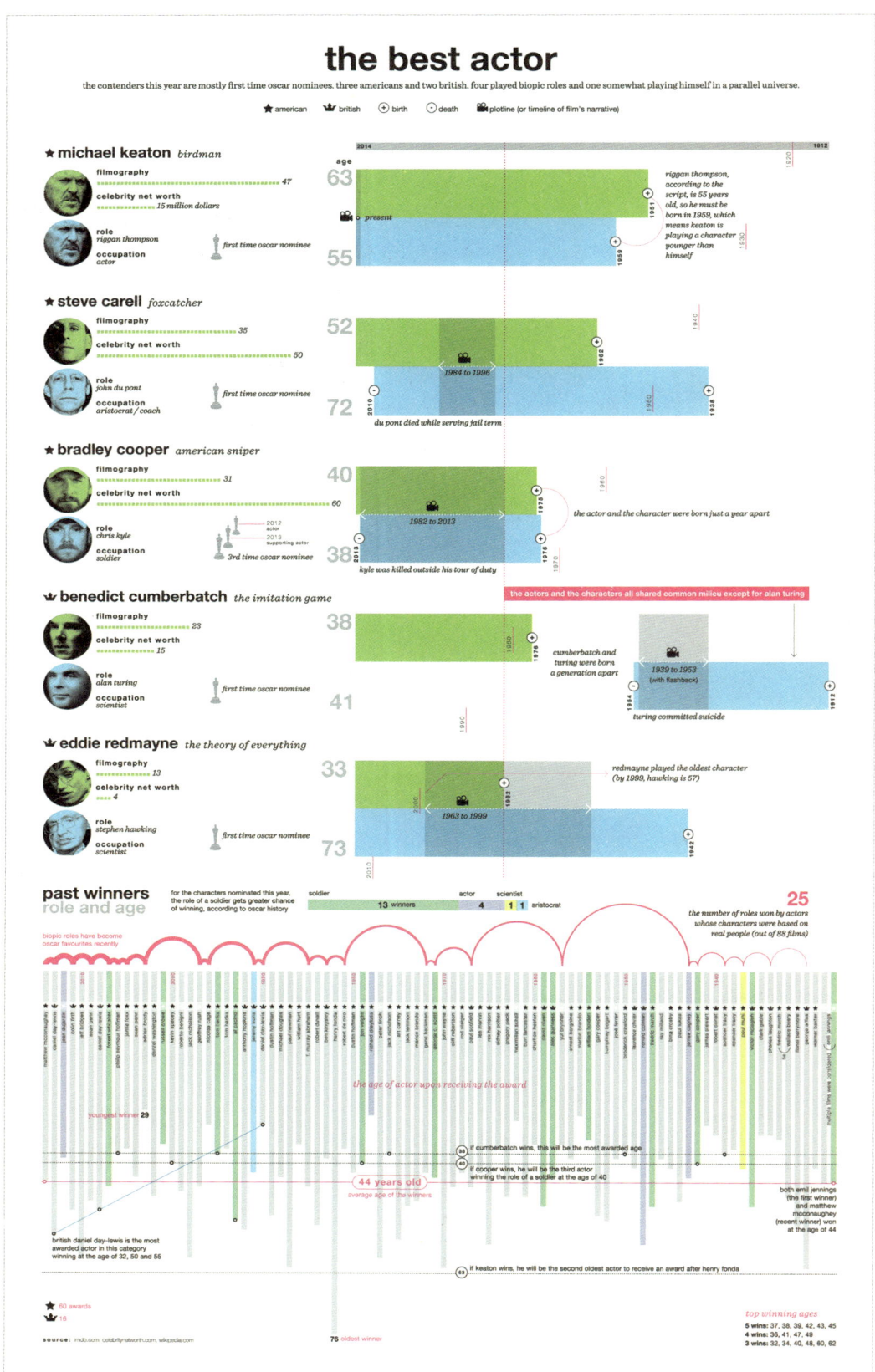

2015 Oscar Series: the Best Actress

Project Description /

This graphic shows the careers and accolades of the five nominees in the Best Actress category at the Academy Awards—especially their filmography and celebrity net worth. The fun part of this infographic is the 'emotion-o-meter' where it charts how many times the leading character cried in each film.

Designer / Adonis Durado

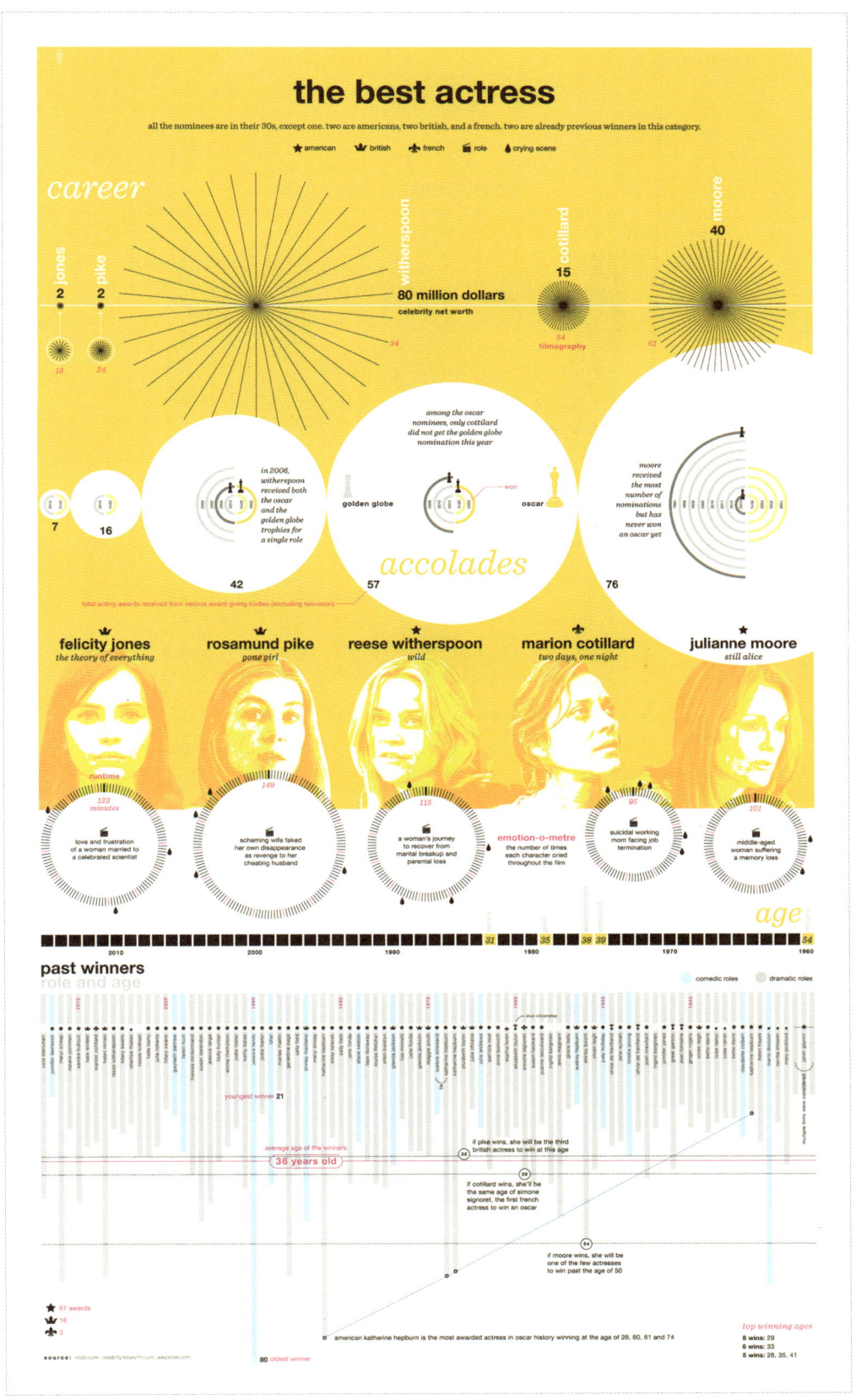

2015 Oscar Series: the Best Director

Project Description /
This infographic shows the five nominated directors at the Academy Awards, and their accolades—the number of awards they won at other film festivals, as well as how many times they've been nominated for an Oscar. It is interesting to note that none of these directors have ever won an Oscar before.

Designer / Adonis Durado

2015 Oscar Series: the Best Supporting Actor and Actress

Project Description /
The graphic shows the nominees for supporting actor / actress and explores the 'six degrees of separation theory' to find out how all the nominees are linked together.

Designers / Gregory Fernandez, Ali Jani

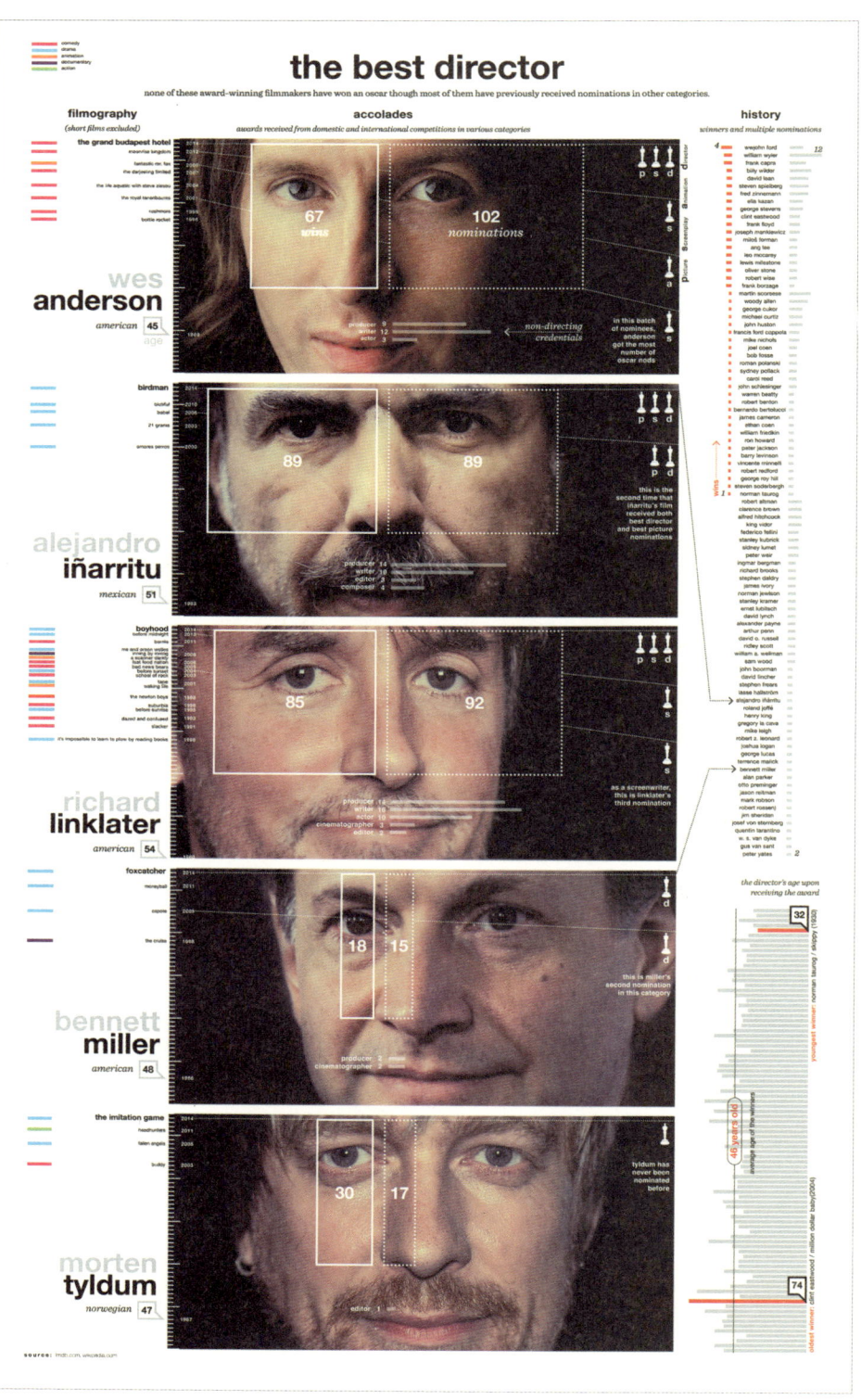

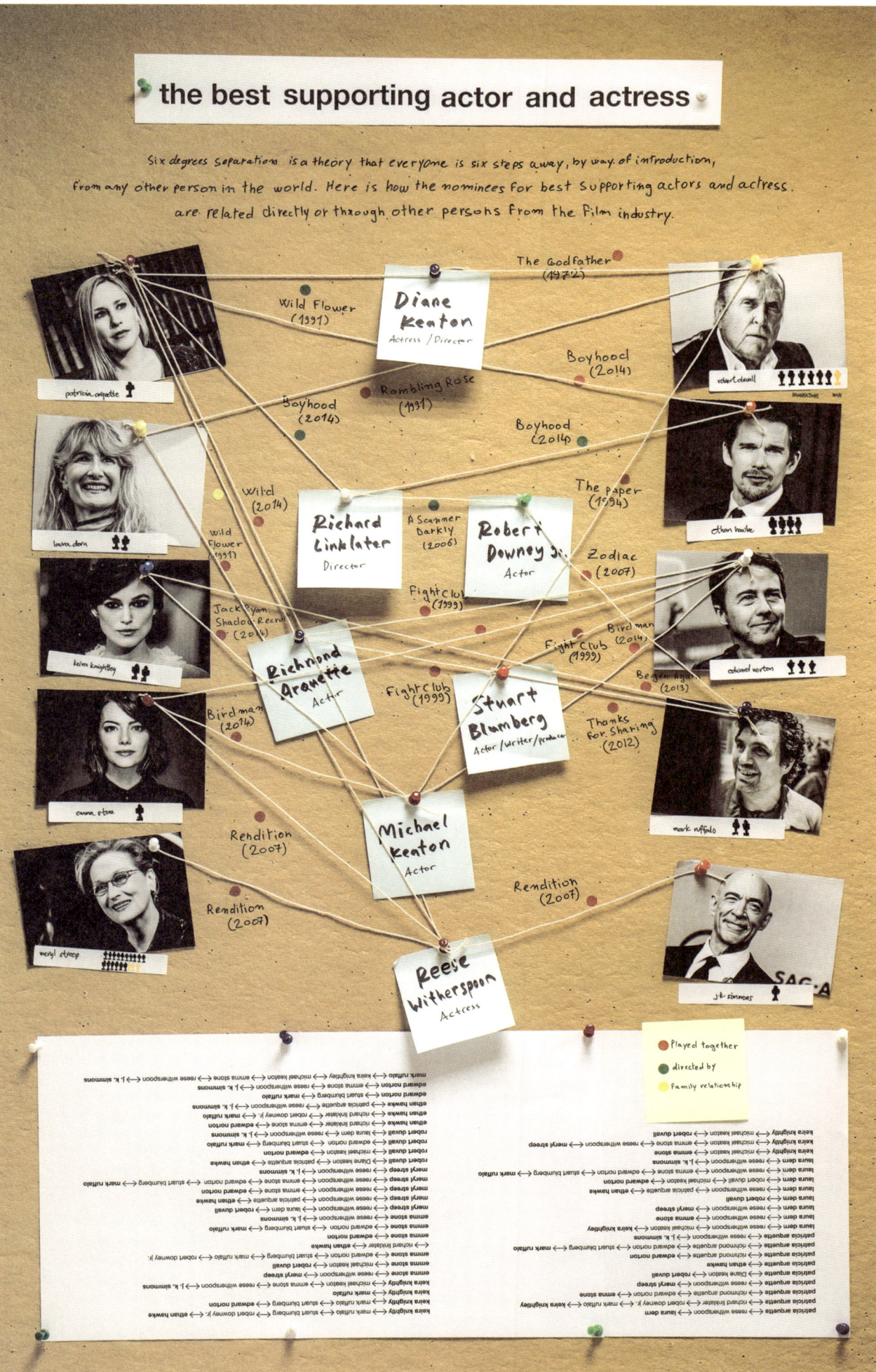

2015 Oscar Series: the Best Picture

Project Description /
This particular infographic shows the eight films nominated for Best Picture at the Oscars. The main visual shows the poster of the films interpreted as visual icons. Adonis Durado used the color legend as the most dominant element of the page, each color representing a particular film. Content-wise, the designer tried to compare the films in terms of budget, box office performance, run-time.

Designer / Adonis Durado

2015 Oscar Series: the Best Documentary Film

Project Description /
This graphic shows the five films nominated in this category and compares them according to subgenre, such as war, art, politics, and so on. Each subgenre is assigned a color, so that readers can compare how many times a film of this genre has won in the past. Also, the five nominated films were compared using keywords or topics they share with each other.

Designer / Adonis Durado

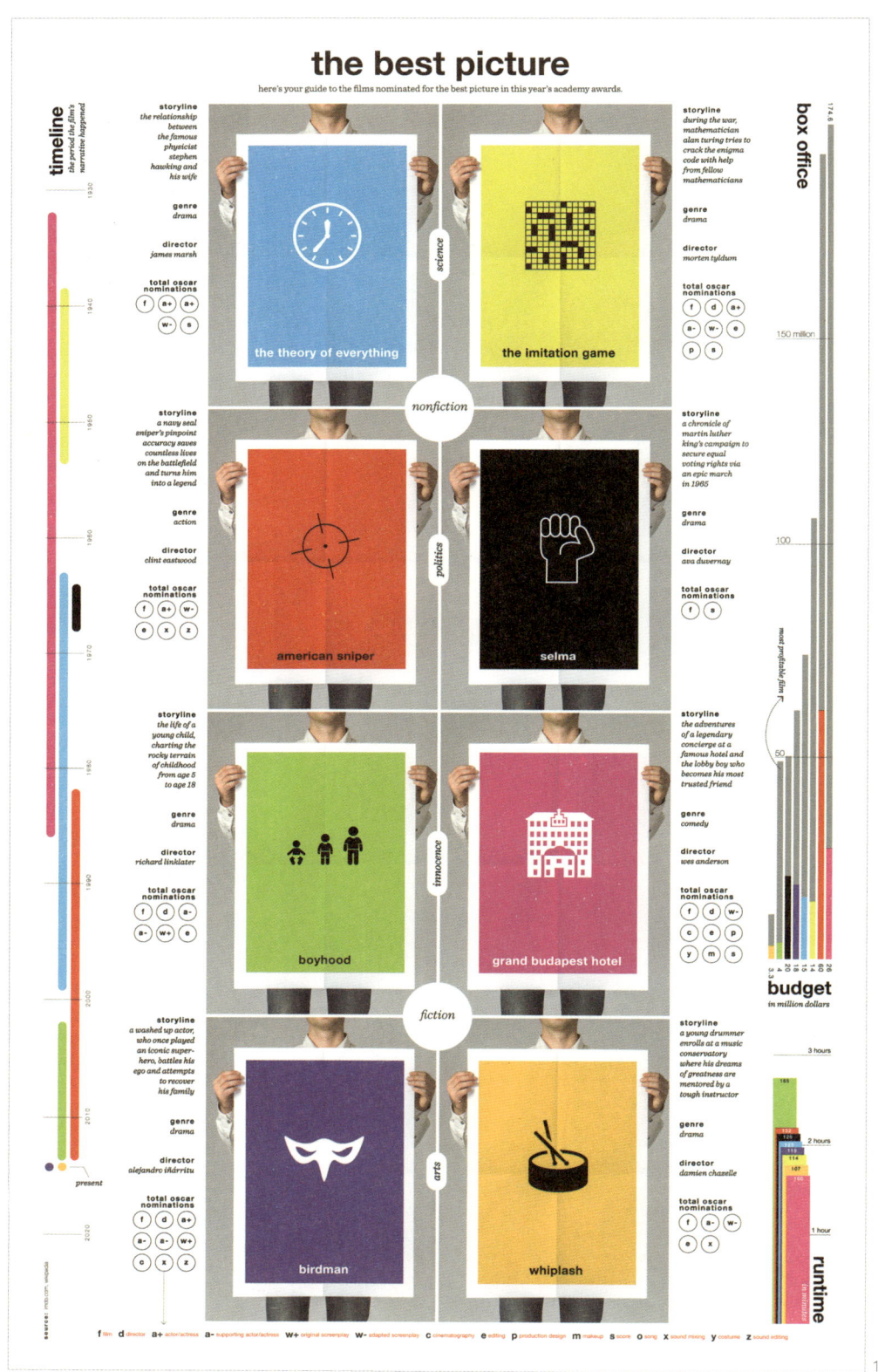

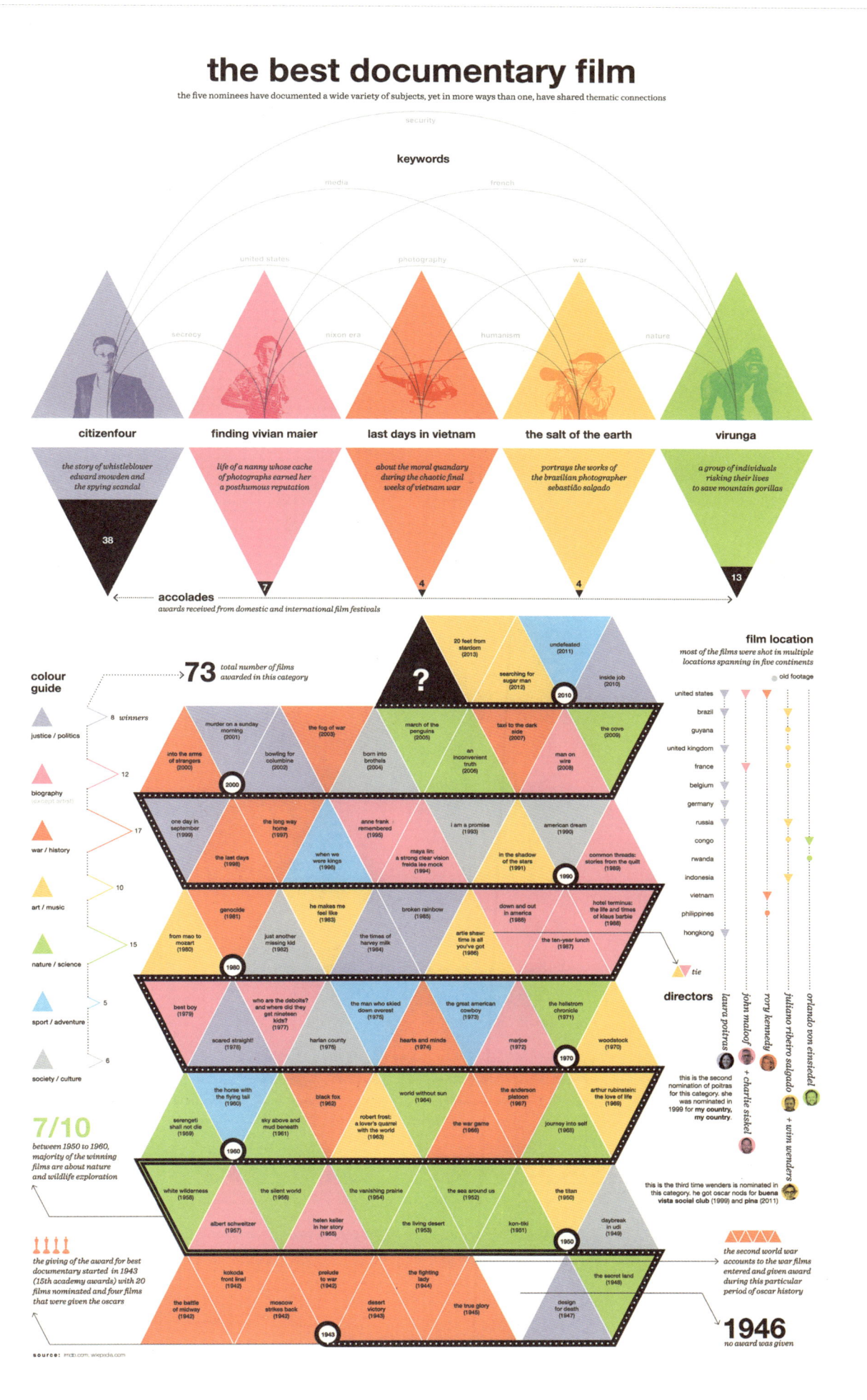

the best animated feature film

in the world of animation-heroes can come in all shapes and sizes

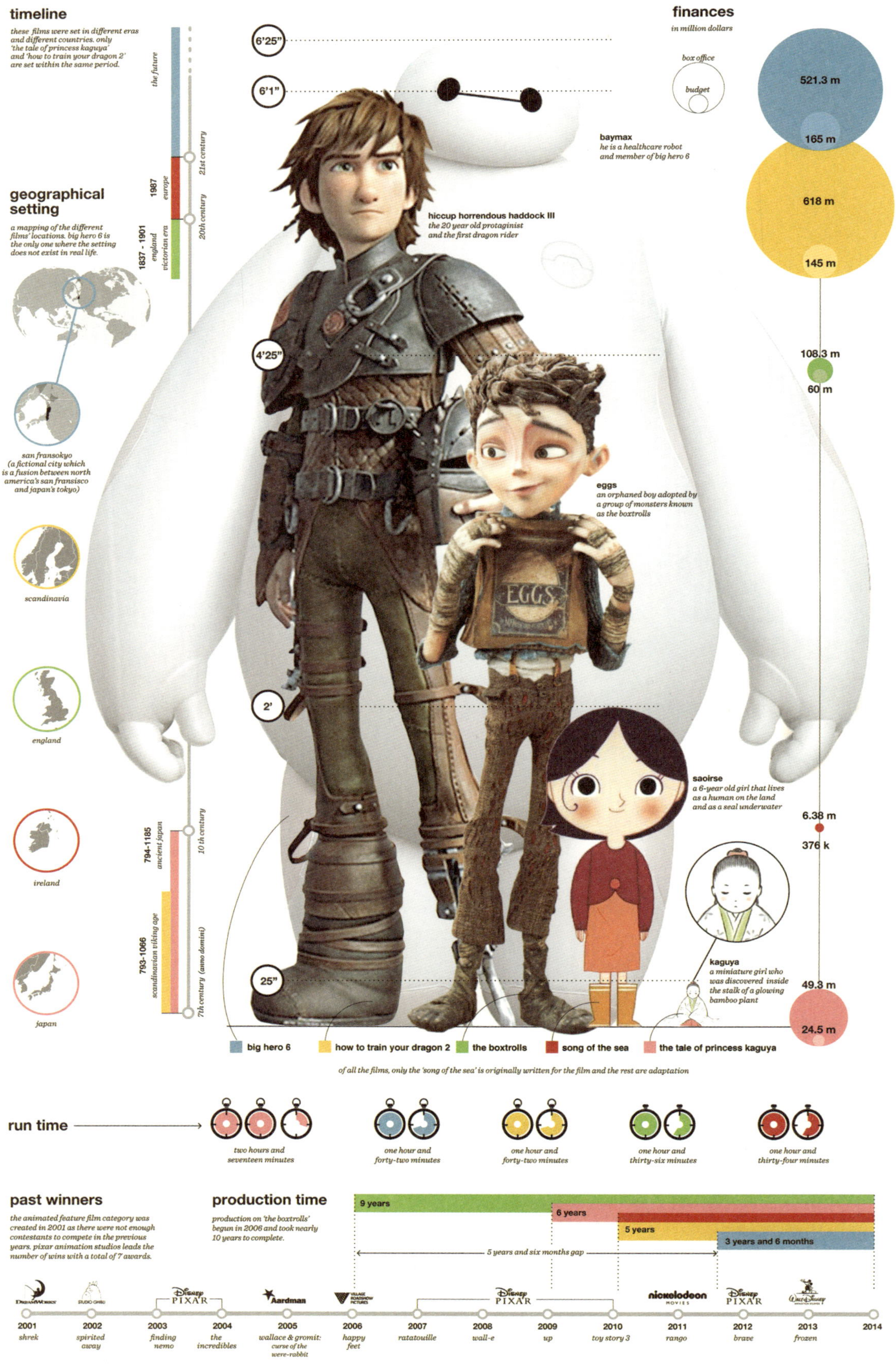

timeline
these films were set in different eras and different countries. only 'the tale of princess kaguya' and 'how to train your dragon 2' are set within the same period.

- the future / 21st century
- 1987 / europe / 20th century
- 1837 - 1901 / england / victorian era
- 794-1185 / ancient japan / 10th century
- 793-1066 / scandinavian viking age / 7th century (anno domini)

geographical setting
a mapping of the different films' locations. big hero 6 is the only one where the setting does not exist in real life.

- san fransokyo (a fictional city which is a fusion between north america's san fransisco and japan's tokyo)
- scandinavia
- england
- ireland
- japan

finances
in million dollars

- box office
- budget

- 521.3 m / 165 m — big hero 6
- 618 m / 145 m — how to train your dragon 2
- 108.3 m / 60 m — the boxtrolls
- 6.38 m / 376 k — song of the sea
- 49.3 m / 24.5 m — the tale of princess kaguya

baymax — he is a healthcare robot and member of big hero 6 (6'1")

hiccup horrendous haddock III — the 20 year old protagonist and the first dragon rider (6'25")

eggs — an orphaned boy adopted by a group of monsters known as the boxtrolls (4'25")

saoirse — a 6-year old girl that lives as a human on the land and as a seal underwater (2')

kaguya — a miniature girl who was discovered inside the stalk of a glowing bamboo plant (25")

- ■ big hero 6
- ■ how to train your dragon 2
- ■ the boxtrolls
- ■ song of the sea
- ■ the tale of princess kaguya

of all the films, only the 'song of the sea' is originally written for the film and the rest are adaptation

run time

- two hours and seventeen minutes
- one hour and forty-two minutes
- one hour and forty-two minutes
- one hour and thirty-six minutes
- one hour and thirty-four minutes

past winners
the animated feature film category was created in 2001 as there were not enough contestants to compete in the previous years. pixar animation studios leads the number of wins with a total of 7 awards.

production time
production on 'the boxtrolls' begun in 2006 and took nearly 10 years to complete.

- 9 years
- 6 years
- 5 years
- 3 years and 6 months
- 5 years and six months gap

2001 shrek — DreamWorks
2002 spirited away — Studio Ghibli
2003 finding nemo — Disney PIXAR
2004 the incredibles
2005 wallace & gromit: curse of the were-rabbit — Aardman
2006 happy feet — Village Roadshow Pictures
2007 ratatouille — Disney PIXAR
2008 wall-e
2009 up
2010 toy story 3
2011 rango — Nickelodeon Movies
2012 brave — Disney PIXAR
2013 frozen — Walt Disney
2014

131
2015 Oscar Series: the Best Animated Film

Project Description /
This infographic compares the heights of the main characters of films, as well as the timeline and setting of the stories. It also compares the budget of each film, and how many years each film took to produce.

Designers / Waleed Rabin, Lucille Umali

132
2015 Oscar Series: the Best Short Films

Project Description /
The infographic shows the 15 films nominated in the three short-film categories—live action, animated, and documentary. The films must not exceed 40 minutes in order to qualify. This infographic uses the image of a cuckoo clock to compare the running time of all the films. At the same time, it incorporates the storyline of the films into the clock's design. The swing of the pendulum is creatively used to identify the film's genre—whether it is comedy (to the left) or drama (to the right).

Designers / Adonis Durado, Winie Ariany

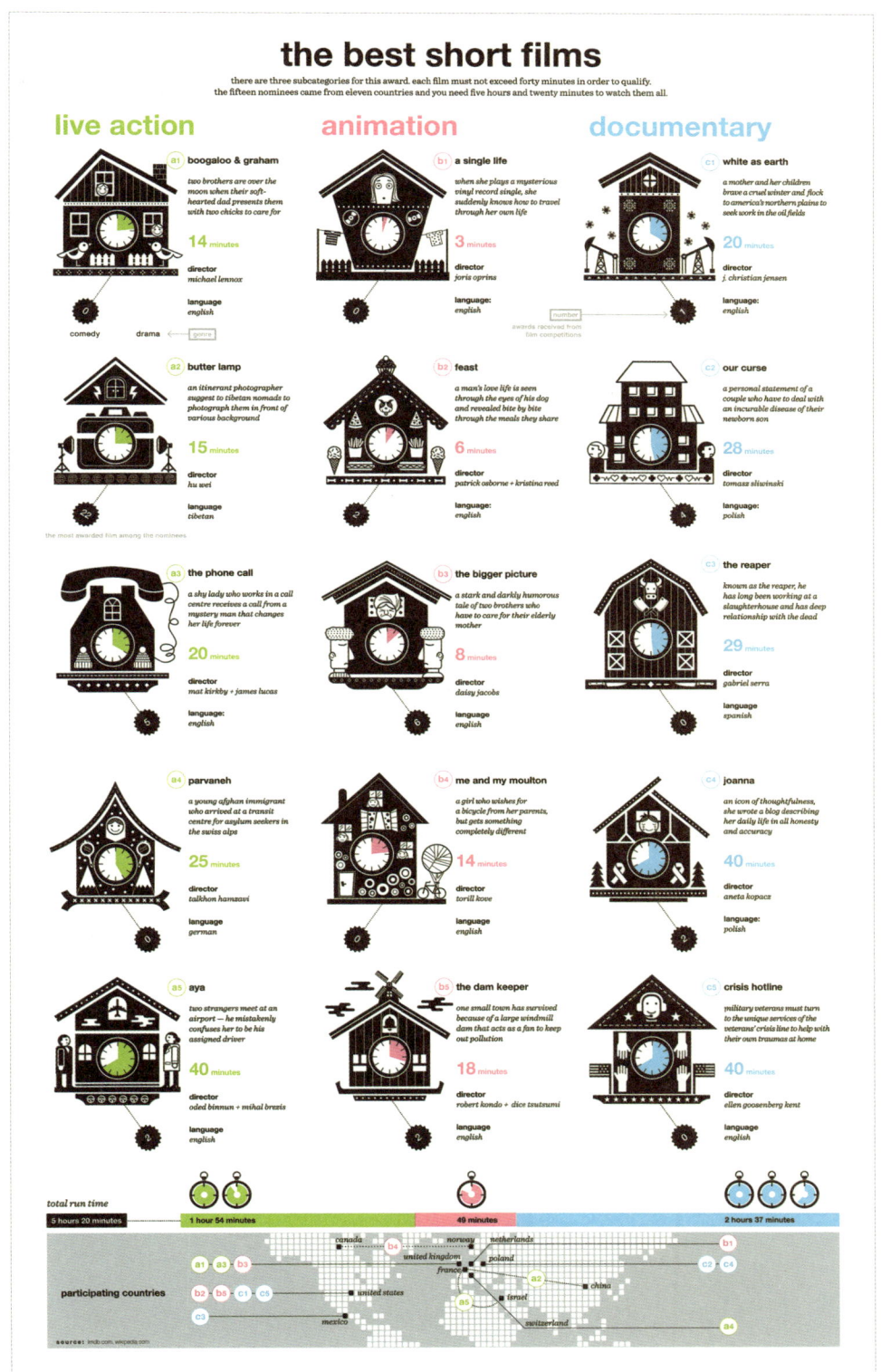

Oscar Fashion

Project Description /
This is a showcase of the gowns worn by winners of Best Actress at the Academy Awards from 2000 to 2015, and who designed them.

Designer / Geri Batara Sonny

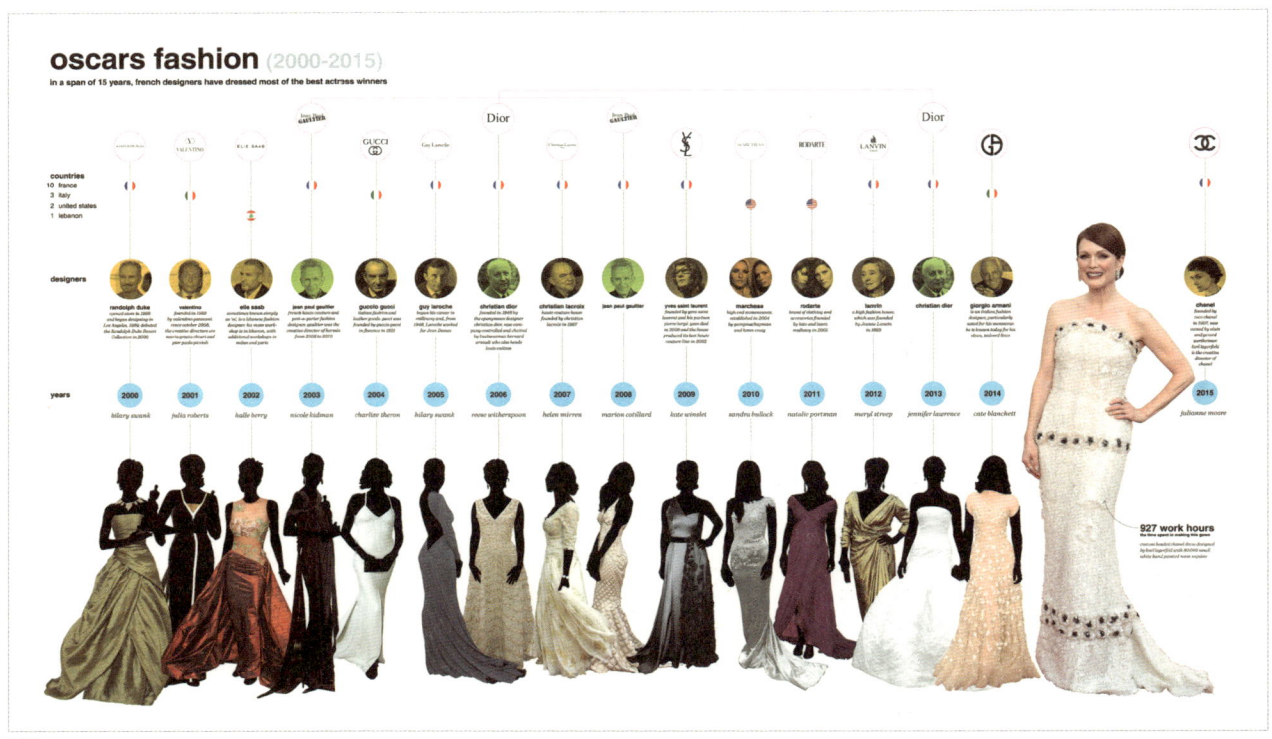

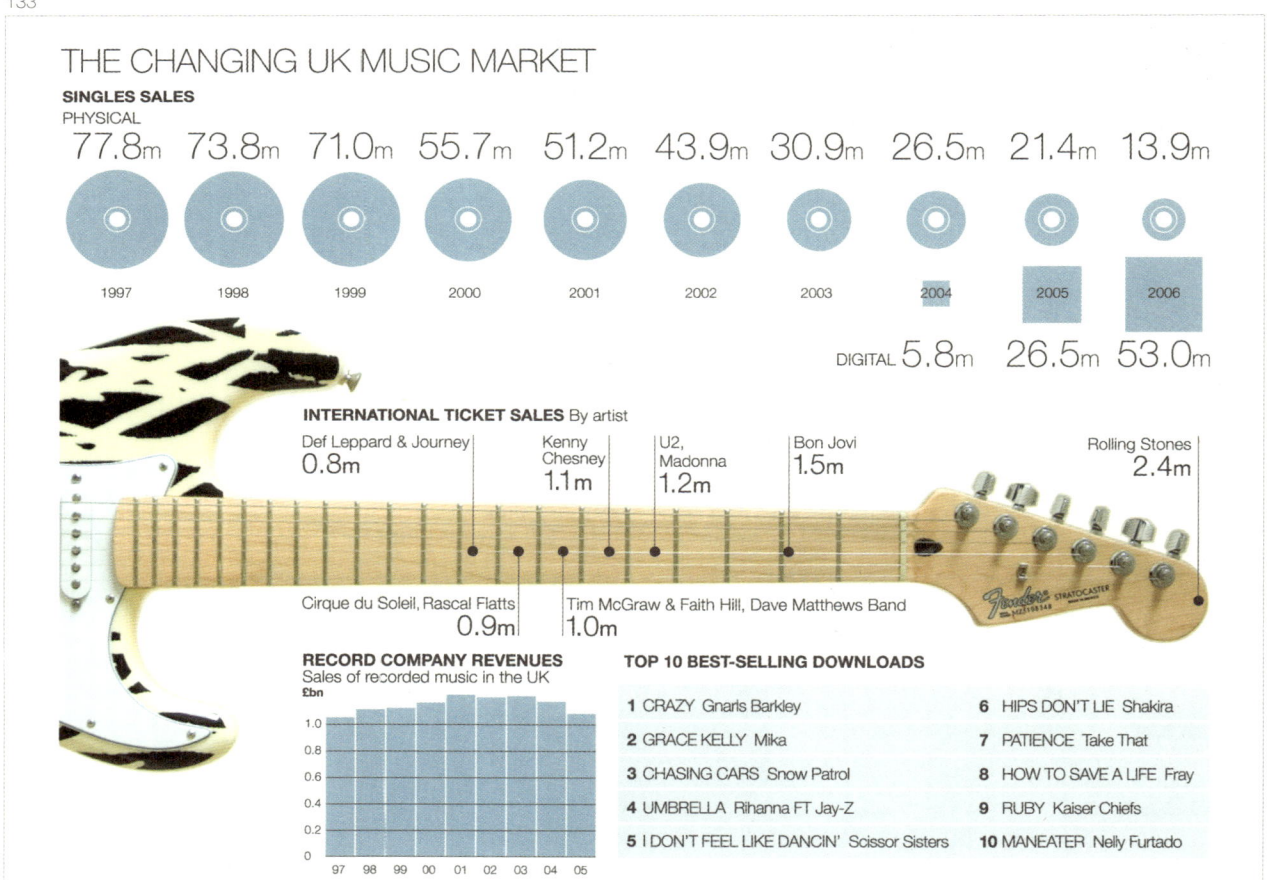

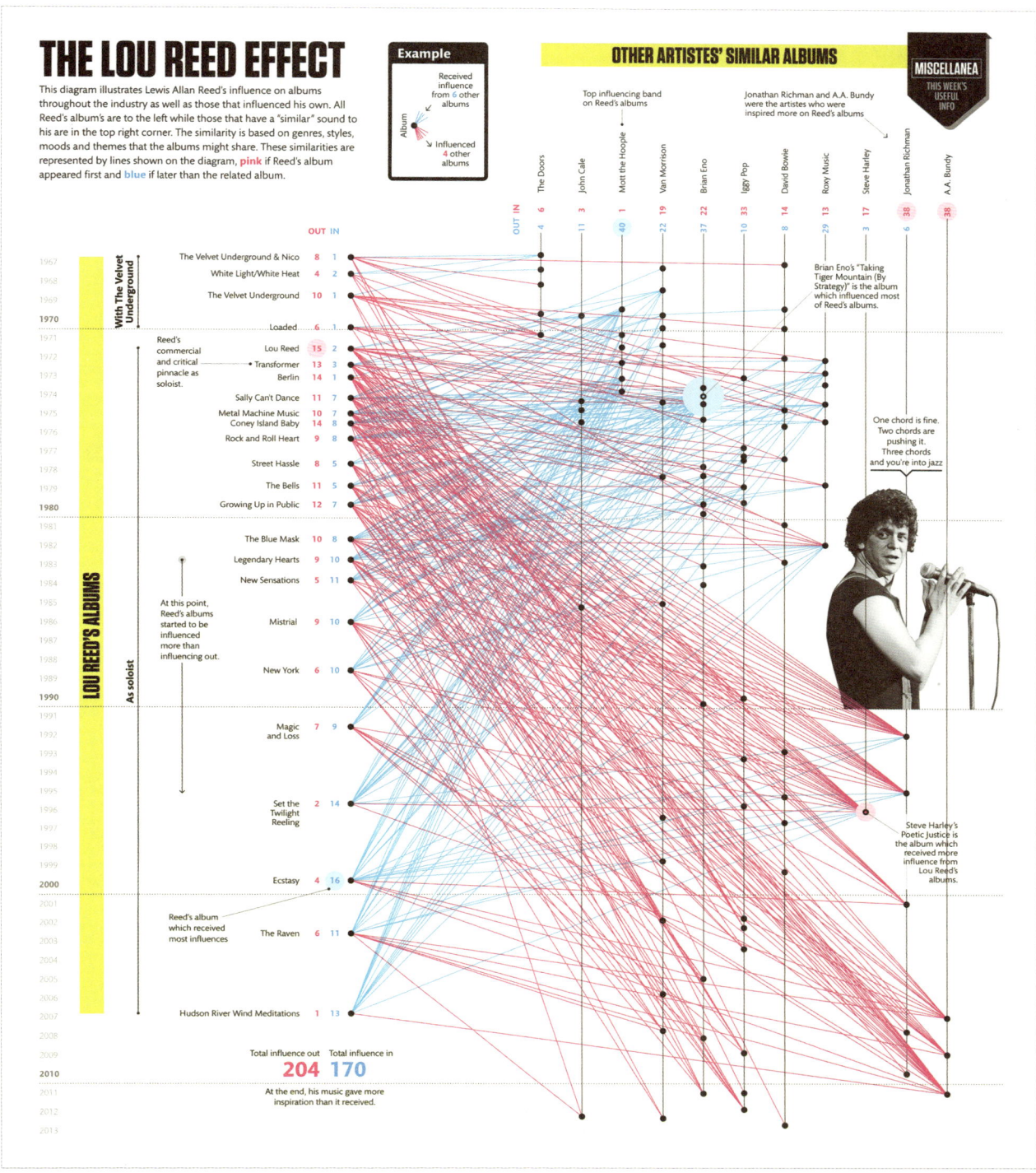

Music Sales

Project Description /
This infographic was for the business section of a Sunday national newspaper on how sales of digital singles had overtaken vinyl sales. Ciaran Hughes wanted a musical visual element to accompany the tables of data he was given, so on the way to work on the train, he decided that a guitar image would make an interesting shape, with the data worked in and around the fret board.

Client / *Sunday Telegraph* newspaper
Designer / Ciaran Hughes

The Lou Reed Effect

Project Description /
When Lou Reed died, Antonio Farach decided to create an infographic showing the rock bands that influenced him most, and the bands he influenced most. All Reed's albums are shown to the left, while those with a 'similar' sound are in the top-right corner. The similarity is based on genres, styles, moods, and themes that the albums might share. The designer uses pink and blue lines to connect the artists with those they have influenced.

Designer / Antonio Farach
Completion / 2013

Mafalda—Who's That Girl

Project Description /
Mafalda, a very famous and beloved cartoon in Latin America, features a very smart girl and a group of her friends, who talk about philosophy, politics, and religion. Published in the newspaper *Tiempo* from Buenos Aires, Argentina, this infographic describes the influences and symbolism of Mafalda and her friends in an easily understandable way.

Designer / Norberto Baruch B.
Completion / 2014

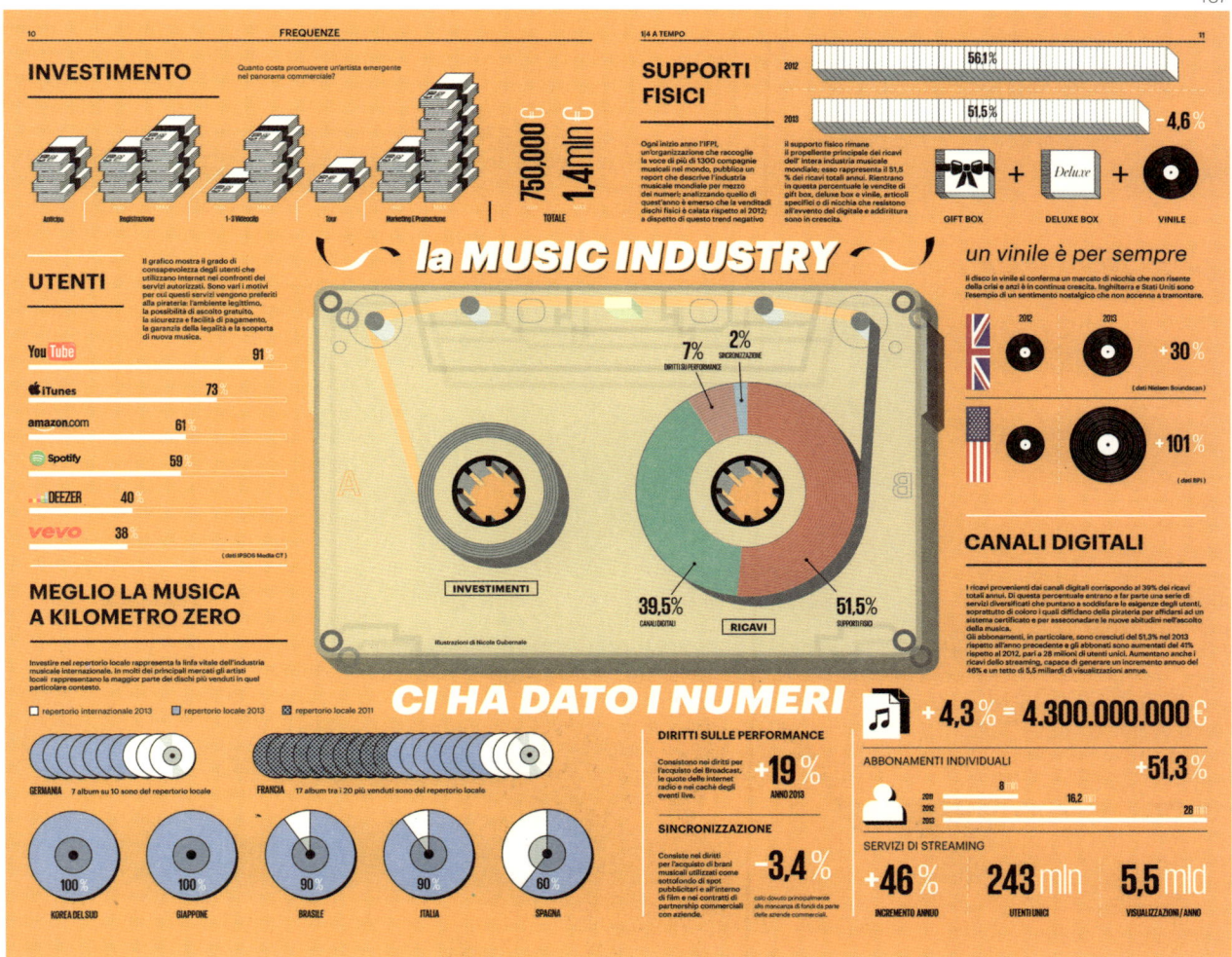

The Music Industry

Project Description /

Part of an editorial experimental project of a music magazine, this unusual infographic visually describes the main investments and revenues of the contemporary music industry. The central part of the infographic, and the main visual subject, is a cassette that shows the percentages of major revenues. Other data is represented on the sides, while a substantial part is dedicated to the growing interest in old vinyl records.

Designer / Nicola Gubernale
Completion / 2014

Statistics about James Bond Movies

Project Description /
The website www.informationisbeautiful.net held a competition to visualize information about James Bond movies, using data provided by the site. When Erik Nylund started this infographic project, he tried to find some shape or form related to the subject that could be be transformed into statistics.

Client / Sydsvenska Dagbladet
Designer / Erik Nylund
Completion / 2012

The 1960s Garage Universe

Project Description /
This infographic features 140 Garage songs of the 1960s. Whether they be punk, moody or psychedelic, they have one thing in common. They contain a couple of the following words in their title: You Don't Love Me Girl So I Cry. If a song title comprises two or more of these words, they are marked and connected with a respective line. Thus, a dynamic figure is born, representing a glimpse of the greatest music of all: 1960s Garage.

Designers / Lana Bragina, Kai Becker
Completion / 2014

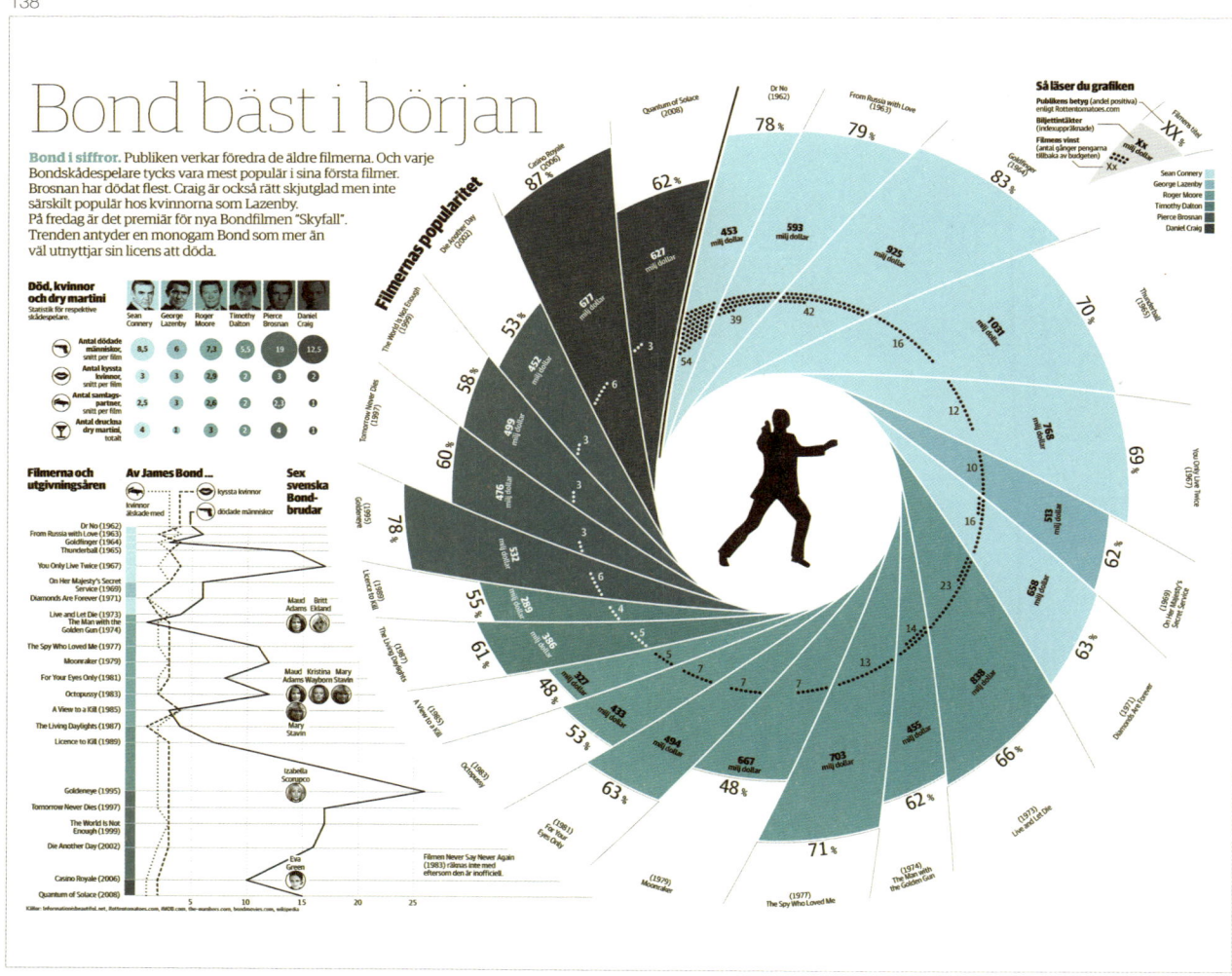

To be Continued

Project Description /

Inspired by someone's research about the top Hollywood films according to their box-office takings, this infographic covered the years from 1980 to 2012, and revealed that the biggest box-office takings were from sequels. The designers collected the information about 320 Hollywood films and then chose the form for the design layout. Though the concept appears quite simple, the design work was more intensive than it sounds.

Client / *Infografika*
Design Agency / Infografika Magazine
Designer / Damir Melnikov
Completion / 2013

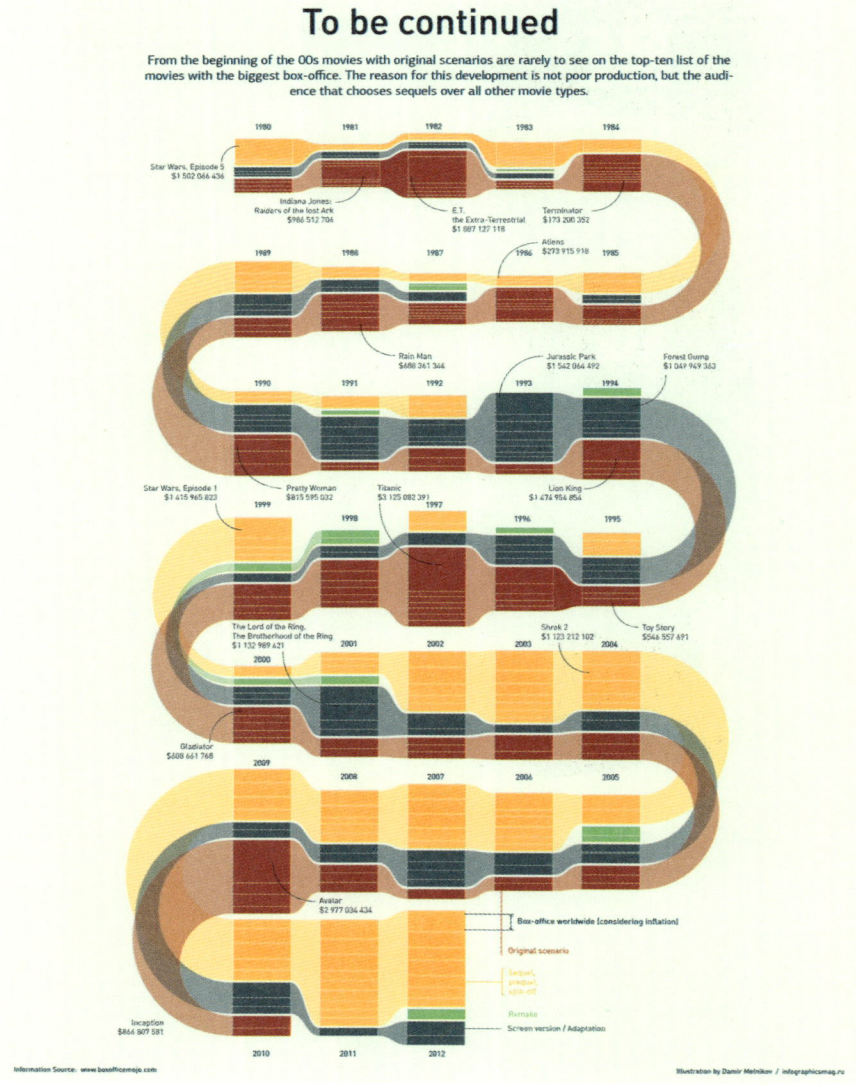

Oscars

Project Description /
The main infographic is a simple table showing all the films in competition at the 2014 Oscars. Almost all graphics in this designer's works are simple and straightforward, using only one color in the work with all other information in black and white.

Client / *Diário Económico*
Designer / Mário Malhão
Completion / 2014

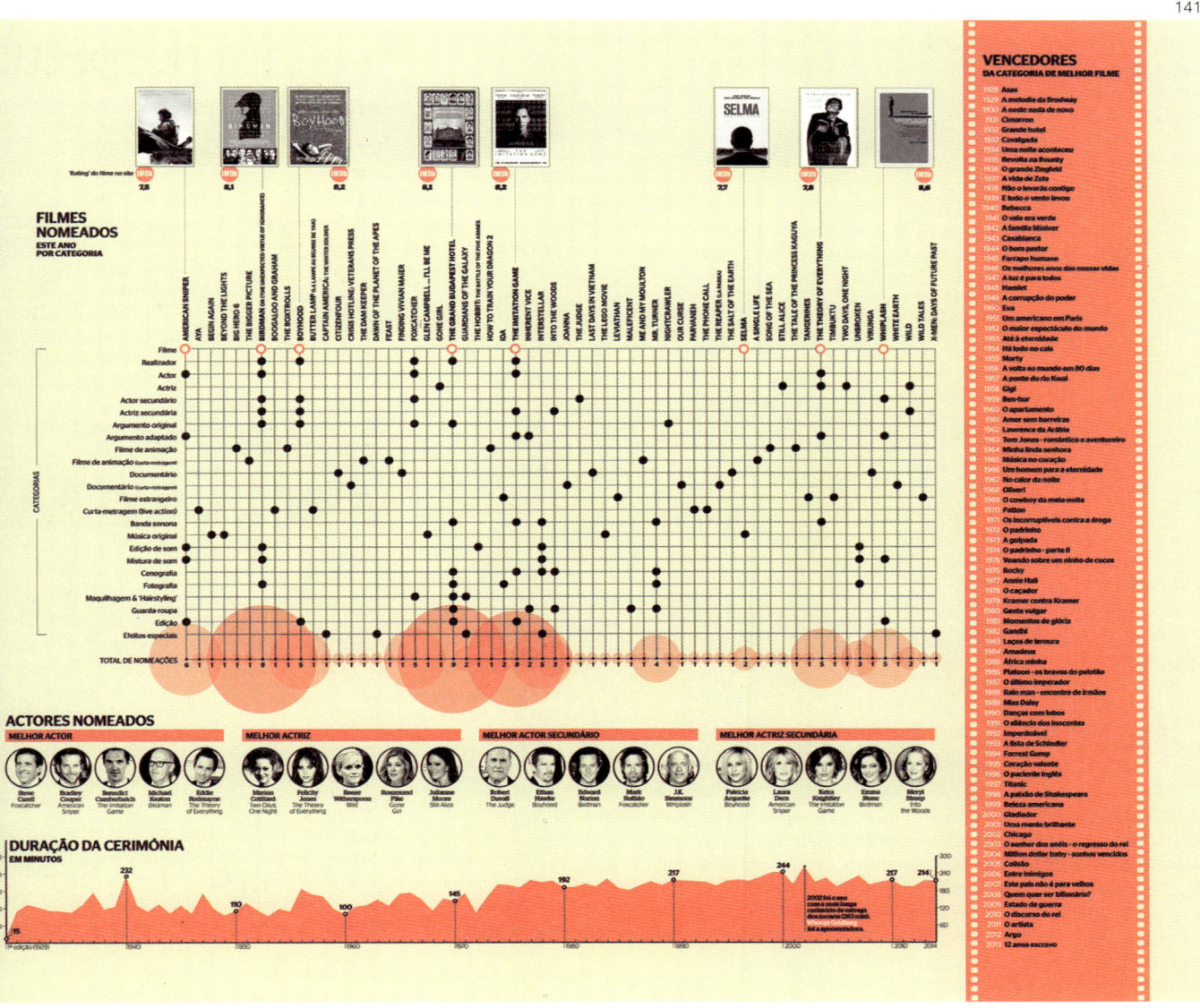

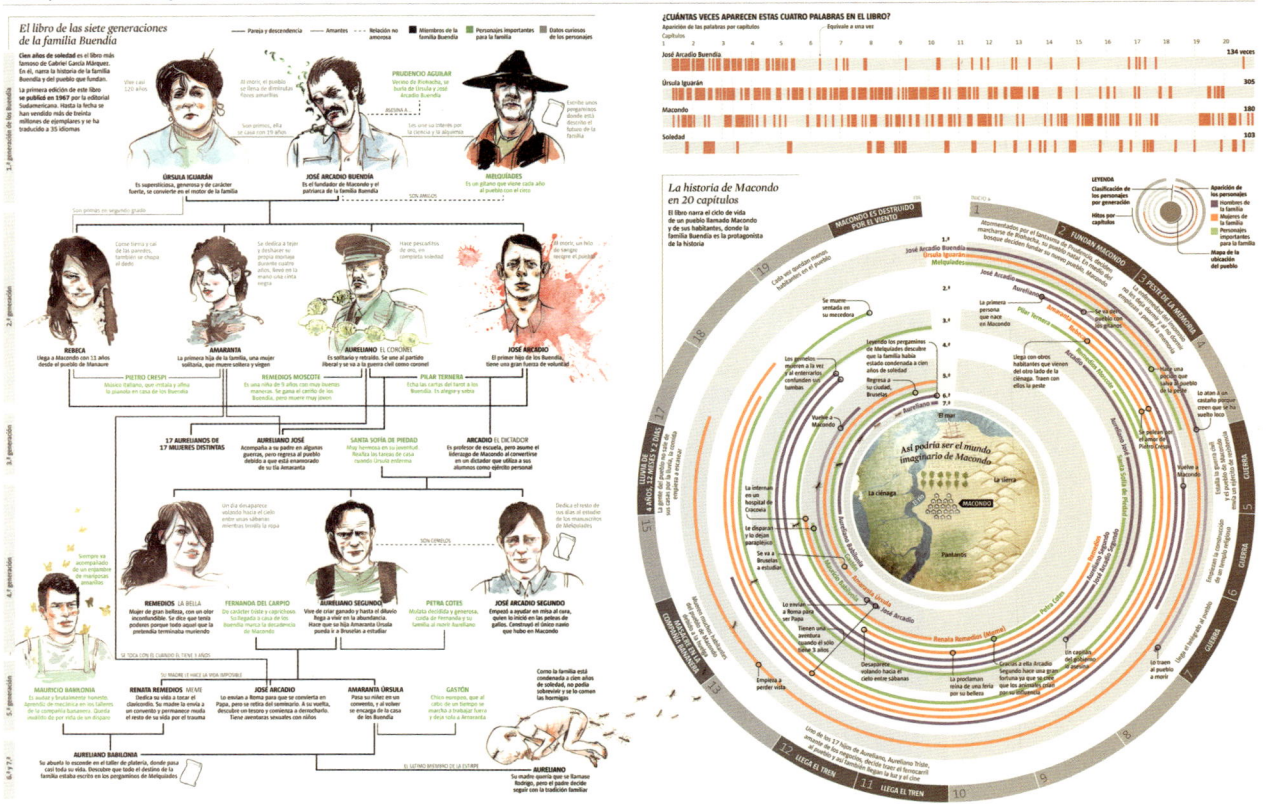

One Hundred Years of Solitude

Project Description /

Due to the age and state of health of acclaimed Colombian author Gabriel García Márquez, the chart was created in anticipation of his death. In this way the designers were able to publish this work (with its extensive documentation) on the day of the writer's death. The infographic summarizes his most famous book: *100 Years of Solitude*. The left side features the complex pedigree of the Buendía family, and the important people linked to these key characters. The main protagonists are drawn according to the descriptions in the book. The right side shows the times that certain key words are repeated in the work. Finally, there is a map of Macondo, the imaginary world where the novel is based. Around the map a pie chart shows the longevity of the main characters and their appearance in the book's chapters.

Client / *La Vanguardia*
Designers / Jaime Serra, Clara Penín, Oriol Malet
Completion / 2014

Bob Dylan Perpetual Tour

Project Description /
The infographic was published to mark the 70th birthday of one of the most influential pop musicians in history. A complete overview of the discography of composer and performer Bob Dylan is presented as a timeline. The line graphs show the successes of those records in major US and UK charts, and the high-profile musicians who have featured in his music over nearly fifty years. The illustration marks the overall aesthetics graph, and a 'Word Cloud' reveals the most used words in Dylan's songs.

Client / *La Vanguardia*
Designers / Jaime Serra, Raul Camañas, Anna Parini

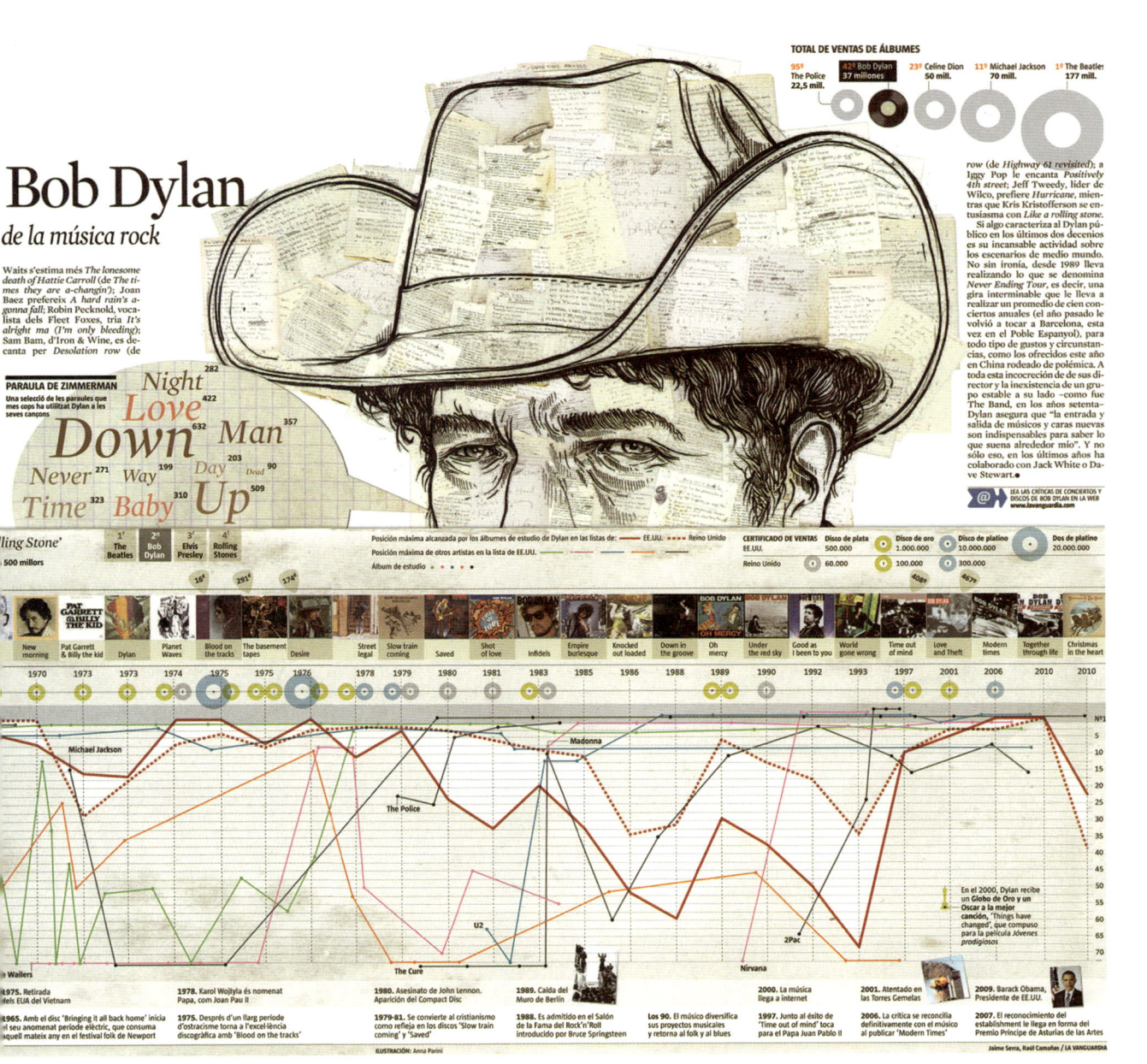

Natural Born Thrillers
A white-knuckled look at what makes a man's heart race.

THE AVERAGE GUY

78% SEXY Number of women who are turned on by scars that accompany high-octane tales

34% Number of men who've spent time in an ER paying the price of an adrenaline rush

Number of guys who've never ridden a roller coaster **12%**

3 Percentage who've ralphed after their dizzying adventure

33 Percentage who got back in line for another round of barfy fun

90 Percentage of wannabe Mavericks who'd gladly fly shotgun in an F-16

1 in 5 Number who'd rather go Verne and probe the depths in a deep-sea submarine

38% Proportion of guys who admit that heights freak them out

4 in 5 Number who'd overcome that phobia if a woman dared them to skydive

88% Number of guys who've gone 100 mph or faster on the highway

1 in 2 Number of guys who've talked a woman into going skinny-dipping

30% Portion who'd be fearless (or drunk) enough to strip down and streak

87% Portion of women who say a taste for adventure is a must-have trait in a guy

45% Portion of gals who say they're the braver mate

42 Percentage of men who say they would swim with sharks—cageless

53 Percentage of men who'd risk a trampling to run with the bulls in Pamplona

64 Percentage of men who've considered a Kilimanjaro summit attempt

12% Number of men who've gone bungee jumping

HALF Segment who harbor fantasies about base jumping

WALK ON WATER (SORT OF)
Looking for a summer thrill without a steep learning curve? Forget about surfing and try stand-up paddleboarding. In a 2013 Outdoor Foundation report, the sport boasted the highest rate of first-time participation of 42 activities surveyed. You'll want to rent a long, wide board for maximum stability, says pro stand-up paddler Girard Middleton, founder of Miami's SoBe Surf. Then find some calm water and start out kneeling if you need to. Odds are you'll be upright in no time. "With the right equipment and conditions," he says, "most people stand easily from the start."

CONQUER COLD FEET
Your parachute is packed and you're about to jump—until you can't. Blame your amygdala—it triggers the release of norepinephrine, a neurotransmitter that overactivates your right prefrontal cortex, leaving you unable to recognize what to do next, says California psychologist John Arden, Ph.D., author of *The Brain Bible*. The solution? Focus on small steps to activate your *left* prefrontal cortex, soothing the amygdala and making the task seem manageable, Arden says. Like this: "I'll step onto the bar, push off, and count." Your anxiety should fade—and then you're flying.

172 MENSHEALTH.COM | June 2014

ILLUSTRATIONS BY TAMER KOŞELI

Your Fighting Chances
All of a man's feints, jabs, and KOs in the ring of life.

THE AVERAGE GUY

58 Percentage of guys who've been sucker punched

31 Percentage who've sunk to kicking a guy in the nuts (oof!)

Top things that make the average guy want to fight:
5. Tie: Someone spilled a secret; a friend cheated with his wife or girlfriend
4. Someone hurt a loved one
3. Someone talked trash about him
2. A trivial matter that escalated
1. A friend went back on his word

7 Number of arguments the average guy has with his partner each year about when to have sex

4 in 5 Number of men who've traded blows defending a woman's honor

Percentage who say they didn't lose— they threw the fight **17**

4% Number of dads who've yelled at their kid's coach

58% Number whose own dads gave them praise for fighting as a kid

55 Percentage of men who have had a fight with their wife or girlfriend while behind the wheel
Top reason: One said the other was a bad driver.

JON STEWART TV celeb the average guy is most afraid to verbally spar with

Rocky Balboa vs. Apollo Creed Average guy's favorite classic fight scene

1 in 5 Number of men who've never put up their dukes

Nolan Ryan vs. Robin Ventura Average guy's most memorable baseball brawl

52 Percentage of men who think fighting has a place in sports (other than hockey)

COUNTER THE COLD SHOULDER
Uh-oh: She's gone quiet. Women default to the silent treatment because they've been socialized to keep the peace, hindering their ability to address conflict head-on, says Audrey Nelson, Ph.D., a gender communications expert. First, Nelson says, acknowledge that she's withdrawn. Then, stress the importance of the relationship—and that she needs to speak up if she feels the same way. Now her silence is implicit. Still nothing? Say you're ready to talk when she is— and scram. Then just wait it out. "You'll put everything back on a level playing field," Nelson says.

TRAMPLE A TROLL
When you can't resist engaging with Internet provocateurs, don't waste time trying to burn them back, says Jay Heinrichs, a corporate communications consultant and the author of *Thank You for Arguing*. Instead, he says, offer praise—it's like an antidote to snark, especially if it's mildly sincere. "Start with something like 'I sense a brain back in there, but your words don't do it justice,'" says Heinrichs. Keep up these left-handed compliments without getting angry or insulting, and you'll leave the flamethrower speechless—and soon, tweetless.

Percentage of men who've intervened to save a buddy from getting pummeled

64% Increase in the average guy's risk of developing heart disease if he nurses a grudge

21 Percentage of men who've fought on social media

Three stupid things *MH* readers have come to blows over:
1. A *Halo* win
2. Turkey stuffing
3. A fart (We told you they were stupid.)

49% Number of men who've gotten into a shouting match with a coworker

Percentage who badly wanted to coldcock the dude **60**

43 Percentage of men who dwell on lost fights

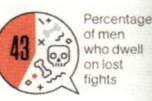
57% Number who regularly beat themselves up over dumb mistakes

1 in 4 Percentage of men who enjoy posting trollish comments

29% Number of (deluded) men who think they'd survive a round with Georges St-Pierre

ILLUSTRATION BY TAMER KOSELI

Smoking Infographic

Project Description /

This infographic was created for the Our Health Patient Portal, a personalized site that offers online health management tools and information. The idea was to design the infographic to reflect the style of the site, integrating flat designs and a modern color palette. It was important to display the information in an engaging way, despite the heavy content. This infographic attempts to inspire change by playing with type, color, and iconography.

Client / Our Health
Designer / Ashley Davis
Completion year / 2015

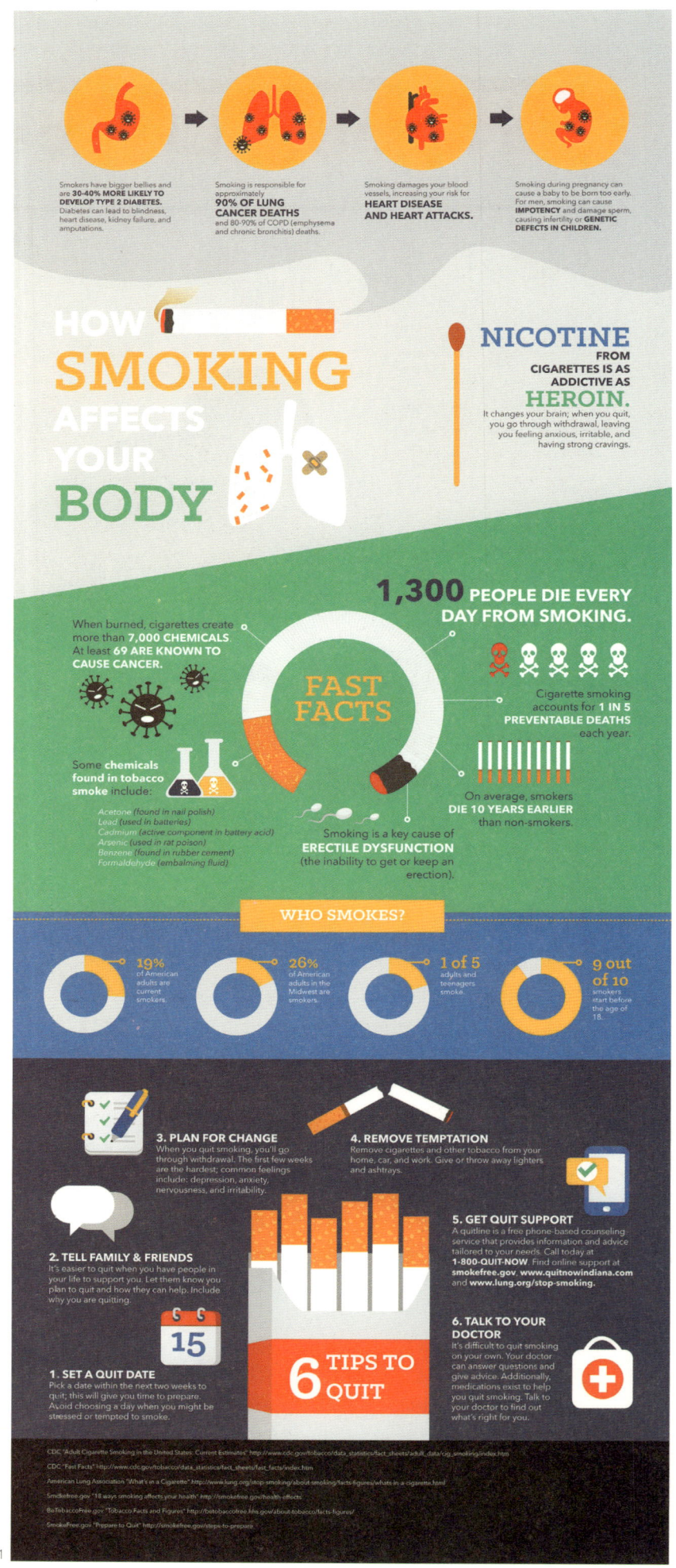

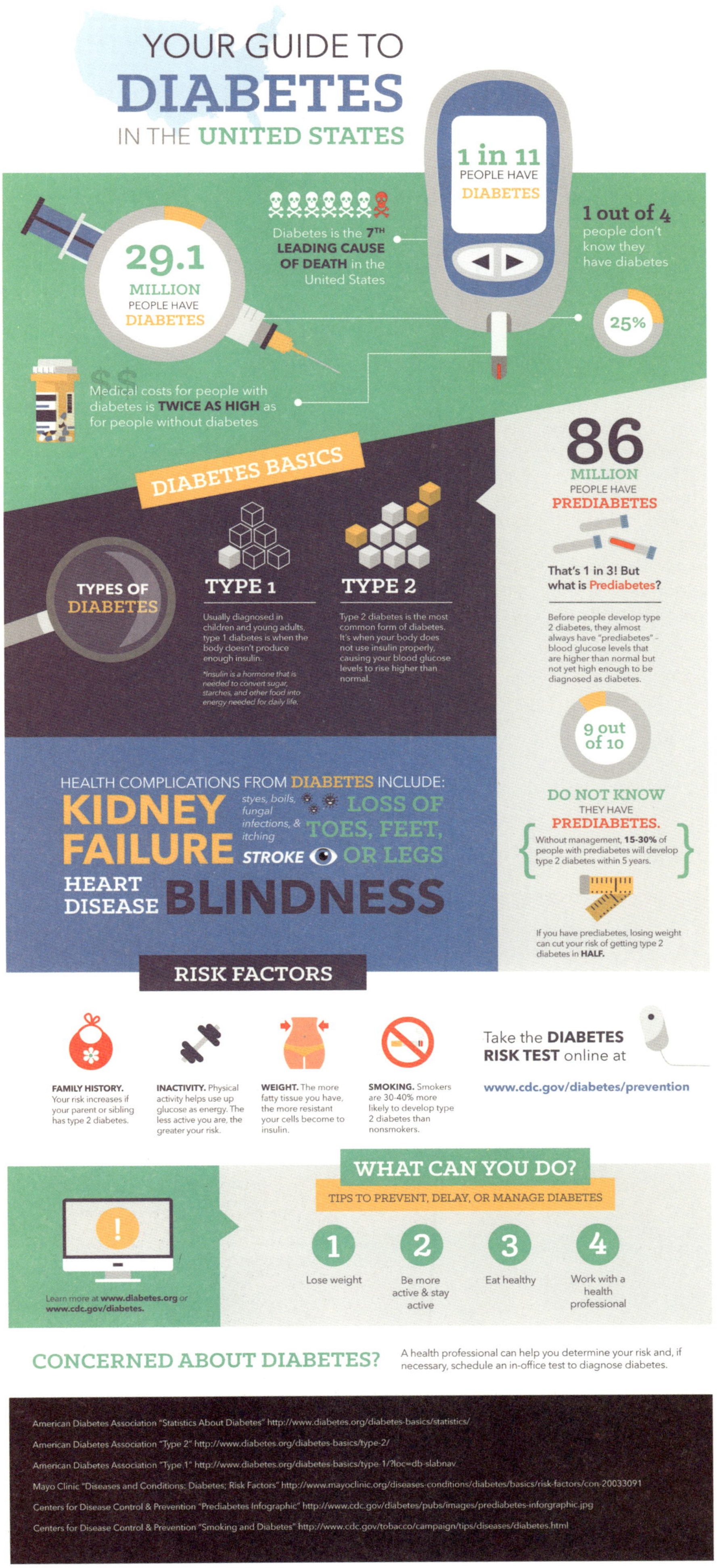

YOUR GUIDE TO DIABETES IN THE UNITED STATES

1 in 11 PEOPLE HAVE DIABETES

29.1 MILLION PEOPLE HAVE DIABETES

Diabetes is the **7TH LEADING CAUSE OF DEATH** in the United States

1 out of 4 people don't know they have diabetes

25%

Medical costs for people with diabetes is **TWICE AS HIGH** as for people without diabetes

DIABETES BASICS

86 MILLION PEOPLE HAVE PREDIABETES

TYPES OF DIABETES

TYPE 1 — Usually diagnosed in children and young adults, type 1 diabetes is when the body doesn't produce enough insulin.

*Insulin is a hormone that is needed to convert sugar, starches, and other food into energy needed for daily life.

TYPE 2 — Type 2 diabetes is the most common form of diabetes. It's when your body does not use insulin properly, causing your blood glucose levels to rise higher than normal.

That's 1 in 3! But what is Prediabetes?

Before people develop type 2 diabetes, they almost always have "prediabetes" – blood glucose levels that are higher than normal but not yet high enough to be diagnosed as diabetes.

9 out of 10 DO NOT KNOW THEY HAVE **PREDIABETES.**

Without management, **15-30%** of people with prediabetes will develop type 2 diabetes within 5 years.

If you have prediabetes, losing weight can cut your risk of getting type 2 diabetes in **HALF**.

HEALTH COMPLICATIONS FROM DIABETES INCLUDE:

KIDNEY FAILURE — styes, boils, fungal infections, & itching — **LOSS OF TOES, FEET, OR LEGS** — STROKE — **HEART DISEASE** — **BLINDNESS**

RISK FACTORS

FAMILY HISTORY. Your risk increases if your parent or sibling has type 2 diabetes.

INACTIVITY. Physical activity helps use up glucose as energy. The less active you are, the greater your risk.

WEIGHT. The more fatty tissue you have, the more resistant your cells become to insulin.

SMOKING. Smokers are 30-40% more likely to develop type 2 diabetes than nonsmokers.

Take the **DIABETES RISK TEST** online at
www.cdc.gov/diabetes/prevention

WHAT CAN YOU DO?

TIPS TO PREVENT, DELAY, OR MANAGE DIABETES

1. Lose weight
2. Be more active & stay active
3. Eat healthy
4. Work with a health professional

Learn more at www.diabetes.org or www.cdc.gov/diabetes.

CONCERNED ABOUT DIABETES?

A health professional can help you determine your risk and, if necessary, schedule an in-office test to diagnose diabetes.

American Diabetes Association "Statistics About Diabetes" http://www.diabetes.org/diabetes-basics/statistics/
American Diabetes Association "Type 2" http://www.diabetes.org/diabetes-basics/type-2/
American Diabetes Association "Type 1" http://www.diabetes.org/diabetes-basics/type-1/?loc=db-slabnav
Mayo Clinic "Diseases and Conditions: Diabetes; Risk Factors" http://www.mayoclinic.org/diseases-conditions/diabetes/basics/risk-factors/con-20033091
Centers for Disease Control & Prevention "Prediabetes Infographic" http://www.cdc.gov/diabetes/pubs/images/prediabetes-inforgraphic.jpg
Centers for Disease Control & Prevention "Smoking and Diabetes" http://www.cdc.gov/tobacco/campaign/tips/diseases/diabetes.html

Ebola Virus

Project Description /

This infographic is about the Ebola virus, and was supervised by Nancy Potvin. Its main purpose was to offer readers a better understanding of the virus. Therefore, several aspects of the disease were covered, such as its history, its transmission (from animal to human, and from human to human), other existing types of Ebola, and a summary of the 2014 outbreak.

There are five types of Ebola. The type responsible for the 2014 epidemic, which is also the most severe type, is the Zaire Ebola virus. Indeed, it has had a mortality rate of 68% since 1976. Even so, by comparing the contagion level with other similar diseases, it is revealed that this illness is far from being the most contagious. This infographic presents different contamination sources, such as the fruit bat, which is the most common.

Since the infographic was meant to appear in a newspaper, the format, folded in half, extends across two pages. The left page presents basic information about the virus, while the right page is essentially intended to inform about the 2014 outbreak. This layout followed the left-to-right reading direction in such a way that readers would be guided throughout the infographic from the introduction to the conclusion.

Designers / Emy Gariepy, Emily Turmel, Renaud Belles-Isles
Completion / 2014

José Mourinho—Winning Also off the Pitch

Project Description /

This graphic was published the day after a study revealed that Mourinho is one of the highest paid coaches in the world. A simple, two-color chart uses a photo of Mourinho and shows how his career grew. Inserted around the main chart is other information, such as salary, sponsorship, and trophies won.

Client / *Diário Económico*
Designer / Mário Malhão
Completion / 2014

The Youngest Coach to Reach 100 Games in the Champions League

Project Description /

The work was published on the day that José Mourinho hit his 100th game in the Champions league. The main chart uses data wins, draws and losses in each season, and the number of goals scored and conceded by the teams in the competition. Other data used shows the trophies won, wages, and the age at which other coaches reached 100 games. The work uses simple graphics and an illustration of Mourinho as the central image.

Client / *Diário Económico*
Designer / Mário Malhão
Completion / 2013

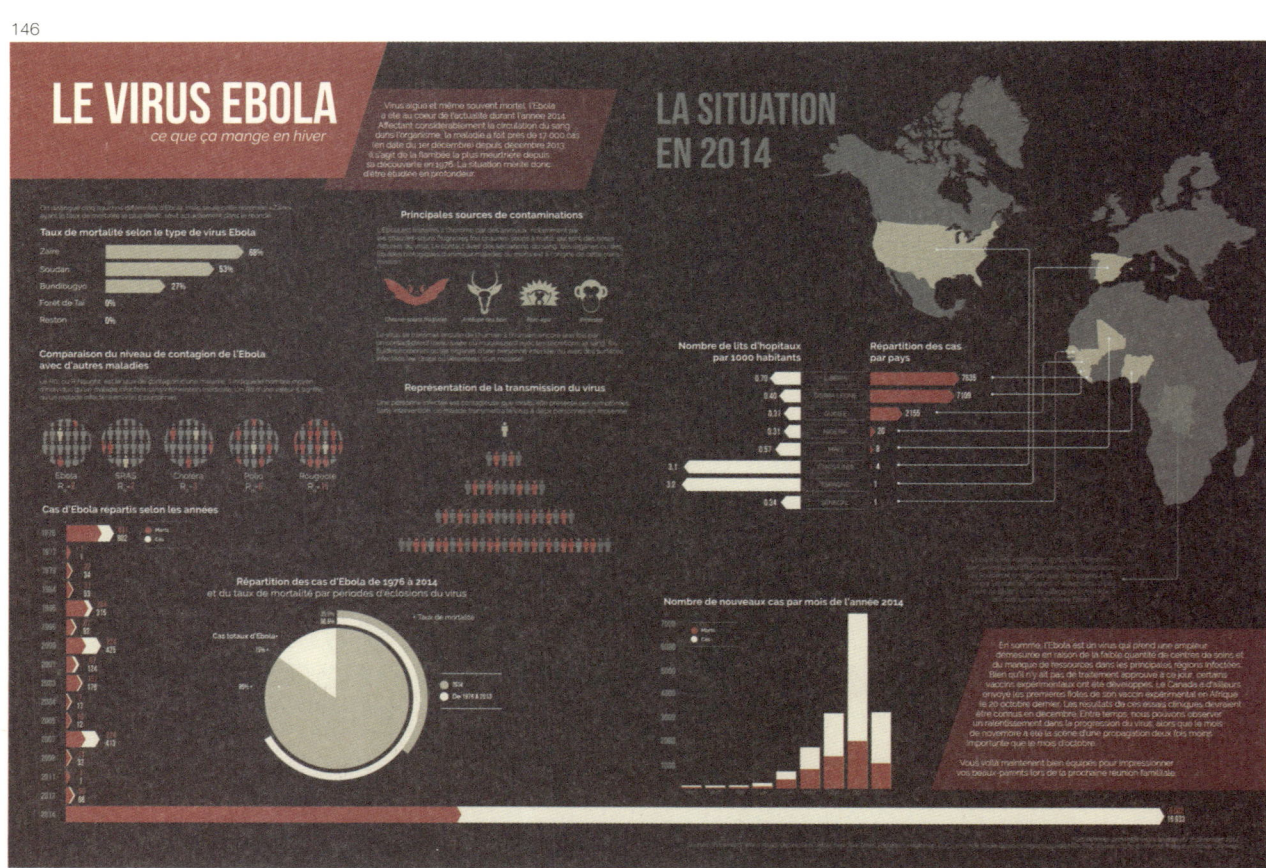

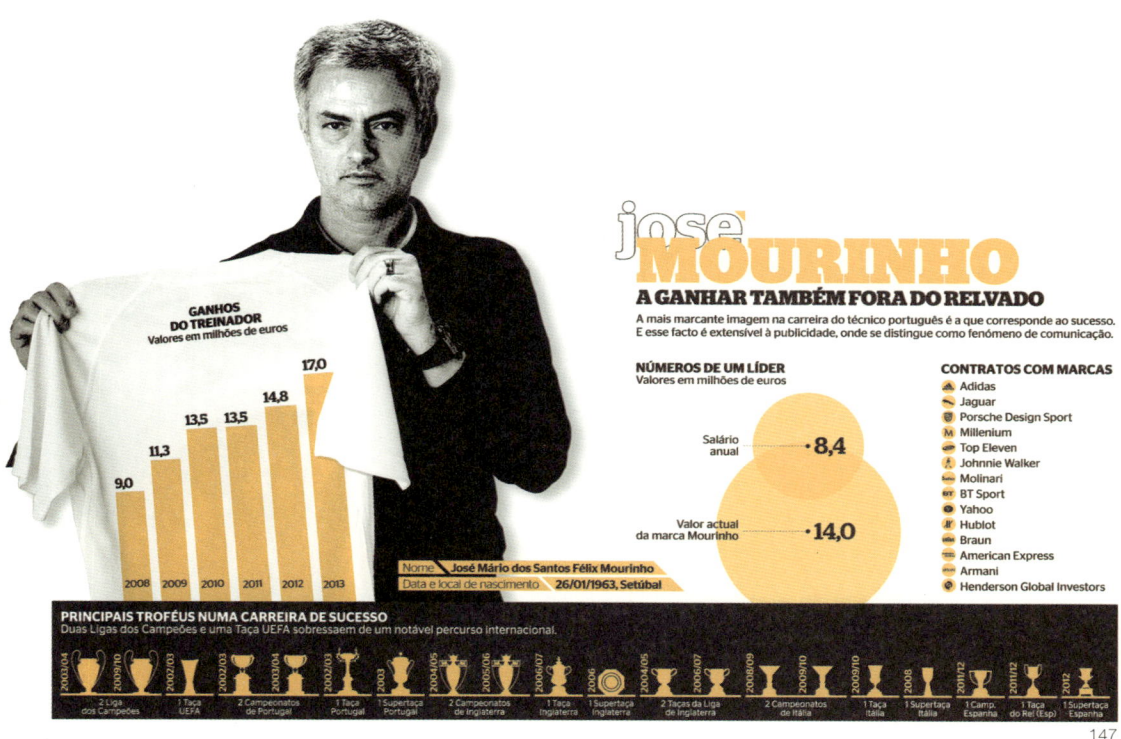

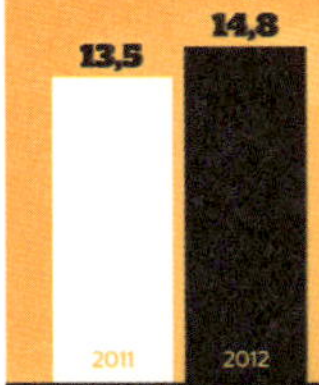

149-1

149-2

149

French Holidays

Project Description /
  What proportion of the French population goes on vacation in summer? Where are they going? What is their budget? What type of accommodation do they choose? And what do the people who stay at home do? Easy Voyage commissioned the designer to visualize the main results of its research into summer holidays. The infographic shows where and how the French will spend their summer in these times of crisis, the growth of the mobile home, the attraction of Britain and the emergence of the 'staycation.'

Client / Easy Voyage
Design Agency / ÉCLAIRAGE PUBLIC
Designer / Nicolas Verrier
Completion / 2014

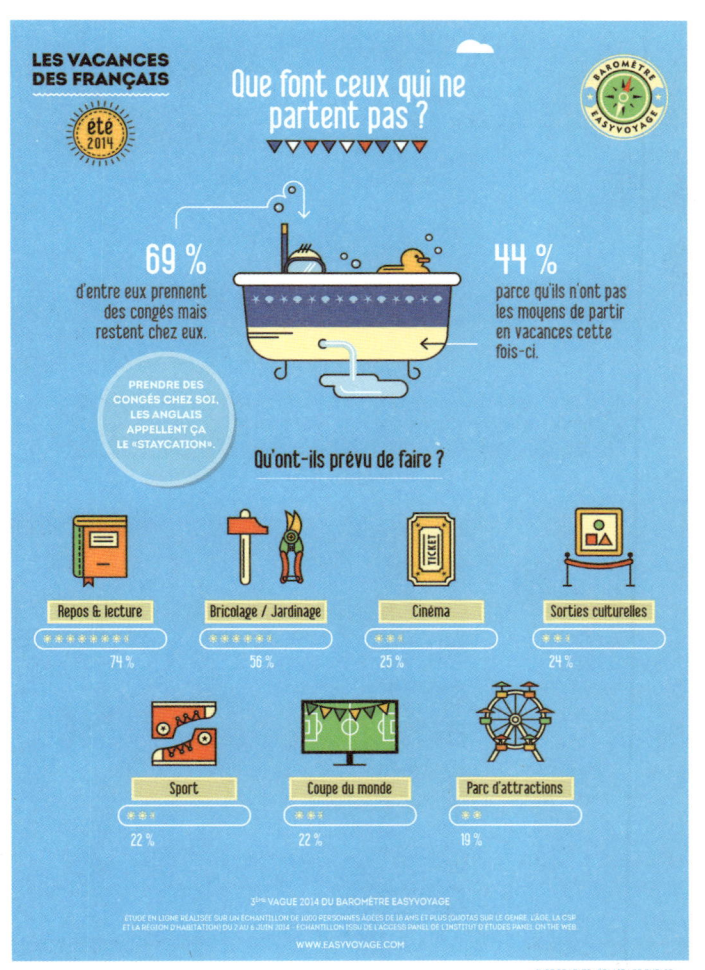

Raiku Editorial Illustrations

Project Description /

Vesa Sammalisto was commissioned to create an infographic-style illustrated spread about the health and welfare of the Finnish populace. The data is drawn not only from national registers, but also from sample material or ready-made statistical data from the National Institute for Health and Welfare (THL). Population studies monitor health and lifestyles among Finns. Some of the population studies also include information from health examinations. The aim is to follow up changes in health behavior both at the level of populations and population groups throughout Finland. The illustration concept is based on the idea of creating a modular laboratory featuring symbolic references to data. The overall form of the illustration reflects and changes along with the topic.

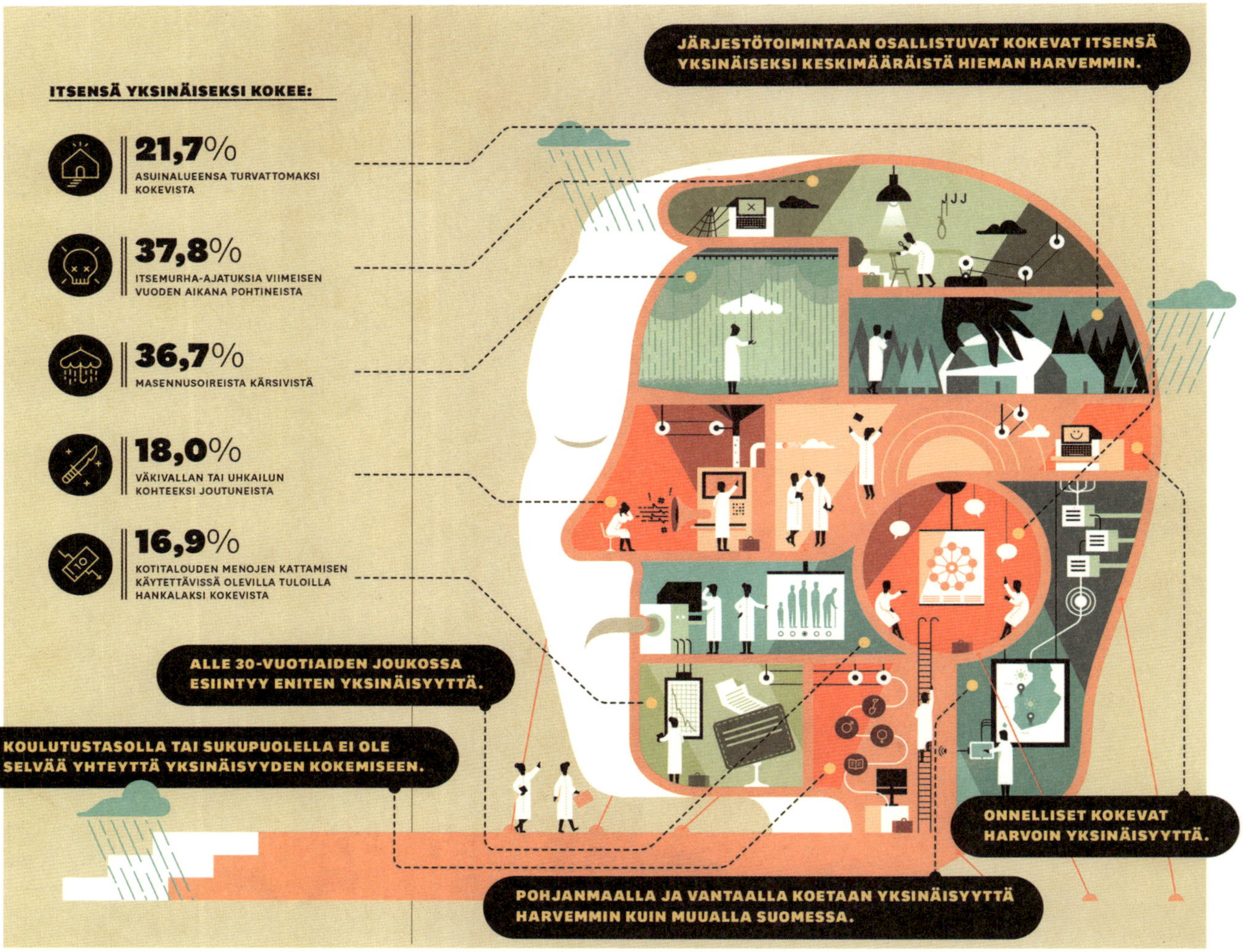

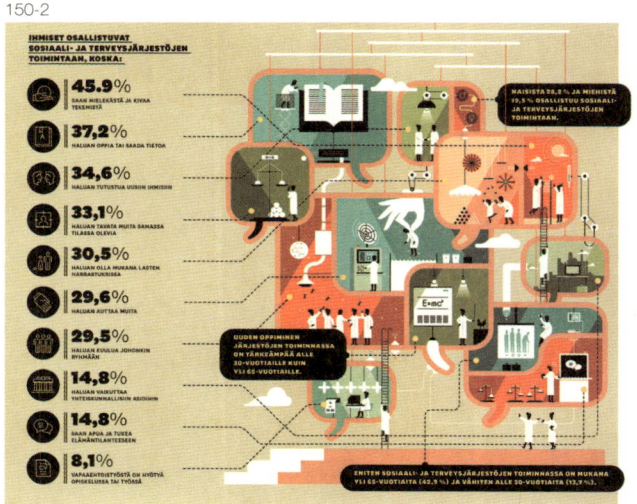

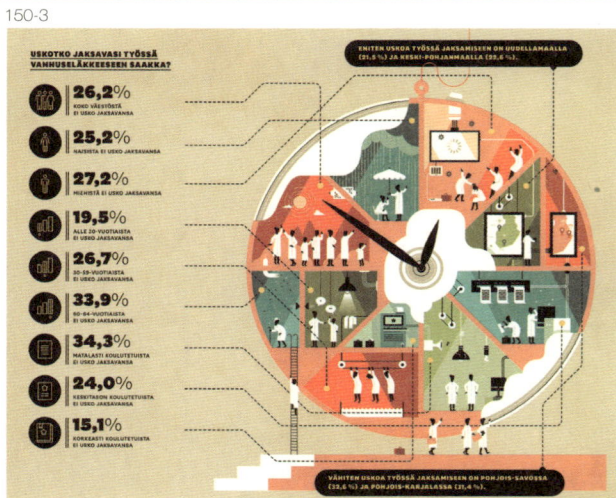

Client / RAY
Designer / Vesa Sammalisto
Completion / 2014

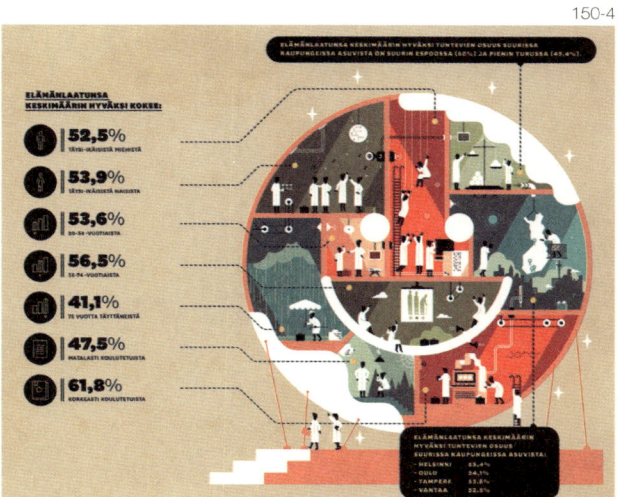

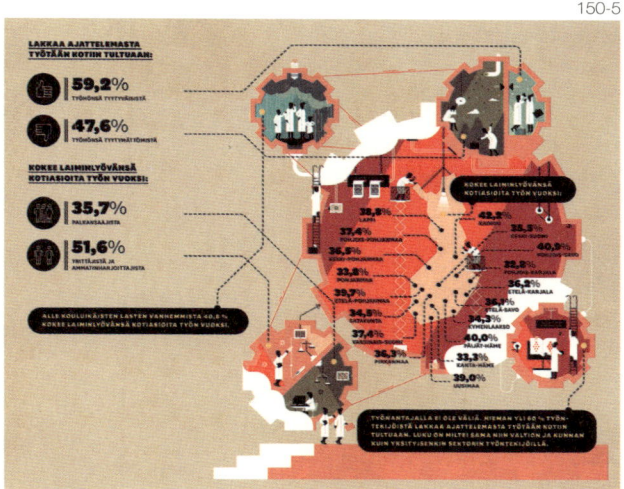

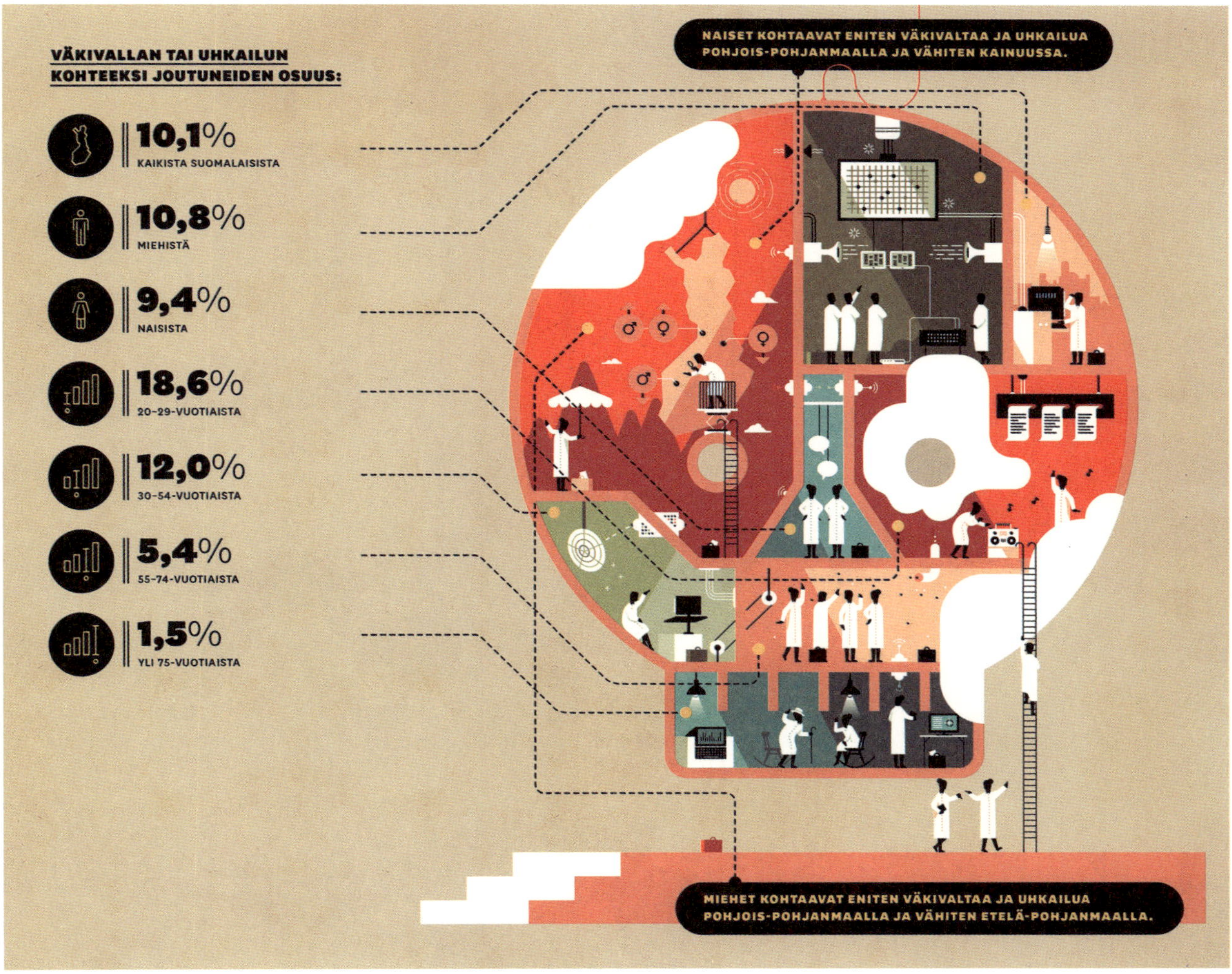

The Portrait of American Travelers Study

Project Description /

The Portrait of American Travelers study provides an in-depth examination of the impact of the current economic environment, prevailing social values, and emerging media habits on the travel behavior of Americans. Differing from past travel studies, the Portrait of American Travelers reveals the underlying motivations that influence travel behavior, with a particular emphasis on how consumers plan, purchase, and share information about their travel experiences. These infographics display some of the information and statistics collected from the study in a creative, unique, and eye-catching way.

Design Agency / MMGY Global
Designer / Catherine Fields
Completion / 2014

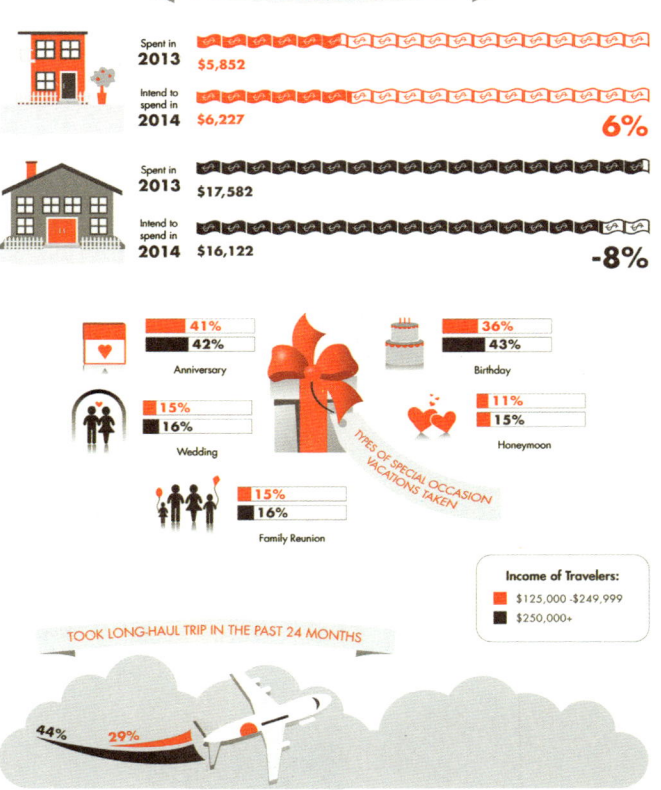

151-1

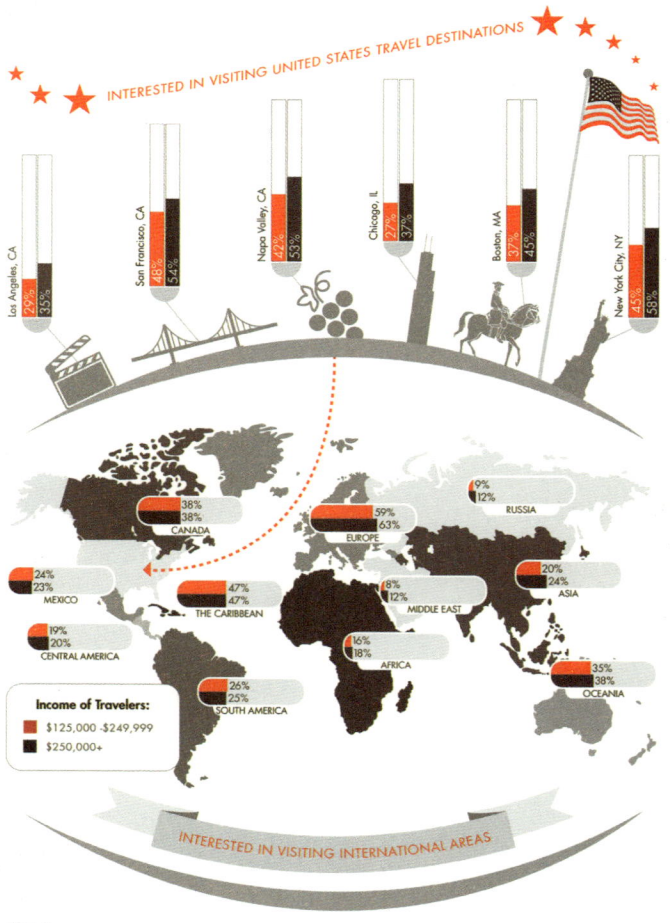

151-2

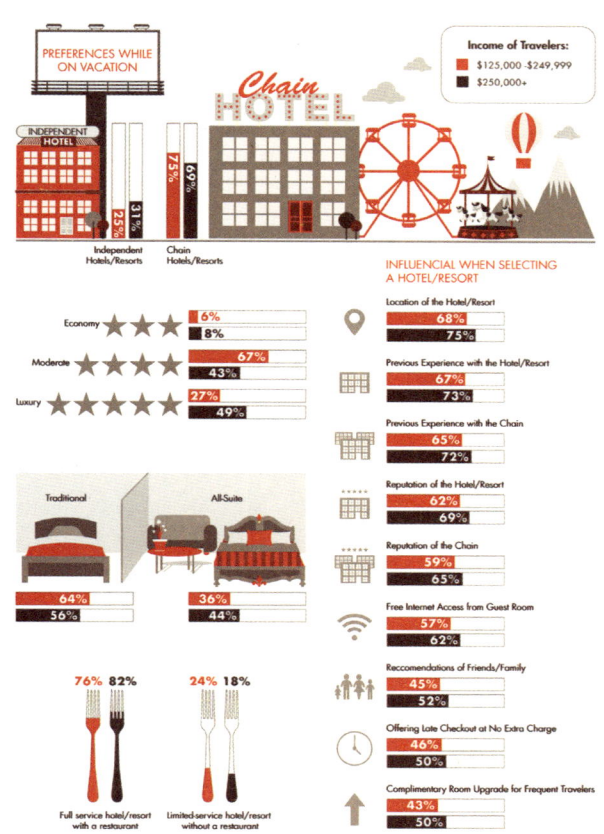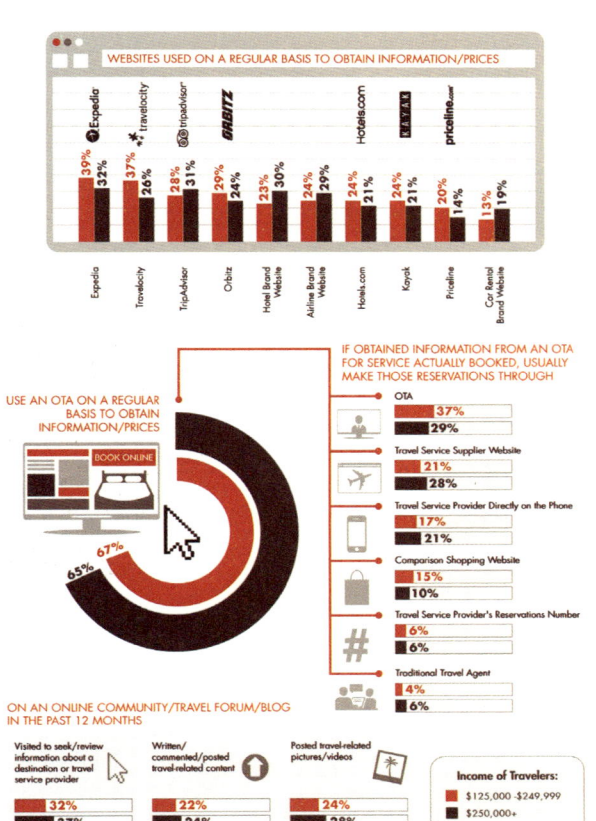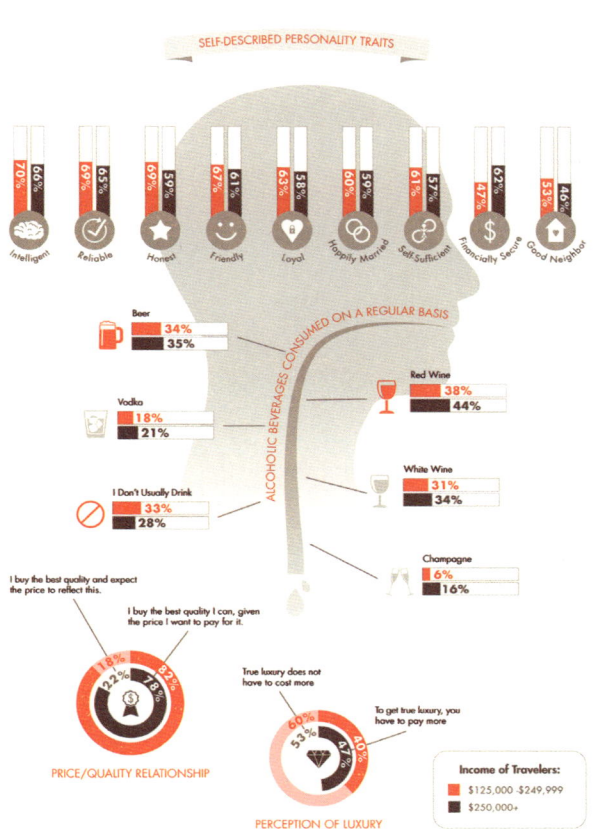

Design X Food

Project Description /

The day before Ryan MacEachern was given a brief to present information on a personal habit over a period of a week, he started a very bland and uninteresting low-carbohydrate diet. He had previously been eating copious amounts of high-fat, high-sugar, colorful junk food, and needed to cut down to a strict diet.

This project explores the nutritional value of the diet, and presents it in a contrasting way: it juxtaposes the dull and boring appearance of the food by presenting the data using colorful vibrant foods. The final products were a perfect bound book with an accompanying poster.

Designer / Ryan MacEachern
Completion / 2013

Aftermarket Education: the MOOC Landscape

Project Description /

The first MOOC launched in September 2008 at the University of Manitoba in Winnipeg. Anyone could attend the class on the web, and 2300 people signed up. In 2011, an artificial-intelligence course at Stanford University enrolled 160,000 students, which inspired one of the instructors to found Udacity.

The courses aren't quite a substitute for a traditional education. At Coursera, one of the largest MOOC providers, 80% of students already hold a bachelor's degree, but only 10% completed the courses they chose, according to co-founder Andrew Ng. But MOOCs can help students learn the skills to do almost anything, or become anybody.

The infographic's clusters represent the number of courses available through nine of the largest MOOC providers in 2014, and every course appears as a dot. The clusters for iTunes U and Udemy, where educators create their own classes, only show the most popular courses.

Client / Popular Science
Design Agency / Beutler Ink
Designers / Tiffany Farrant-Gonzalez, Michelle LeClerc, Jefferson Mok
Completion / 2013

Ranking of Genera Equity

Project Description /

This visual data shows the difference in work opportunities between men and women. How many women in Mexico have been to university? This study covers the status in this decade. Do women have more opportunities than before, or do they still experience the same discrimination? This graphic was created for International Women's Day in 2014.

Design Agency / Diario La Razón de México
Designer / Diana Estefanía Rubio
Completion / 2014

A Statistical Day in Estonia

Project Description /

What does life look like in Estonia during one statistical day?

A story appeared in a newspaper about one average day in the Republic of Estonia. A lot of statistical material was gathered in the course of writing the story, which had to be put forward as a whole. This grew into the idea of putting all of the events into a single picture.

This illustration and infographic describes what is happening in Estonia, on average, on a given day—how many children are born, how many people die, how many people get married, and how many couples get divorced. It also shows the number of traffic accidents, how many crimes are committed, how much public transportation is used, and so on.

Design Agency / AS SL Õhtuleht
Designer / Ingvar Meen

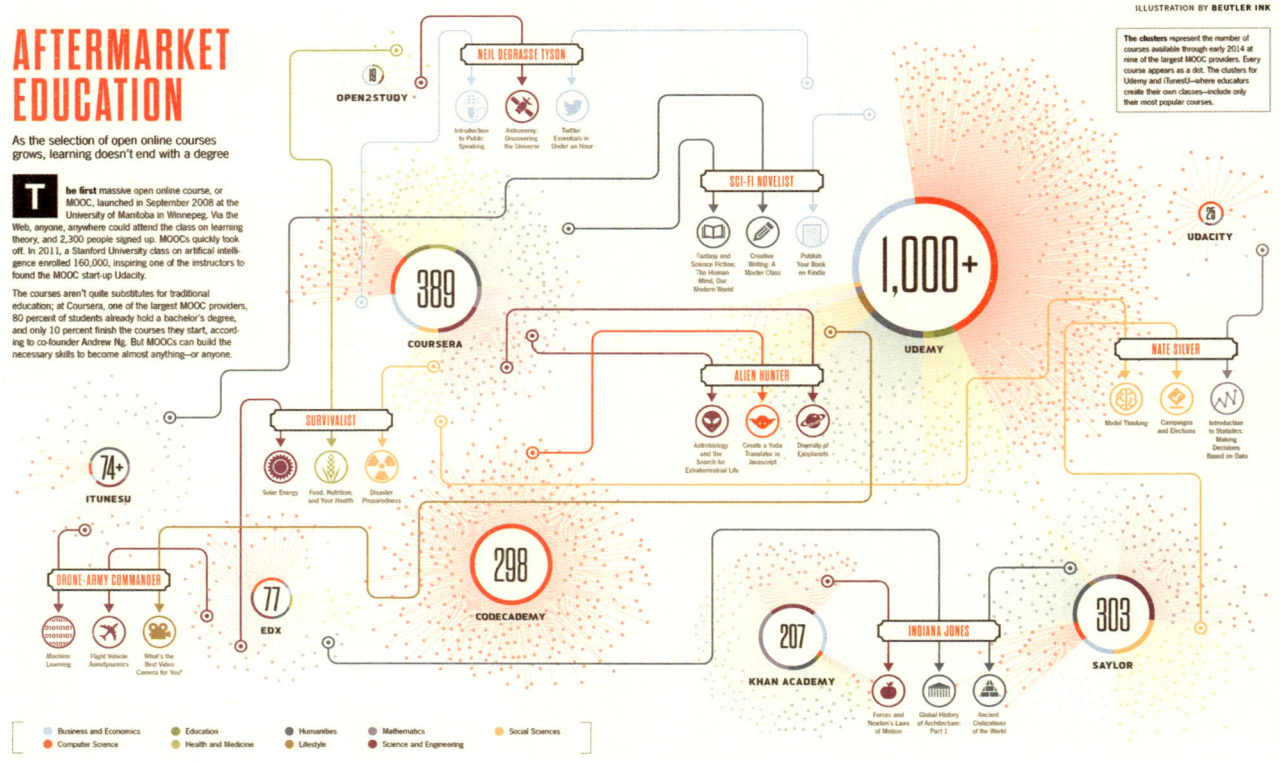

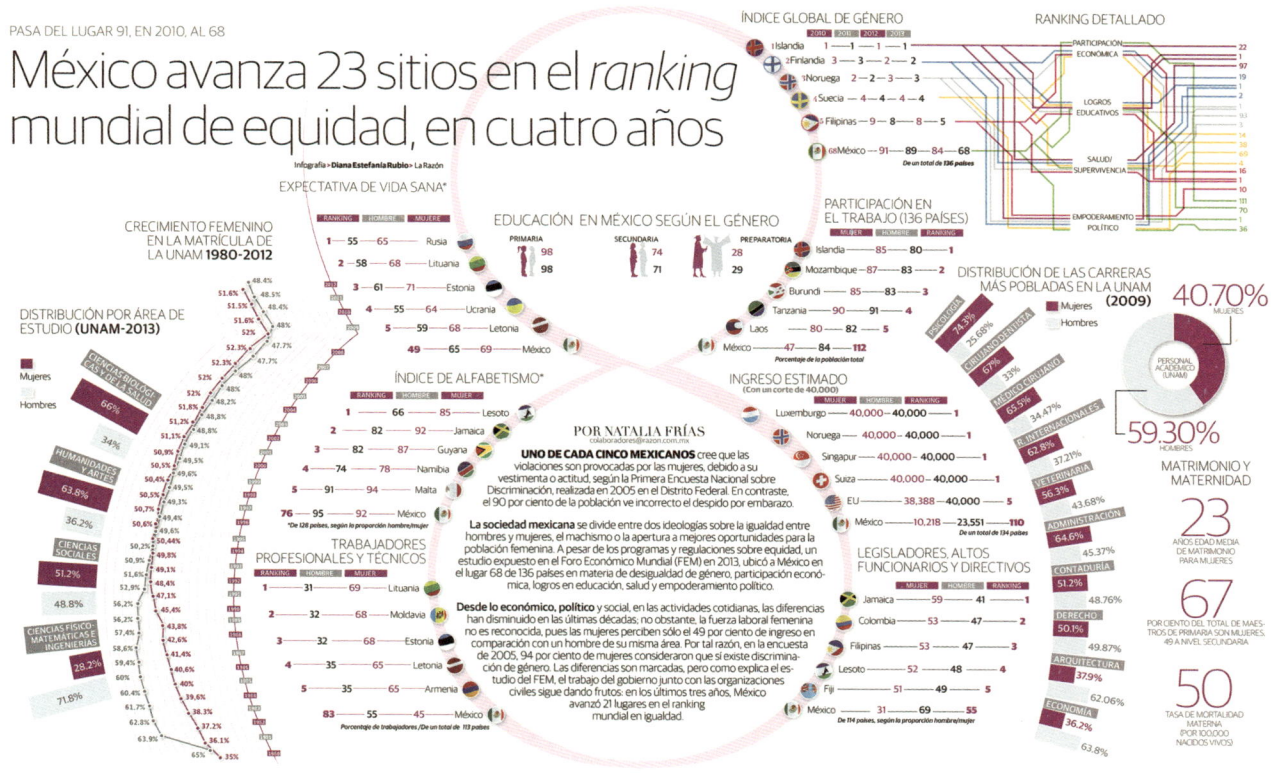

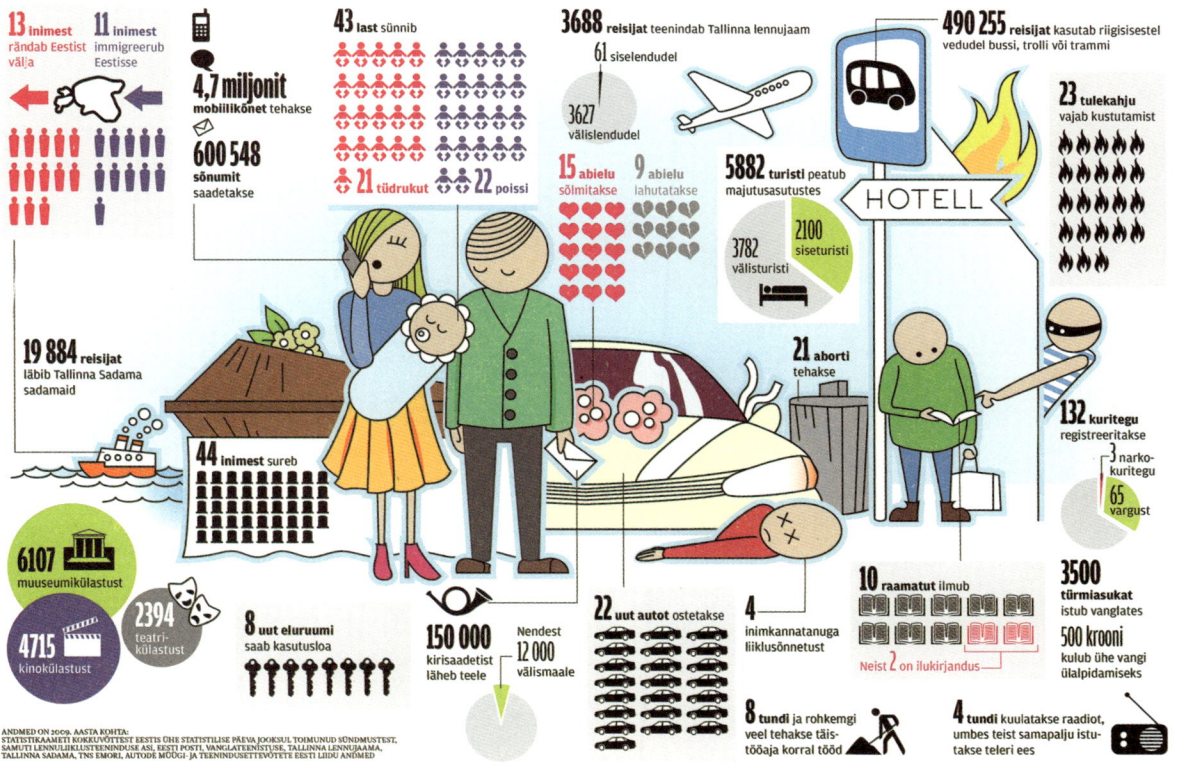

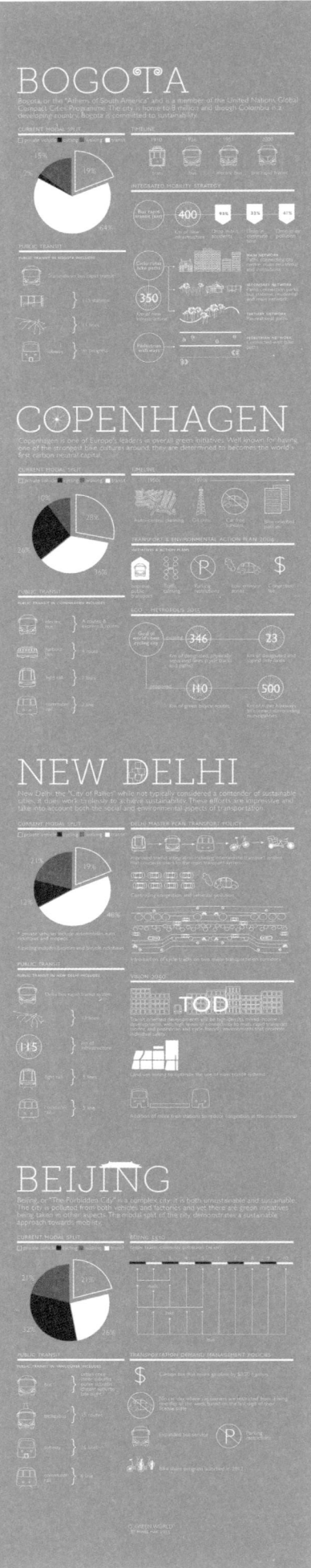

O' Green World

Project Description /

Sustainable transportation is of utmost importance in this day and age, in light of the environmental issues that we face and the choices that we have to make. O' Green World is a brief look at the history and policies of some of the world's major cities with successful multi-modal transport systems. The creative direction for this infographic came from the understanding that most proposed transit policies were news pieces that were presented to the public in either text or oral media, such as on a city website, in election platforms, in public meetings, and so on. Renée Mak wanted to create something that transformed verbose and technical policies into something digestible for the average person, and so she created an illustration-based, tablet-optimized infographic to leverage the modern method of obtaining news via the Internet. To keep people interested and connected with their city, she introduced city-specific illustrations that were merged with typography, and kept a balance between descriptive text, illustrations, and number-based data.

Designer / Renée Mak
Completion / 2012

Qatar

Project Description /

Over the last few years, Qatar has become a powerful country under the guidance of three major emirates. A land famous for being rich in oil, today it represents much more than that. The illustration reflects the history of Qatar, and its development from a country of pearl fishermen to becoming a significant power in the world with its own airline, Qatar Airways, and its own Doha-based broadcaster, Al Jazeera. Each big step in the history of this country has been represented by each letter that together make the word 'Qatar'. Each letter has been designed as one floor of a building, the building itself being the country Qatar has become today.

Client / IL—Il Sole 24 ORE
Designers / Francesco Franchi, Laura Cantadori, Giacomo Gambineri
Completion / 2013

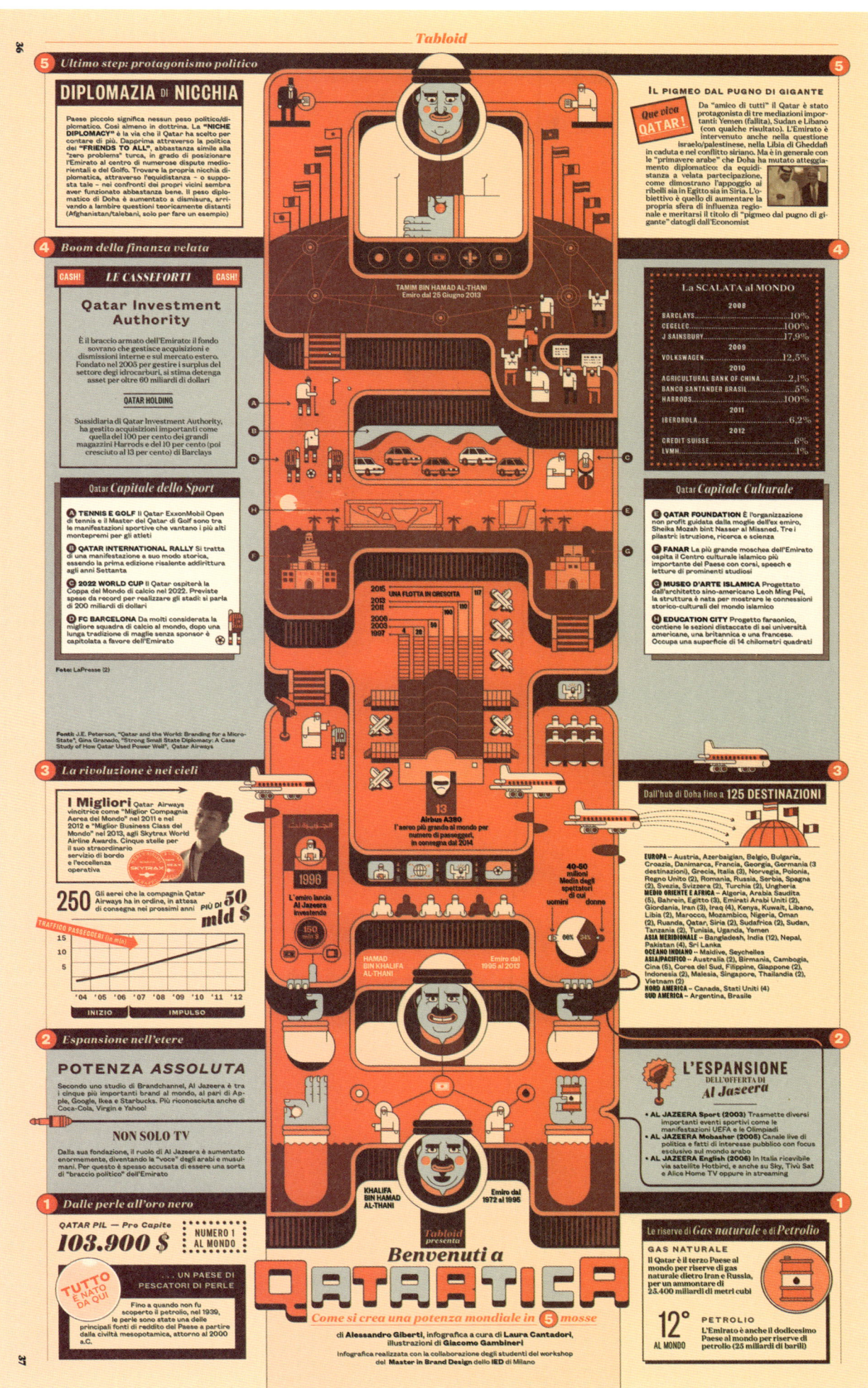

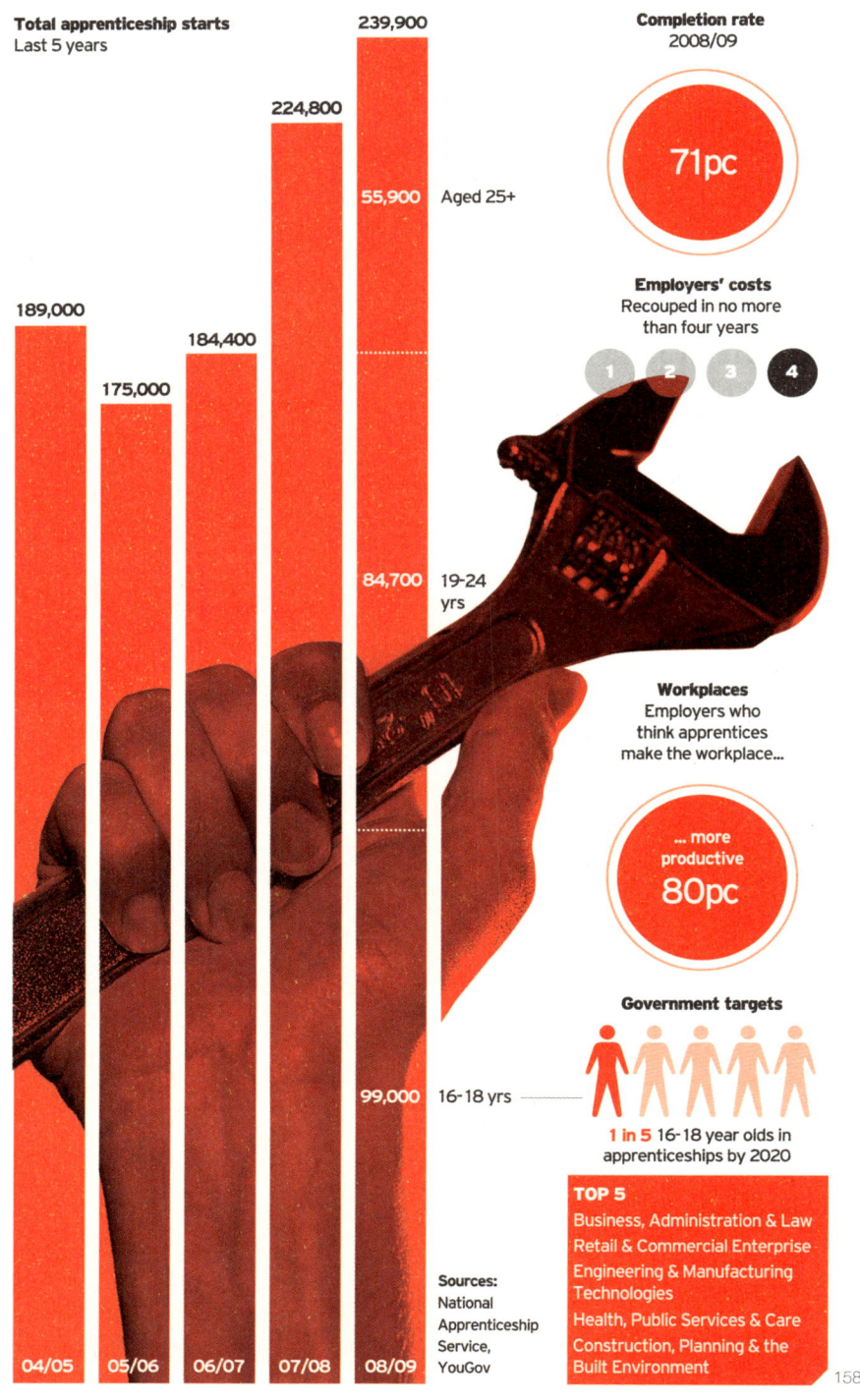

Workers Arise

Project Description /
This was a front-page graphic for the business section of a national newspaper that went with an article about apprentices in the workplace. Ciaran Hughes loved the work of Russian designer Rodchenko, and the space he had to fill lent itself to a strong image of manual work.

Client / *Daily Telegraph* newspaper
Designer / Ciaran Hughes

My City of Tomorrow

Project Description /
What do French students think the city of tomorrow should look like? What is their dream city? What is a smart city in their eyes? The Real Estate and Sustainable Development Chair of ESSEC, led by Professor Ingrid Nappi-Choulet, surveyed students about their vision of the future city. The survey's main finding, reflected in the infographic, is a strong concern for the environment, which will likely lead to future life choices.

Client / ESSEC Business School
Design Agency / ÉCLAIRAGE PUBLIC
Designer / Nicolas Verrier
Completion / 2014

Ma ville de demain

COMMENT LES ÉTUDIANTS IMAGINENT TRAVAILLER ET VIVRE DANS LA VILLE DE DEMAIN.

🍃 LA POLLUTION DE L'AIR PRÉOCCUPE FORTEMENT LES ÉTUDIANTS

ILS POURRAIENT REFUSER UNE OFFRE D'EMPLOI DANS UNE VILLE...

- si l'air y est de mauvaise qualité — 54 %
- si la nature n'est pas assez présente — 42 %

ILS SONT PRÉOCCUPÉS PAR LES PICS DE POLLUTION DE L'AIR :

- 76 % des étudiants français
- 81 % des étudiants d'Île-de-France

87 % accorderont de l'importance au calme, à l'espace et à la qualité de l'air au moment de choisir leur lieu de vie.

🍃 POUR EUX, UNE VILLE INTELLIGENTE EST...

- **DURABLE** en harmonie avec son environnement naturel — 62 %
- **TECHNOLOGIQUE** et ultra-connectée — 19 %
- **DENSE** favorisant les déplacements doux — 19 %

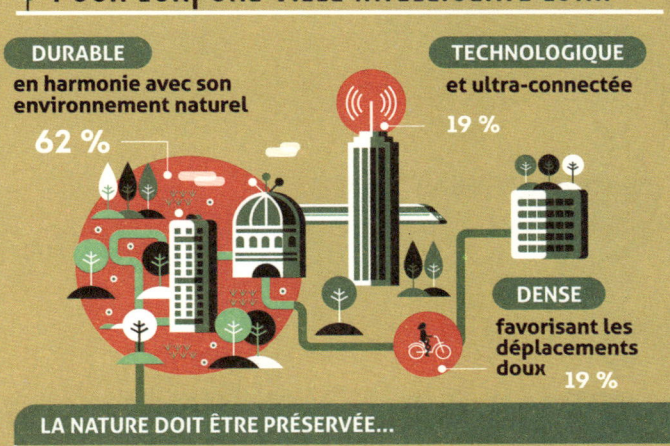

LA NATURE DOIT ÊTRE PRÉSERVÉE...

- dans les villes — 90 %
- autour des villes — 87 %
- sur les bâtiments — 63 %

🍃 QUELLE EST LEUR VILLE RÊVÉE ?

EN FRANCE
1. PARIS 15 %
2. LYON 7 %
3. BORDEAUX 7 %
4. TOULOUSE 6 %

À L'ÉTRANGER
1. NEW-YORK 11 %
2. LONDRES 9 %
3. SYDNEY 3 %
4. BARCELONE 3 %

🍃 VIVRE ET TRAVAILLER DANS LA VILLE DE DEMAIN

DANS LA VILLE DE DEMAIN, QU'IMAGINENT-ILS FAIRE DEPUIS LEUR DOMICILE ?

- **Faire leurs courses** — 23 % (♂ 28 % / ♀ 19 %)
- **Télétravailler** — 20 % (♂ 26 % / ♀ 15 %)
- **Étudier** — 12 % (♂ 16 % / ♀ 8 %)

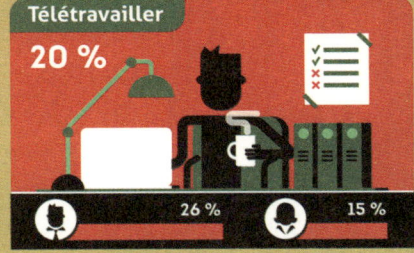

Enquête réalisée en ligne du 25/06 au 10/07/2014 par Harris Interactive pour la Chaire Immobilier et Développement Durable de l'ESSEC, dirigée par le professeur Ingrid Nappi-Choulet, auprès d'un échantillon représentatif de 1000 étudiants français post-bac. 54 % sont des femmes et leur moyenne d'âge est de 21 ans.

ESSEC BUSINESS SCHOOL — *Chaire Immobilier et Développement Durable*

INFOGRAPHIE ÉCLAIRAGE PUBLIC

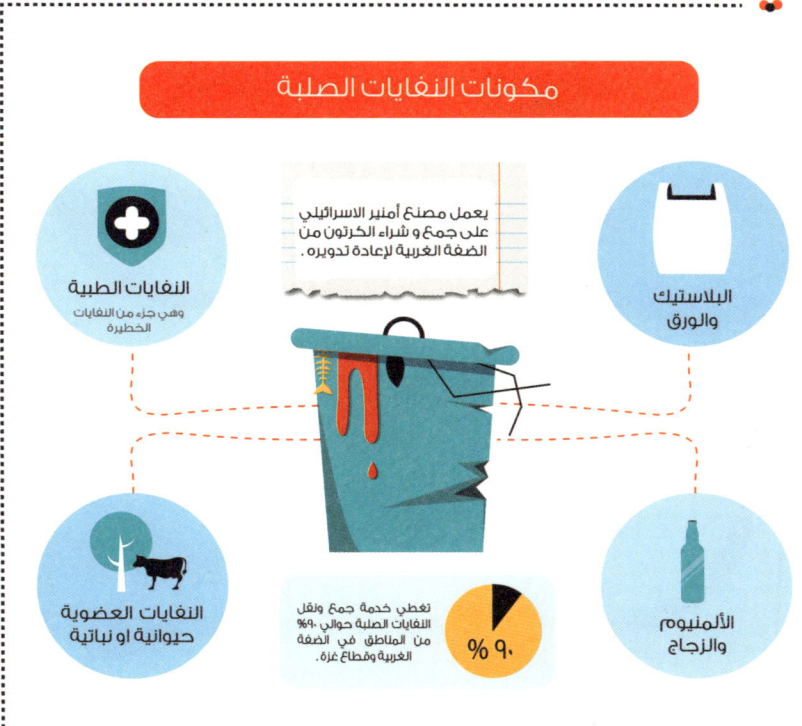

Solid Waste Status in Palestine

Project Description /
This project was based on the information from the joint service council for solid-waste management in Ramallah and Al Bireh governorates. The design is about waste in Palestine. It is divided into several parts, which are the types of solid waste, how to get rid of the waste, the components of solid waste, a general background on landfills, and the solid-waste sector in Palestine.

Designer / Duaa R. Hattab
Completion / 2013

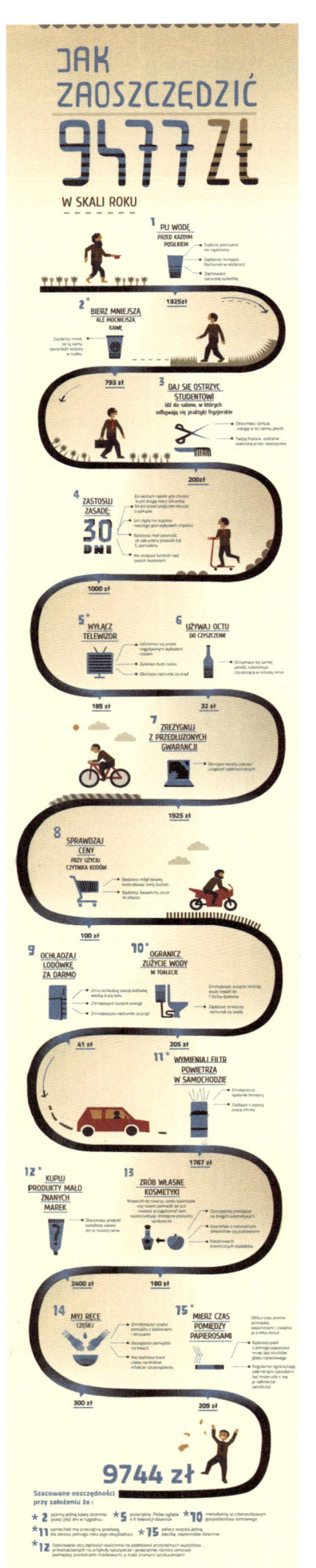

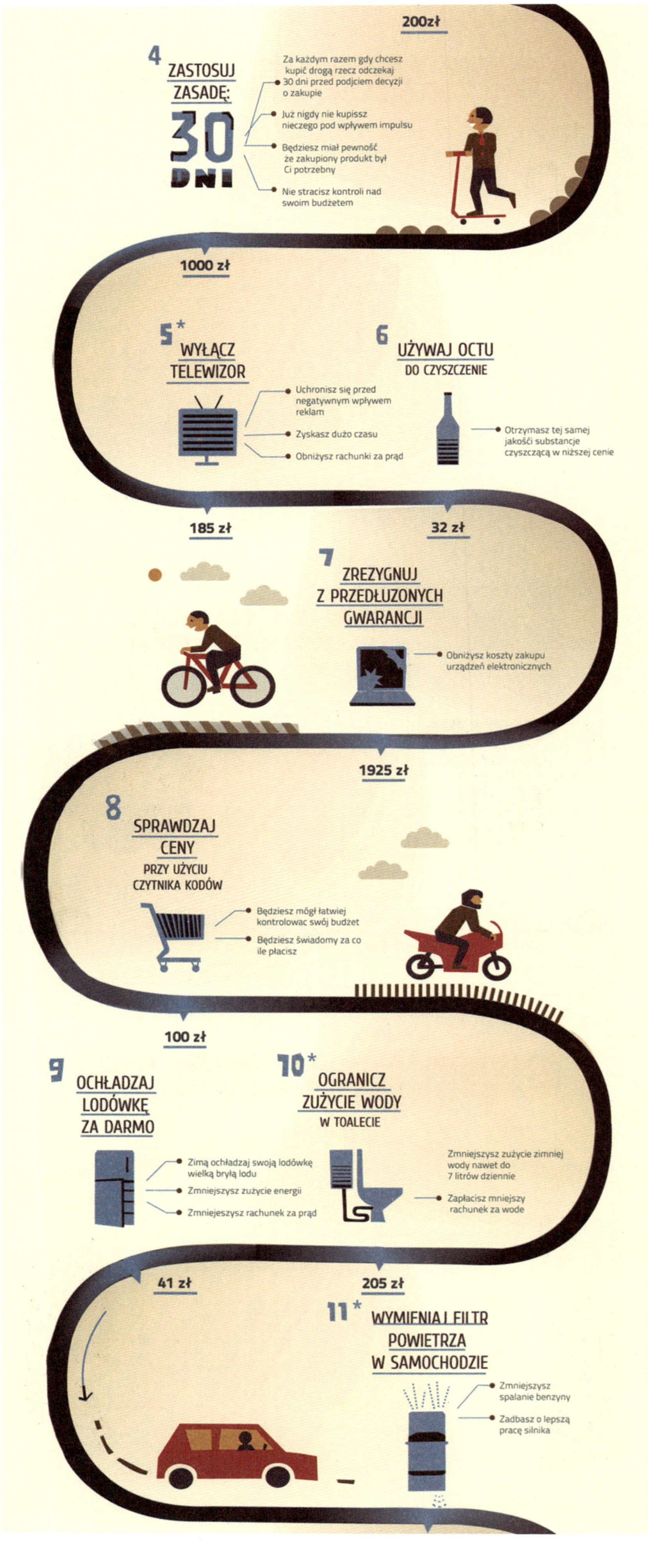

How to Save 9477 Zloty

Project Description /
These days there are a lot of articles with smart tips for saving money. This is a topic that, no doubt, interests all of us. For the most part information about saving money is delivered in a very serious way. The purpose of creating this infographic was to offer information on saving money in a more humorous way. It shows how to save 9477 Polish zloty in very unusual ways that are not very practical or useful, but funny and original. It reveals that it is possible to save money during the winter by using a big cube of snow from outside instead of wasting money on electricity for the fridge. The suggestions are placed along an alley, which symbolizes the path from being poor to being rich. It uses a variety of simple icons to represent the central idea of each money-saving suggestion.

Client / Wirtualna Polska
Designer / Karolina Kot
Completion / 2012

How Food Trends Change Eating Habits

Project Description /
The designers tried to understand the relationship between four main topic areas of food: health (the impact of food on consumer health); social (the level of social interaction focused on food); economy (how much specific kinds of food impact on household economies); time (how much time is spent on eating). Data found on nine trends from the 1980s to 2013 shows the impact on each area of interest during these years. Observing the flow of the lines, the designers developed some possible scenarios to inspire new ideas and new projects about the big topic of food.

Client / Politecnico di Milano
Designers / Emanuele Bianchi, Cenk Basbolat, Francesca Carbonara, Jacopo Grilli, Giovanni Piemontese
Completion / 2014

Beekeeping in Oman

Project Description /
Antonio Farach was commissioned to produce an infographic about traditional beekeeping in Oman, to be published in the newspapers *Times of Oman* and *Al Shabiba* as a double page spread for Oman's National Day celebrations. In the infographic, there are two methods of Omani beekeeping shown, one using a hollow date palm trunk and the other using a branch. It used three-dimensional representation to help readers understand the two methods easily.

Client / *Times of Oman*
Designers / Antonio Farach, Winie Ariany, Sreemanikandan Satheendranathan

Generation Y

Project Description /
The Millennials, made up of those who were born from the 1980s, began their career atypically. They had a good education, and were starting their careers at a time when companies were willing to offer benefits and salaries above average, including bonuses, awards, and flexible hours. With the global financial crisis, the market cut the excess. The number of vacancies decreased, and the new generation had to make concessions.

Client / *Época* magazine
Designers / Marco Vergotti, Rodrigo Fortes, Gerson Mora e Alexandre Lucas
Completion / 2012

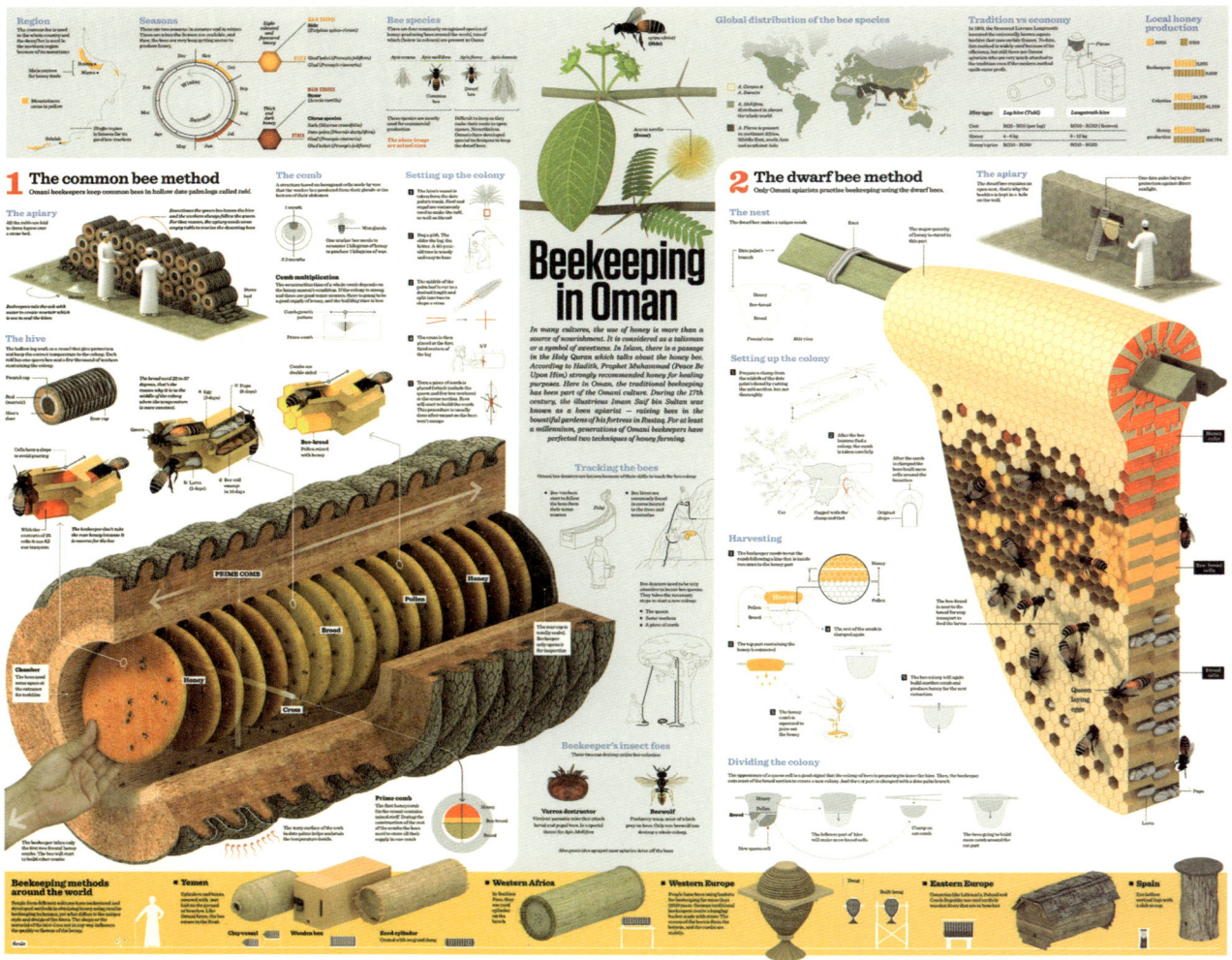

Obesity Emergency

Project Description /
Obesity has become a worldwide phenomenon, and this infographic explores this health emergency. It explains the causes, the tips to avoid it, the health costs, and the top 10 risk factors of death.

Client / *La Repubblica*
Designer / Annalisa Varlotta
Completion / 2014

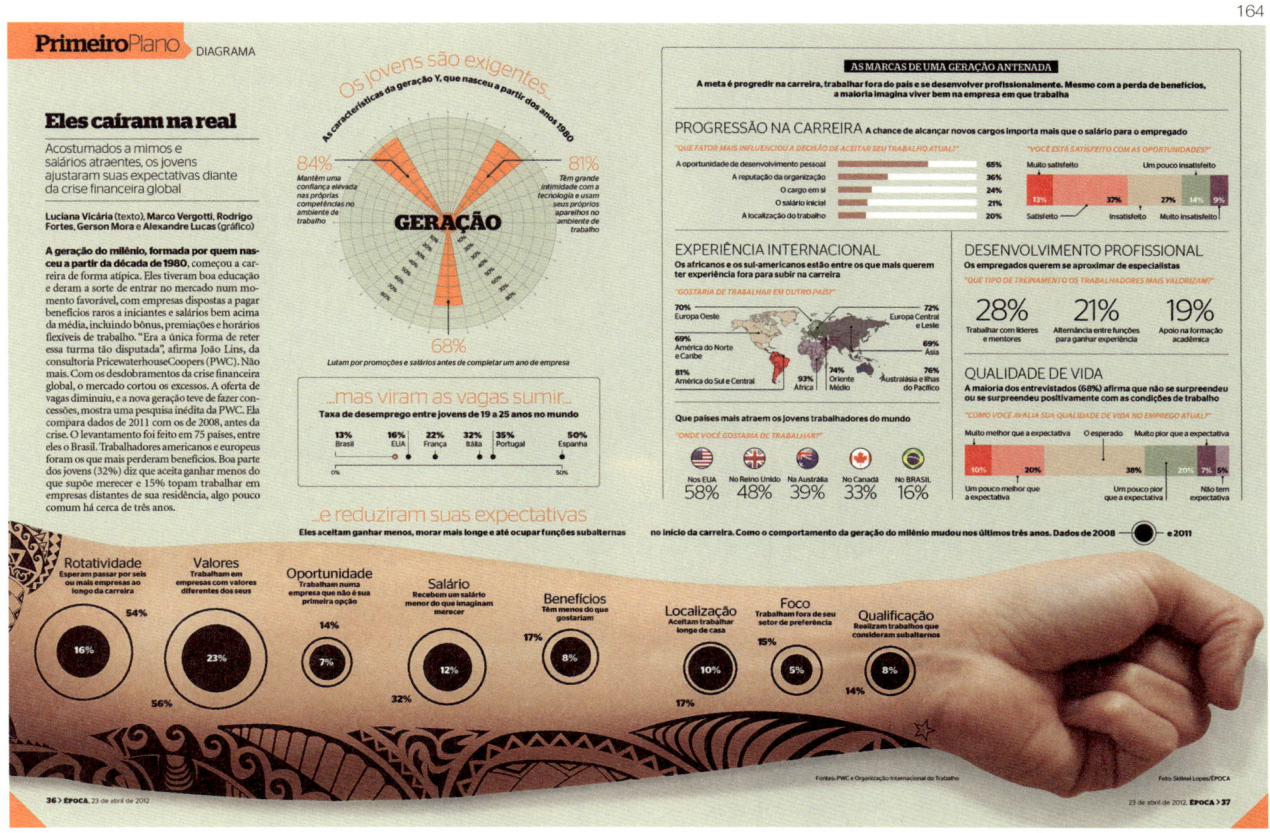

25 Years of Collected Debris

Project Description /

An Ocean Conservancy initiative each September has more than half a million people around the world mobilizing to collect waste that has been dumped into the seas and waterways. The marine debris is then sorted into categories, classified and numbered. On the Ocean Conservancy's 25th anniversary, Ocean Conservancy made an inventory of the tons of garbage collected in the past quarter century to better understand the specifics of the pollution issue.

Client / Ocean Conservancy
Design Agency / ÉCLAIRAGE PUBLIC
Designer / Nicolas Verrier

The Rise of the Silver Surfers

Project Description /

Apia Insurance wished to share its research on how people aged 50+ use the Internet. Landscape format was used, which is unusual for infographics. The approach was to have the information illustrative and free-floating, not boxed into organized panels.

Client / King Content, Apia Insurance
Design Agency / RussellTate.Com
Designer / Russell Tate
Completion / 2014

How Much Does Our Life Really Cost?

Project Description /

The infographic was designed to break down simple day-to-day tasks, from making a sandwich to using electronic devices, into cost per use to show an overall look at how expensive life is in Israel. The number-heavy data needed a smart and simple approach. Simple icons, shapes, and colors identify the products, so that the viewer can easily focus on the numbers next to each task, understanding the prices by the simple mathematic symbols shown next to each icon.

Client / The Markerweek
Designer / Yael Shinkar
Completion / 2012

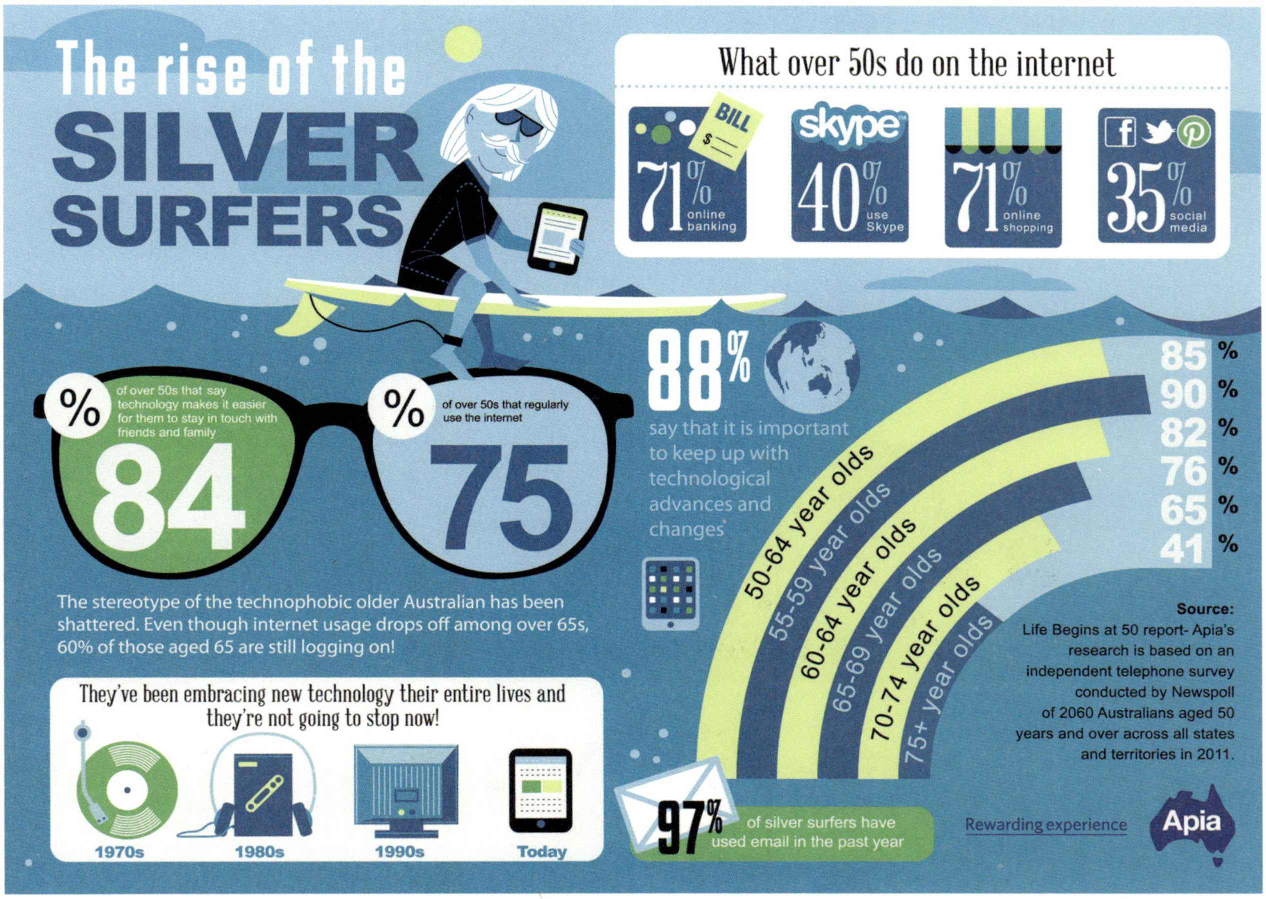

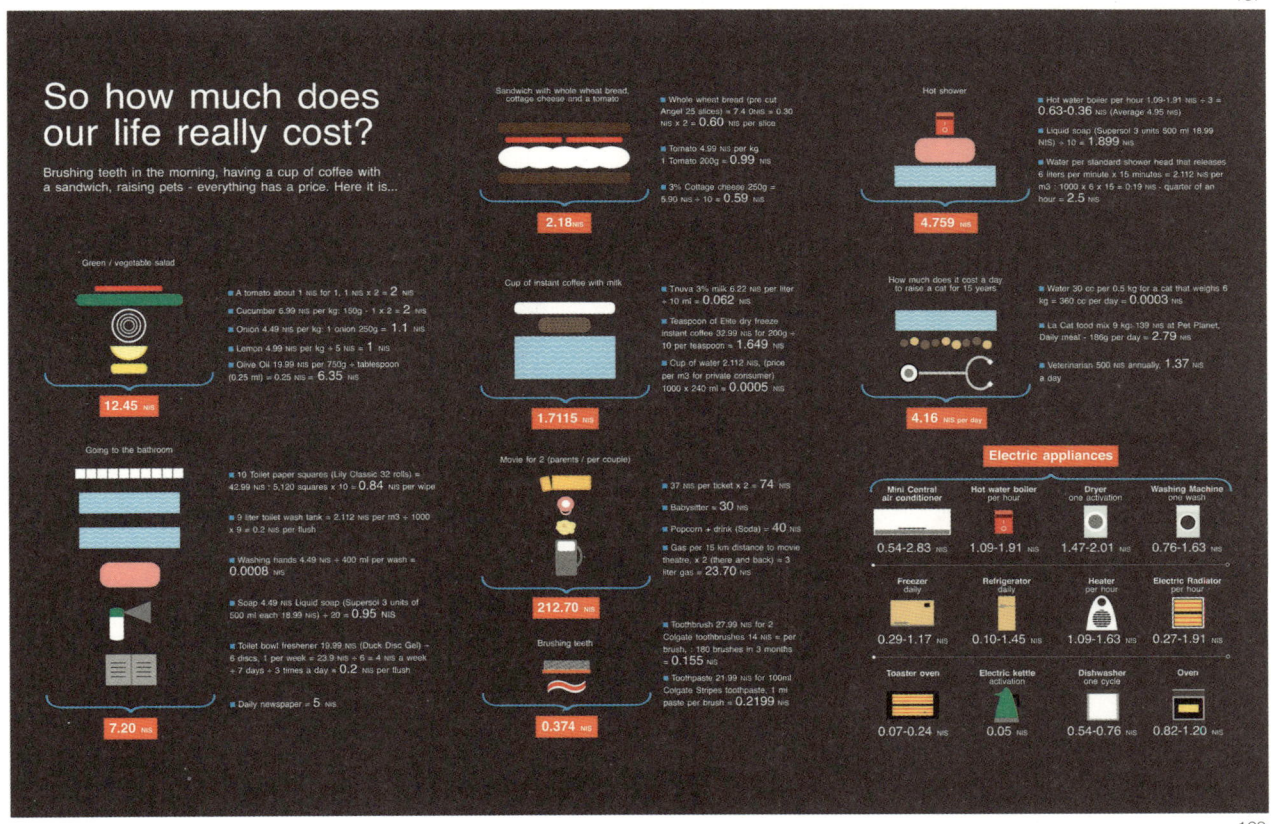

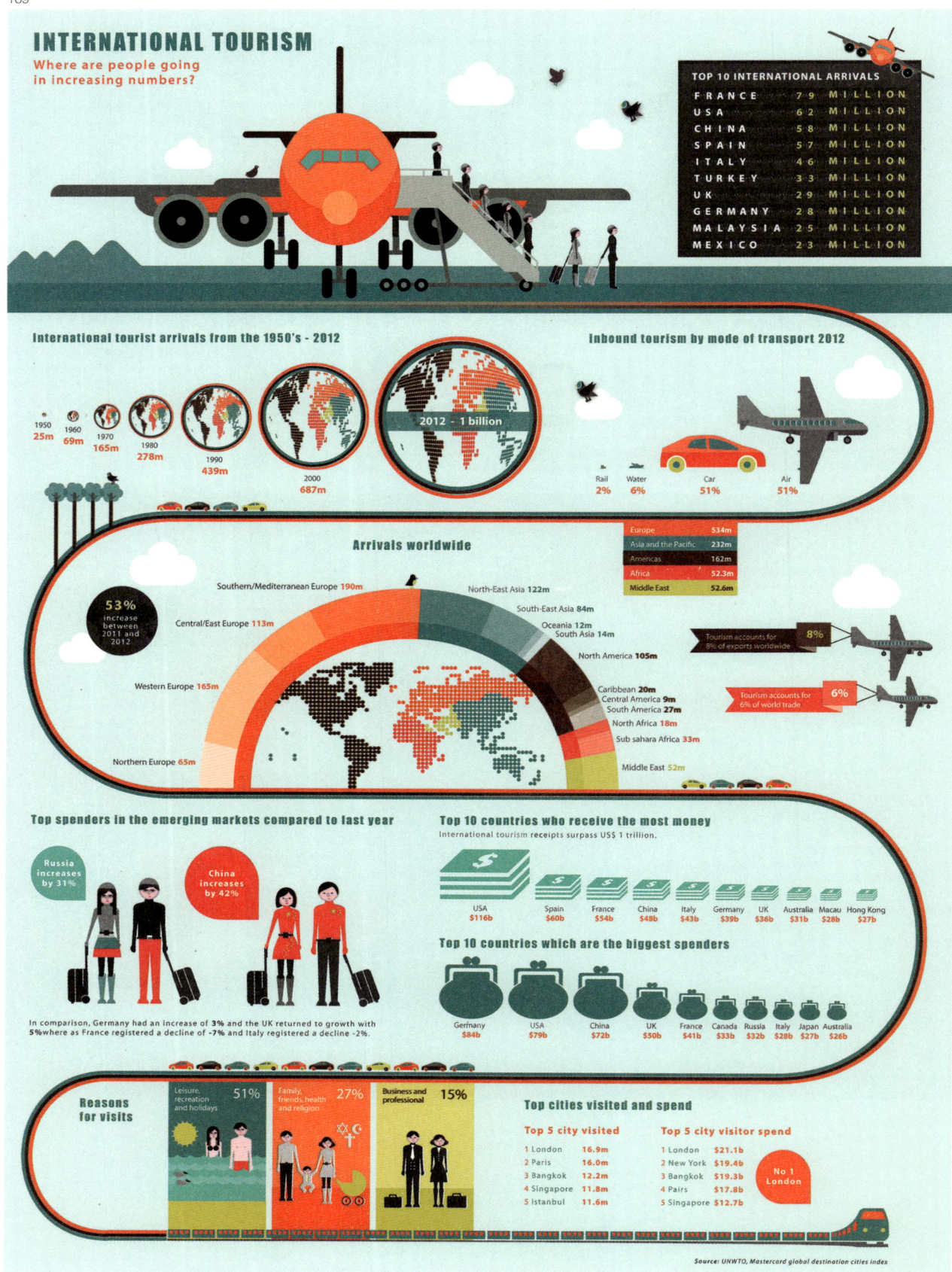

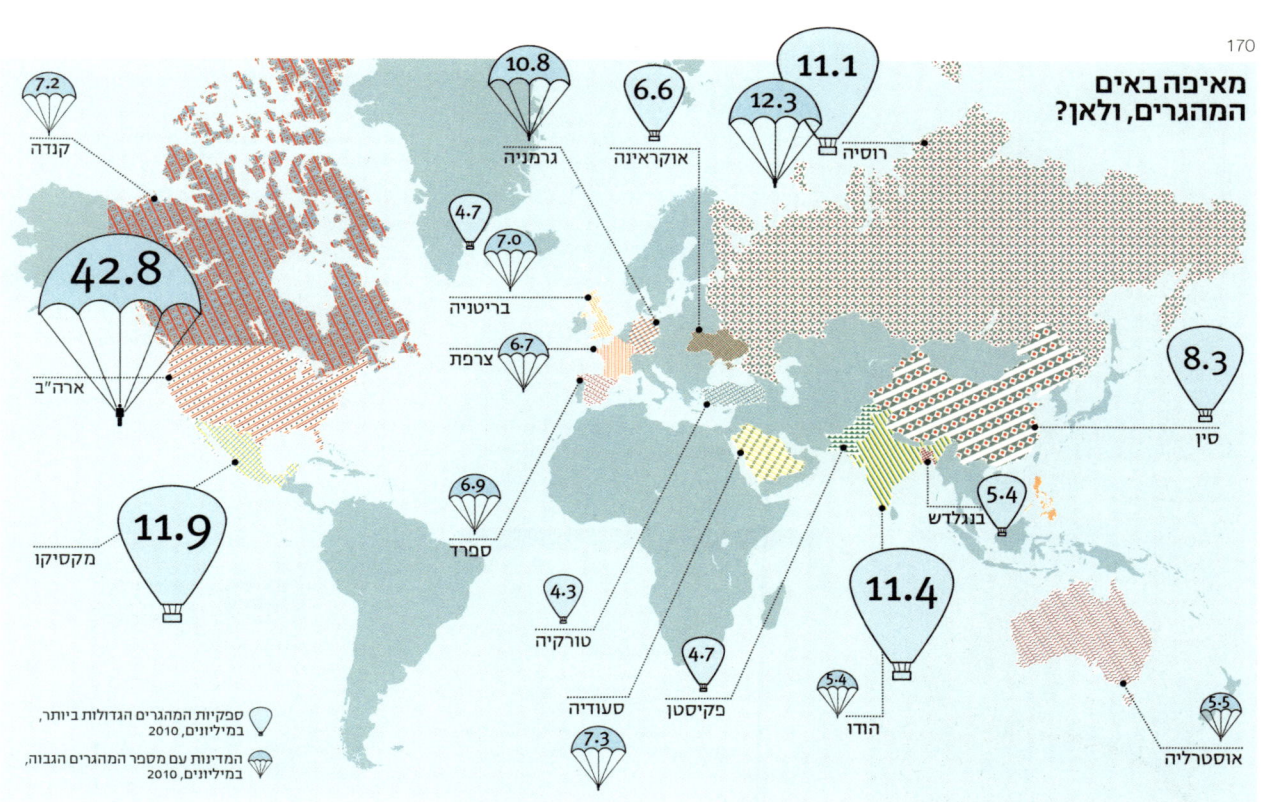

169
International Tourism

Project Description /
According to the World Tourism Organization and Mastercard Global Destinations Cities Index, one billion people will travel across an international border as a tourist. That means one in seven people on the planet will participate in world travel, an activity that just a few decades ago was exclusively for the rich. Reasons for the upswing include increasing prosperity in developing countries such as China. The infographic shows who is traveling, where they are going, and why.

Design Agency / Blink Designs
Designer / Stephanie Halpern
Completion / 2013

170
The Immigrants' Journey

Project Description /
Hundreds of millions of people are leaving home to reach other countries. They work and live there, challenging thoughts on nationalism. The map of the world is divided into colors. The hot-air balloons show where the immigrants originally came from, and the parachutes indicate their destinations. Finding the right icon to portray the immigrants' journey was a challenge. Yael Shinkar managed to define the concept by using the hot-air balloon and parachute metaphors, helping the reader to understand the immigrants' journeys.

Client / The Markerweek
Designer / Yael Shinkar
Completion / 2012

What's the Particulate Matter?

Project Description /

The World Health Organization (WHO) recently updated its database of ambient air pollution in cities, causing quite a stir when its findings revealed that air quality in most cities of the world is getting progressively worse. Several news outlets ran reports that focused on the top 10 most polluted cities of the world—but the most interesting data from WHO's release is not only which cities are at the top of the 'most polluted' list, but also how pollution is affecting human population levels.

A new infographic from Dalberg examines the impact of particulate matter (PM)—tiny particles suspended in the Earth's atmosphere—on human life.

Why should we care about PM? While PM is not the only air pollutant, it is a key indicator of long-term air quality and health risks. In fact, our lives could depend on it; WHO estimates that 'reducing annual average PM10 concentrations from levels of 70 micrograms, common in many developing cities, to the WHO guideline level of 20 micrograms, could reduce air-pollution-related deaths by around 15%.' (PM10 particles are smaller than 10 microns in diameter).

The analysis of WHO's latest data suggests that the human impact of PM pollution is greater in the top 20 polluted cities than in the next 80 cities combined. PM pollution in these top 20 cities (all of which are located in developing countries) is also responsible for more than half of the overall PM pollution impacting on human life.

Client / Dalberg
Designer / Mayuresh Patole
Completion / 2014

171-1

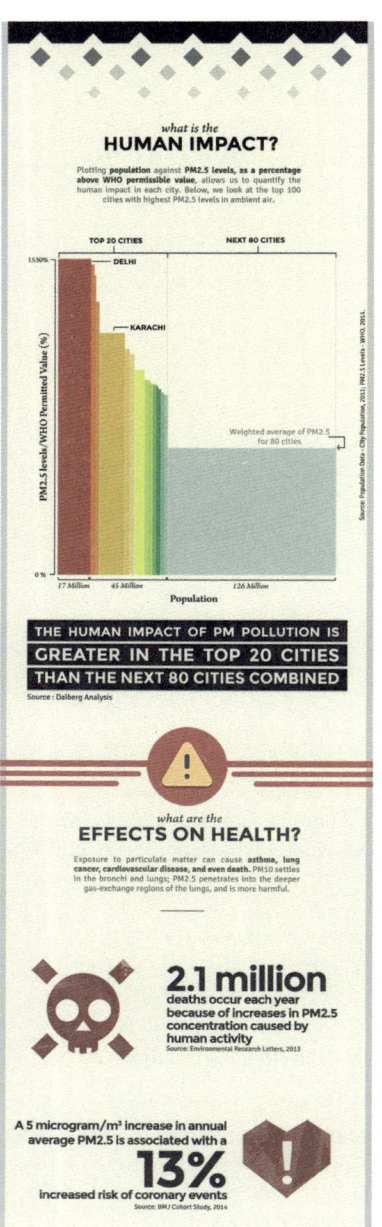

171-2

171-3

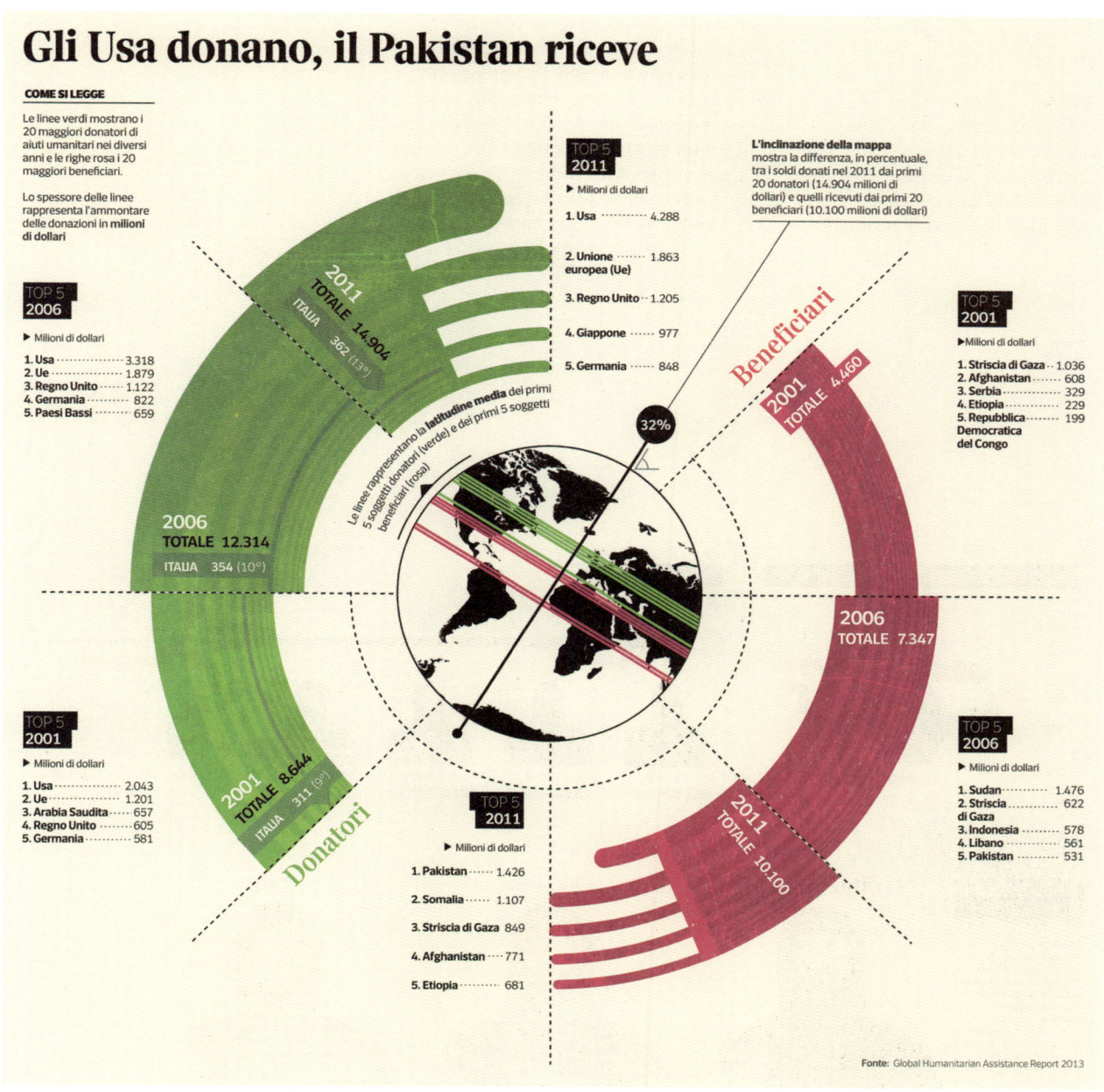

[172 – 176]
Client / La Lettura—*Corriere della Sera*
Designer / Mónica Serrano
Completion / 2013 — 2014

172

Humanitarian Aid

Project Description /

In this infographic, the green lines show the 20 largest donors of humanitarian aid in different years and the pink shows the top 20 beneficiaries. The thickness of the lines represents the amount of donations in millions of dollars. The USA was the main donor in the last decade, followed by the European Union as a whole. However, the beneficiaries have changed over the years in response to different crises, such as natural disasters or military conflicts. The idea was to illustrate this data as two arms helping each other to gain balance.

Muslim Veil

Project Description /

The infographic shows the veils that women should use in public places, according to survey respondents in some Middle East countries. They range from the most conservative to the least conservative, using a range of wefts to visualize the differences. The woman presents different veils chosen in a particular country, and their amplitude reflects the percentage. This infographic not only provides the statistical information, but it also clearly illustrates how women are supposed to look in particular countries.

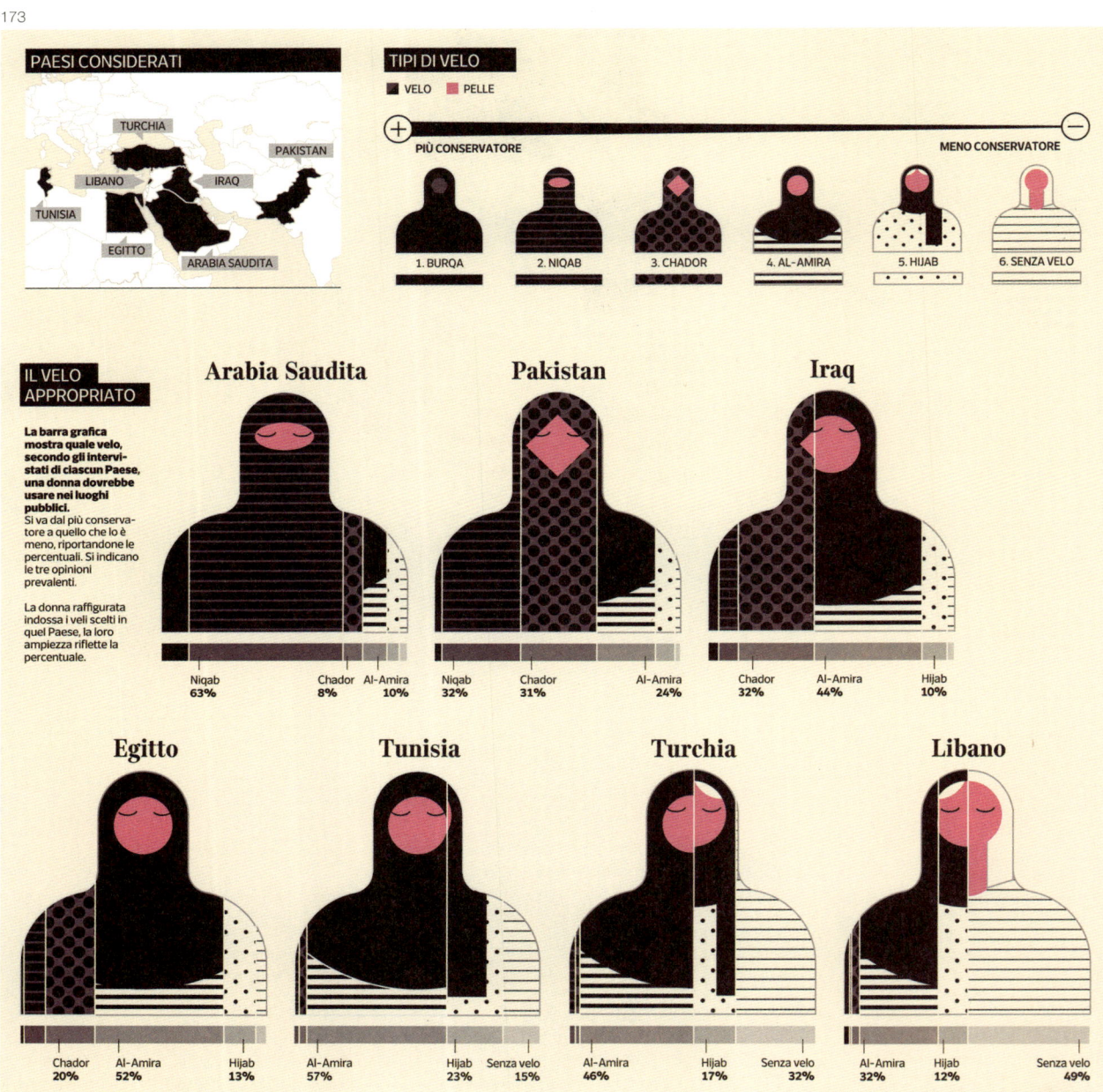

Tourist Inflows

Project Description /
How did the economic crisis affect European holidaymakers? This infographic covers the full spectrum of consequences of the crisis—from the people who were not affected at all (such as Austrians) to those who gave up going on vacations, through to those affected in some way (changing their destination or reducing their stay). As an example, most Italian and Greek people spent their vacation time in their own countries.

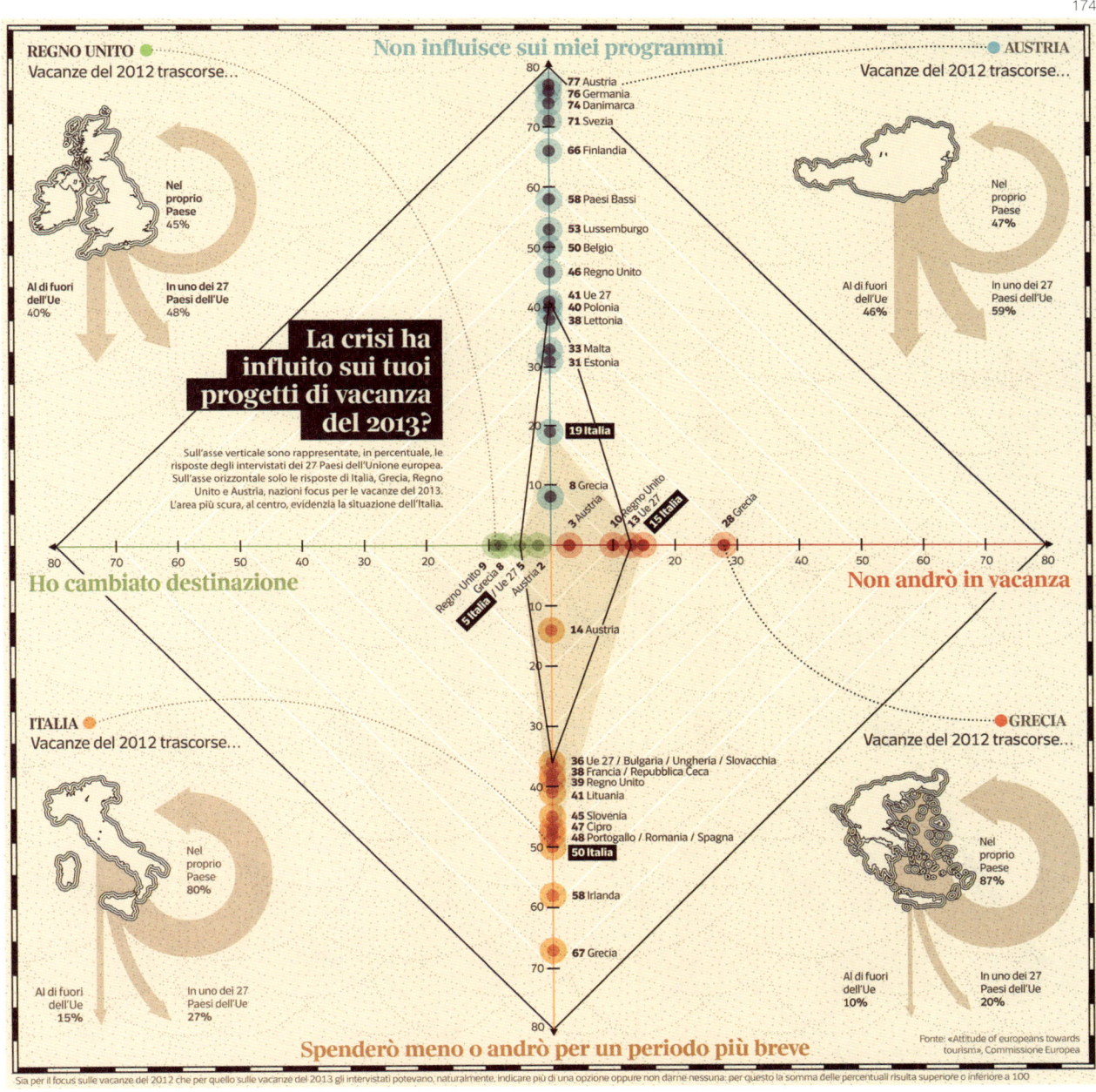

Pets in the EU

Project Description /

This is a snapshot displaying the number of domestic animals per 100 inhabitants in the European Union, with each rhombus representing a country. Belgium, the Netherlands and Italy are in the top three for pet ownership, showing a preference for birds. However, cats are more abundant in the total account. In this infographic, color was used to transmit joy and variety, and little black silhouettes of animals were used to symbolize the most common pet in a particular country.

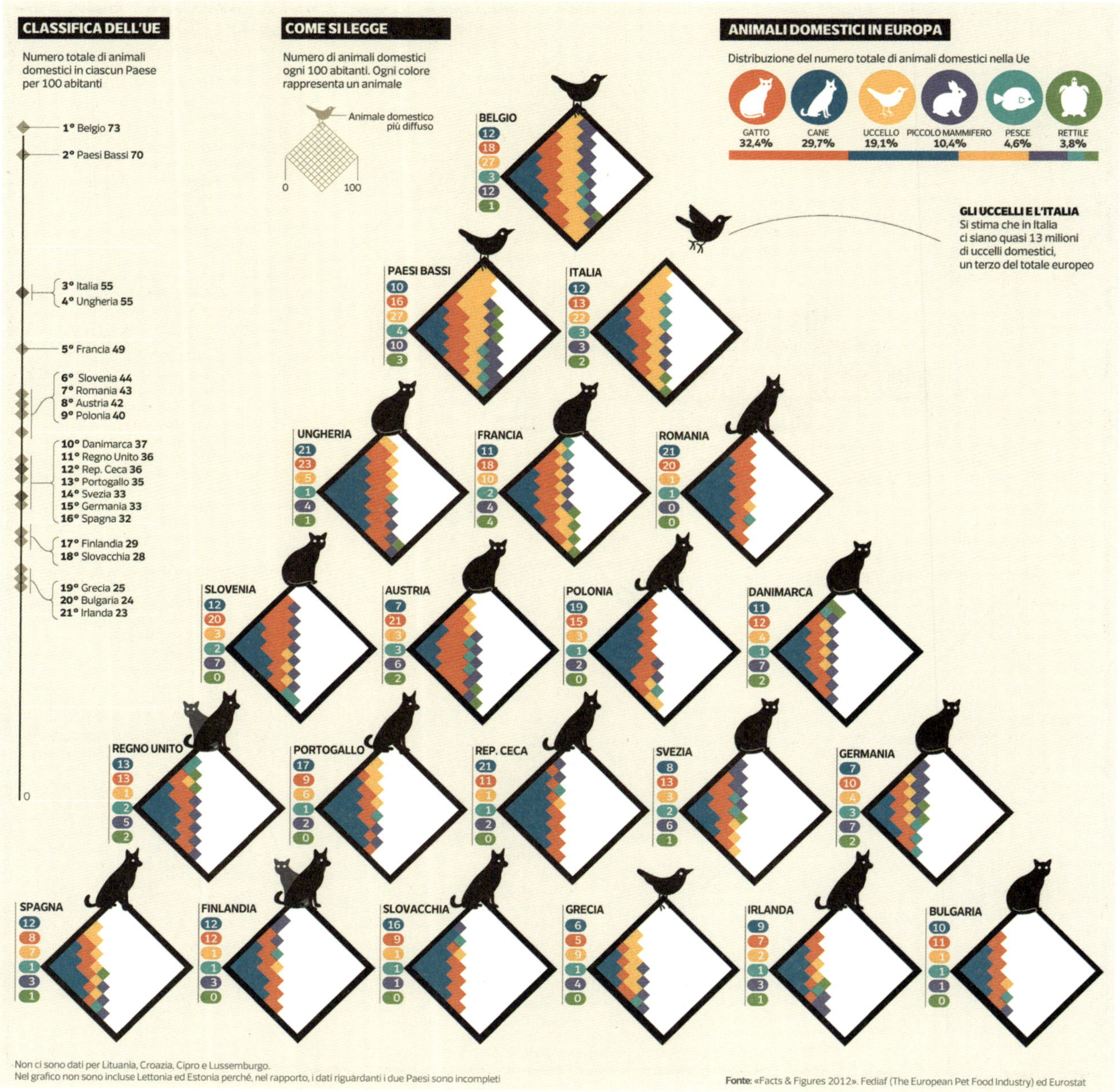

The Rainbow Index

Project Description /

The aim of this infographic, published in the dominical supplement of *Corriere della Sera*, was to illustrate the breadth of LGBT (lesbian, gay, bisexual and transgender) rights. A completed flag represents those who enjoy equal rights and an uncompleted flag is for those who don't. The data, obtained from the Rainbow Country Index Ranking 2012 from the ILGA (International Lesbian and Gay Association) Europe, is also accompanied by the number of LGBT associations and pride events in each country.

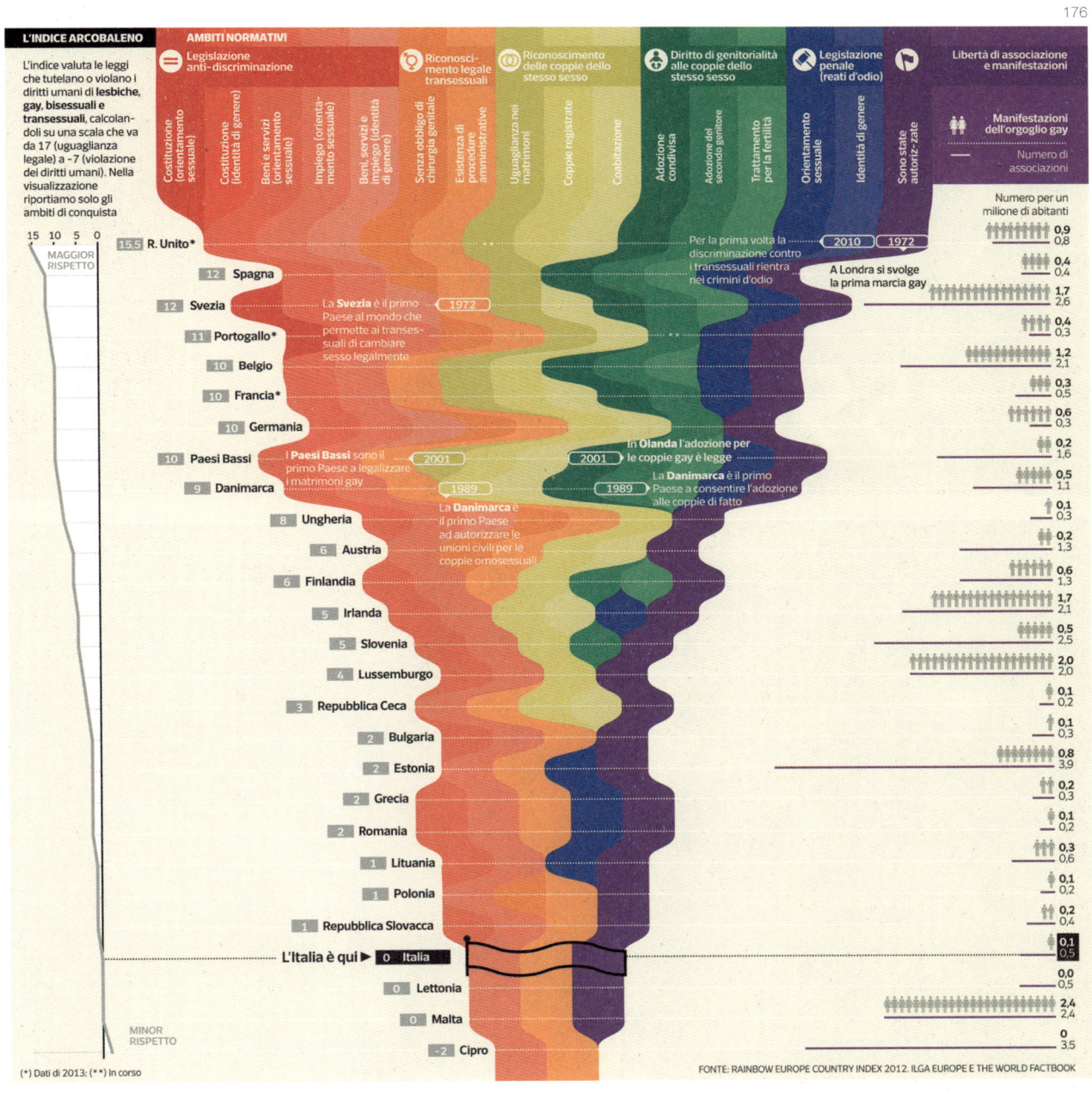

177

Ilha Formosa

Project Description /
Designed as an introduction to Taiwan, this infographic set includes a book, bookmark, and poster. Very different from other publications about Taiwan, it's not a tourist guide or a boring government-published book. This collection of nice, delicate-paper illustrations is interesting and informal, but also clear in delivering the information about Taiwan.

Designer / Tien-Min Liao

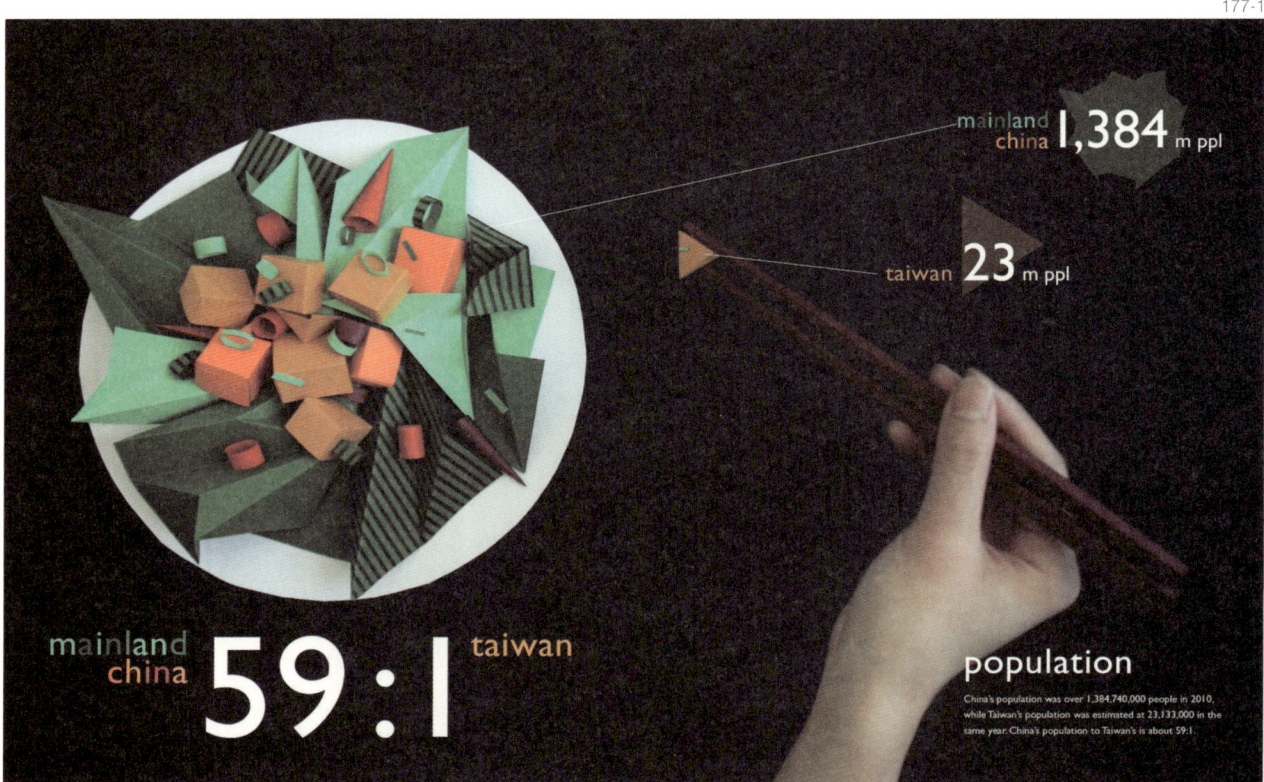

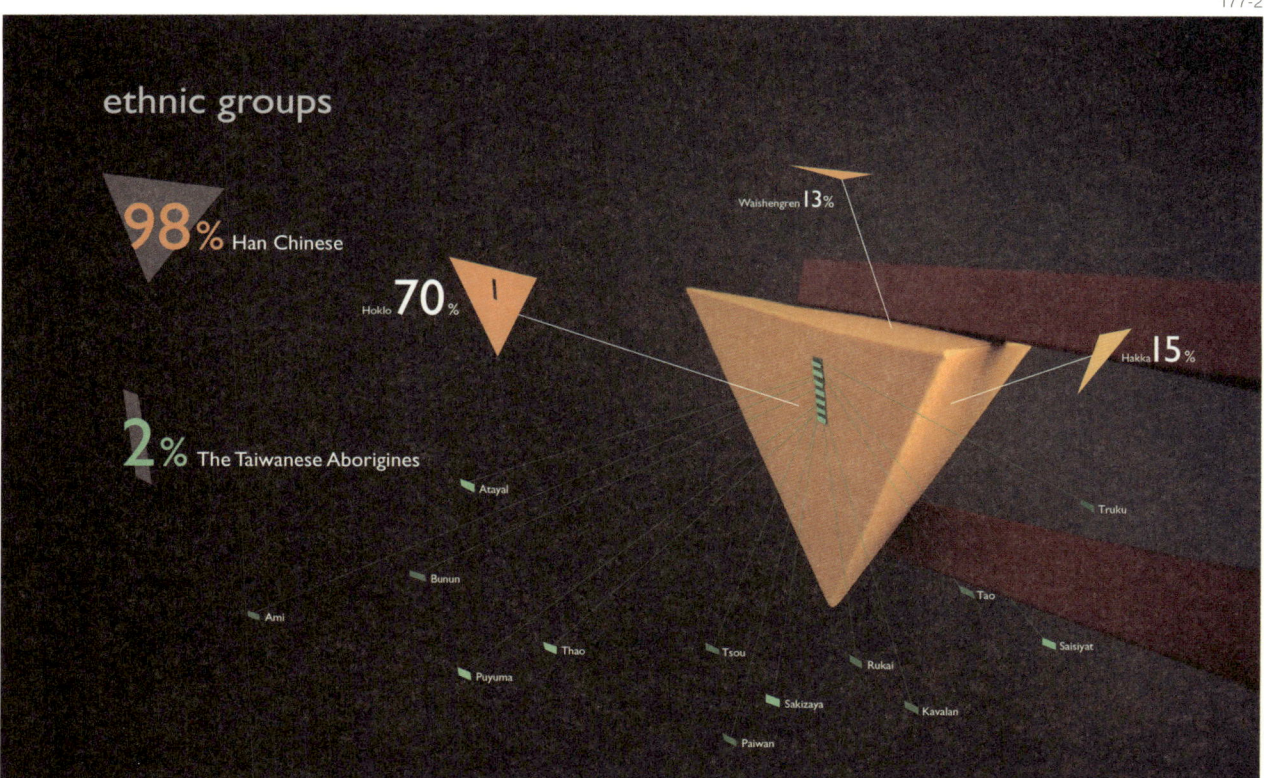

"Ilha formosa"

means "Beautiful Island" in Portuguese. Taiwan was known as Formosa in the past.

Hillside and Mountains occupy 2/3 area of the island.
Over 1/2 area is forest land area.
Only 1/3 area is plains.

rains

thunderstorm

The annual rainfall in Taiwan is 2,150 mm, about 2.6 times the world average in rainfall. However, about 80% of the rainfall is concentrated from May to October.

Meiyu – The East Asian rainy season
The occurrence of Meiyu is the result of annual monsoon movement in east Asia. Each year, the winter monsoon which comes from northeast meets the summer monsoon which comes from southwest, thus causing the consistent precipitation for about two months during the late spring and early summer. This phenomenon is called Meiyu.

177-5

TVBS News
FTV News
CtiTV News
SET News
ERA News
ETTV News
USTV News

24h news stations ×7

In recent years, Taiwan has a reputation for its freedom in news media. According to Reporters Without Borders, the Press Freedom Index in Taiwan is one of the top fews in Asia. Despite a relatively small news media market, Taiwan has seven 24/7 news channels, compared to the amount both in the United States and the Great Britain which is three in total. Taiwan also acquires a highest density of SNG (Satellite News Gathering) trucks.

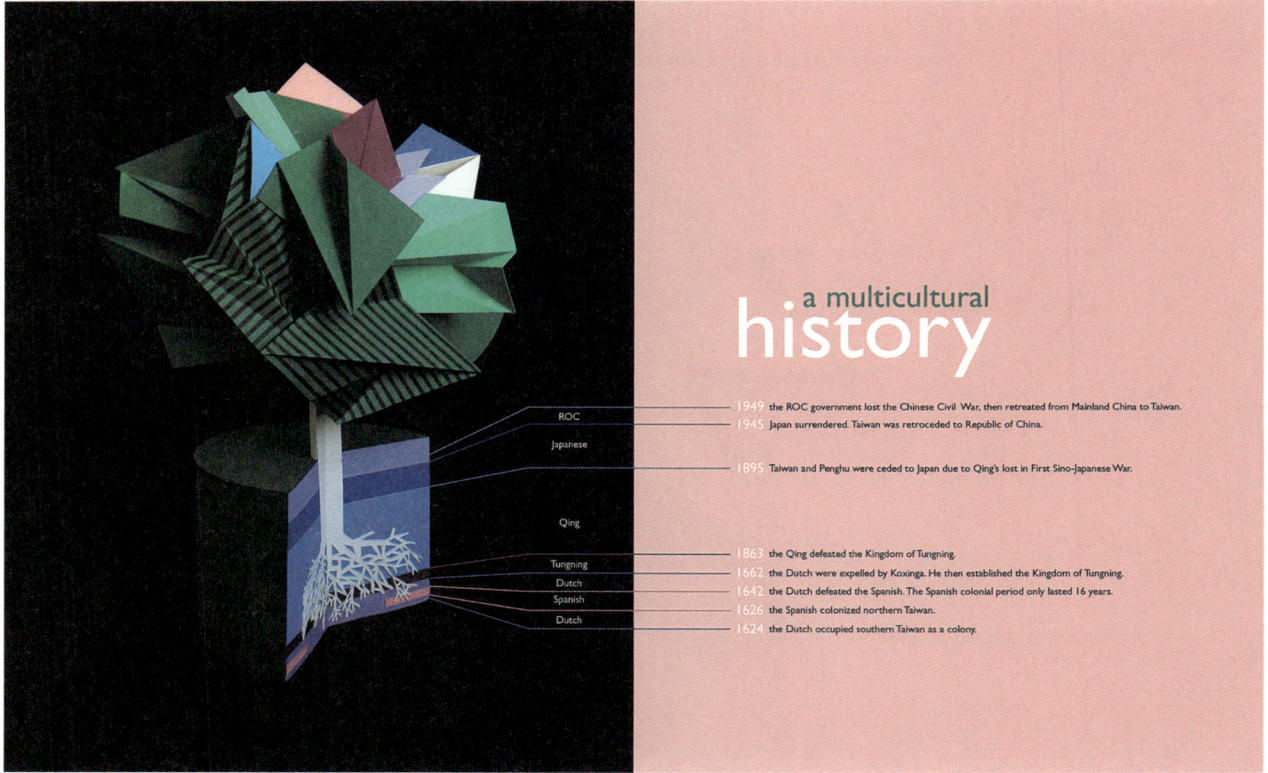

177-6

a multicultural history

ROC   1949 the ROC government lost the Chinese Civil War, then retreated from Mainland China to Taiwan.
Japanese   1945 Japan surrendered. Taiwan was retroceded to Republic of China.
             1895 Taiwan and Penghu were ceded to Japan due to Qing's lost in First Sino-Japanese War.
Qing
             1863 the Qing defeated the Kingdom of Tungning.
Tungning   1662 the Dutch were expelled by Koxinga. He then established the Kingdom of Tungning.
Dutch   1642 the Dutch defeated the Spanish. The Spanish colonial period only lasted 16 years.
Spanish   1626 the Spanish colonized northern Taiwan.
Dutch   1624 the Dutch occupied southern Taiwan as a colony.

cycling around the **entire island**

Cycling around the entire island has become more and more popular in recent years. Some students do it as a celebration for their graduation, while more people view it as a challenge and adventure. The ages of the participants are from nine to eighty years old. It usually takes 6–12 days to finish. The total lenghth is about 1,200km.

177-7

16,000
tons of tea leaves / year

Taiwanese people consume 16,000 tons of tea leaves each year, equivalent to the weight of 3,200 adult Asian Elephants. This number does not even include the tea that is sold in the teashops and convenient stores.

* The average weight of an adult African Elephant is about 5 Tons.

177-8

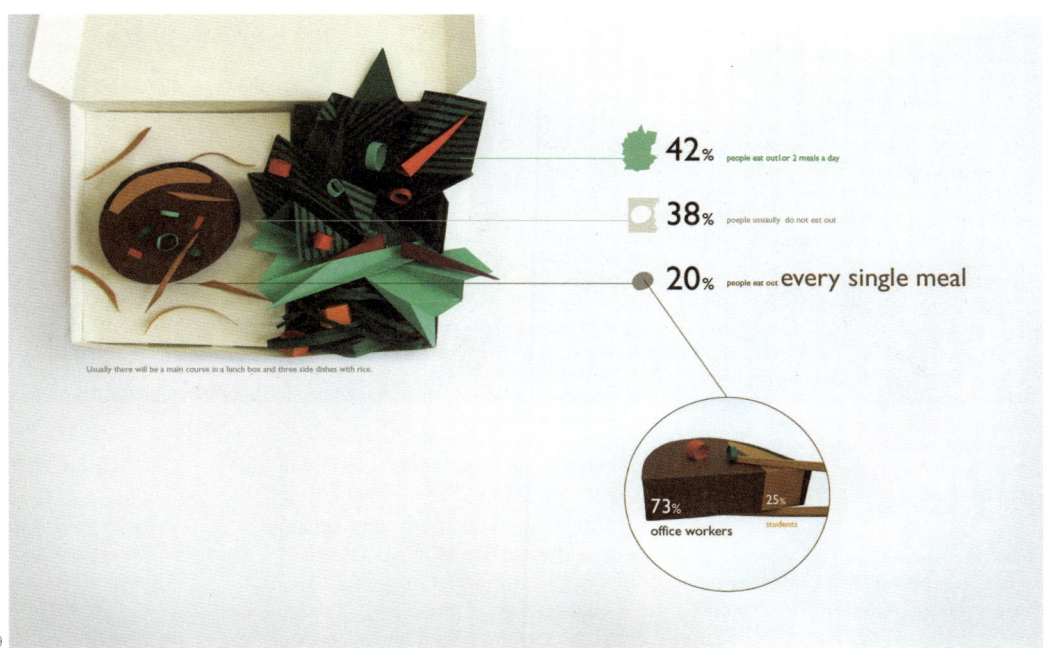

- 42% people eat out or 2 meals a day
- 38% poeple usually do not eat out
- 20% people eat out **every single meal**

Usually there will be a main course in a lunch box and three side dishes with rice.

73% office workers 25% students

177-9

Black Market

Project Description /

For this article, Irina Shirokova thoroughly researched the subject before beginning work on her design. Only after realizing the whole 'picture' did she start to create infographics about the main types of trafficking worldwide. Shirokova had limited time, so she decided to create a very simple map. She used small illustrations as symbols: a bleeding elephant or polar hare to indicate poaching points; naughty girls to represent prostitution; and production places of fake 'ADIDAS' as a symbol of global counterfeit points in the world.

Designer / Irina Shirokova

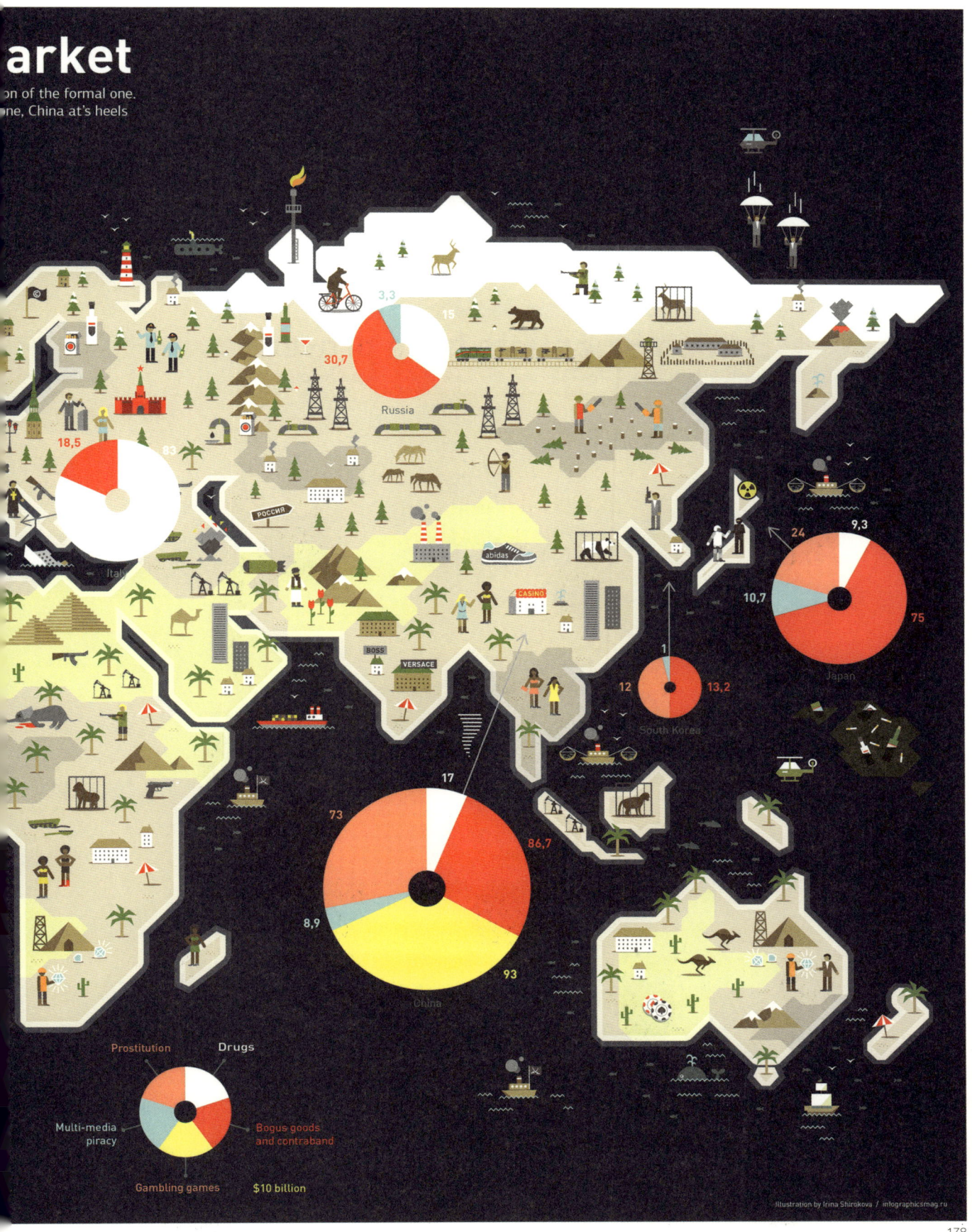

[178 – 180]
Client / *Infografika*
Design Agency / Infografika Magazine
Completion / 2012

Harm of Drugs

Project Description /

The idea of making an infographic about the harmful effects of drugs was inspired by scientific research created by a team of talented, independent, British scientists, who discovered 16 criteria for damaging human health. The designers analyzed the research and shortened the list to 11 points, which they decided to visualize as randomly situated, colored '3-D' pikes.

What piqued the designers' interest the most was the fact that alcohol could inflict much more serious damage on someone's life than any other drugs.

The research refuted the rumors and misconceptions that drugs were more dangerous than alcohol. In fact, alcohol had the most harmful effects.

Designers / Igor' iinnqqiitt Kosyrev, Slava Novikov

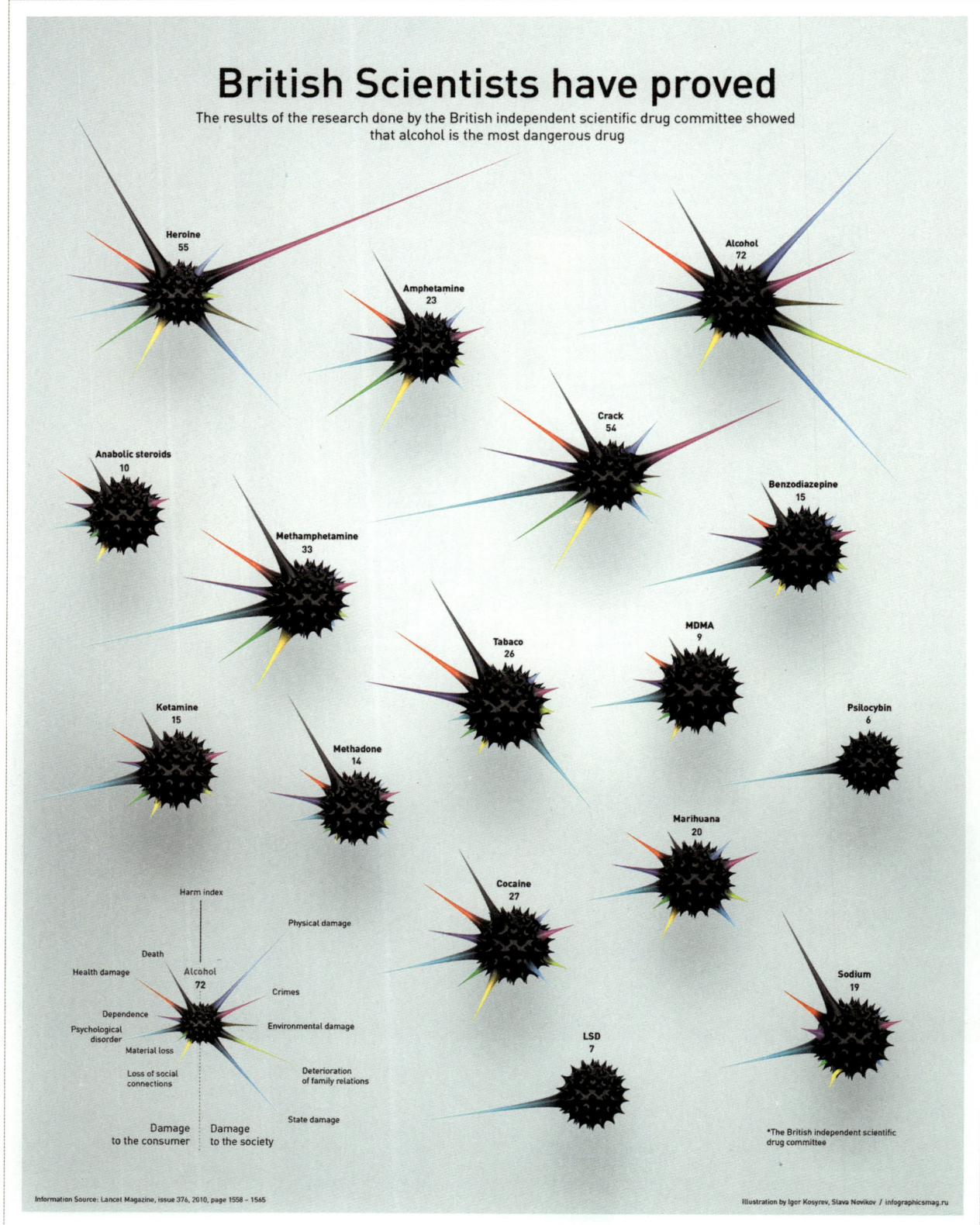

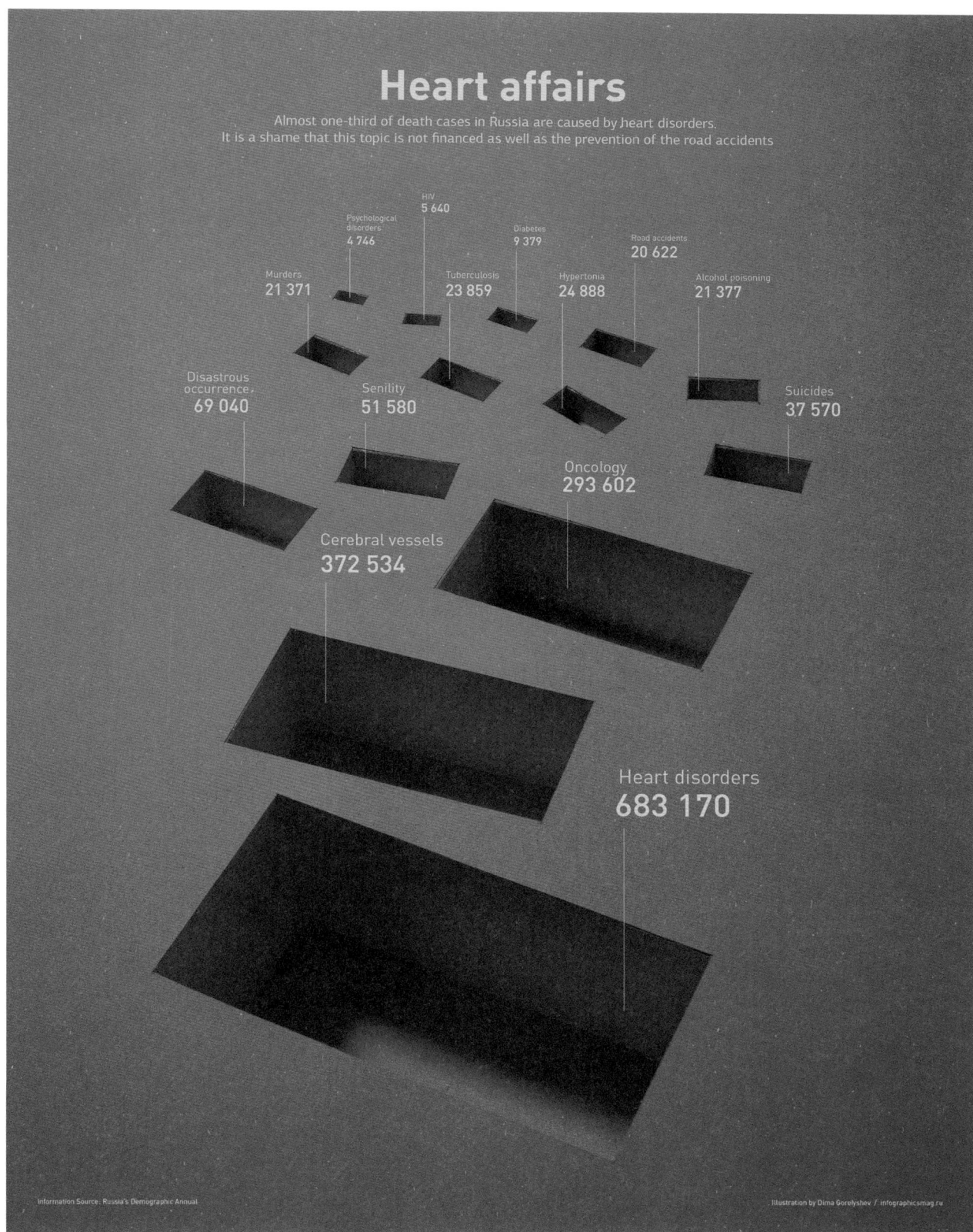

Heart Affairs

Project Description /

This infographic article was created for the magazine's 'hand-made' section, where every piece is a 'real' creative product, crafted by hand rather than computer, and able to be used as an art-project in real life. The project's theme was the principal causes of death in Russia, and designer Dima Gorelyshev used red cardboard for her design, creating slots as if they were real human graves. In the Russian media it's commonly believed that there are more deaths from car accidents, AIDS or murder than any other cause, which isn't completely true. An analysis of the statistics found that the number of deaths caused by cardiovascular diseases is much higher. The aim of the infographic was to encourage people to start paying attention to their health: to give up alcohol, drugs, and cigarettes, and to start getting fit and healthy.

Designer / Dima Gorelyshev

Abasto Cartography

Project Description /
Cartografías Abasto is intersted in the history of the Abasto Market Supplier, an old market located in the geographic center of modern-day Buenos Aires which used to supply fruit and vegetables to the city. Originally built in 1893, the market was a huge beautiful construction. Many political and social changes forced the market to close and reopen several times, but it was the main wholesale provider until its permanent closure in 1984. In 1998 a shopping mall called 'Abasto Shopping' was built where the market had been before; the improvements respected the market external walls and structure. The mall continues to operate today.

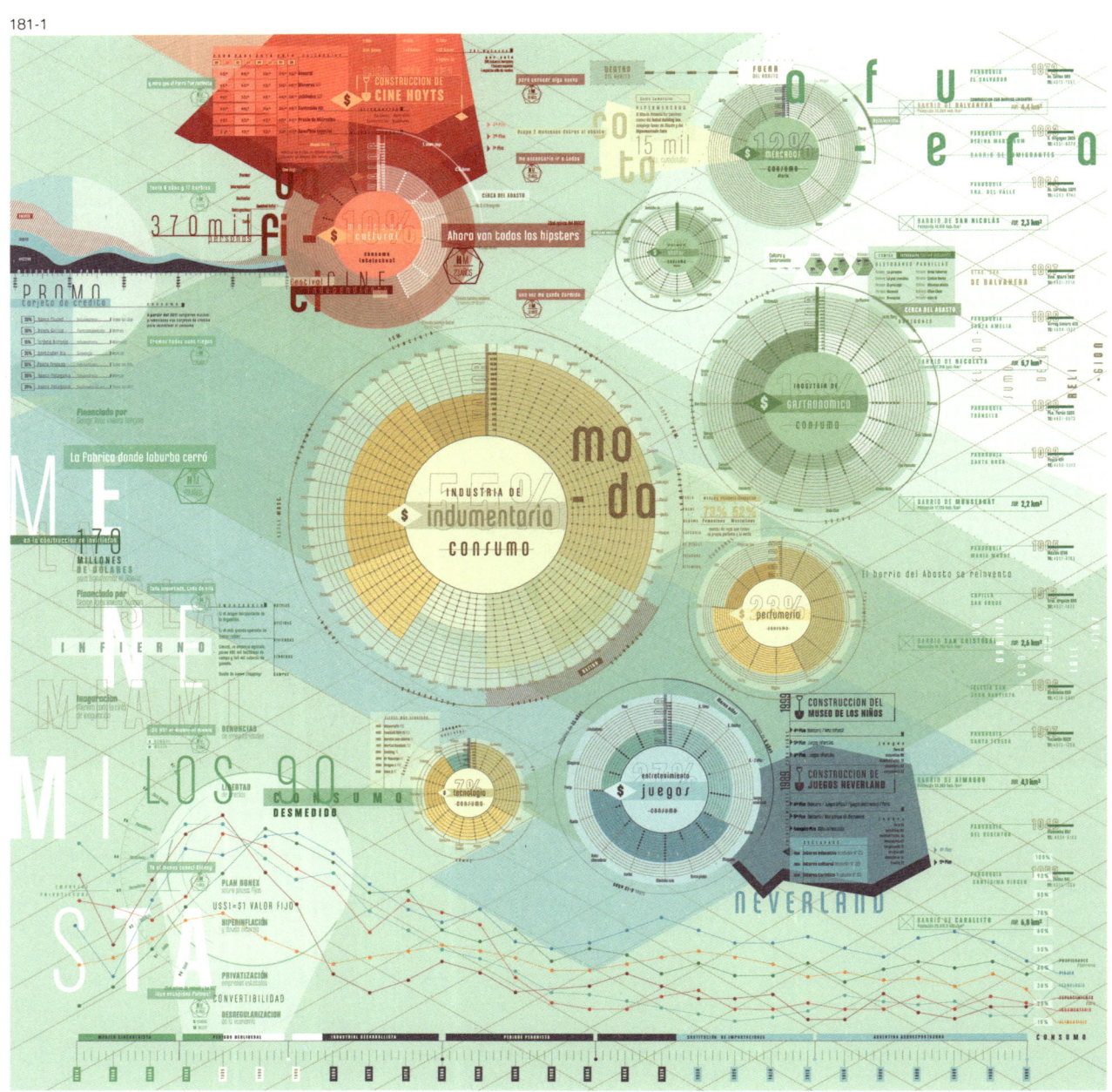

181-1

The project has three infographics. The first one is about the competition between the different spheres of consumption. The second is about the different cultural and tourist circuits that were generated around the present 'Abasto'. The last one is about how the policy measures, European migrations and social changes influenced the transformation of the territory.

Designer / Julieta Bernstein
Completion / 2014

Client / *Infografika*
Design Agency / Infografika Magazine
Completion / 2013

Dangerous Sex

Project Description /

The designers of this infographic were interested in HIV / AIDS. They found an online article that stated that AIDS did not exist as an illness. There were a large number of comments on the post, and it was clear that some readers didn't know the difference between HIV and AIDS. The infographic shows how HIV infection occurs and the effects of AIDS on the body; it also gives relevant statistics in Russia.

Designer / Nonna Khismatullina

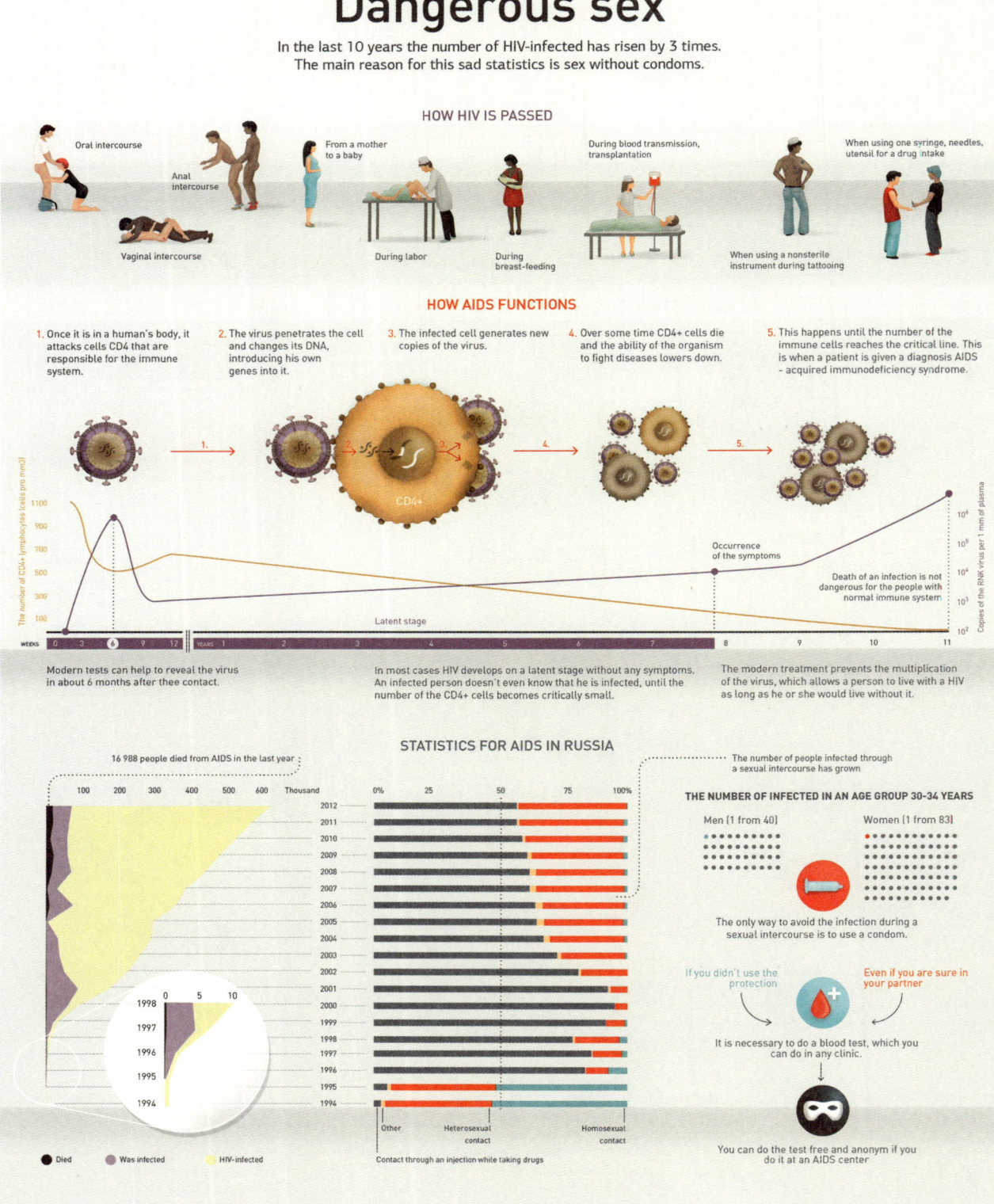

We be of One Blood, Thou and I

Project Description /

Everyone knows that blood is needed for surgeries, but the percentage of people who make blood donations in Russia is very low. Why is this the case? The designers suspect this is because of the bad reputation of Russia's medical system. This infographic was created to draw more attention to the issue, and to encourage people to make blood donations. The designers compared the quantities in blood banks in the West with those in Russia.

Designer / Olga Stozharova

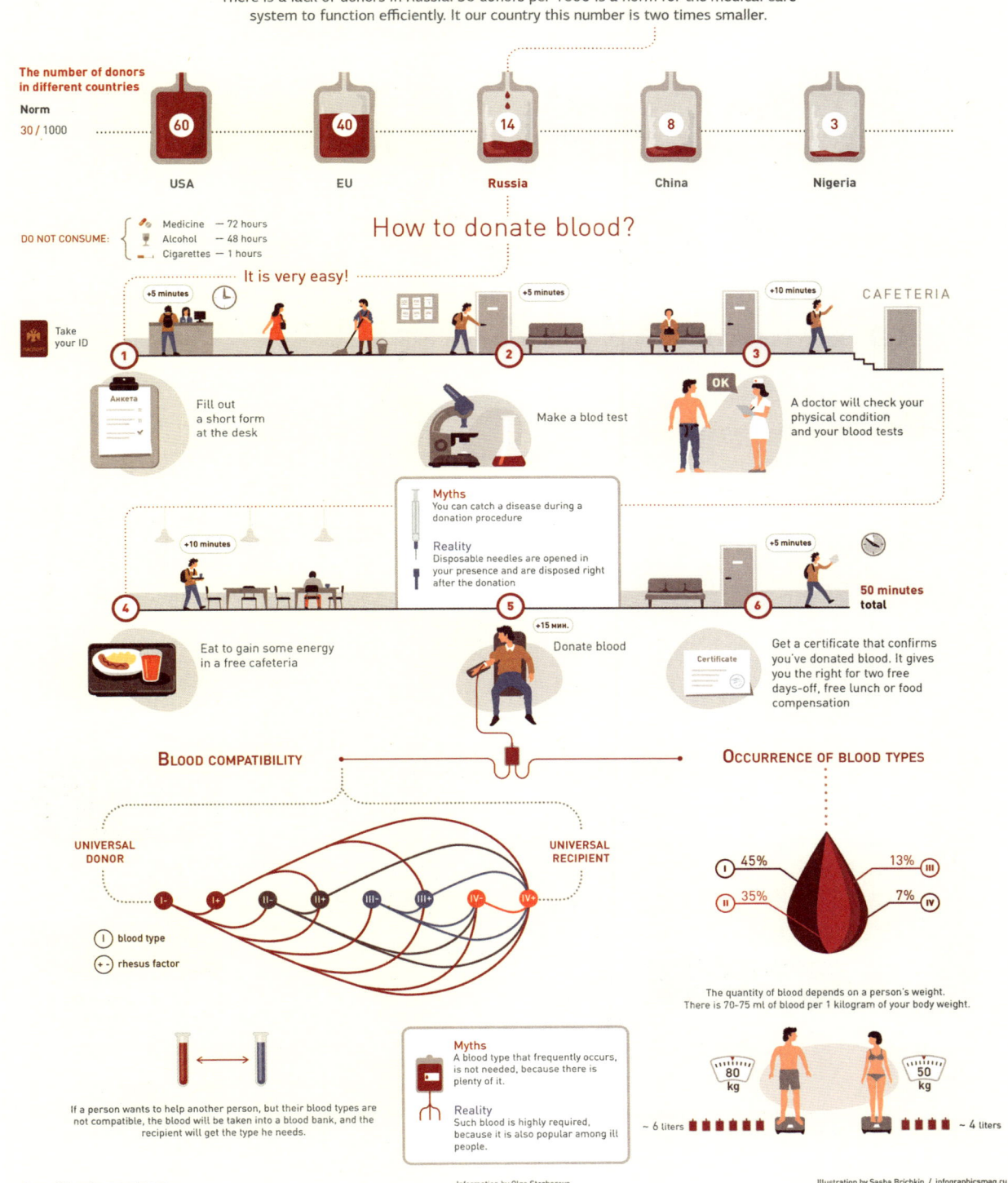

The Pension System in Russia

Project Description /

This infographic aims to teach readers about how the pension system works in Russia, so they won't wonder why they have such a small pension when they are old. The purpose of this article was quite difficult, so the designer chose a simple, friendly layout. It was designed as if it was drawn by hand by a smart person, who knows this theme well.

Designer / Andrey Mashanov

Repair your cart in December; in July your sledge remember

Most part of Russians do not think about their future pension. The result of such carelessness can be very sad – average pension in Russia right now is 9 800.

Do you ever think how you will support yourself when you get old?
- 44%
- 20%
- 33%
- 3%

20% – Yes, I have thought about it and I'm doing something about it right now
44% – Yes, I have thought about it, but I do not do anything about it
33% – No, I don't think about it
3% – Can't answer

EMPLOYER
officially declared salary: 30 000 ₽

Pension contributions **22%** → **PENSION FUND** (pfrf.ru)

Do you save money for the time when you get older?
- 13% – Yes, I do
- 59% – I want to, but I have no such opportunity
- 6% – I could, but I don't want to
- 11% – Can't answer
- 11% – I can't and I don't want to

Where do you keep the funded component of retirement pension?
- 63% – Left at the Pension Fund of the Russian Federation
- 9% – Transferred money to a private pension fund
- 28% – Don't know where it is

16% PAYG COMPONENT
Only 10% of the money transferred to this part is saved on your personal account. The money isn't actually stored. State just commits to certain responsibilities.
*These responsibilities are adjusted according to an index based on inflation rate.

Money from the PAYG component are used to pay pensions to today's pensioners

6% THE FUNDED COMPONENT OF RETIREMENT PENSION
Money is stored on your account; you can place this money under management.

Through which sources do you support yourself when you are retired?*
- 72% – Government pension
- 35% – I continue working
- 22% – Savings
- 18% – Help of the kids and relatives
- 5% – Pension from a private pension fund
- 4% – Income from a real estate
- 4% – Income from investments, stocks and so on
- 9% – Hard to say

*Several answers are possible.

PRIVATE PENSION FUND
Places money under the management of several asset management companies and takes a certain per cent for that.
A private pension fund is considered to be able to choose a better asset management company.

ASSET MANAGEMENT COMPANY
Invests money from the funded component of retirement pension into financial instruments and takes its per cent for that.

"Vneshekonombank" State management company
Money goes under its management automatically, if you do not apply to the State Pension Fund about transferring money into another asset management company or to a private pension fund.

Management results for 2011:
- −9,86% – −7,63% — The range of activity of 97 companies
- −17,83% – −7,69% — The range of activity of 55 companies
- 5,47% – 5,9% — Two strategies

YOUR FUTURE PENSION WILL CONSIST OF THREE PARTS

3 278 ₽ + **6 665 ₽** + **12 683,8 ₽***

- Get all people of the retirement age with a job tenure of 5 years
- Money that the government owes you by the time you retire. Government will divide it by 216. This is the number of months you live after the retirement according to the government
- this part consists of insurance fees (from salaries) and income from investments. The result will be divided by 216

*In case the income from investments will annually exceed inflation by 5%

The calculations are made for the salary of 30 000 for the time span of 30 years

TOTAL: 22 626,8 ₽

It is approximately 80% of the 30 000 rubles salary

WEAK POINT

Payments to the Pension Fund cover only **70,8%**

The rest part is supplied by the government that uses profit from the export of resources → The population gets older, which means the Pension Fund will get more and more imbalanced

Once oil price crush, the government won't be able to compensate this difference. In this case the basic part will become smaller, as well as the PAYG component. Only the funded component of the retirement pension is safe form this influence, in case you place it under the management of a management company or a private pension fund

Small and Old

Project Description /

Nastya Mikheeva chose this topic for an infographic in response to a Russian plane crash that had sparked much debate about how bad planes were in Russia. The planes have a reputation for being old, uncomfortable and unreliable, so the designer decided to research information about international and Russian airlines, concentrating on the age of the aircraft fleets.

The infographic focuses on the large airlines with flights from Russia to Europe. The designer discovered that the Russian airlines compared favorably with the international fleets. Russian airlines have more new aircraft than Ryanair or Lufthansa, for example.

Designer / Nastya Mikheeva

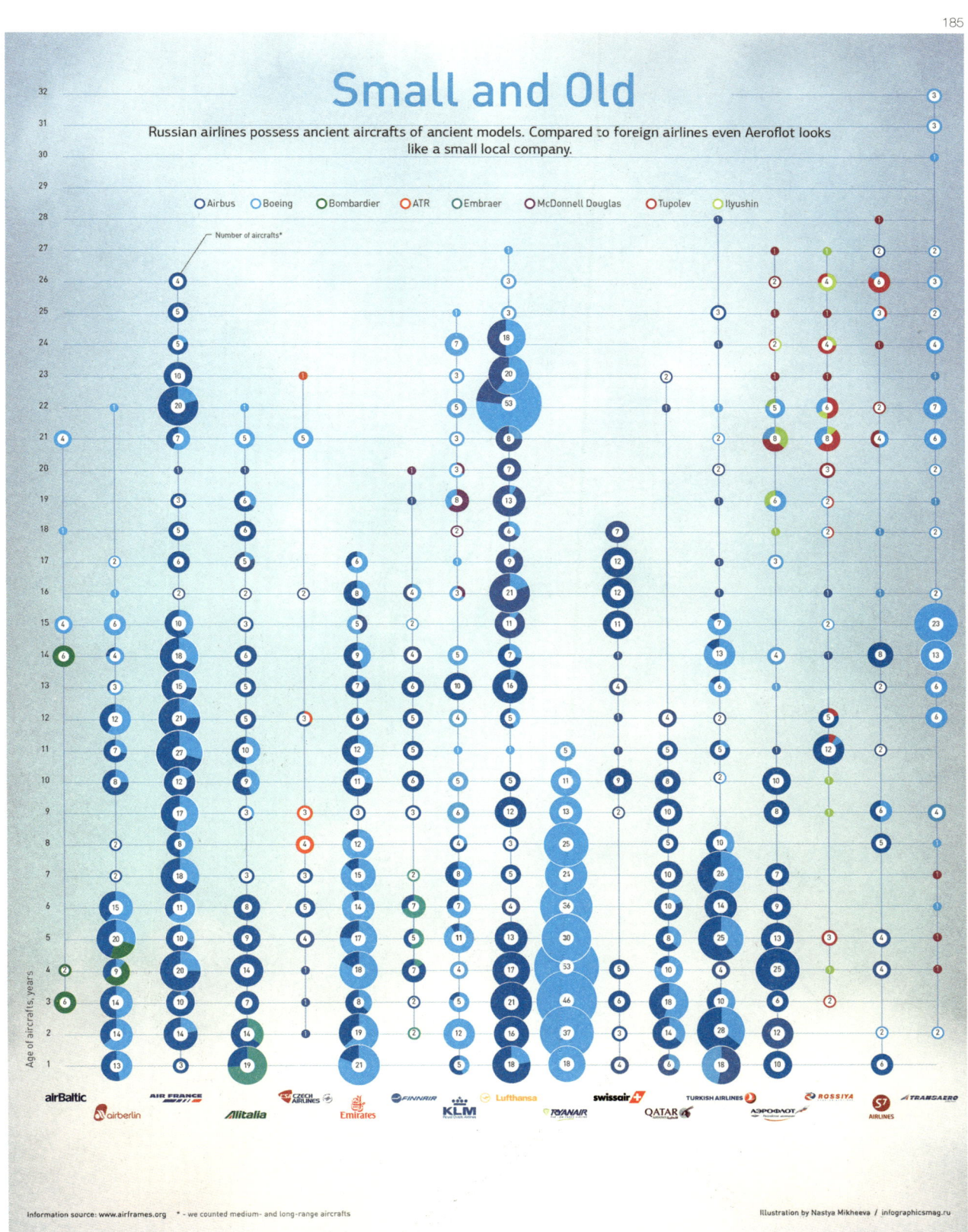

Rainy Days

Project Description /

As genuine Petersburgers, the designers love to talk about weather. It's well known that their city has a bad reputation when it comes to weather, so they decided to find out if the rumours were true or not. The designers used information from the Worldwide Meteorology Organization to research data about rainy days in different cities, and discovered that Saint Petersburg has almost the same weather conditions as Moscow.

The designer used simple umbrellas as symbols in their infographic. They needed to do a photo shoot outside in summer, and Saint Petersburg was very warm and sunny at this time. So they wet the pavement near their office and added some additional signs while photo editing in Photoshop.

Designers / Kristina Moskvina, Artyom Koleganov

The Meter is Running

Project Description /

The theme of this infographic emerged after the designers paid an electricity bill. They thought the bill was huge, and were very curious about which devices had such high energy use. They made a list of popular household appliances and attentively researched their technical instructions. Then they estimated the average person's daily usage, and multiplied numbers to get the final result. Every device and square of lighting in the project was made of cardboard, which looks interesting and three-dimensional.

Designer / Dima Gorelyshev

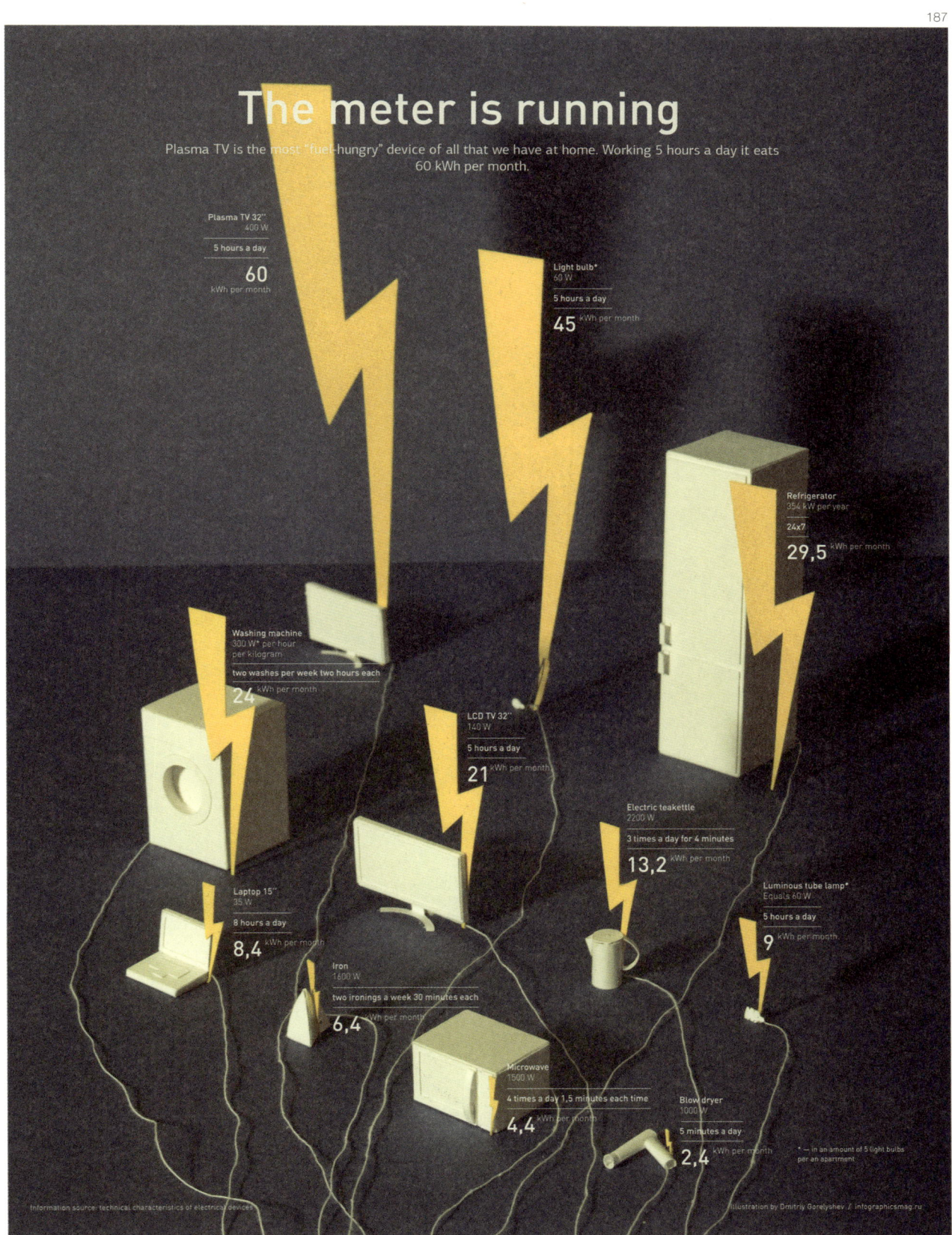

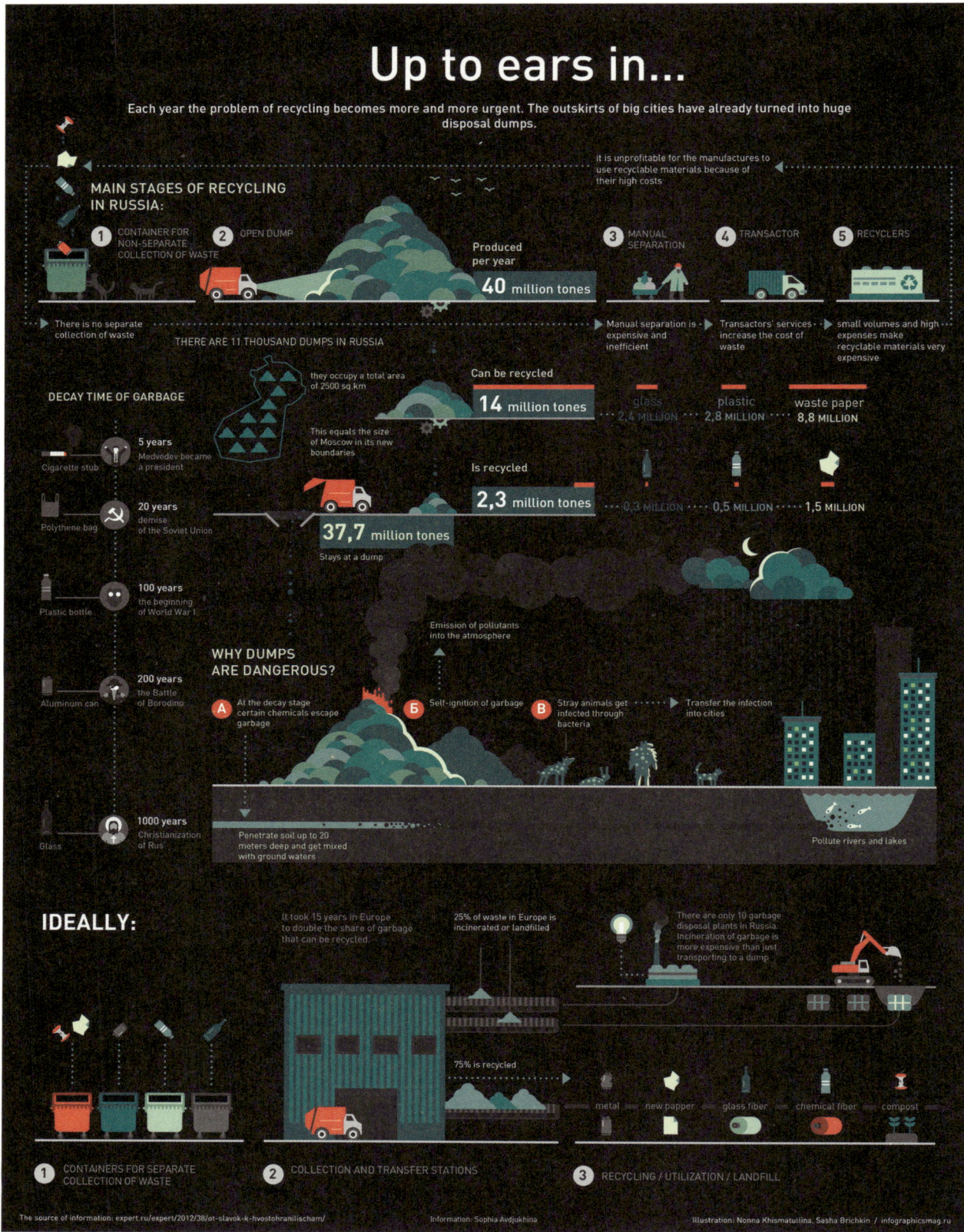

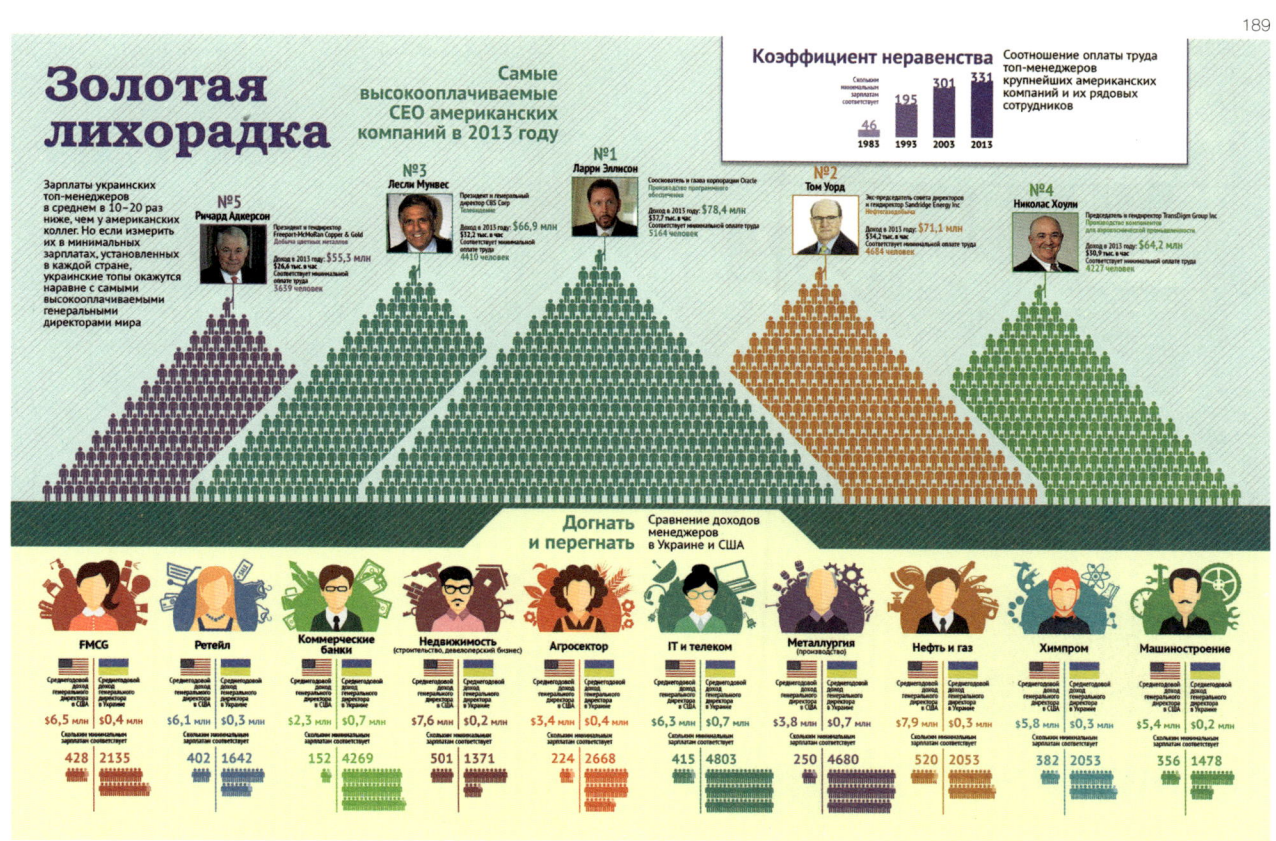

Up to Ears

Project Description /
Though the necessity of bikeways in cities is a hot topic with progressive urban communities, this infographic concentrates on the trash problem, which is much more important for Saint Petersburg and other large cities in Russia. The designers used the infographic to explain why Russia doesn't have the custom of separating trash by type, and tried to demonstrate what would happen if nothing changes. They compared information about Russia with that of western developed countries.

Designers / Nonna Khismatullina, Sasha Brichkin

Highly Paid Professions

Project Description /
This project compared the salaries of Ukrainian and American CEOs. The US dollar represents the minimal salaries in each industry, and the human silhouette was designed as a symbol of different industries.

Client / *Focus* magazine
Design Agency / Focus Media LLC
Designer / Lizaveta Bukreeva
Completion / 2014

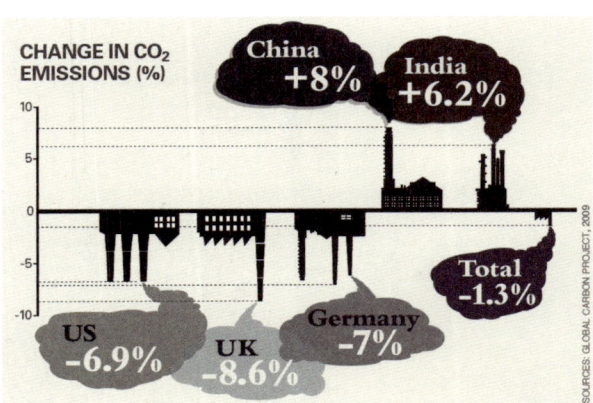

190-1

190-2

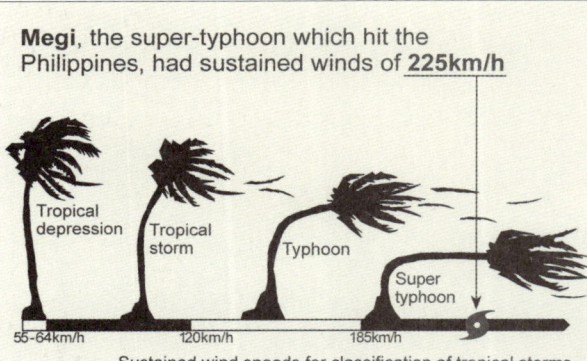

190-3

190-4

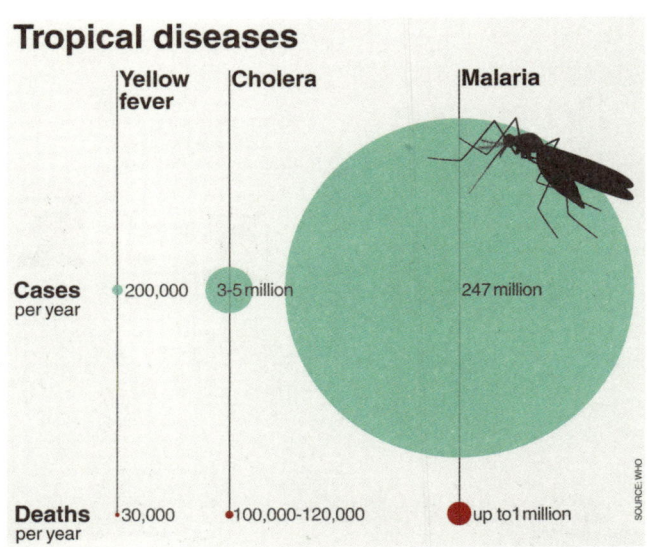

190-5

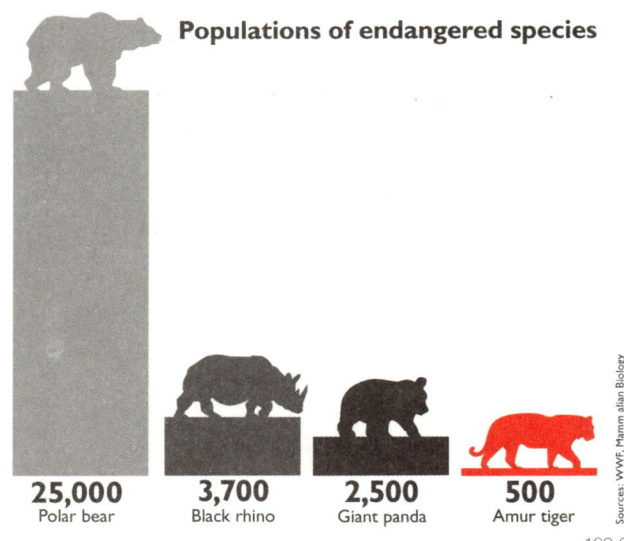

190-6

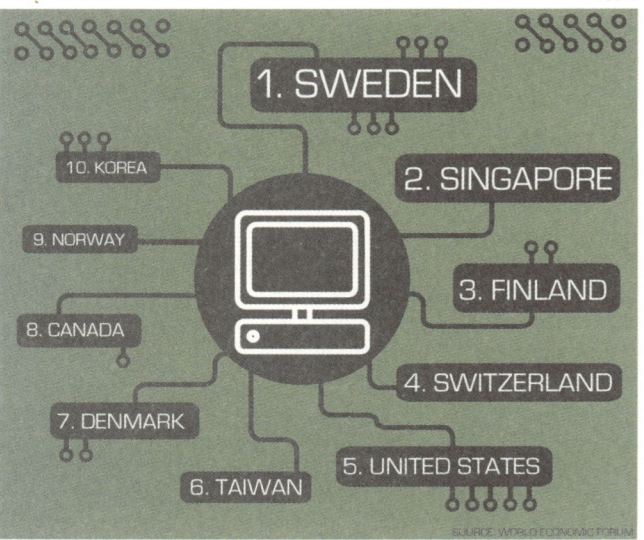

190-7

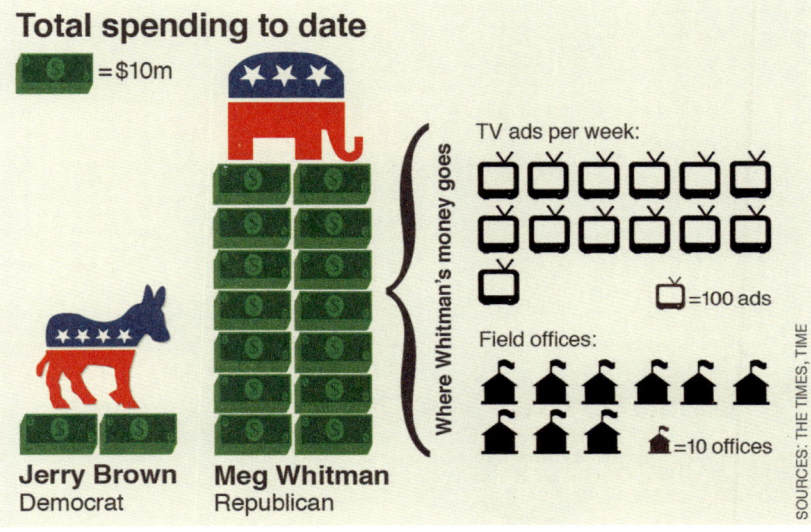

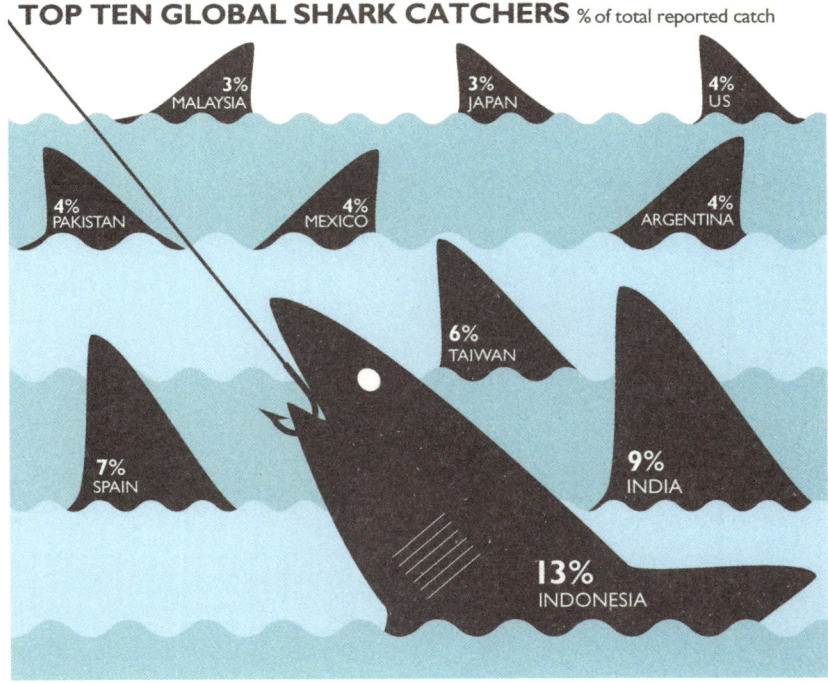

190

The Chartist

Project Description /
This project is a weekly slot in the current affairs and culture magazine dealing with a newsworthy subject. The aim of the design is to visualize a piece of information or a set of statistics, looking at something from a different perspective or highlighting a statement.

Client / *New Statesman* magazine
Designer / Henrik Pettersson
Completion / 2012

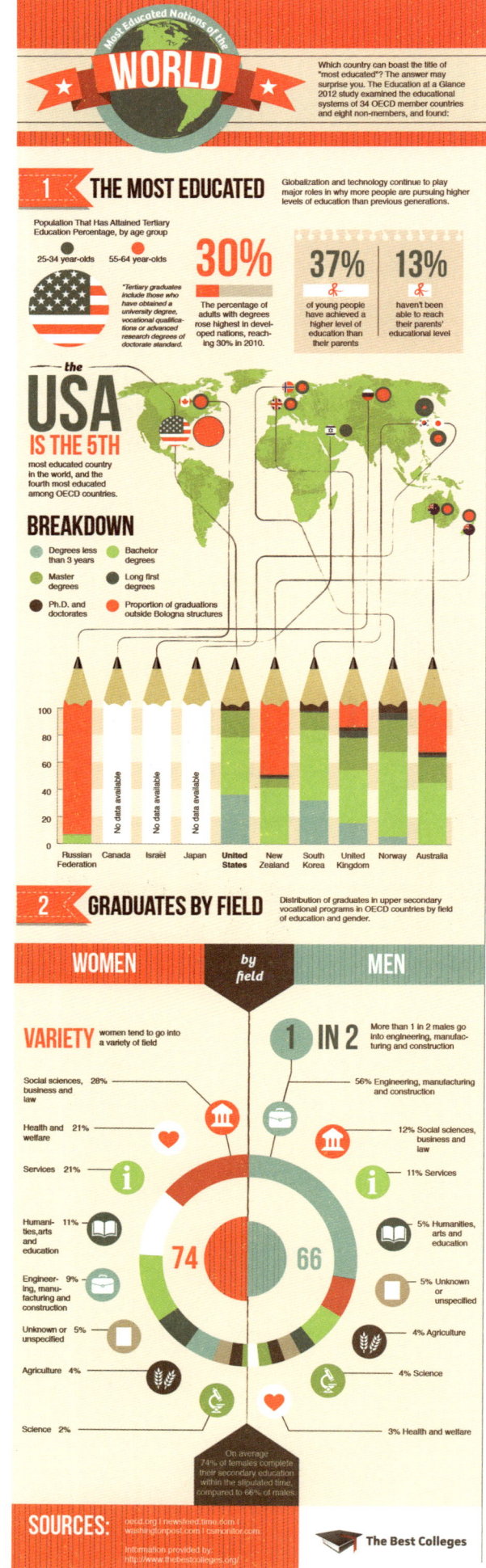

Most Educated Nations of the World

Project Description /

This infographic is an overview of the surprising results of research into 'Which country can boast the title of most educated?.' Globalization and technology play a major role, and the United States is the 5th most educated nation. The design displays the facts by using a lot of different tables and diagrams, which work with colors and drawing lines.

The Social Media Missing Link in MBA Programs

Project Description /

The University of Massachusetts Dartmouth interviewed 70 of the nation's top MBA schools to learn more about their social media use. The results showed the great power of social media, and as a result they decided to cut their traditional advertising costs, and increase their future investment in social media. The design uses many icons to attract readers and help them understand the information quickly.

The Sustainability of La Stampa

Project Description /

The infographic shows the sustainable printing processes of the Italian newspaper *La Stampa*, and appeals to the newspaper industry to be aware of the project's sustainability. The designer used tree and wood as the design element to emphasize that saving paper is saving trees.

Client / *La Stampa*
Designer / Gianluca Seta
Completion / 2012

Leishmaniasis

Project Description /

This scientific infographic is based on Andrea Mastrangelo and Daniel Salomon's article 'Contribution of social anthropology to eco-epidemiological comprehension of an American Tegumentary Leishmaniosis outbreak at '2.000 ha', Iguazú, Argentina.' The article discusses the exposure of the disease, the methods of transmission, prevention and control.

The infographic is aimed at professionals such as doctors or nurses, since the information does not focus on teaching the existence of the vector, but shows different views of the problem from an epidemiological and anthropological standpoint. The infographic design is based on a graphic narrative divided into zones, which explain the levels of risk of exposure, from the habitat of the parasite in the jungle to residential areas. The complex information is simplified by using encyclopedic character illustrations and plane figures for the statistics graphs.

Designer / Mosettig Tamara
Completion / 2014

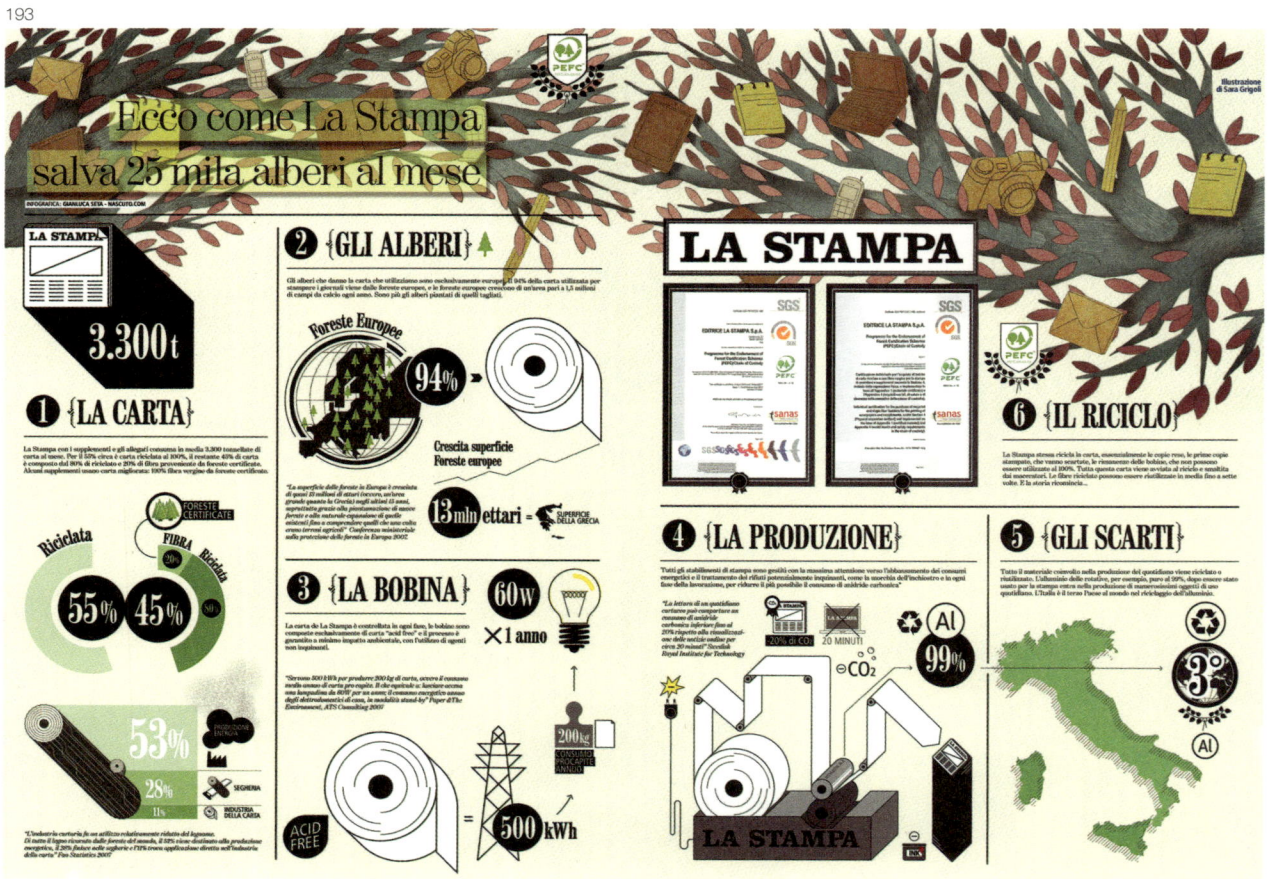

BROTE DE LEISHMANIASIS 2000 HA PUERTO IGUAZÚ

CONTRIBUCIÓN DE LA ANTROPOLOGÍA A LA COMPRENSIÓN ECOEPIDEMIOLÓGICA DE UN BROTE DE LEISHMANIASIS TEGUMENTARIA AMERICANA EN LAS **"2.000 HECTÁREAS"**, PUERTO IGUAZÚ, ARGENTINA

350 millones

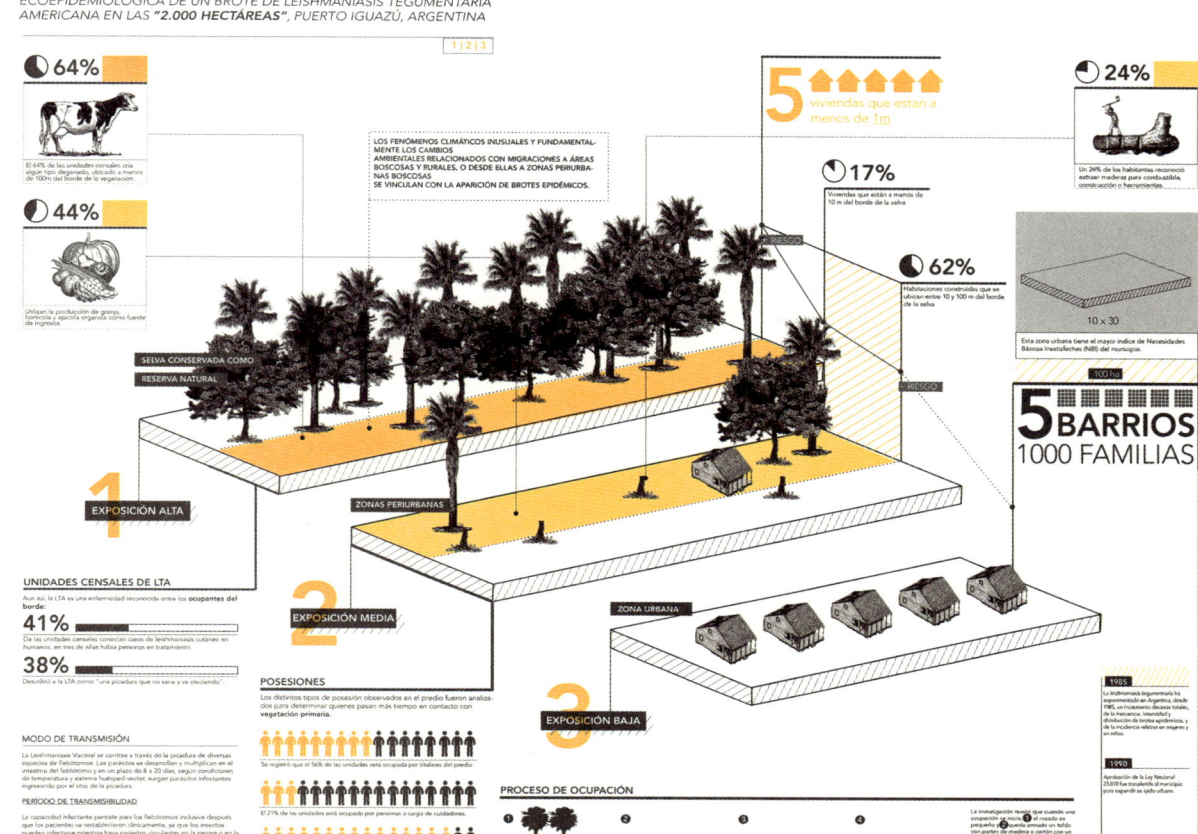

CONCLUSIONES: la información social recabada se considera crítica para planificar acciones de prevención, vigilancia y control con participación comunitaria.

The Map of Sustainability

Project Description /

The report concerned contradictions in the modern world regarding energy—how big countries need and consume enormous quantities of energy, while at the same time some countries have no access to modern energy systems. The infographic aimed to illustrate the statistics for CO_2 emissions as well as the electricity production of the world's biggest, most important countries. The total CO_2 emissions by country were corelated with the national population, showing how some countries contaminate a huge amount despite having a relatively small population, and vice versa. The total production of electricity by country was related with the presence of fossil fuel resources to produce the electricity, showing the relative cleanliness of the produced electricity. The infographic in the lower part illustrates the situation of the countries that have not had access to modern

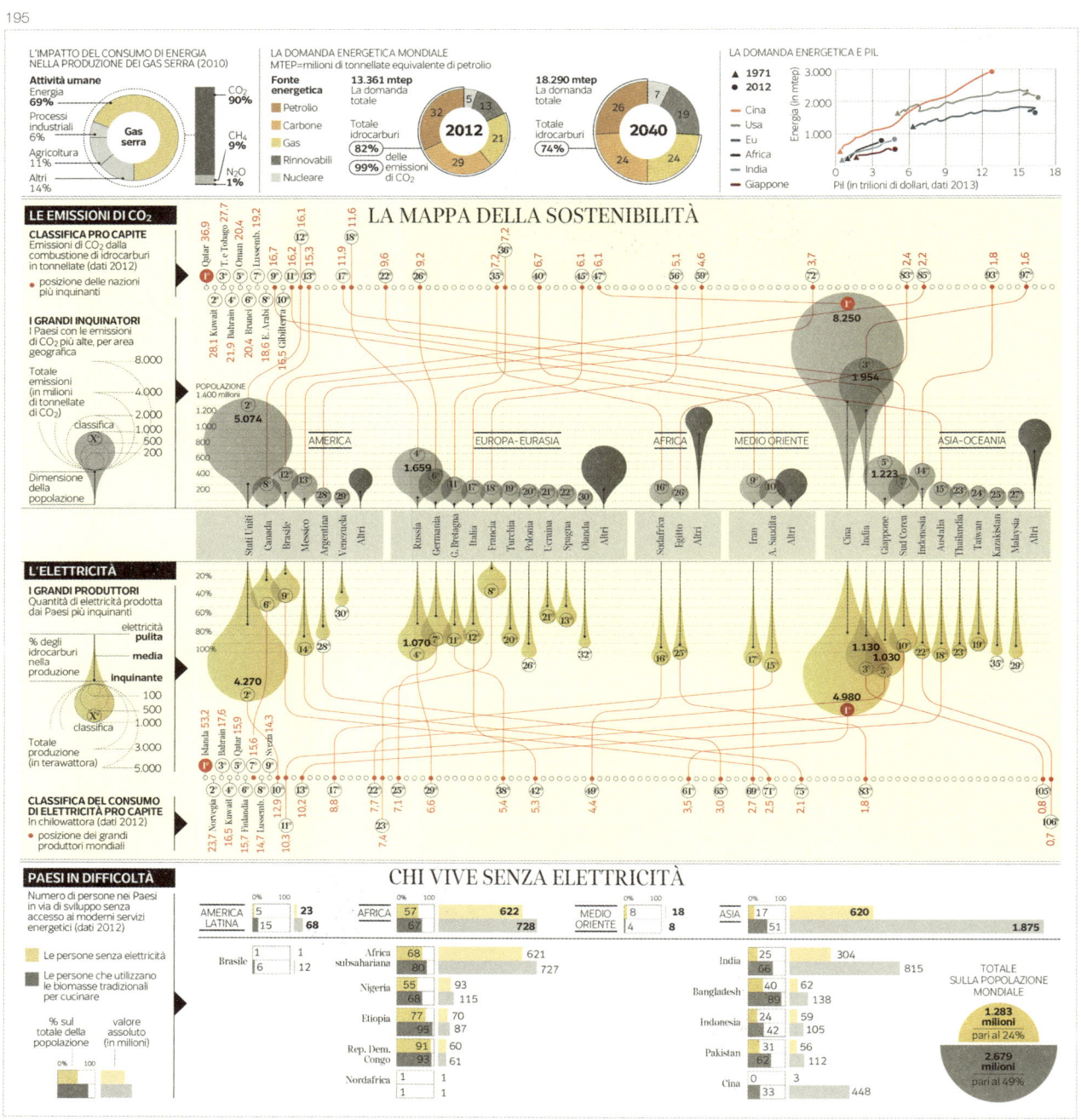

Design Agency / Corriere Della Sera
Infographic newsroom
Completion / 2015

energy systems, and that still use biomasses as a source of their daily energy supply.

Designer / Nicolas Vargas

The Map of Solidarity

Project Description /

Expo 2015, held in Milan, required a huge commitment of the public and private sectors but also of the society. Many activities were promoted and supported with the help of volunteers. This infographic was intended to illustrate the extent of not-for-profit activity in the Italian territory, dividing the data of the organizations and the human capital by region. The hand of the volunteer (as the main concept) represents the total number of not-for-profit organizations in the region: those organizations are divided per activity (fingers) and per legal form (cake inside the hand). The area graphic down the hands represent the human capital engaged by region; divided by typology, they show the main role of the voluntary force in the not-for-profit organizations. It also illustrates how many volunteers are engaged by region for each 10,000 people. The lower part of the graphic illustrates the profile of the Italian volunteer, considering the sex, the age range, the education level, and the occupational situation.

Designer / Nicolas Vargas

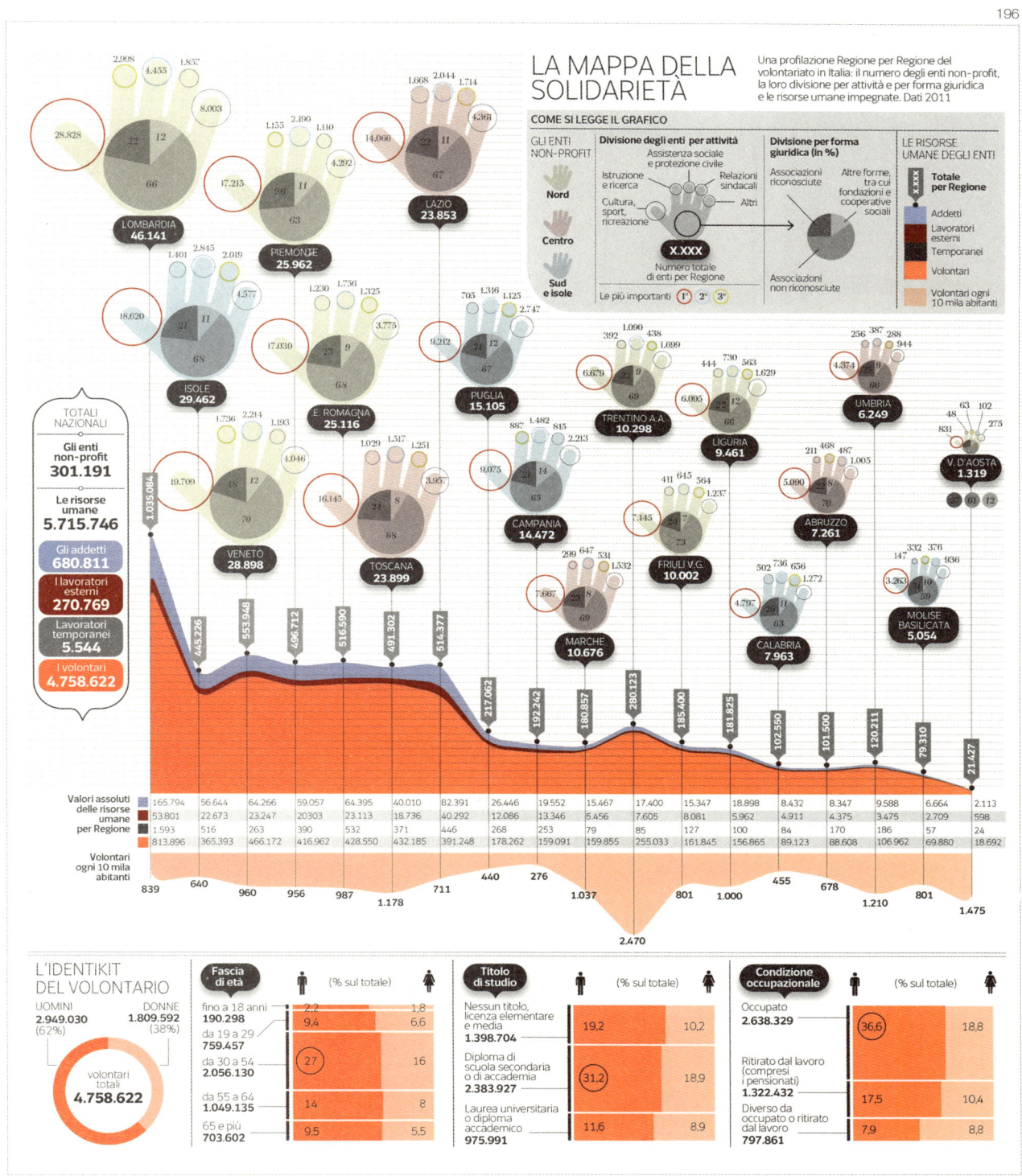

Urban Gardens

Project Description /

The urban garden has gained a lot of attention in modern society for many reasons. Many cities in Europe have designated some public ground for citizens to cultivate their own products. 'Do it yourself' agriculture has become a practice that's not just limited to farmers and people in the country; today, in metropolitan areas, people have started to cultivate not just decorative plants but also fruits and vegetables. This infographic illustrates this modern phenomenon, explaining the different types of urban gardens that people can easily create on their own properties. The design also introduces the 10 most important rules to take care of the garden. Finally, it develops the concept of the calendar of sowing, illustrating the right time to sow the seeds, depending on the type of plant. The calendar gives some main examples, with detailed and important information about their cultivation.

Designer / Sabina Castagnaviz

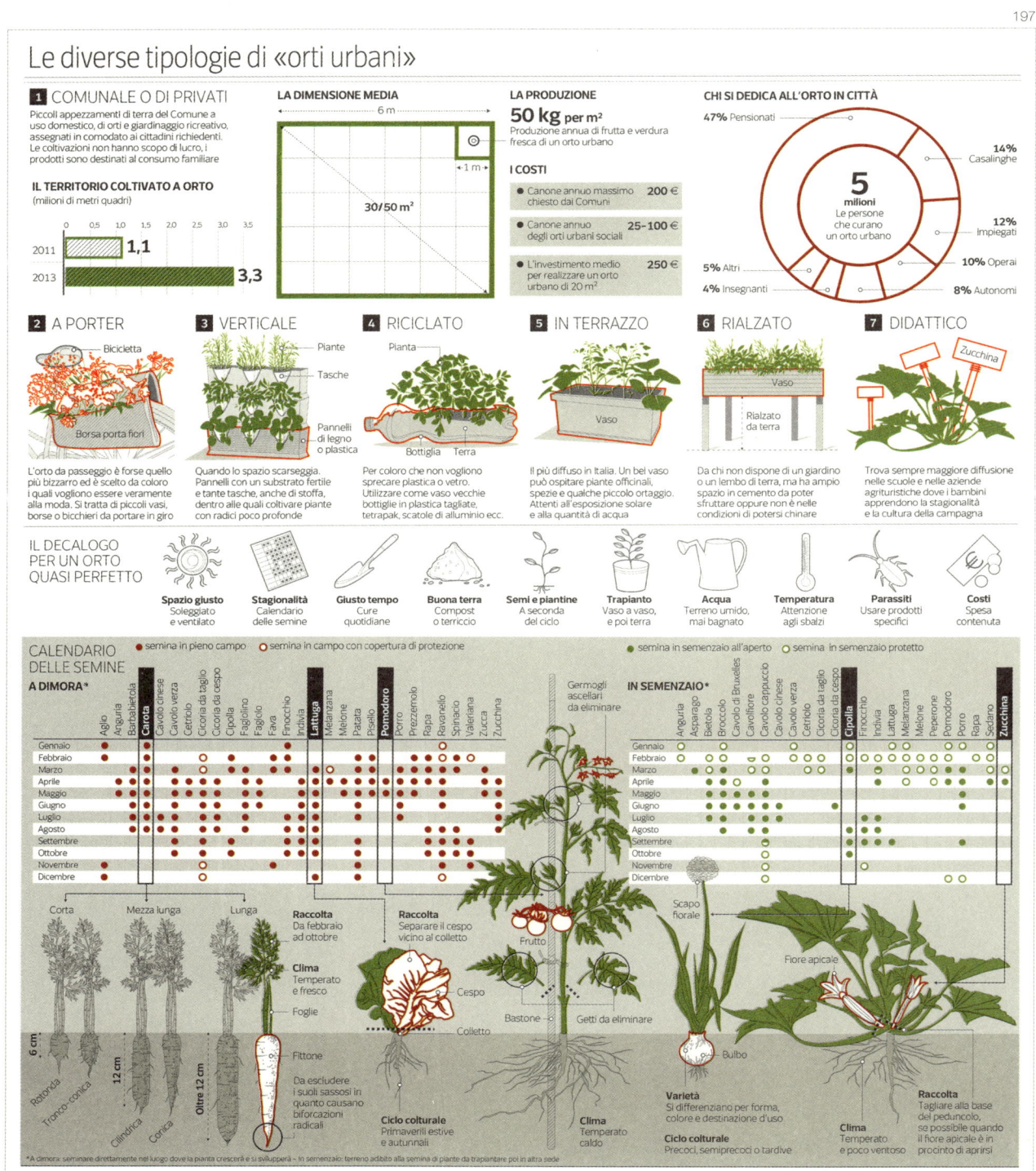

Tourism in Italy

Project Description /

This infographic focuses on the people that come to Italy to enjoy what the country has to offer, and the tendency of visitors to look for new models of tourism experience. For modern-day tourists, it's not just about eating good food or visiting great museums, but also experiencing the Italian way of life. A new tourism model in Italy gives visitors the opportunity to live in the old cities, where the hotel rooms are individual historic houses. In the upper part of the infographic, the arrivals are divided by continent and by country of origin, reporting the average nights of stay. In the lower part, the arrivals are divided by region, related again with the average nights of stay. The dolls wearing regional clothes around the country represent the new model of experience tourism, indicating the number in each region.

Designer / Sabina Castagnaviz

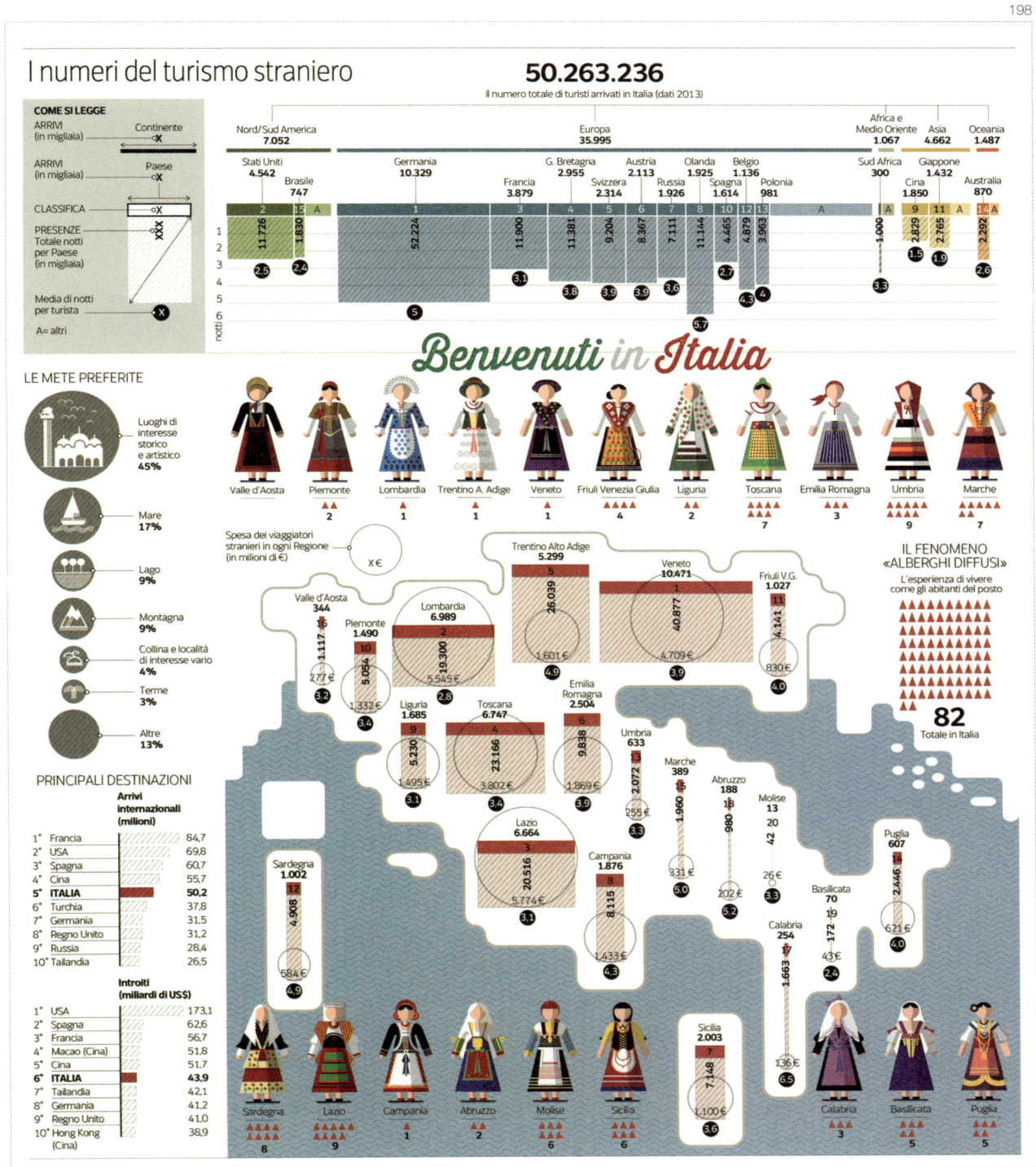

Mediterranean Diet

Project Description /

Studies suggest that the benefits of the Mediterranean diet don't stop on the wellness sphere, but also have positive environmental impacts as a sustainable way of eating. This infographic aims to explain the main characteristics of the Mediterranean diet, and the daily quantities that should be consumed from each family of products. A bar graph on the right side of the pyramid illustrates how the adoption of the Mediterranean diet has changed in the Mediterranean countries. The lower part of the graphic explores the issue of the diet's sustainability. Proponents of the Mediterranean diet argue that people consume more products that contaminate less, and fewer products that contaminate a lot; while Mediterranean diet skeptics argue that consuming a lot of products that contaminate less is, in the end, simply the same as consuming fewer products that contaminate a lot.

Designer / Sabina Castagnaviz

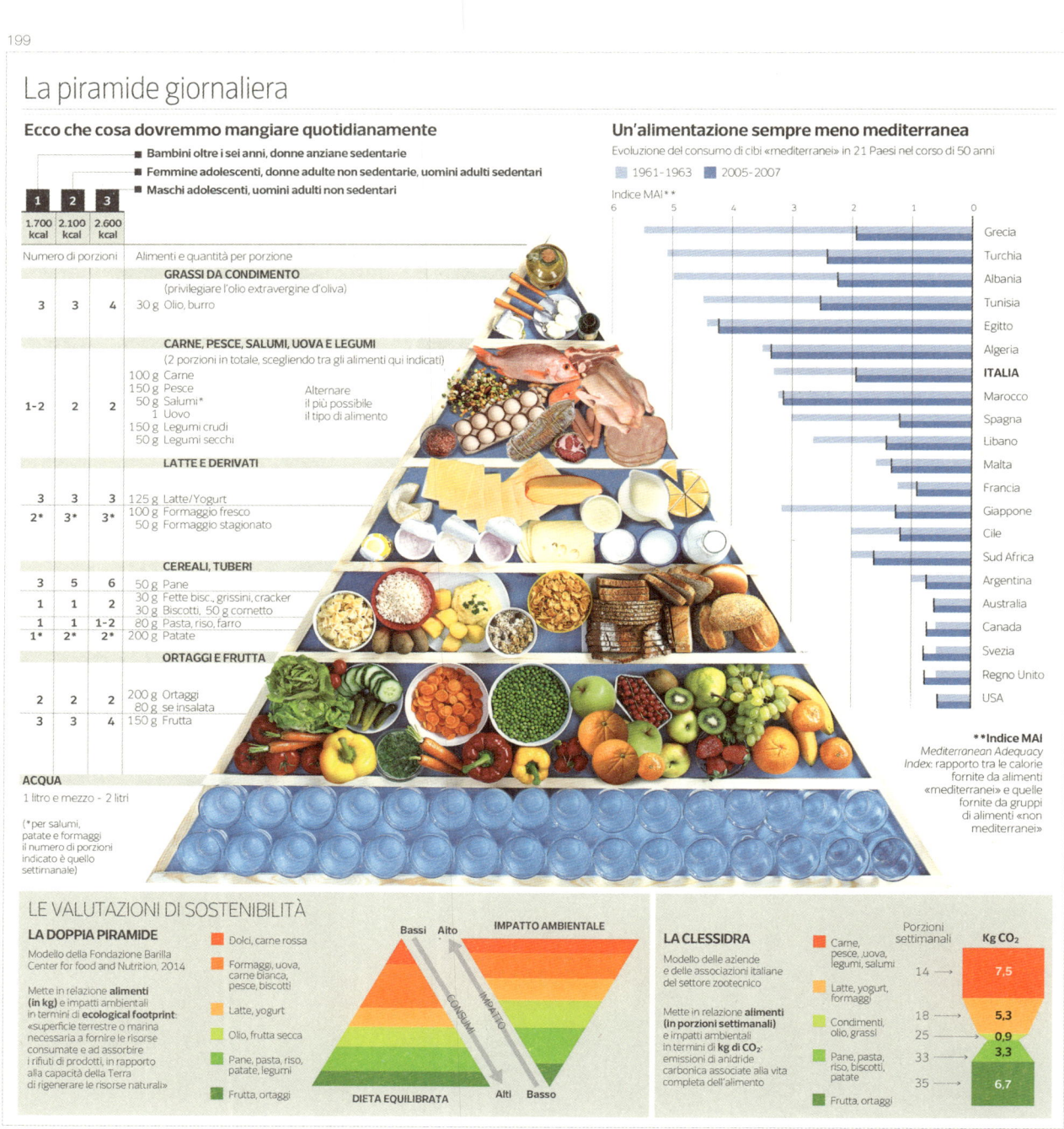

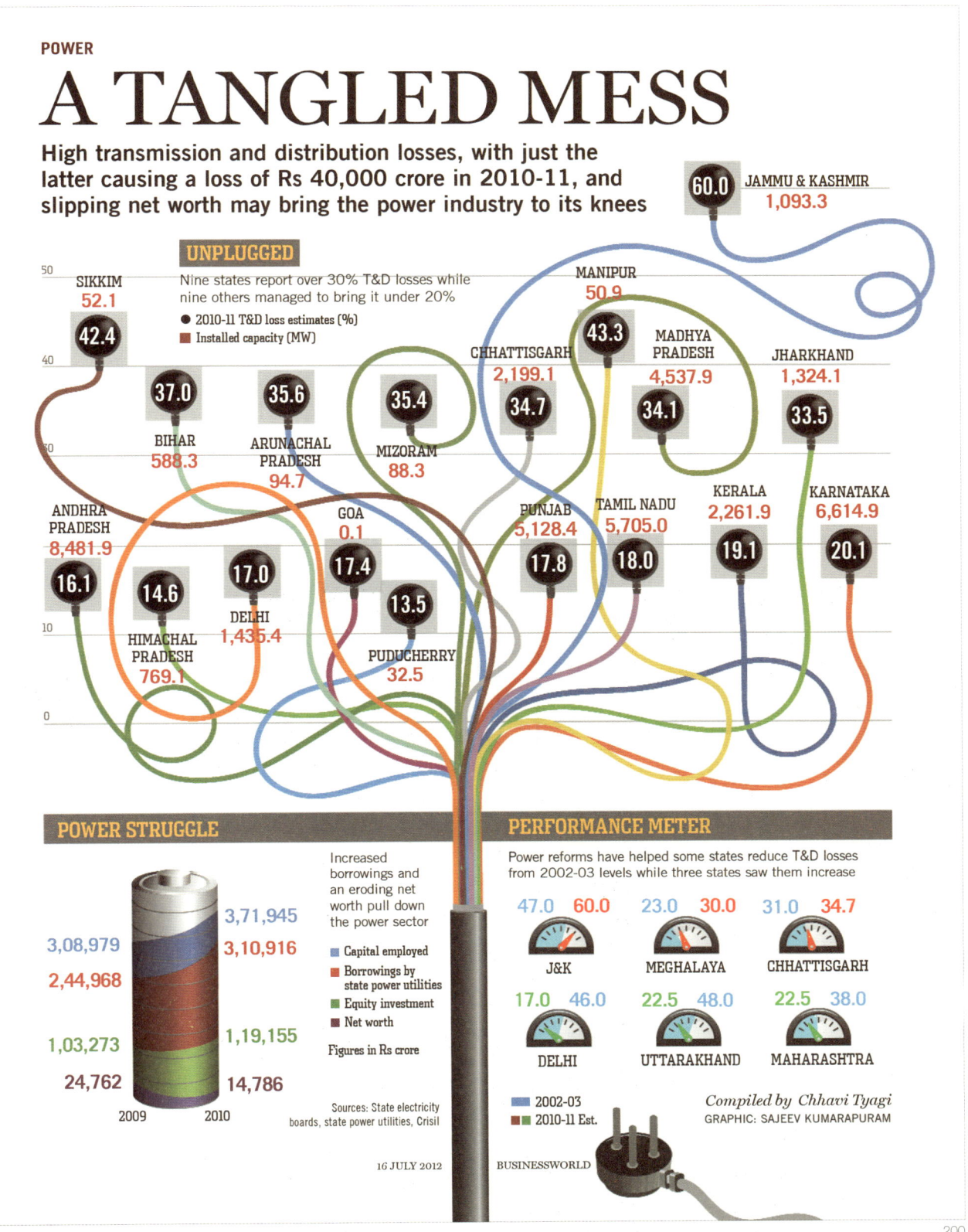

Power Distribution

Project Description /

This infographic depicts the state of India's troubled electricity industry, which at the time was losing more than $6 billion per year, with no clear solution in sight. The design of the graphic reflects the chaos. Multicolored cables represent the various states, each of which has its own power policy, with the embattled Kashmir region at the top. It includes snapshots of how the industry has changed in the past decade, and identifies the top three best and worst-performing states.

Client / *Business World* magazine
Designer / Sajeev Kumarapuram
Completion / 2012

What's in the Customer's Mailstream?

Project Description /
Marketers are often good at understanding what makes a mail piece stand out, but it's not always apparent what that piece needs to stand out against. The purpose of this infographic is to show marketers what the US mailstream really looks like, so they have a clear picture of the kind of mail their target customers would be receiving, and it would help marketers create mail marketing strategies.

Client / United States Postal Service
Design Agency / Lowe Campbell Ewald
Designers / Grayson Cardinell, Jude Buffum

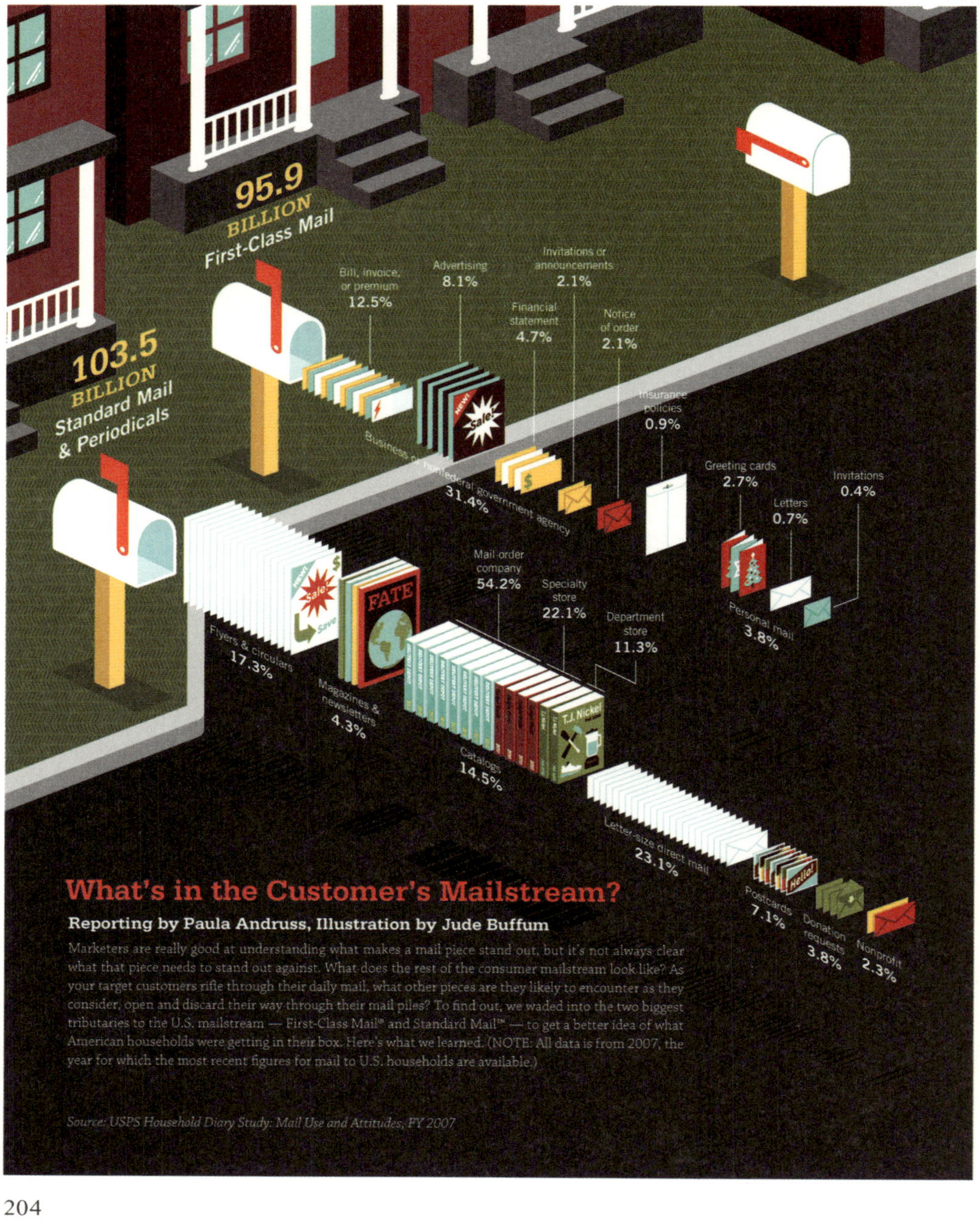

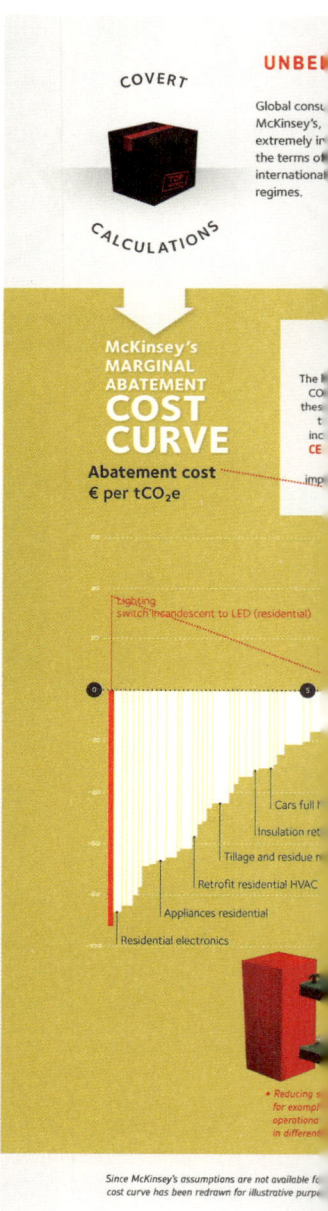

Greenpeace McKinsey's Curve

Project Description /

The Marginal Abatement Cost (MAC) curve is a bar chart that describes a set of different options available to reduce carbon emissions. MAC curves feature a succession of different steps, each one being a different potential measure, with its height representing its cost and its width representing the amount of carbon abatement it could deliver.

Greenpeace highlighted some issues with the McKinsey's curve, such as the lack of transparency in the calculations or the over-simplification of the representation of an economy. The top part of the visualization reveals three main reasons why the McKinsey's Marginal Abatement Cost curve is not a reliable tool. In the main section the different issues are represented with columns highlighted in the graph, each one with an illustration to convey the message contained in the description boxes.

Client / Greenpeace UK
Design Agency / Density Design Research Lab
Designers / Veronica Clarin, Luca Masud, Mario Porpora

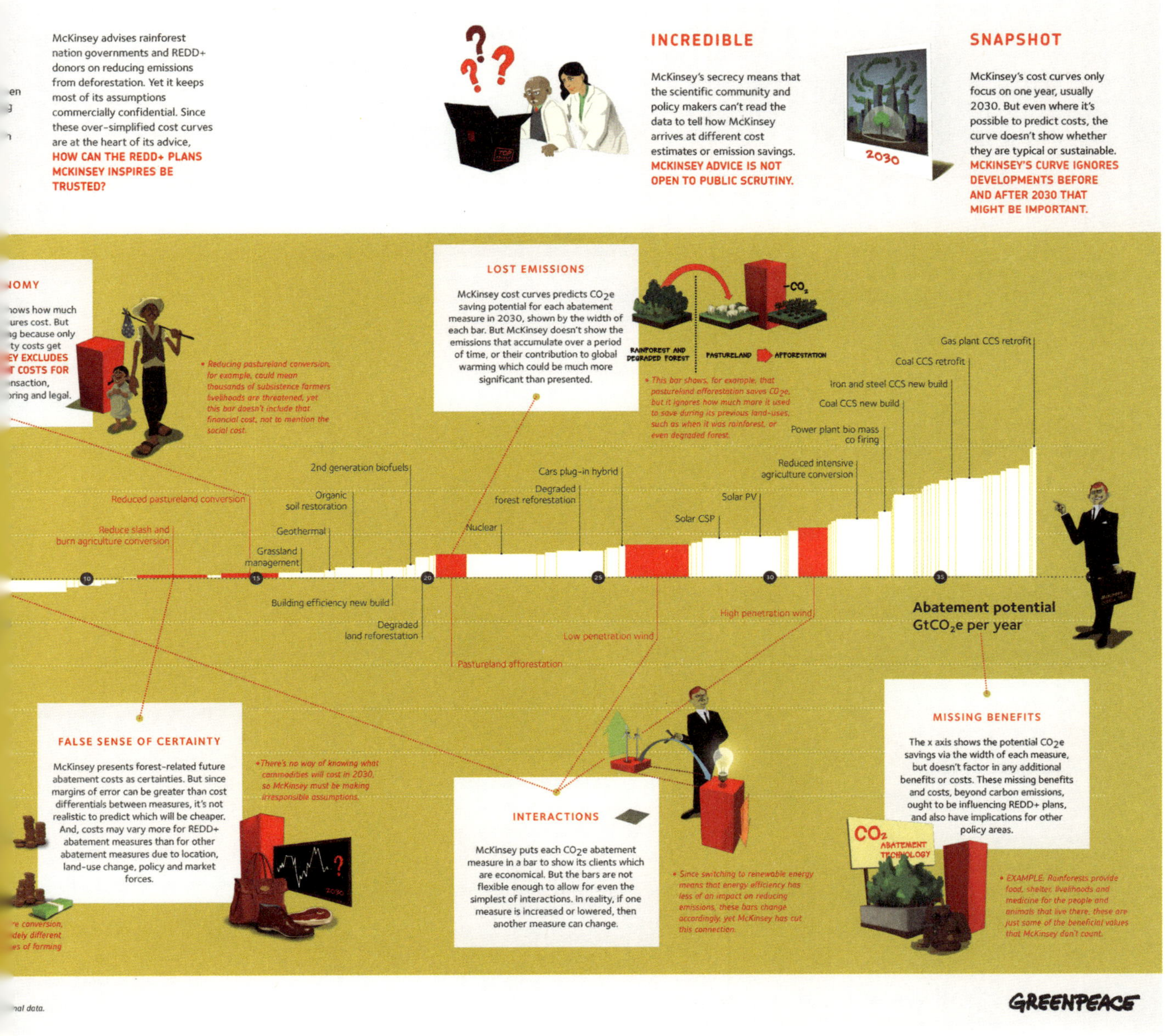

Life Issues

Project Description /

This work aims to evoke sympathy from readers about some of the difficult issues in life; the illustrations help to present the content more clearly and make the work more visually interesting. 'Non smoking' shows that quitting smoking should not just be for a while, but for a lifetime. 'Go on a Diet' explores the reasons why some people fail to lose weight. 'Give up Drinking' asks readers to consider whether they are in charge of their drinking, or whether the alcohol is in charge of them. 'Save Money' explores how much money people save every month, and the purpose of their saving. The text at the bottom of each infographic offers a conclusion for each theme, expressing the designer's personal thoughts.

Designer / Sangseob Lee
Completion / 2014

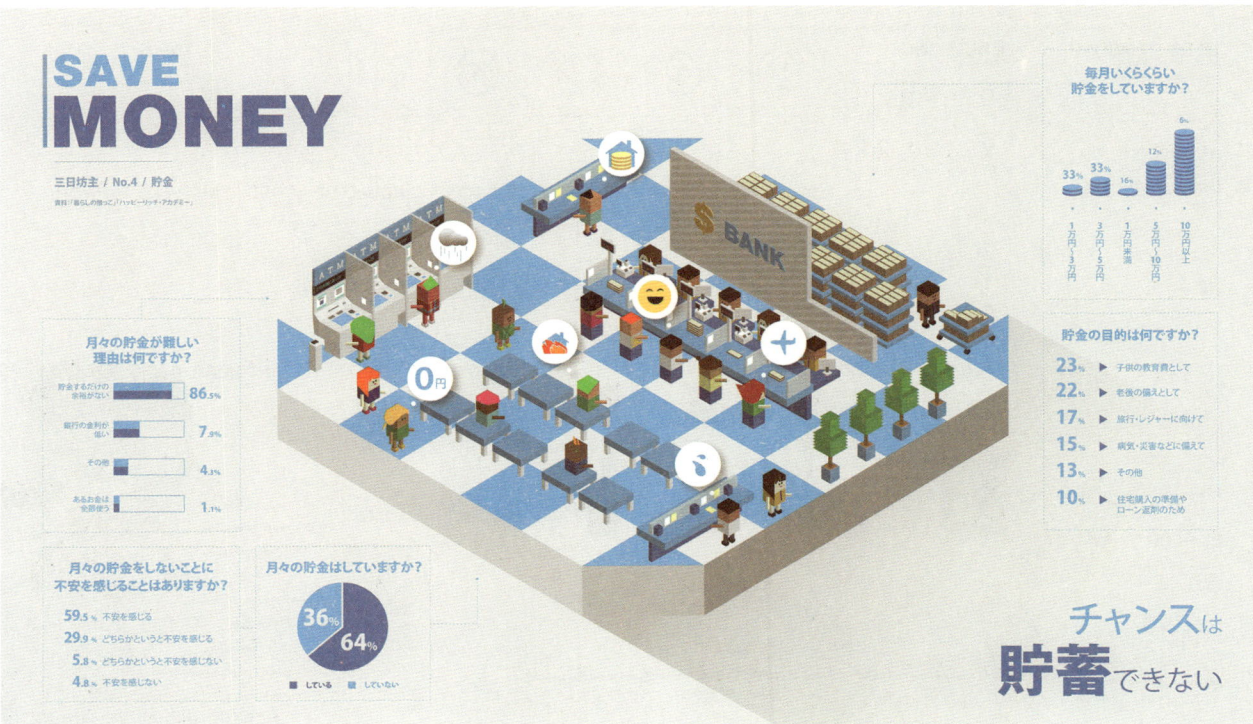

Bullying

Project Description /

This infographic about bullying was created after a long process of research and investigation. The most relevant data was taken to explain the topic, after collecting information from different sources such as newspapers, magazines, websites, publications, and books. This information was translated into visual elements. Handwriting, collage, crafts, and altered photographs featured in the infographic scheme, with the child-like aesthetic providing a good contrast with the maturity of the subject.

Designer / Bárbara Villoslada

C.S.I. South Africa

Project Description /

CSI South Africa aims to graphically and creatively convey the increasing crime rate in the country. The infographic is designed in the form of a crime scene, using iconic symbols associated with the various categories of crime depicted in the poster. Some of the featured felonies include murder, assault, car-jacking, corruption, drug and sex crimes; each is displayed in the infographic with the total convictions recorded. With composition and hierarchy as key priorities, a dominant set of graphics was matched with minimal text to convey the data simply and systematically.

Client / Cape Peninsula University of Technology
Designer / Maxine Koen
Completion / 2013

CSI: SOUTH AFRICA

Total Crime 2012:

1. Murder
15 609

43 people are murdered on average everyday in South Africa. The World Murder Average is 7.6 per 100 000 people. The South African Murder Average is 36.5 per 100 000

2. Assault
373 691

Assault is the most common contact crime (assault, murder, attempted murder, sexual offence and robbery)

3. Commercial Crime
88 068

About R650 billion has been lost to corruption since 1994. That's nearly R13 000 per South African (50.6 million people)

4. D.U.I.
69 232

Crime involving driving under the influence of drugs and alcohol has increased by 155.7% since 2004

5. Robbery
154 122

House robbery is the most feared crime by South African households. This is followed by burglary, street robbery, murder and sex crimes

6. Sex Crimes
64 419

601 606 sex crimes were reported across S.A between 2004 and 2012, with Durban Central, Mitchells Plain and Umlazi being the highest areas

7. Hijacking
10 426

The top carjacking provinces are Gauteng, Kwazulu Natal and Eastern Cape. Booysens in Gauteng is the no. 1 hijacking hotspot in the country

8. Drug Crimes
175 823

Drug related crimes have increased by a staggering 158% since 2004, with almost half occurring in the Western Cape alone

More than 2 million crimes were reported in South Africa during 2012

Top 10 Most Dangerous Areas in South Africa

01. Mitchells Plain (WC)
02. Cape Town CBD (WC)
03. Durban CBD (KZN)
04. Johannesburg CBD (GT)
05. Hillbrow (GT)
06. Park Road (FS)
07. Honeydew (GT)
08. Pretoria CBD (GT)
09. Phoenix (KZN)
10. Rustenburg (NW)

Total Crimes (2004-2012)

Top Crime Provinces 2012

1. Gauteng
2. Western Cape
3. Kwazulu-Natal
4. Eastern Cape
5. Freestate
6. Mpumalanga
7. Limpopo
8. North West
9. Northern Cape

References: South African Police Department. 2012. Crime Statistics Overview RSA 2011/2012. SAPS [Online]. Available: http://www.saps.gov.za/statistics/reports/crimestats/2012/downloads/crime_statistics_presentation.pdf. [18 April 2013]; Crime Stats.

Animal and Human Relationships

Project Description /
This is an exploration on human and animal cognition. This series of five informational designs demonstrate that animals are surprisingly more like us than one might have thought. Each design measures 45.72 × 109.22 centimeters (18 × 43 inches). These graphs explore various facts and situations that relate to humans and the specified animal. Graphs and data are plotted in unique and unexpected ways to make the information more attractive and interesting to readers.

Client / Honors Thesis
Designer / McKenzie Smith
Completion / 2013

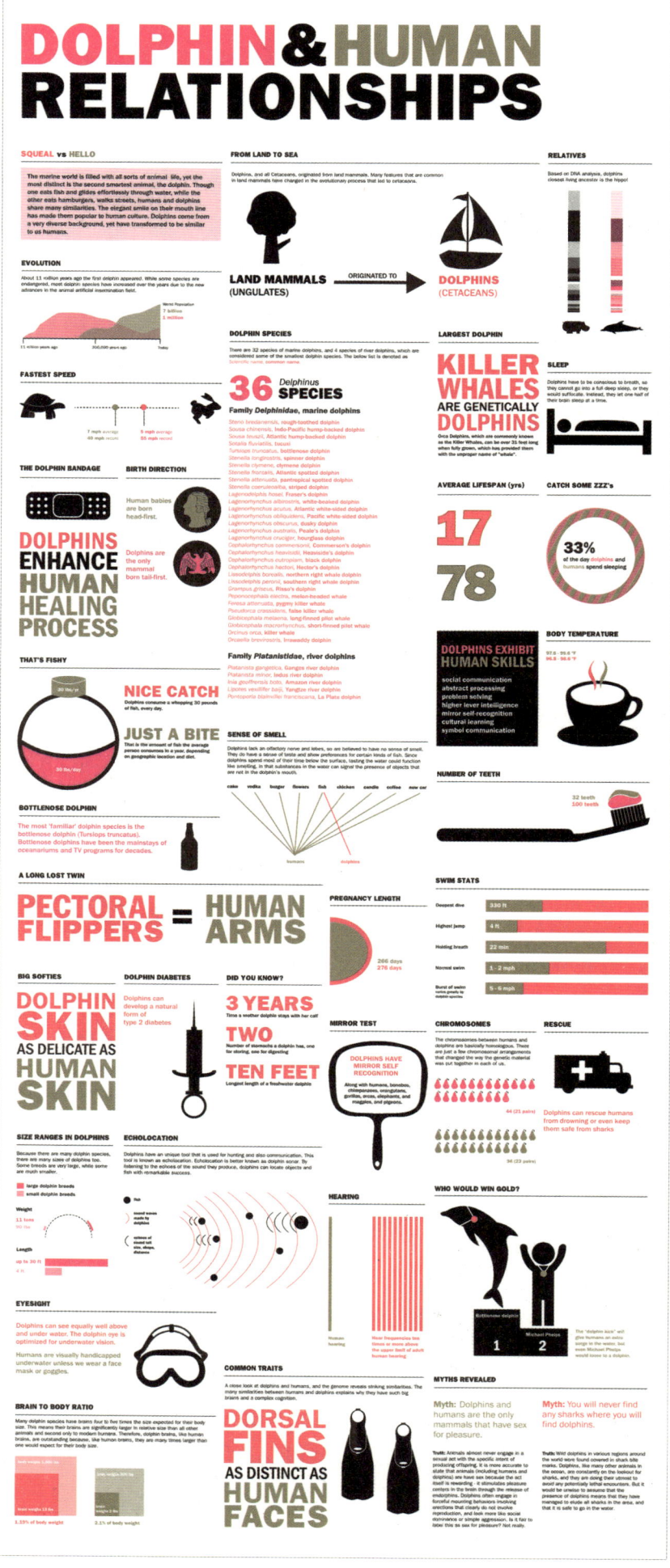

DOG & HUMAN RELATIONSHIPS

RUFF vs HELLO

Why do humans and dogs have such a close bond? Why do so many people find such comfort and happiness from their dogs? Dogs became associated with early humans thousands of years ago and have formed exceptionally close relationships. Numerous people feel a strong emotional connection to dogs and have evolved a predisposession for a close symbiotic relationship with dogs. The unique relationship between these two species is the result of our hunting and gathering past. You can thank your ancestors for your pet Fido.

DOG BREEDS

The term dog breed is used to refer to natural breeds or landrance, which arose through time in response to a particular environment that included humans, with little or no selective breeding by humans.

151 Canis lupus familiaris **BREEDS**

EVOLUTION

About 12,000 years ago, dogs were first domesticated. Dogs provided early humans with a guard animal, source of food, and fur. Humans greatly outnumber dogs.

World Population
7 billion
400 million

220,000 years ago — 12,000 years ago — Today

DOGS CAME FROM THE WOLF

BREED SIZE
- small
- medium
- large

BREED GROUP
- herding
- sporting
- working
- hound
- non-sporting
- terrier
- toy

LIVING ENVIRONMENT
1. Good for active families. Especially for active and social people.
2. Play well with intactive families and singles, especially seniors. Gentle for apartments, and quiet alone. Independent.
3. Great for families with small children. Very social and always there for you.
4. Take slight caution, can be overpowering or sometimes ferocious. Often extremely loyal.

BRAIN POWER

DOG INTELLIGENCE = 2 YEAR OLD CHILD

MATURITY
The average time (in years) it takes to reach maturity.
- small
- medium
- large

OBESITY
Overweight dogs are the norm in America these days. If this doesn't surprise you, you'll be equally unmoved to learn that canine obesity closely mirrors human obesity. And like humans, overweight dogs assume health risk factors ranging from diabetes to coronary dysfunction, not to mention a lifespan shortened by an average of 1.8 years.

U.S. POPULATION
IN THE U.S. THERE ARE
78.2 MILLION DOGS

DNA SEQUENCING
Dog nose prints are as unique as human fingerprints, both are used to identify one another.

BREED DIFFERENCES
There are greater difference between great danes and pugs than weasels and walrus.

weasel — walrus
great dane — pug

MOST LOVED
LABS FAVORITE BREED
in United States, Canada, and United Kingdom

UNDERSTAND THE SAME LANGUAGE
RUFF!
sit, stay, shake, speak, come, up, down, potty, good, bad, back, no, out, get it, drop it, leave, lay down, roll over, dad, mom

A PART OF THE FAMILY
- 34% go on family vacation
- 23% have signatures included in greeting cards
- 62% get gifts from their owners during Christmas
- 10% are in a photo in their owners wallet
- 50% of dalmations are deaf in one or both ears
- 26% get birthday presents
- 27% are in the family photo
- 36% watch television

TRUE LOVE
16% of owners buy a vehicle based on the convenience of their dog in mind

37% of owners have a picture of their dog displayed in their home

CHROMOSOMES
78 (39 pairs)
46 (23 pairs)

HEALTH BENEFIT
DOGS LOWER BLOOD PRESSURE

GOOD EARS
1/600 SECONDS The time it takes a dog to locate the source of a sound
ONE MILLISECOND The time it takes a human to locate the source of a sound

DOGS IN THE HOUSEHOLD
39% of households have at least one dog
- 12% of those households have three or more dogs
- 28% of those households have two dogs
- 60% of those households have one dog

VISION
MYTH
DOGS ARE COLOR BLIND
They can actually see in color, just not as vividly as humans. It is similar to our vision at dusk.

BREED SIZE
SMALLEST Chihuahua
LARGEST Irish Wolfhound

BONE ANATOMY
AROUND **320** Depending on the claw and tail
206 Bones in the human body

[list of bones]

FASTEST SPEED
7 mph average / 9 mph average
40 mph max / 42 mph max

AVERAGE LIFESPAN (yrs)
12
78

EYESIGHT
Based on the placement of eyes, there are different visual fields, measured by facing forward.
250 degrees
200 degrees

PREGNANCY LENGTH
266 days
63 days

HEART RATE (bpm)
- 60 - 100 large dog breeds
- 100 - 140 small dog breeds
- 60 - 80 humans

BODY TEMPERATURE
97.6 - 99.6 °F
101 - 102.2 °F

HEALTH
SEROTONIN rises in humans from playing with a dog

SIX MILLION Number of dogs that are diagnosed with cancer each year

DR. FIDO Dogs can smell cancer, predict seizures, and even small blood sugar fluctuations

MOST COMMON DOG NAMES
MAX
Marley, Bella, Buddy, Molly, Rocky, Bailey, Maggie, Jake, Daisy, Charlie, Sophie, Jack, Sadie, Toby, Chloe, Cody, Buster, Lola, Duke, Zoe, Cooper, Abby, Riley, Ginger, Harley, Roxy, Bear, Gracie, Tucker, Coco, Murphy, Sasha, Lucky, Lily, Oliver, Angel, Sam, Princess, Oscar, Emma, Teddy, Annie, Winston, Rosie, Sammy, Ruby, Rusty, Lady, Sparky

WORD ORIGIN
BITCH FEMALE DOG

The origin of the term is Middle English "bicche", which derived from Old English "bicce".

The true definition of the word "bitch" was a female dog, or more generally a female canine (female wolf, female coyote). The word "dog" actually defined the male of the canine species.

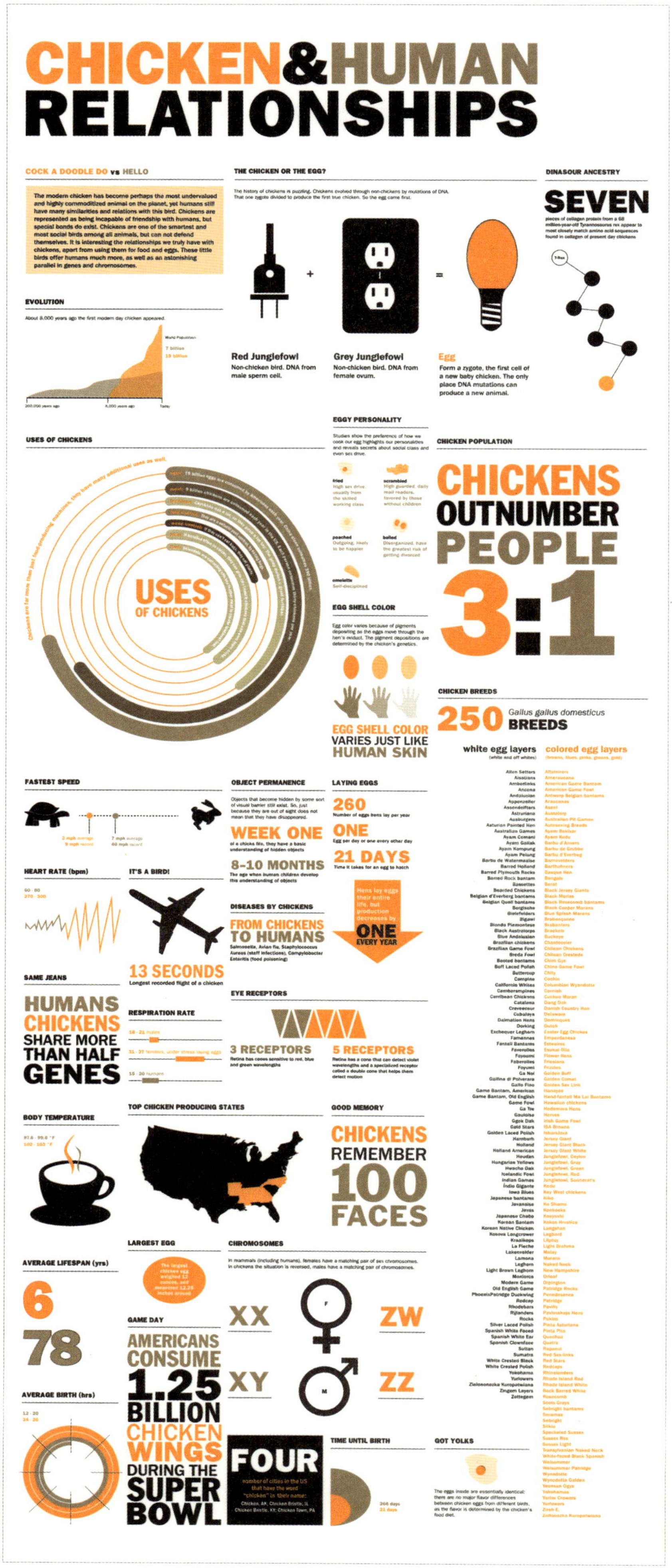

CHICKEN & HUMAN RELATIONSHIPS

COCK A DOODLE DO vs **HELLO**

The modern chicken has become perhaps the most undervalued and highly commoditized animal on the planet, yet humans still have many similarities and relations with this bird. Chickens are represented as being incapable of friendship with humans, but special bonds do exist. Chickens are one of the smartest and most social birds among all animals, but can not defend themselves. It is interesting the relationships we truly have with chickens, apart from using them for food and eggs. These little birds offer humans much more, as well as an astonishing parallel in genes and chromosomes.

THE CHICKEN OR THE EGG?

The history of chickens is puzzling. Chickens evolved through non-chickens by mutations of DNA. That one zygote divided to produce the first true chicken. So the egg came first.

DINOSAUR ANCESTRY

SEVEN pieces of collagen protein from a 68 million-year-old Tyrannosaurus rex appear to most closely match amino acid sequences found in collagen of present day chickens

EVOLUTION

About 8,000 years ago the first modern day chicken appeared.

Red Junglefowl — Non-chicken bird. DNA from male sperm cell.

Grey Junglefowl — Non-chicken bird. DNA from female ovum.

Egg — Form a zygote, the first cell of a new baby chicken. The only place DNA mutations can produce a new animal.

USES OF CHICKENS

EGGY PERSONALITY

Studies show the preferences of how we cook our egg highlights our personalities and reveals secrets about social class and even sex drive.

- **fried** — High sex drive, usually from the skilled working class
- **scrambled** — High guarded, daily meal readers, favored by those without children
- **poached** — Outgoing, feels to be happier
- **boiled** — Disorganized, have the greatest rate of getting divorced
- **omelette** — Self-disciplined

CHICKEN POPULATION

CHICKENS OUTNUMBER PEOPLE 3:1

EGG SHELL COLOR

Egg color varies because of pigments depositing as the eggs move through the hen's oviduct. The pigment depositions are determined by the chicken's genetics.

EGG SHELL COLOR VARIES JUST LIKE HUMAN SKIN

CHICKEN BREEDS

250 BREEDS *Gallus gallus domesticus*

white egg layers (white and off-whites)
colored egg layers (browns, blues, pinks, greens, gold)

Altem Setters, Altsteirer, Ambelisha, Ancona, American Game Bantam, American Game Fowl, Antwerp Belgian bantams, Appenzeller, Araucana, Ascel, Assendeiftsers, Asturiana, Australorp, Australian Pit Game, Auszuigens, Ayam Bekisar, Ayam Cemani, Ayam Kedu, Barbu d'Anvers, Ayam Kampung, Barbu de Grubbe, Ayam Pelung, Barbu d'Everberg, Barbu de Watermaal, Barnevelder, Barred Holland, Barred Plymouth Rocks, Basque Hen, Bassette, Bergai, Beared Chickens, Black Jersey Giants, Belgian d'Everberg bantams, Black Marble, Belgian Quail bantams, Black Rosecomb bantams, Bergische, Black Sedan Roosters, Bielefelders, Blue Spanish Moroms, Zigavi, Boblesquenne, Blondo Piemontese, Bodjurnos, Black Australorps, Boxtails, Blue Andalusian, Brabancone, Brazilian chickens, Brazilian Game Fowl, Chilean Chickens, Breda Fowl, Chilean Dresdels, Booted bantams, Chin-Eye, Buff Laced Polish, Chims Game Fowl, Buttercup, Chitu, Campine, Coshin, California Whites, Columbian Wyandotte, Cambourgnoise, Concroli, Cantbean Chickens, Coucou Maran, Catalena, Dong Dos, Crevecoeur, Danish Country Hen, Cubalaya, Delaware, Dalmatian Hens, Derbygogosh, Dorking, Dutch, Eschequer Leghorn, Faster Egg Chicken, Famenas, Empondoroos, Faraoni Bantams, Estonian, Favenelles, Faroese Fin, Fayoumi, Filipino, Feneudiles, Finsnes, Foyum, Golden Buff, Gaillina di Polverara, Golden Comet, Gallo Fino, Hamburg, Game Bantam, American, Hard-feathered Ma Lai Bantams, Game Bantam, Old English, Hawaiian chickens, Game Fowl, Hedbennes Hens, Ga Tre, Horse, Guulaka, Holk Game Fowl, Ggos Dok, ISA Brown, Gold Stars, Islandanal, Golden Laced Polish, Jersey Gol, Hamborth, Jersey Giant Black, Holland, Jersey Giant White, Holland American, Jungielfowl, Ceylon, Houdan, Jungielfowl, Grey, Hungarian Yellows, Jungielfowl, Green, Hwacho Oak, Jungielfowl, Red, Icelandic Fowl, Jungielfowl, Sonnerat's, Indian Games, Kadz, Iowa Blues, An Ghamo, Japanese bantams, Kankasha, Javanaise, Kaycuchi, Jess, Kukoa bustuka, Japanese Chabo, Langshan, Korean Bantam, Langshan, Korean Native Chicken, Lappas Godana, Kosove Longcomeas, Lophant, Kraakepel, Lapano, La Fleche, Light Sussex, Lakenfelder, Maby, Lamona, Marans, Leghorn, Naked Neck, Light Brown Leghorn, New Hampshire, Mozotena, Orloff, Modern Game, Orpington, Old English Game, Patridge Rocks, Phoenix/Partridge Dukwing, Penedesenca, Redcap, Partridge, Rhodebars, Pavily, Rijlanders, Pashonaga Hera, Rocks, Poslins, Silver Laced Polish, Poncil, Spanish White Faced, Red Ser-bira, Spanish White Ear, Red Stars, Spanish Clorenfian, Redcap, Sultan, Rapanui, Sumatra, Rhode Island Red, White Crested Black, Rhode Island White, White Crested Polish, Rock Barred White, Yokohama, Rosecomb, Yuricowers, Seabright bantams, Zielonorozka Kuropatwiczna, Sasenez, Zingem Layers, Seebright, Zottengem, Serpert Longish, Shamo, Speckled Sussex, Sussex Rio, Sultan, Transylvanian Naked Neck, White Faced Black Spanish, Wyandotte, Wyandotte, Golden, Yokohama, Wyandotte, Silver, Yurikawers, Zach II, Zielonorozka Kuropatwiczna

FASTEST SPEED

2 mph average / 9 mph record (tortoise)
7 mph average / 45 mph record (rabbit)

OBJECT PERMANENCE

Objects that become hidden by some sort of visual barrier still exist. So, just because they are out of sight does not mean that they have disappeared.

8-10 MONTHS — The age when human children develop this understanding of objects.

LAYING EGGS

260 — Number of eggs hens lay per year
ONE — Egg per day or one every other day
21 DAYS — Time it takes for an egg to hatch

Hens lay eggs their entire life, but production decreases by **ONE EVERY YEAR**

HEART RATE (bpm)

60 - 80
275 - 300

IT'S A BIRD!

13 SECONDS — Longest recorded flight of a chicken

DISEASES BY CHICKENS

FROM CHICKENS TO HUMANS

Salmonella, Avian flu, Staphylococcus Aureus (staff infections), Campylobacter Enteritis (food poisoning)

EYE RECEPTORS

3 RECEPTORS — Retina has cones sensitive to red, blue and green wavelengths

5 RECEPTORS — Retina has a cone that can detect violet wavelengths and a specialized receptor called a double cone that helps them detect motion

SAME JEANS

HUMANS CHICKENS SHARE MORE THAN HALF GENES

RESPIRATION RATE

18 - 21 males
31 - 37 females, under stress laying eggs
13 - 20 humans

BODY TEMPERATURE

97.6 - 99.6 °F
105 - 107 °F

TOP CHICKEN PRODUCING STATES

GOOD MEMORY

CHICKENS REMEMBER 100 FACES

LARGEST EGG

The largest chicken egg weighed 12 ounces, and measured 12.25 inches around

CHROMOSOMES

In mammals (including humans), females have a matching pair of sex chromosomes. In chickens the situation is reversed, males have a matching pair of chromosomes.

XX ♀ ZW
XY ♂ ZZ

AVERAGE LIFESPAN (yrs)

6
78

AVERAGE BIRTH (hrs)

12 - 20
24 - 36

GAME DAY

AMERICANS CONSUME 1.25 BILLION CHICKEN WINGS DURING THE SUPER BOWL

TIME UNTIL BIRTH

FOUR — number of cities in the US that have the word "chicken" in their name: Chicken, AK; Chicken Bristle, IL; Chicken Bristle, KY; Chicken Town, PA

GOT YOLKS?

The eggs inside are essentially identical; there are no major flavor differences between chicken eggs from different birds, as the flavor is determined by the chicken's food diet.

200 days
21 days

PIGEON & HUMAN RELATIONSHIPS

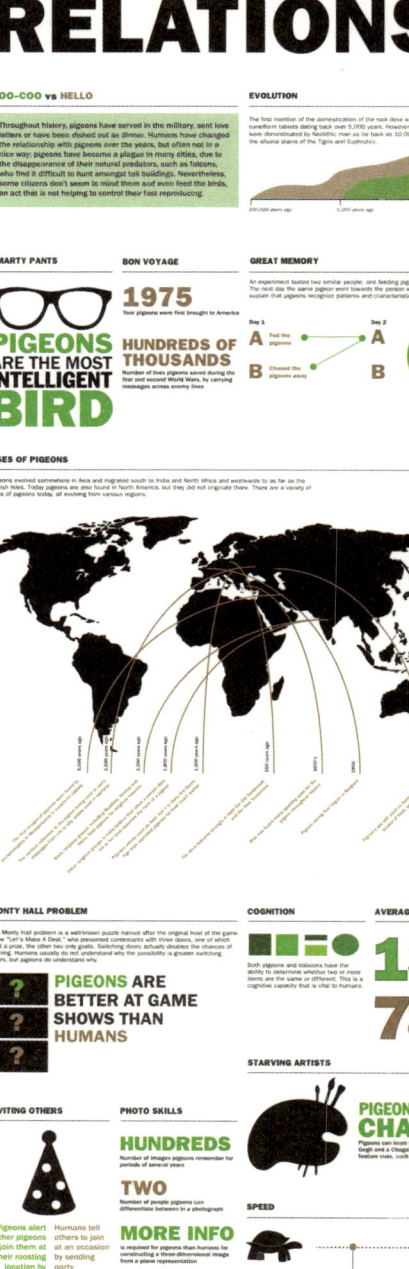

COO-COO vs **HELLO**

Throughout history, pigeons have served in the military, sent love letters or have been dished out as dinner. Humans have changed the relationship with pigeons over the years, but often not in a nice way; pigeons have become a plague in many cities, due to the disappearance of their natural predators, such as falcons, who find it difficult to hunt amongst tall buildings. Nevertheless, some citizens don't seem to mind them and even feed the birds, an act that is not helping to control their fast reproducing.

EVOLUTION

The first mention of the domestication of the rock dove was found in Mesopotamian cuneiform tablets dating back over 5,000 years. However, it is likely that rock doves were domesticated by Neolithic man as far back as 10,000 years ago in the alluvial plains of the Tigris and Euphrates.

SMARTY PANTS

PIGEONS ARE THE MOST INTELLIGENT BIRD

BON VOYAGE

1975 — Year pigeons were first brought to America

HUNDREDS OF THOUSANDS — Number of lives pigeons saved during the first and second World Wars, by carrying messages across enemy lines

GREAT MEMORY

An experiment tested two similar pigeons, one feeding pigeons, one chasing. The next day the same pigeon went towards the person who fed them. This explain that pigeons recognize patterns and characteristics of a person's face.

Day 1: A Fed the pigeons / B Chased the pigeons away
Day 2: A / B

USES OF PIGEONS

Pigeons evolved somewhere in Asia and migrated south to India and North Africa and westwards to as far as the British Isles. Today pigeons are also found in North America, but they did not originate there. There are a variety of uses of pigeons today, all evolving from various regions.

MONTY HALL PROBLEM

The Monty Hall problem is a well-known puzzle named after the original host of the game show "Let's Make A Deal." A contestant is presented with three doors, one of which held a prize. The other two only goats. Switching doors actually doubles the chances of winning. Humans usually do not understand why the possibility is greater switching doors, but pigeons do understand why.

PIGEONS ARE BETTER AT GAME SHOWS THAN HUMANS

COGNITION

Both pigeons and baboons have the ability to determine whether two or more items are the same or different. This is a cognitive capacity that is vital to humans.

AVERAGE LIFESPAN

13
78

STARVING ARTISTS

PIGEONS PREFER CHAGALL — Pigeons can learn to distinguish between Gogh and a Chagall paintings, based on feature cues, such as color and patterns.

INVITING OTHERS

Pigeons alert other pigeons to join them at their roosting location by using actions and noises.

Humans tell others to join at an occasion by sending party invitations

PHOTO SKILLS

HUNDREDS — Number of images pigeons remember for periods of several years

TWO — Number of people pigeons can differentiate between in a photograph

MORE INFO

is required for pigeons than humans for constructing a three-dimensional image from a plane representation

SPEED

7 mph average / 40 mph record (tortoise)
40 mph average / 92.5 mph record (pigeon)

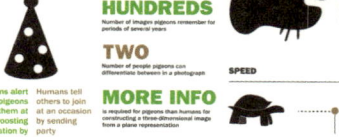

GOOD EYESIGHT

Ultraviolet, a part of the spectrum that humans cannot see. This explains why pigeons have far-better eyesight than humans.

AVERAGE POOP PER YEAR

How much poop does the average human and pigeon poop in one year? A whole lot!

= 10 pounds
25 pounds

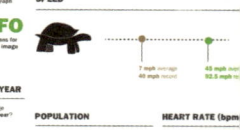

POPULATION

THERE ARE ROUGHLY ONE MILLION PIGEONS NYC

HEART RATE (bpm)

60 - 80
600
Beat their wings up to 10 times per second, and fly up to 16 hours without stopping

HUMAN DISEASES

Three human diseases are known to be associated with pigeon droppings:
histoplasmosis
cryptococcosis
psittacosis

TIME UNTIL BIRTH

9 months
18 days incubated by both parents

GOT MILK?

Both pigeon parents produce "crop milk", which is made by a sloughing of fluid cells from the lining of the crop and regurgitated to the young.

MIRROR TEST

PIGEONS HAVE MIRROR SELF RECOGNITION (but only after extensive behavioral conditioning)

FUN FACTS

1. Pigeons can recognize all 26 letters of the English language
2. Pigeons are the only bird that do not have to lift their head to swallow water
3. They are bred, raised and trained as good as Thoroughbred Horses

EGGS

TWO — Number of pigeon eggs in each clutch, pigeon eggs are white

EIGHT — Number of clutches pigeons can produce each year under optimal conditions

10 DAYS — after mating, a pigeon will lay the eggs, which are incubated for 18 days by both parents

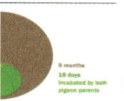

DIET

PIGEONS RELY ON HUMANS FOR FOOD AND SOME PLANTS

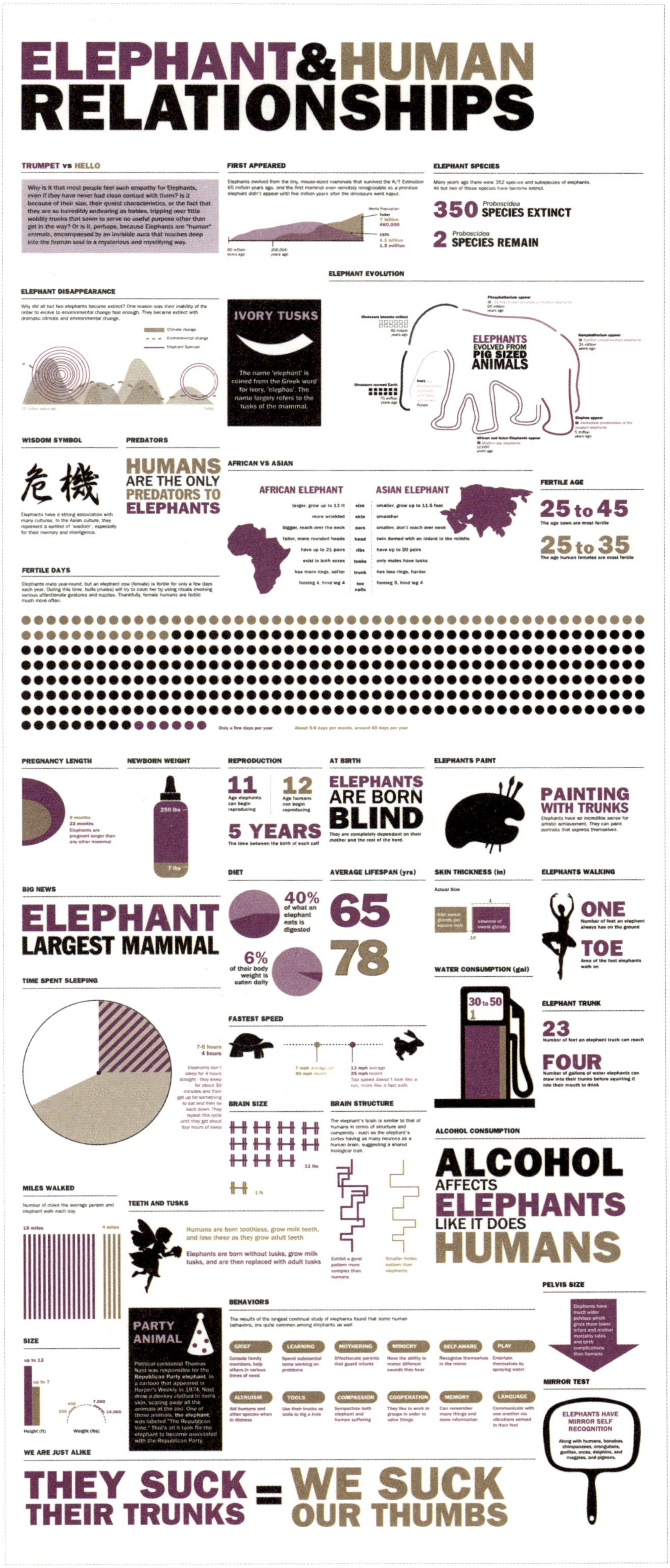

ELEPHANT & HUMAN RELATIONSHIPS

TRUMPET vs HELLO

Why is it that most people feel such empathy for Elephants, even if they have never had close contact with them? Is it because of their size, their coyest characteristics, or the fact that they are so incredibly endearing as babies, tripping over little wobbly trunks that seem to serve no useful purpose other than get in the way? Or is it, perhaps, because Elephants are "human" animals, encompassed by an invisible aura that reaches deep into the human soul in a mysterious and mystifying way.

FIRST APPEARED

Elephants evolved from the tiny, mouse-sized mammals that survived the K/T Extinction 65 million years ago, and the first mammal even remotely recognizable as a primitive elephant didn't appear until five million years after the dinosaurs went kaput.

ELEPHANT SPECIES

Many years ago there were 352 species and subspecies of elephants. All but two of these species have become extinct.

350 Proboscidea SPECIES EXTINCT

2 Proboscidea SPECIES REMAIN

ELEPHANT DISAPPEARANCE

Why did all but two elephants become extinct? One reason was their inability of the order to evolve to environmental change fast enough. They became extinct with dramatic climate and environmental change.

- Climate change
- Environmental change
- Elephant Species

IVORY TUSKS

The name 'elephant' is coined from the Greek word for ivory, 'elephas'. The name largely refers to the tusks of the mammal.

ELEPHANT EVOLUTION

ELEPHANTS EVOLVED FROM PIG SIZED ANIMALS

WISDOM SYMBOL

危機

Elephants have a strong association with many cultures. In the Asian culture, they represent a symbol of 'wisdom', especially for their memory and intelligence.

PREDATORS

HUMANS ARE THE ONLY PREDATORS TO ELEPHANTS

AFRICAN VS ASIAN

	AFRICAN ELEPHANT		ASIAN ELEPHANT
larger, grow up to 13 ft		size	smaller, grow up to 11.5 feet
more wrinkled		skin	smoother
bigger, reach over the neck		ears	smaller, don't reach over neck
fatter, more rounded heads		head	twin domed with an indent in the middle
have up to 21 pairs		ribs	have up to 20 pairs
exist in both sexes		tusks	only males have tusks
has more rings, softer		trunk	has less rings, harder
foreleg 4, hind leg 4		toe nails	foreleg 5, hind leg 4

FERTILE AGE

25 to 45 The age cows are most fertile

25 to 35 The age human females are most fertile

FERTILE DAYS

Elephants mate year-round, but an elephant cow (female) is fertile for only a few days each year. During this time, bulls (males) will try to court her by using rituals involving various affectionate gestures and nuzzles. Thankfully, female humans are fertile much more often.

Only a few days per year   About 5-6 days per month, around 66 days per year

PREGNANCY LENGTH

9 months   22 months. Elephants are pregnant longer than any other mammal

NEWBORN WEIGHT

250 lbs   7 lbs

REPRODUCTION

11 Age elephants can begin reproducing

12 Age humans can begin reproducing

5 YEARS The time between the birth of each calf

AT BIRTH

ELEPHANTS ARE BORN BLIND They are completely dependant on their mother and the rest of the herd.

ELEPHANTS PAINT

PAINTING WITH TRUNKS Elephants have an incredible sense for artistic achievement. They can paint portraits that express themselves.

BIG NEWS

ELEPHANT LARGEST MAMMAL

DIET

40% of what an elephant eats is digested

6% of their body weight is eaten daily

AVERAGE LIFESPAN (yrs)

65
78

SKIN THICKNESS (in)

Actual Size

ELEPHANTS WALKING

ONE Number of feet an elephant always has on the ground

TOE Area of the foot elephants walk on

TIME SPENT SLEEPING

FASTEST SPEED

7-8 hours   4 hours

7 mph average cut   13 mph average
40 mph recent   25 mph recent
Elephants don't sleep for 4 hours straight - they sleep for about 30 minutes and then get up for something to eat and then lie back down. They repeat this cycle until they get about four hours of sleep   Top speed doesn't look like a run, more like a fast walk

WATER CONSUMPTION (gal)

30 to 50

ELEPHANT TRUNK

23 Number of feet an elephant trunk can reach

FOUR Number of gallons of water elephants can draw into their trunks before squirting it into their mouth to drink

BRAIN SIZE

H H H H H
H H H H H
H

13 lb
1 lb

BRAIN STRUCTURE

The elephant's brain is similar to that of humans in terms of structure and complexity - such as the elephant's cortex having as many neurons as a human brain, suggesting a shared biological trait.

Exhibit a gyral pattern more complex than humans   Smaller, familiar system than elephants

ALCOHOL CONSUMPTION

ALCOHOL AFFECTS ELEPHANTS LIKE IT DOES HUMANS

MILES WALKED

Number of miles the average person and elephant walk each day.

15 miles   4 miles

TEETH AND TUSKS

Humans are born toothless, grow milk teeth, and lose these as they grow adult teeth

Elephants are born without tusks, grow milk tusks, and are then replaced with adult tusks

PARTY ANIMAL

Political cartoonist Thomas Nast was responsible for the Republican Party elephant, in a cartoon that appeared in Harper's Weekly in 1874. Nast drew a donkey clothed in lion's skin, scaring away all the animals at the zoo. One of those animals, the elephant, was labeled "The Republican Vote." That's all it took for the elephant to become associated with the Republican Party.

PELVIS SIZE

Elephants have much wider pelvises which gives them lower infant and maternal mortality rates, and birth complications than humans

BEHAVIORS

The results of the longest continual study of elephants found that some human behaviors, are quite common among elephants as well.

GRIEF	LEARNING	MOTHERING	MIMICRY	SELF-AWARE	PLAY
Console family members, help others in various times of need	Spend substantial time working on problems	Affectionate parents that guard infants	Have the ability to mimic different sounds they hear	Recognize themselves in the mirror	Entertain themselves by spraying water

ALTRUISM	TOOLS	COMPASSION	COOPERATION	MEMORY	LANGUAGE
Aid humans and other species when in distress	Use their trunks as tools to dig a hole	Sympathize both elephant and human suffering	They like to work in groups in order to solve things	Can remember many things and store information	Communicate with one another via vibrations sensed in their feet

MIRROR TEST

ELEPHANTS HAVE MIRROR SELF RECOGNITION

Along with humans, bonobos, chimpanzees, orangutans, gorillas, orcas, dolphins, and magpies, and pigeons.

WE ARE JUST ALIKE

THEY SUCK THEIR TRUNKS = WE SUCK OUR THUMBS

Spanish Emigration Flow

Project Description /

This infographic aims to deconstruct and represent emigration from Spain between 2008 and 2013. The designer used four variables to visualize the total number of emigrations: time, quantity, destination, and social group. The graphic is a timeline that is fragmented by year, measuring the volume of people leaving Spain for specific parts of the world. This enables the reader to identify the type and extent of emigration at any specific time according to destination. The people outflow is divided into two groups: nationals (Spanish born), represented in yellow; and internationals (non-Spanish born), represented in red.

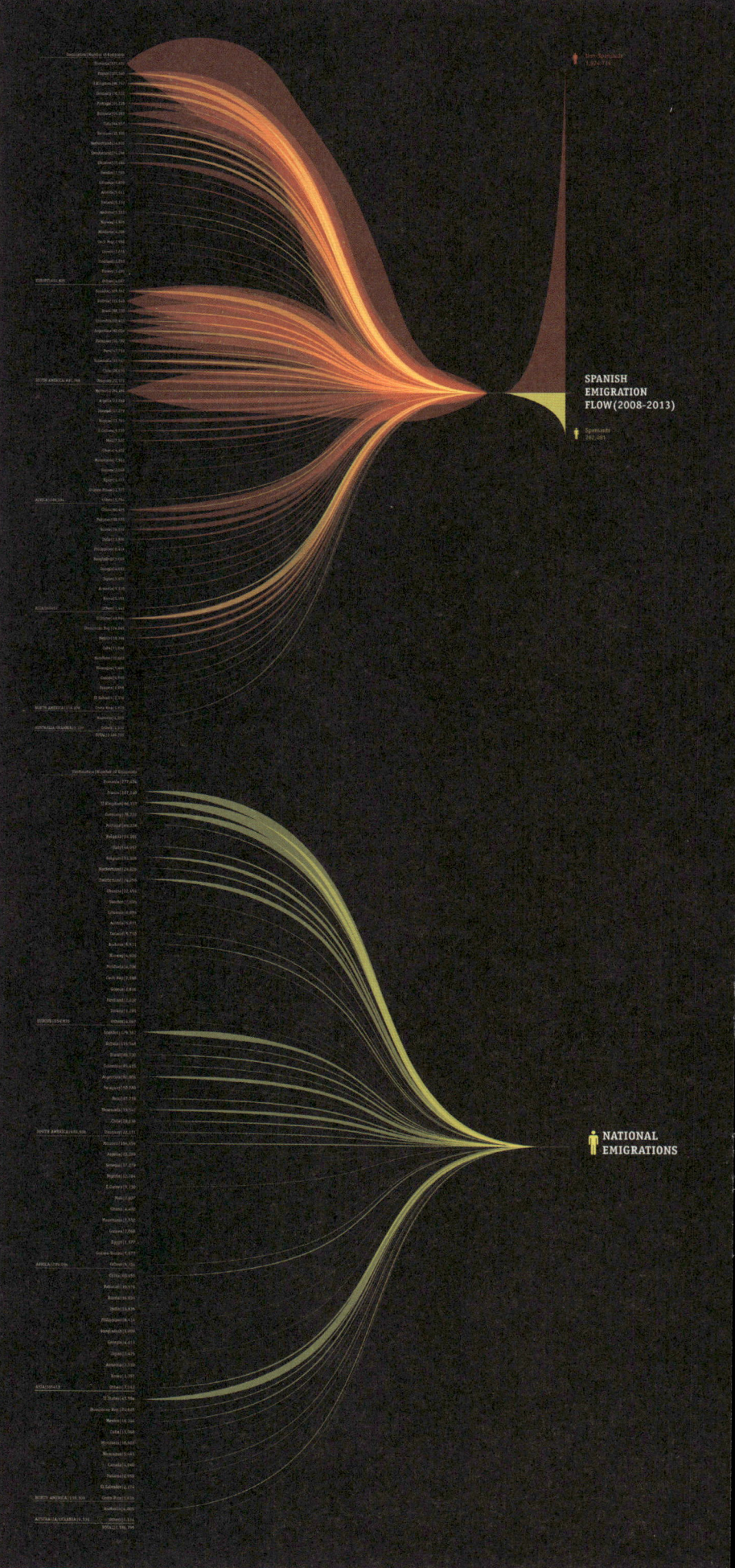

Designer / Rafael Cordoba
Completion / 2014

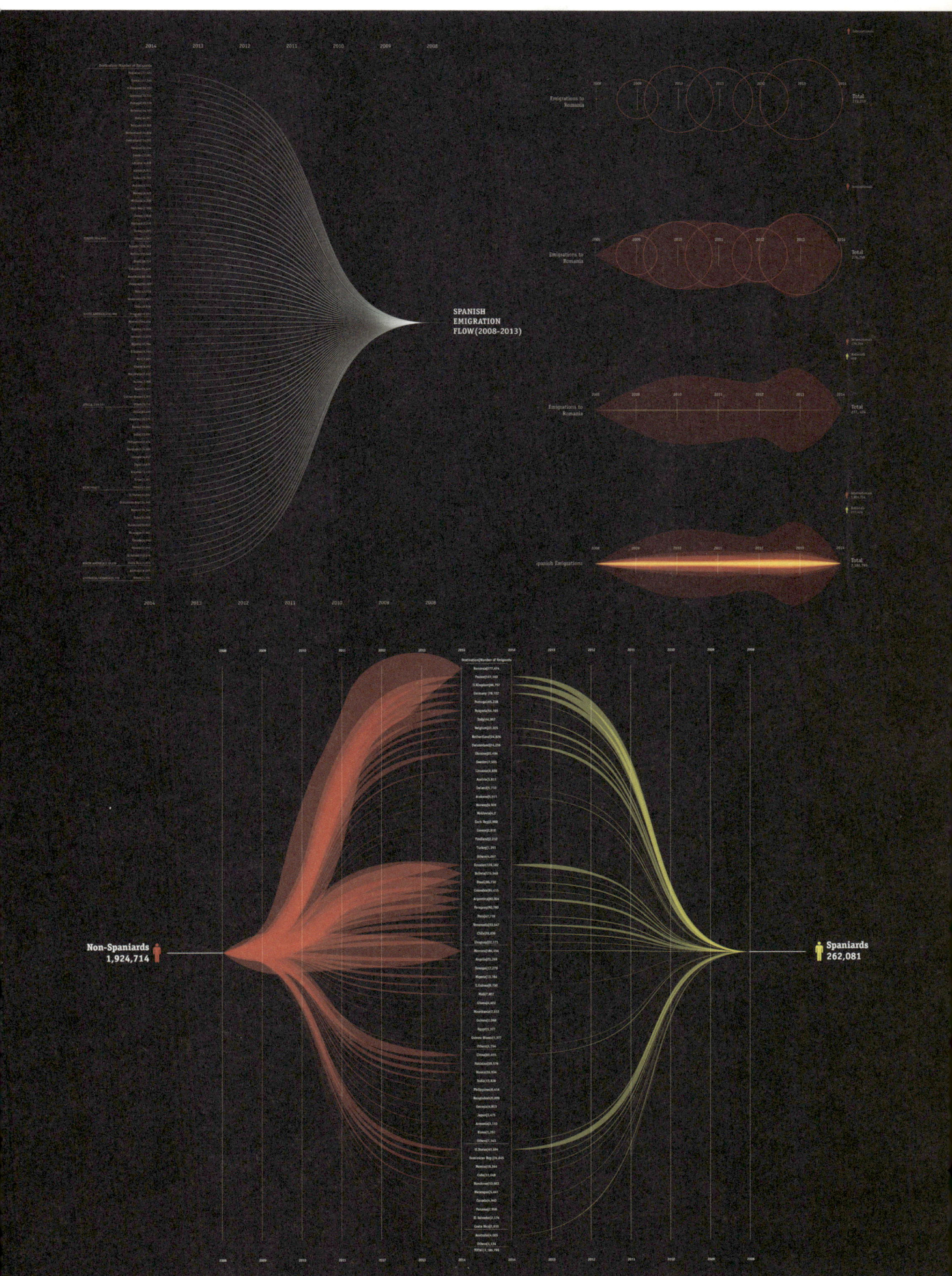

208	209	210

Are You Ready to Retire?

Project Description /
 Illustrating a global survey that shows that Indians are the most well-prepared for their retirement, this graphic uses simple line drawings and watercolors to achieve an informal look.

Client / *Economic Times Wealth*

Did You Lie on Your Resume?

Project Description /
 The tough job market is forcing many employees to fudge their job applications—for example, by hiding or exaggerating details of employment. This project illustrates a survey conducted by global consultancy firm Hill & Associates.

Client / *Economic Times Wealth*

The Latex Thing

Project Description /
 The condom was vaulted into the spotlight recently when Bill Gates put out a call for inventors to come up with a next generation model that 'enhances pleasure' and promotes 'regular use'. In this graphic, the *Times of India's Crest Edition* examined how the world regards the condom.

Client / *Times of India (The Crest Edition)*

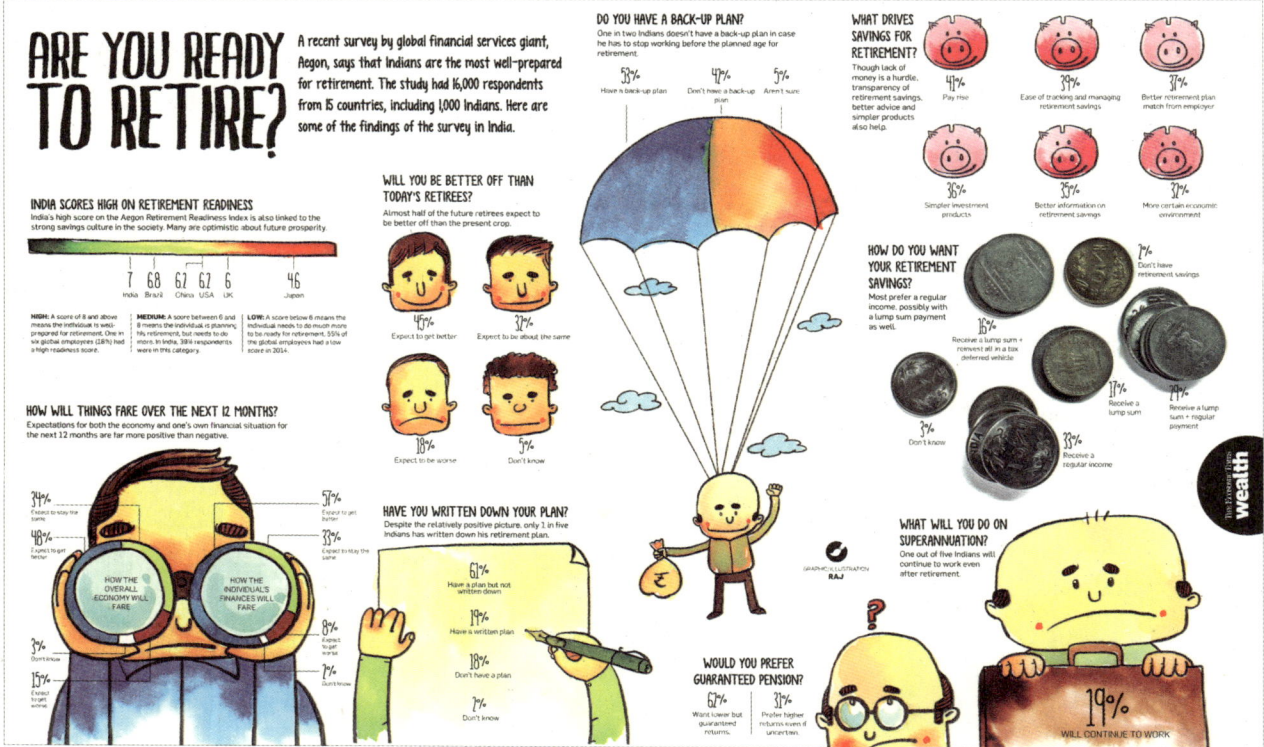

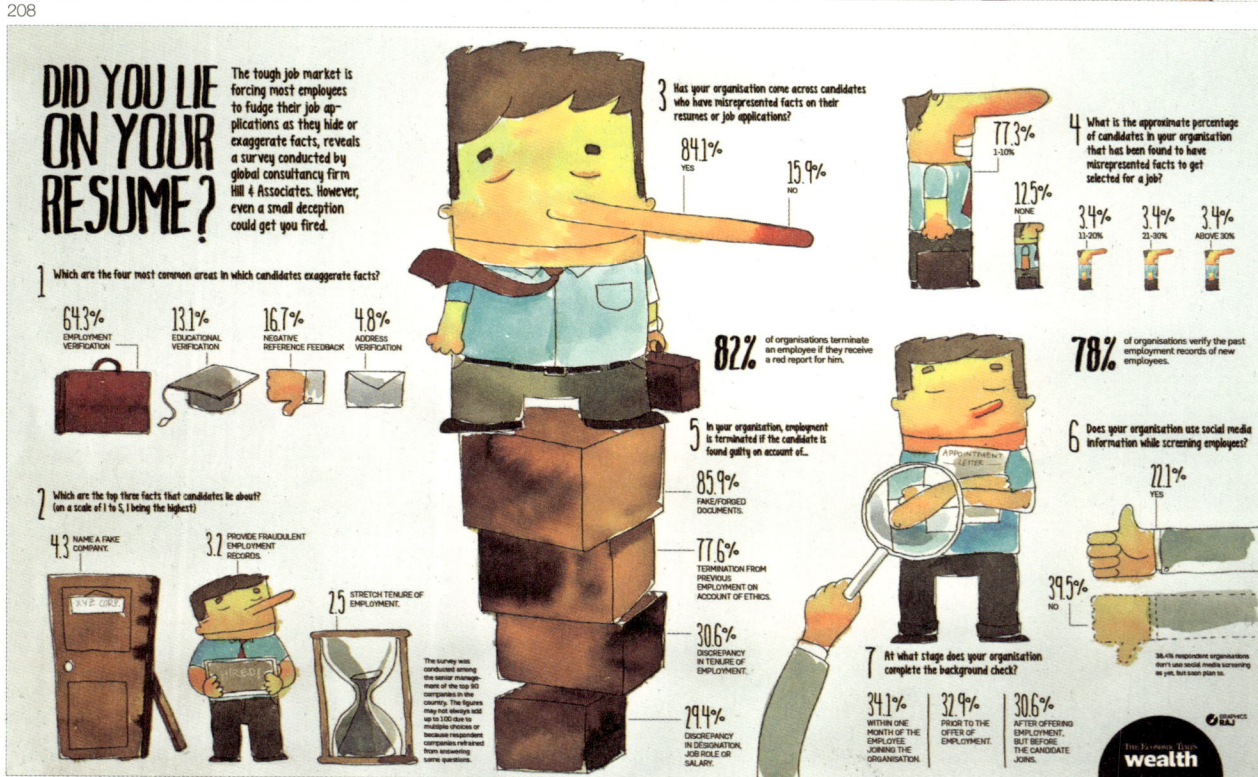

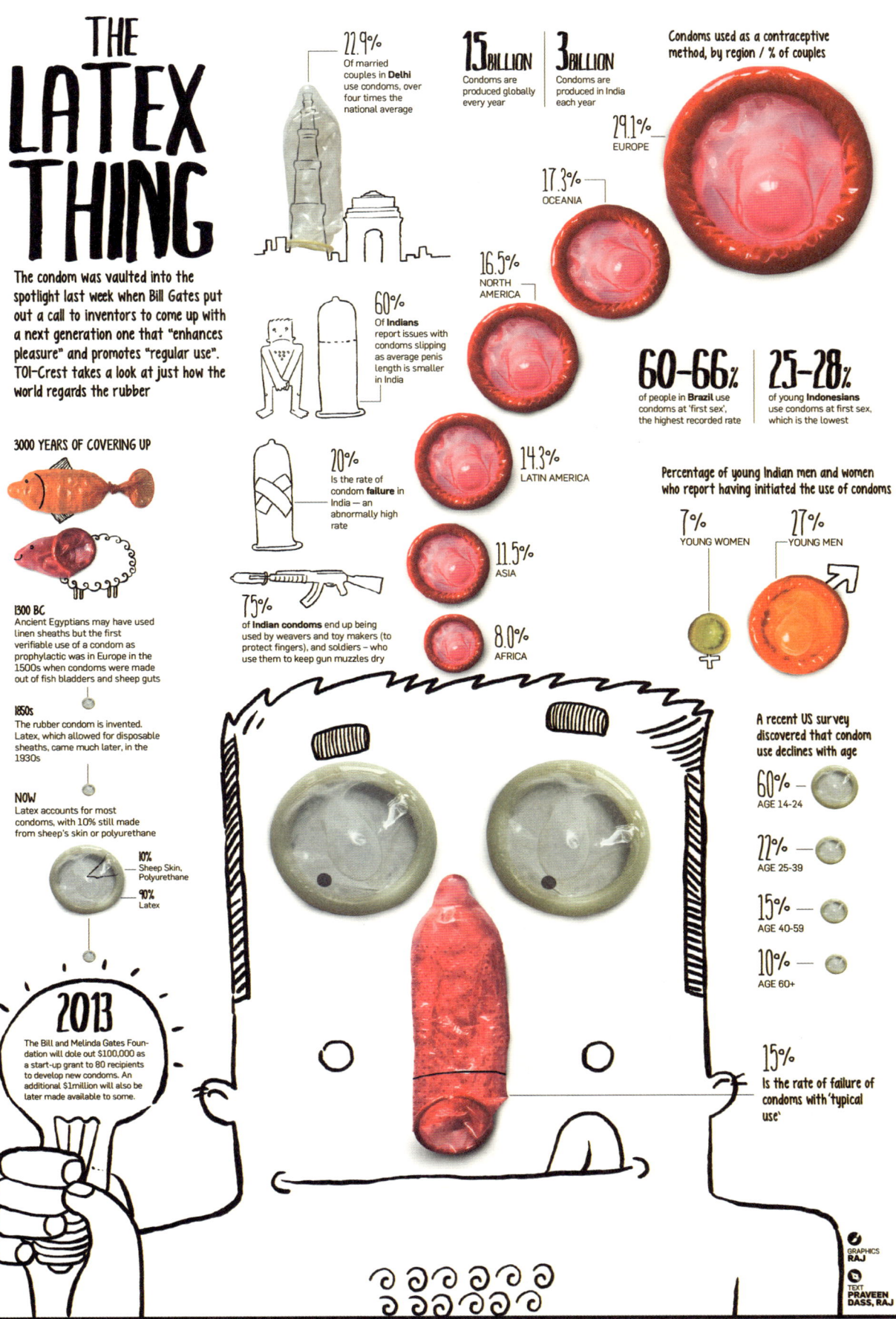

How to Make A CV

Project Description /
This project shows how to make an interesting and impressive CV —essential to landing a good job, especially for people who work in visual industries such as infographics and photography.

212

Happiness and Bliss

Project Description /
This simple Venn diagram illustrates the project's theme by combining images of breasts, with the overlapping section representing a vagina. The designer just uses simple breast pictures to express the theme of the work, which is intended to catch the reader's eye and make them understand it easily.

213

Luchi

Project Description /
This pie chart graphic shows a deep-fried flatbread made of wheat flour called *luchi*, a typical cuisine of Bengal. The designer makes use of the actual food picture instead of the graph to let the simple work much more vivid and attractive.

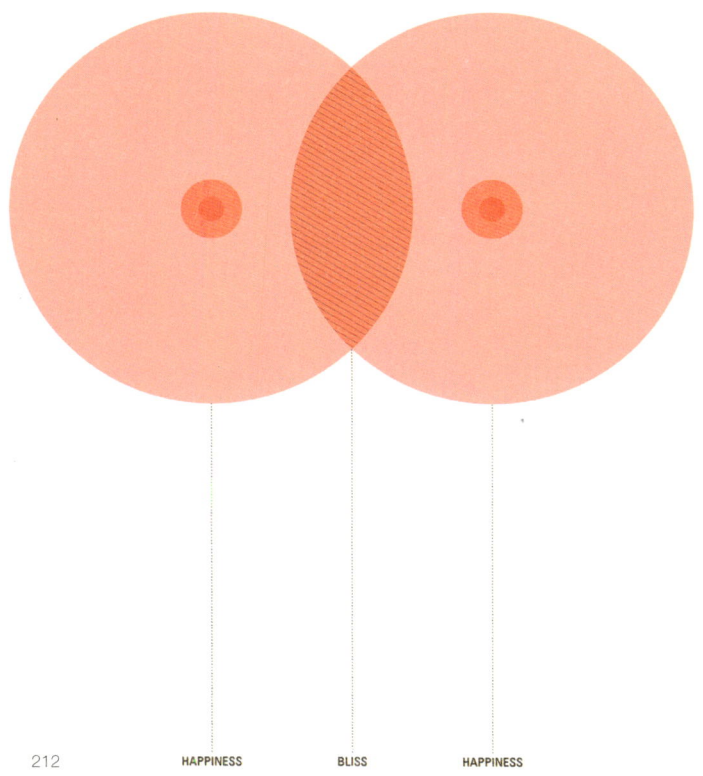

HAPPINESS   BLISS   HAPPINESS

214

Men Like It Best

Project Description /
This graphic illustrates the results of a survey about men's preferences regarding their partner's pubic hair. Not many designers could think of using pubic hair to express this theme directly. Although the graph looks very simple, it explains the content comprehensively.

215

Malaria

Project Description /
This infographic depicts the impact of malaria, an infectious disease characterized by cycles of chills, fever, and sweating, caused by a protozoan of the genus Plasmodium in red blood cells, which is transmitted to humans by the bite of an infected female anopheles mosquito.

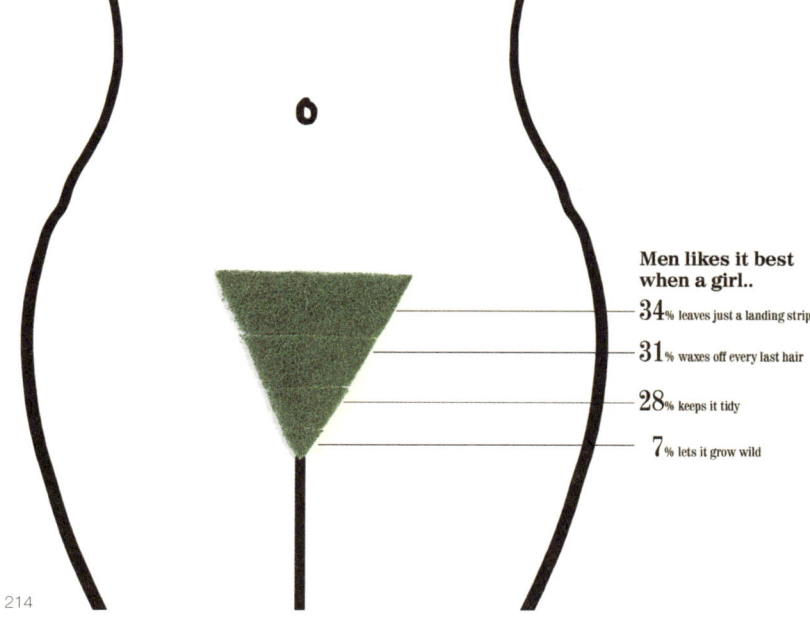

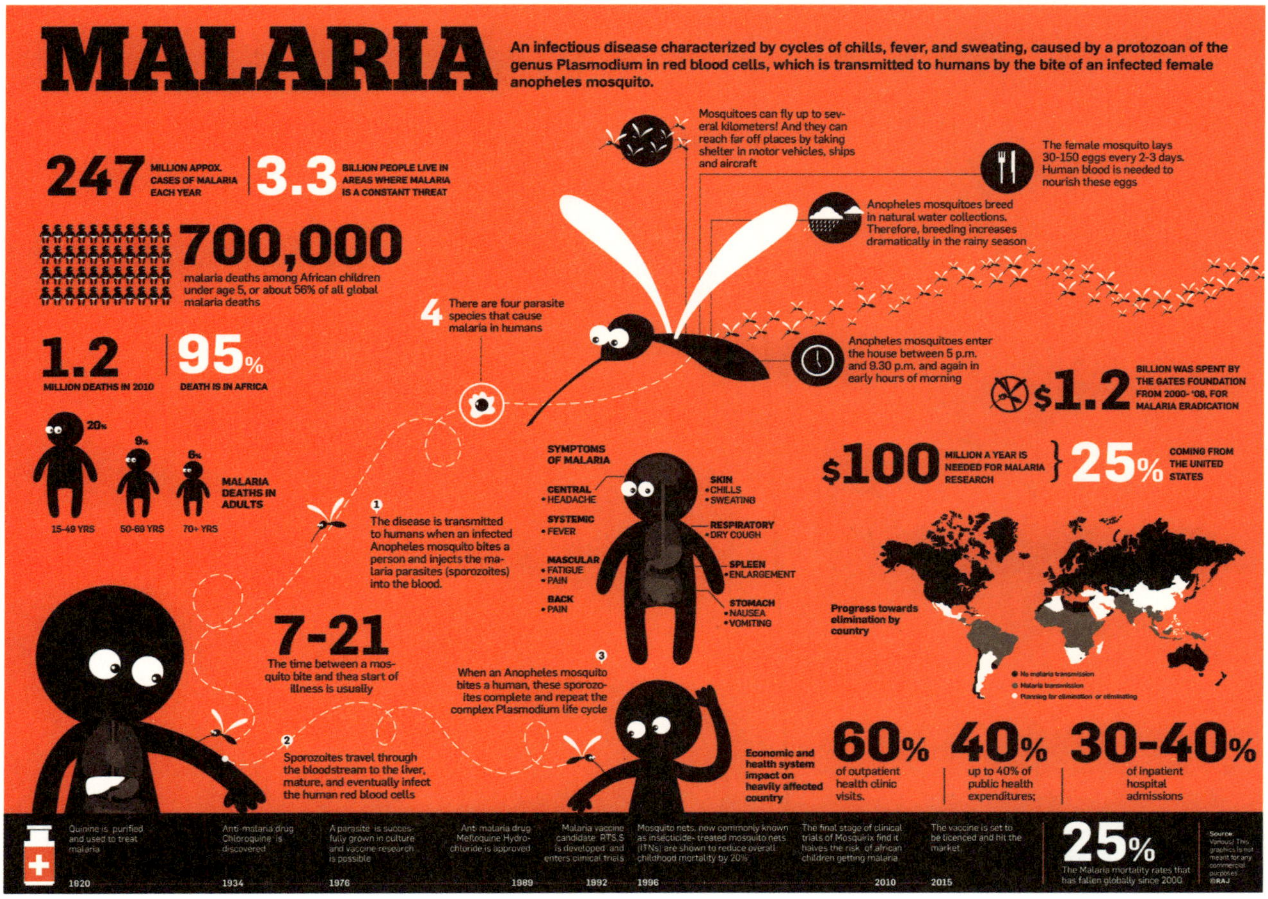

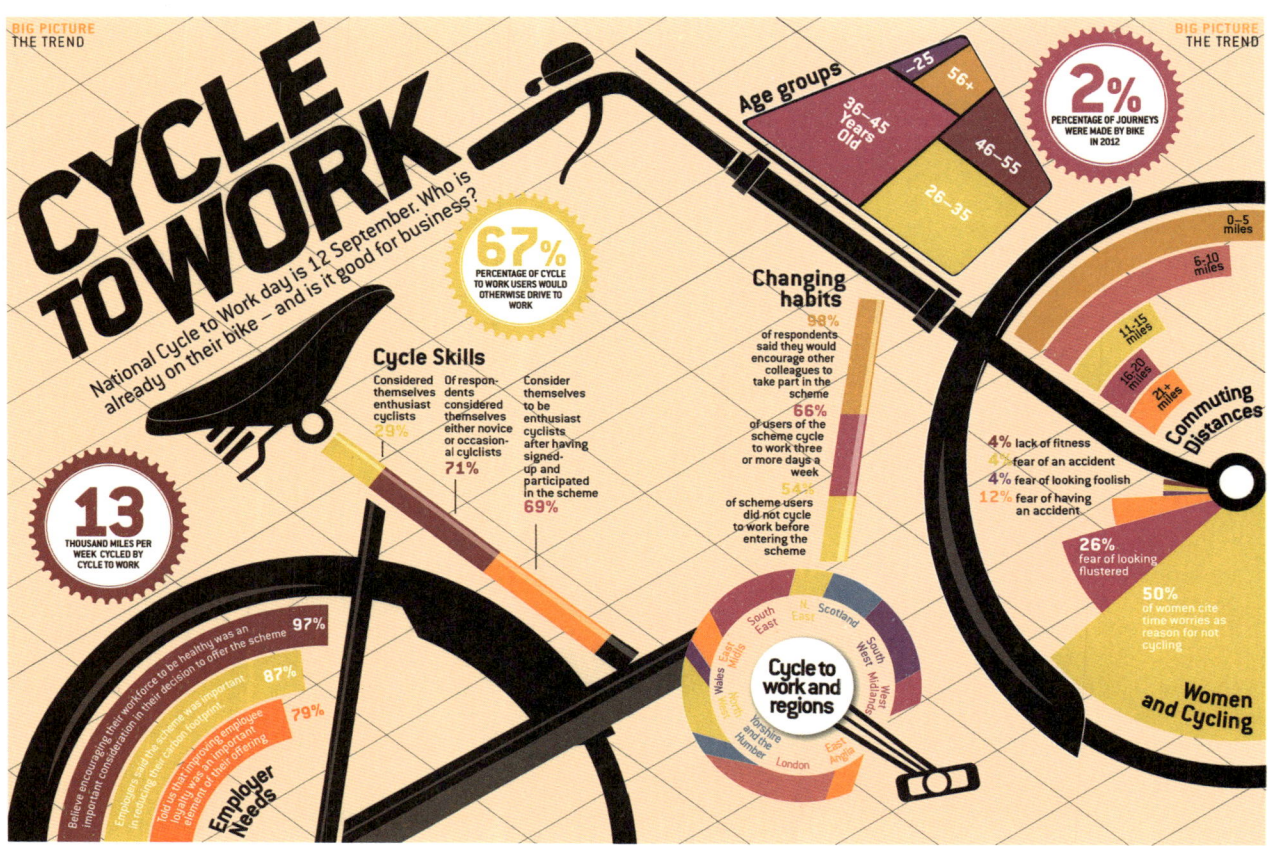

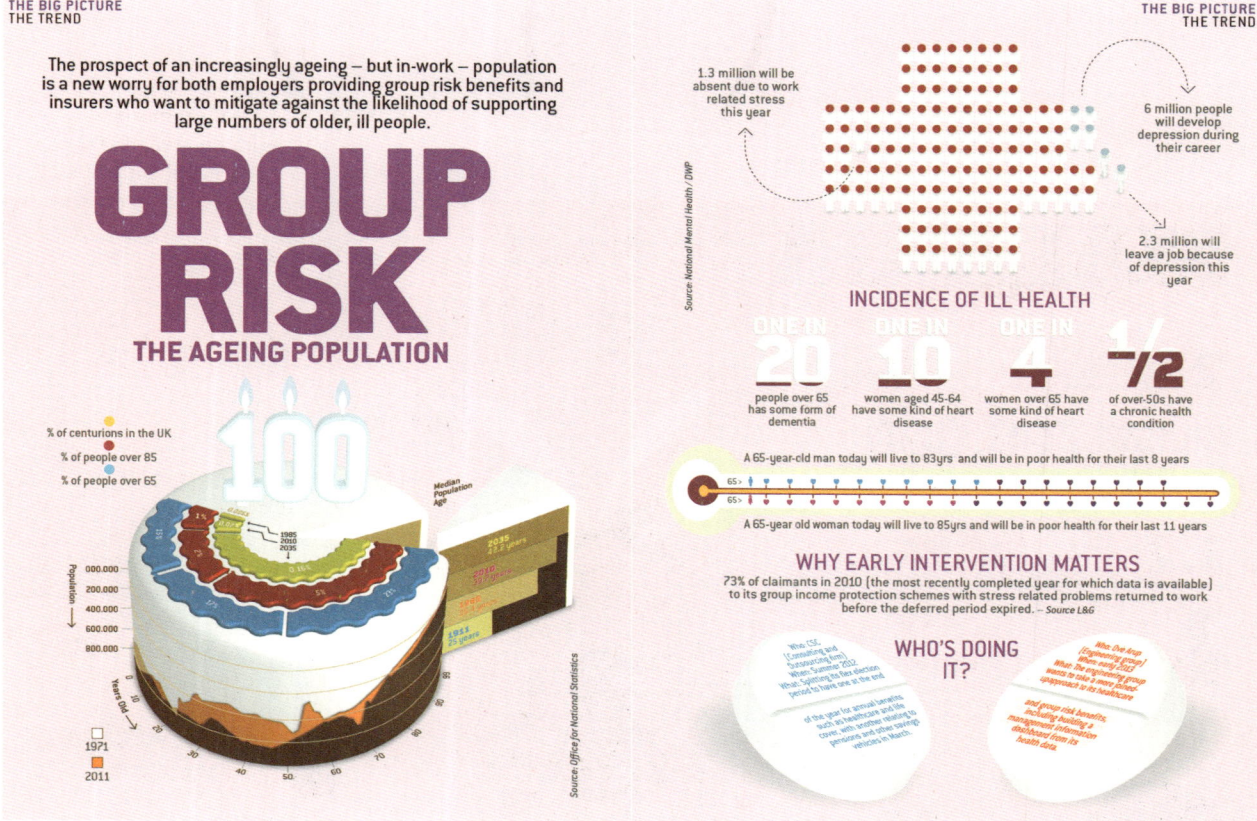

[216 – 218]
Client / *Reward* magazine, Newsquest Specialist Media
Designer / Hugo Camacho
Completion / 2013

216

The Trend—Cycle to Work

Project Description /
This infographic examines the trend of cycling to work in the UK on the occasion of the 'Cycle to Work Day' 2013. It shows the details about how and why people cycle when commuting and why employers should support them by offering cycling incentive schemes as part of their benefits package.

217

The Trend

Project Description /

The prospect of an increasingly ageing workforce is a new worry for both employers providing group risk benefits and for insurers who want to mitigate against the likelihood of supporting large numbers of older and ill people. This infographic illustrates key findings from a research project about an ageing population.

218

The Trend in Financial Sector Workplace Benefits

Project Description /

The infographic shows key findings about workplace benefits and rewards in the financial sector in the UK. Beyond the popular public perception of overpaid bankers, the financial sector is one where more than a million staff still need motivation.

219

Recent Progress with Anti-Cancer Vaccines

Project Description /

This infographic was published in the scientific journal *Oncoimmunology*. It shows the recent promising developments in the area of anti-cancer vaccines, and the benefits combining them with conventional chemotherapy to fight cancer effectively. The initial task was to highlight the benefits of combining therapies, but Andriy Nemchenko always tries to provide context for any infographic he designs. Here, he has analyzed several different forms of cancer, and how bad they are (number of patients and mortality numbers), compared with investment into research. Additionally, he has listed three of the most common treatments of cancer: surgery, radiotherapy, and chemotherapy, along with anti-cancer vaccines. The last section expands on the anti-cancer vaccines and the state of their development. Finally, the depiction shows the combined effect of the vaccines with the powerful drugs destroying the main villain—cancer.

Client / Taylor & Francis LLC
Designer / Andriy Nemchenko
Completion / 2012

Drinks of Death

Project Description /

Project Description /
This infographic illustrates the connection between alcohol and traffic accidents in Buenos Aires, Argentina. The main objective is to raise awareness of the issue among young people (about 18 to 27 years old), and the secondary objective is to reduce traffic accidents and promote the use of a designated driver. The strategy used in the design was to demonstrate the effects of alcohol on a driver.

Designer / Russel Daniela
Completion / 2013

The Average Resident in Helsingborg

Project Description /
The goal of this project was to illustrate data about residents in Helsingborg, Sweden. The editorial text analyzed the information and the infographic highlighted the regional averages. The designer's idea was to present the numbers as the anatomy of the resident.

Client / Helsingborgs Dagblad
Designer / Erik Nylund

▶ HELSINGBORGAREN I GENOMSNITT
Statistik om stadens befolkning, angivet i procent. **Så stor andel av helsingborgarna...**

Hälsa och livsstil

- röker varje dag. **16**
- mår psykiskt dåligt. **18**
- äter frukt minst fem gånger om dagen. **9**
- joggar minst en gång i månaden. **Tio procent** spelar fotboll. **32**
- känner sig orolig över brottsutvecklingen. **Var femte** tycker det är otäckt att vistas ute sent på kvällarna. **33**
- är feta, det vill säga har en BMI över 30. (BMI, body mass index, är vikten i kg delat med längden i meter i kvadrat.) **12**
- umgås med vänner utanför familjen varje vecka. Men ungefär **en femtedel** av helsingborgarna saknar en nära vän som man kan prata med om allt. **63**
- har varit på semester i Sverige eller utomlands en vecka senaste året. **64**

Kultur

- går på teater minst två gånger om året. **20**
- besöker biblioteket minst fyra gånger om året (bara Lundaborna och Kalmarborna är flitigare besökare). **34**
- har tillgång till dator hemma. **Hälften** av helsingborgarna använder internet dagligen på sin fritid. **80**
- går på bio minst fyra gånger om året. **42**
- läser böcker varje vecka. **76**

Allmänt

- är födda i ett annat land än Sverige. 1990 var andelen **11 procent**. **20**
- är män respektive kvinnor. **49/51**
- studerar. **20**
- är gifta. **34**
- förvärvsarbetar, av dem i arbetsför ålder. **69**
- var arbetslösa i juli 2011. Motsvarande siffra för 1996 är **13 procent**. **8**

Boende

- äger sin bostad. **60**
- bor i bostadsrätt. **20**
- har tillgång till bil. **77**
- bor i hyresrätt. Lika många bor i villa eller radhus. **40**
- är ensam i hushållet, **26 procent**.

Ekonomi

- tjänar mindre än 15 000 kronor i månaden. **15**
- tjänar mer än 50 000 kronor i månaden. **3**
- skulle inte klara av en oväntad utgift på 8 000 kronor utan hjälp eller lån. **17**
- är miljonärer, enligt tre år gammal statistik, vilket motsvarar nästan 22 000 personer. **18**
- bor i hushåll som spenderar mer än 1 000 kronor i veckan på mat. **39**
- spenderar mer än 2 000 kronor om året på välgörenhet. **8**

Övrigt

41 år
Medelåldern.

81 år
Medellivslängden (78,64 år för män och 83,17 för kvinnor).

1,89
Så många barn föder den genomsnittliga Helsingborgskvinnan, vilket är lägre än riksgenomsnittet som ligger på **1,98 barn**.

20 527 kronor
Så hög var den genomsnittliga månadslönen 2009. Bland kvinnorna är medelinkomsten lägre än bland männen: **17 050 kronor** mot **24 300** kronor i månaden. Riksgenomsnittet är **21 008 kronor**.
Som inkomst räknas lön, sjukpenning, föräldrapenning, a-kassa och liknande (men kapitalinkomster ingår inte).

Statistiken gäller den vuxna befolkningen. Uppgifterna om inkomst, medelålder, antal barn per kvinna med mera bygger på folkbokföringsregistrets siffror. Övriga siffror har hämtats ur olika undersökningar där ett urval helsingborgare (minst ett par hundra personer) har tillfrågats om sina vanor. Dessa undersökningar har genomförts av Statistiska centralbyrån, Region Skåne, SOM-institutet, TNS-Sifo, Helsingborgs stad och Yougov på uppdrag av olika myndigheter och företag. Ibland antyder statistiken att helsingborgarna skiljer sig från genomsnittssvensken, men oftast faller skillnaden inom felmarginalen. Riksnittet anges därför enbart om skillnaden är statistiskt säkerställd.

Onlus Bhalobasa

Project Description /
The content of the project is based on the development of various infographics for the Association ONLUS Bhalobasa in Perignano (PI) in Italy. The theme is to express the values and methodology of the work of volunteers and the association by a series of illustrations. The association uses these to make social presentations and publications. The style used is flat design, a very good compromise between aesthetics, functionality, and comprehensibility, as the infographics are targeted mainly at primary school children.

Client / Association ONLUS Bhalobasa
Designer / Valentina Teleschi
Completion / 2015

223

Where Do Designer Dogs Come From?

Project Description /

Morkies, cockapoos, chiweenies… These dog breeds might not have serious names but they're a serious business, as shown in this infographic. Known as 'hybrid' or 'designer' dogs, these canines are bred with a purpose—to optimize the best qualities of each parent breed.

Unlike some mixed breeds, designer dogs are generally born from two purebred parents. Labradoodles, for instance, were first bred from Labradors (which are common guide dogs) and poodles (with a low-shed coat) to be hypoallergenic. Puggles, a cross between a pug and a beagle, usually have the muzzle of a beagle, which can eliminate breathing problems often associated with the short-nosed pug.

Not all hybrids are desirable. Designer-dog critics say genetic experimentations are exacerbating the problem of puppy mills. For instance, when a puggle inherits a short snout from a pug and the hunting instincts from the beagle, it may not have a respiratory system that's equipped to handle all the exercise it needs. These unwanted dogs often end up in shelters.

Despite the controversy, designer breeds have made a mark on the $60 billion pet market by commanding high prices that often exceed their purebred counterparts. And so long as the market continues to demand cavachons, pekeapoos and schnoodles, they are here to stay.

Client / TIME magazine
Designer / Heather Jones
Completion / 2014

224

Horn & Antler Development

Project Description /

This infographic describes the difference between the growth processes of horns and antlers. It focuses on big game animals in North America, and was based on research containing fairly complex information. Even though there are similarities in these animals, there are also great differences, and this infographic focuses on these differences in order to best communicate the fascinating nature of horn and antler growth. The designer wanted to engage the audience in a fun way and still communicate lots of information to people of all ages, especially children. Text was converted into illustrative elements wherever possible, and the written form was only used when necessary and in small snippets.

Designer / Spencer Shores
Completion / 2013

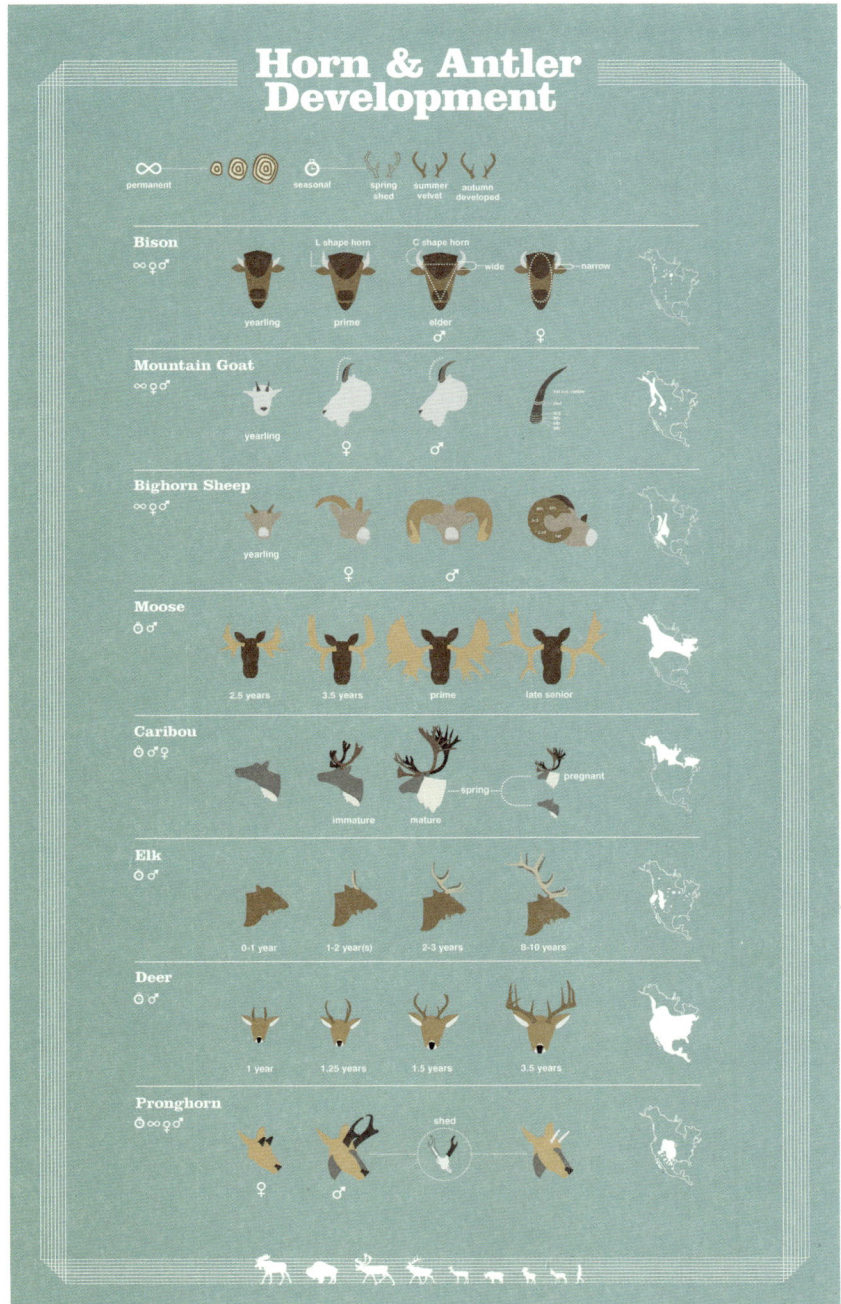

Help, Call Noah

Project Description /

The United Nations declared 2010 to be the year of biodiversity, celebrating biological diversity and its value for life on Earth. With the intention of raising public awareness, this infographic represents a part of the 'red list' of endangered wild species, according to the International Union for the Conservation of Nature. Animals are grouped by continent, and for each one, the infographic identifies its environmental status and the greatest dangers to its survival, with a particular focus on human activities.

Client / *Il Sole 24 Ore*
Designer / Laura Cattaneo

IL GREEN REPORT — ANALISI GRAFICA

TUTTE LE CAUSE DI ESTINZIONE
Gli animali a rischio sono minacciati da vari fattori. Per ognuno abbiamo indicato quali sono

URBANIZZAZIONE – La crescita delle aree cittadine danneggia e frammenta molti habitat.

INQUINAMENTO – Un serio problema per specie marine, anfibi e insetti, sensibili agli agenti chimici.

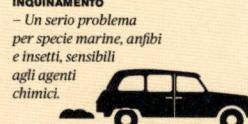

SPECIE ALIENE – L'introduzione artificiale di una specie in un ecosistema può distruggerne gli equilibri.

CAMBIAMENTO CLIMATICO – Investe specie marine sensibili alla temperatura e gli uccelli migratori.

Aiuto, chiamate Noè

Il 2010 è l'anno mondiale della biodiversità. A ricordarci che se scompare una specie, l'intero ecosistema può subire danni irrimediabili: senza api non avremmo frutta, caffè, cotone. La "lista rossa" degli animali a rischio è lunga. Ecco una mappa aggiornata e alcuni casi-simbolo. Ma ve lo immaginate un mondo senza elefanti?

— *di* **Francesco Franchi** *e* **Daniele Lorenzetti** | *illustrazioni di* **Laura Cattaneo**

CHE RICCA LA BARRIERA
Nella mappa, i luoghi in cui la ricchezza di specie viventi (marine e terrestri) è maggiore. Alti livelli di biodiversità si registrano soprattutto nelle foreste equatoriali e lungo la Grande barriera corallina.
● hotspot di biodiversità

COSA SUCCEDERÀ SE CONSERVIAMO...
● gli hotspot protetti ● tutte le foreste tropicali
● tutti gli hotspot

CHI SPARISCE E CHI NASCE
Come da 600 milioni di anni cambiano le famiglie
● origine ● estinzione

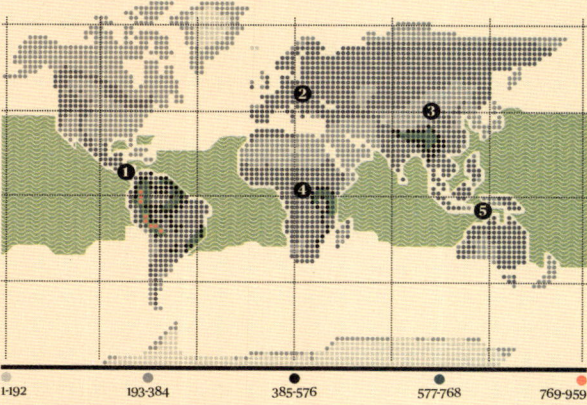

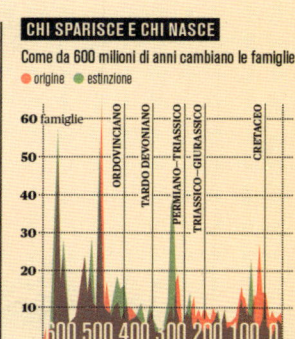

❶ **Americhe** — *Epidemia silenziosa dal polo ai tropici*

Ⓐ LONTRA DI MARE
Enhydra lutris
La riduzione delle popolazioni di lontra marina causa il proliferare di ricci, una delle loro prede principali. Troppi ricci depauperano le riserve di kelp e macroalghe.

Ⓑ ARMADILLO GIGANTE
Priodontes maximus
Un mammifero simbolo dell'ecosistema amazzonico, classificato come *endangered* nella lista rossa Iucn. La caccia indiscriminata e la riduzione degli habitat lo minacciano.

Ⓒ ORSO GRIZZLY
Ursus arctos horribilis
Negli ecosistemi sub-polari come l'Alaska l'orso grizzly è al vertice della catena alimentare. È una "specie ombrello": dalla sua sopravvivenza dipende quella di molte altre.

ATTENZIONE, INSETTI VULNERABILI
L'Iucn (unione mondiale per la conservazione della natura) valuta periodicamente le specie potenzialmente a rischio. Ecco le percentuali di quelle minacciate secondo la Red List del 2008

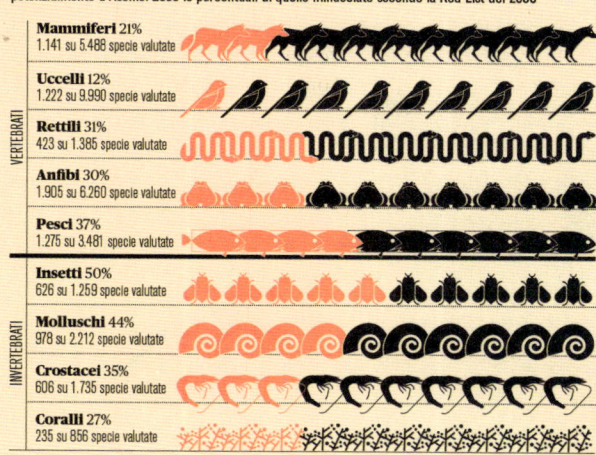

VERTEBRATI
- **Mammiferi** 21% — 1.141 su 5.488 specie valutate
- **Uccelli** 12% — 1.222 su 9.990 specie valutate
- **Rettili** 31% — 423 su 1.385 specie valutate
- **Anfibi** 30% — 1.905 su 6.260 specie valutate
- **Pesci** 37% — 1.275 su 3.481 specie valutate

INVERTEBRATI
- **Insetti** 50% — 626 su 1.259 specie valutate
- **Molluschi** 44% — 978 su 2.212 specie valutate
- **Crostacei** 35% — 606 su 1.735 specie valutate
- **Coralli** 27% — 235 su 856 specie valutate

MEDICINA ALTERNATIVA
– La medicina tradizionale cinese usa ancora parti di animali: soprattutto ossa e corna.

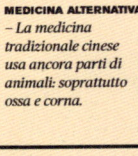

PERDITA HABITAT
– La deforestazione e la riduzione di habitat strangolano la biodiversità.

SVILUPPO AGRICOLO
– L'espansione di aree agricole causa la perdita di foreste e specie indigene.

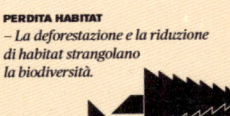

CACCIA E PESCA
– Bracconaggio e traffico illegale di parti di animali sono una piaga globale.

❷ Europa – *Tornano gli ululati, soffrono le rane*

Ⓐ APE
Apis mellifera

Non ancora a rischio, ma in rapido declino: tra le cause l'inquinamento, i pesticidi e le epidemie parassitarie. La loro scomparsa sarebbe un disastro per l'impollinazione, da cui dipende la vita di fiori e frutti.

Ⓑ LUPO ITALICO
Canis lupus italicus

Caso esemplare di successo delle strategie di tutela, il lupo è tornato a popolare gli Appennini e vaste aree europee. Il bracconaggio è stata la prima minaccia per la specie.

Ⓒ PELOBATE FOSCO
Pelobates fuscus insubricus

La sottospecie del pelobate italico, tipica della Pianura padana, soffre come molti altri anfibi la distruzione di habitat umidi e viene predata da specie introdotte artificialmente quali tartarughe e rane toro.

❸ Asia – *Là dove regnavano le tigri*

Ⓐ TIGRE
Panthera tigris

È la specie simbolo della lotta per la biodiversità: ne restano 3mila esemplari adulti. Estinte tre delle nove sottospecie. Il bracconaggio per la medicina tradizionale è una vera piaga.

Ⓑ PANDA GIGANTE
Ailuropoda melanoleuca

La popolazione totale si attesta tra i mille e i duemila individui. È giudicato "in pericolo di estinzione". Le minacce: distruzione dell'habitat e caccia per la preziosa pelle.

Ⓒ ANTILOPE TIBETANA
Pantholops hodgsonii

La popolazione di questa specie che vive sugli altopiani del Tibet si attesta sui 100mila capi. Viene cacciata per la fine lana, lo *shatoosh*. Le corna sono usate nella medicina cinese.

❹ Africa – *Il destino delle specie "carismatiche"*

Ⓐ RINOCERONTE NERO
Diceros bicornis

Fino a metà del XX secolo diffusissimo nelle savane africane, questo mammifero è arrivato sulla soglia dell'estinzione. Il corno viene usato nella medicina tradizionale cinese.

Ⓑ LEONE
Panthera leo

Il suo areale, un tempo esteso all'intera Eurasia, si è ridotto all'Africa subsahariana. L'Iucn lo considera "vulnerabile": la sua riduzione minaccia l'equilibrio dell'ecosistema.

Ⓒ ELEFANTE AFRICANO
Loxodonta africana

Gli esperti ne stimano in natura circa 400mila esemplari rispetto agli 1,3 milioni degli anni 70. Il bracconaggio per commercio di avorio mostra una recrudescenza.

❺ Oceania – *Se cambia la geografia degli atolli*

Ⓐ CORALLI
Scleractinia

L'ordine comprende 26 famiglie. Il degrado della Grande barriera minaccia un intero ecosistema: pesci, molluschi, cavallucci marini. Effetti anche sulla geografia degli atolli.

Ⓑ CASUARIO
Casuarius casuarius

Non solo predatori ma anche erbivori possono essere in pericolo: il casuario è fondamentale perché disperde, attraverso le feci, i semi delle piante di cui si nutre.

Ⓒ DIAVOLO DELLA TASMANIA
Sarcophilus harrisii

Questo marsupiale, un tempo diffuso anche in Australia, vive oggi solo in Tasmania. In pericolo per la caccia e la diffusione del tumore facciale infettivo, è a rischio estinzione.

Hot Air Balloon

Project Description /
Today, we live in an era of technology where we are constantly worried about the next big hi-tech innovation. For this infographic, designer David Santos decided to go back in time and explore a whole new different device, currently undervalued, the hot air balloon. He devised the project mainly because the hot air balloon is a familiar topic many think they know all about, but facts about their operation are still largely unknown.

Designer / David Santos
Completion / 2012

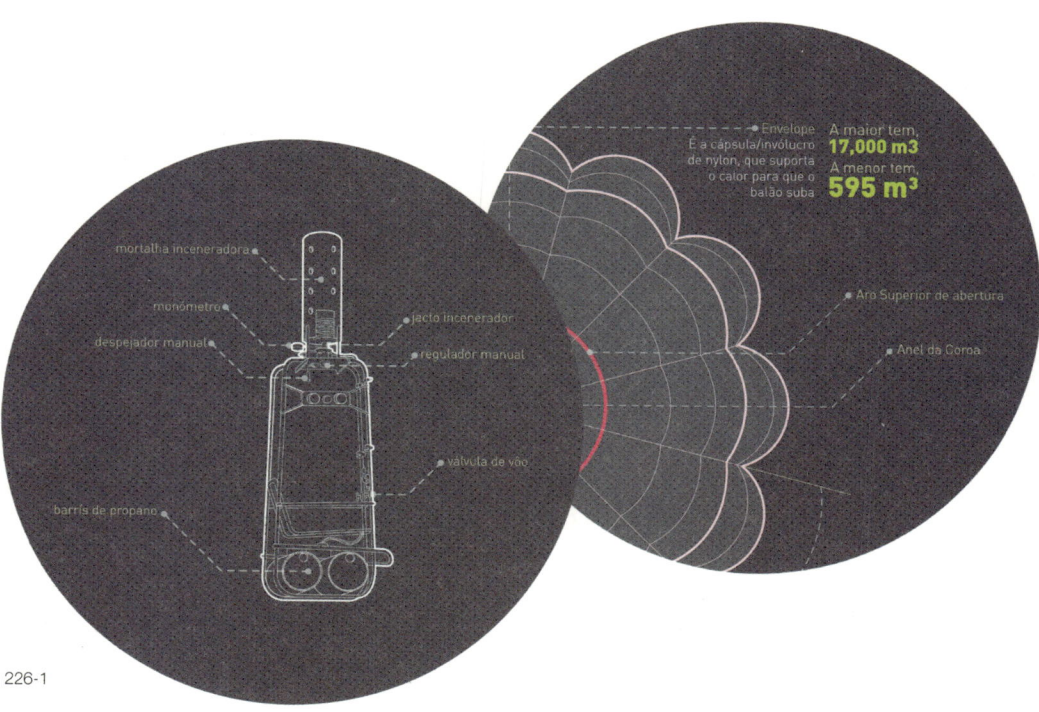

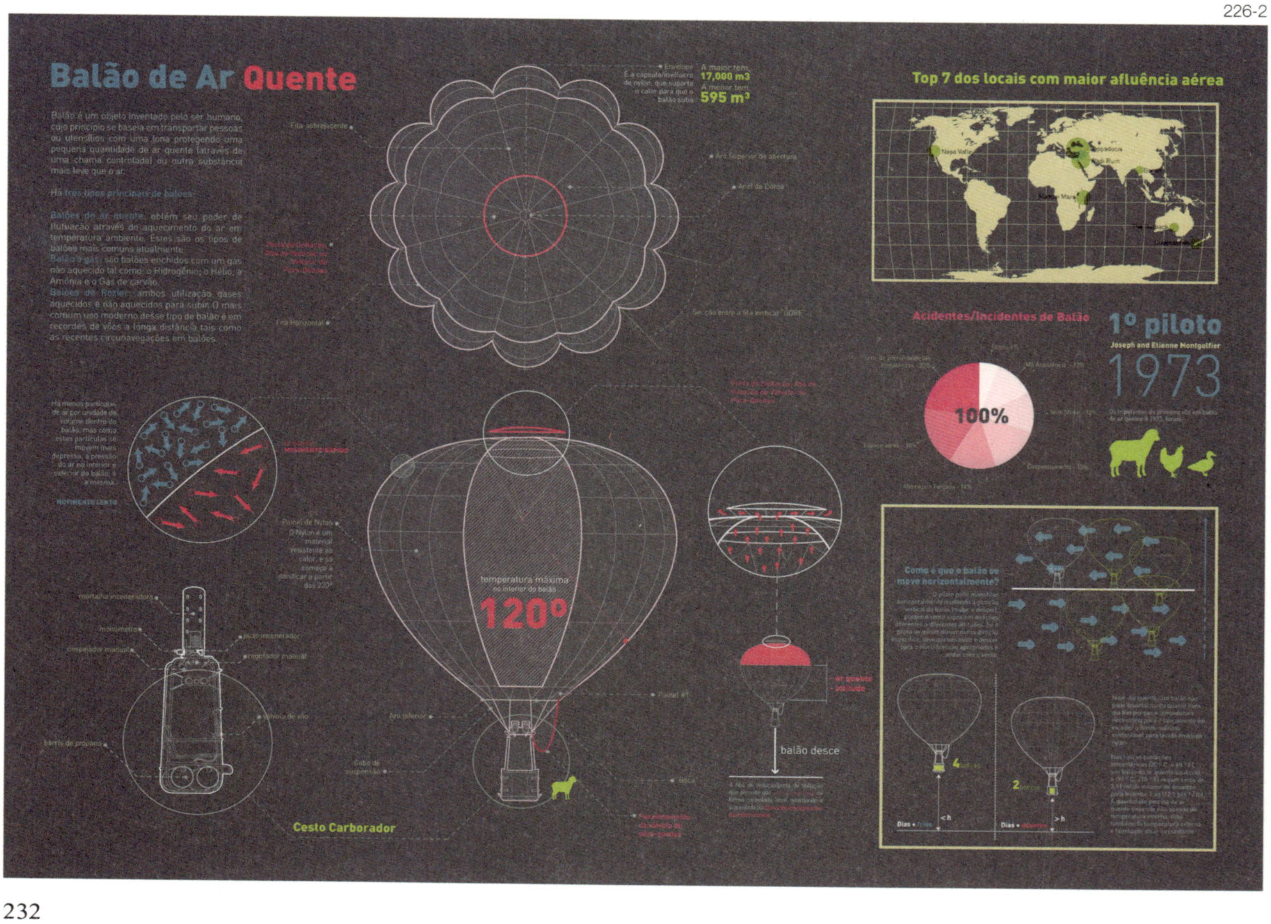

Wars for Water

Project Description /

This infographic was developed with the collaboration of the Foreign Affairs newsroom of the *Corriere Della Sera*. The report was about the state of world conflicts over water as a fundamental resource for future socio-economical development but also as a source of political problems. Since most of the countries have to share river basins, decisions about the water taken by one country (for example, the construction of a dam or effluent put into a river upstream) can directly affect other countries. The infographic in the upper part shows the hottest conflict spots in the world over surface water, as well as the boundaries of the transnational subterranean aquifers. The infographic in the lower part analyzes conflicts of water around the world, identifying the time period, the cause and the geographical area of the conflict.

Design Agency / Corriere Della Sera Infographic newsroom
Designer / Nicolas Vargas
Completion / 2015

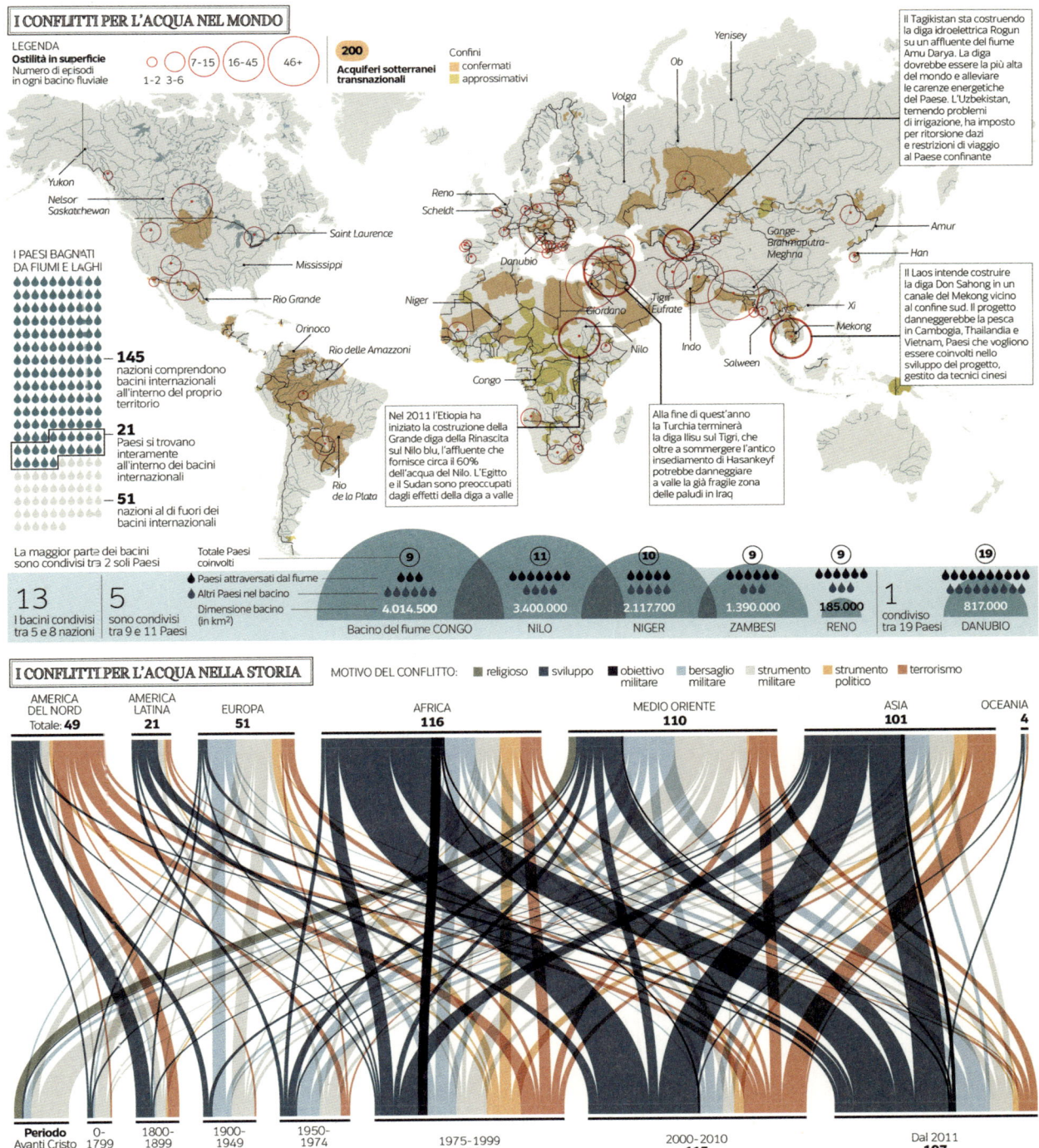

Brief History of the Universe in Thirteen Moments

Project Description /
The infographic about the evolution of the universe was designed for *Público* newspaper for its 25th special anniversary edition, where time and science were the themes. The idea was to touch on the history of the universe in several important steps, trying a more conceptual approach rather than a scientific one. The consistent use of patterns and iconography allowed the designer to explore a less common visual design identity, somewhat different from what we are used to seeing on these subjects. The pattern that she used to represent the big bang was, in fact, based on the image of the cosmic inflation that is known.

Client / *Público*
Designer / Cátia Mendonça
Completion / 2015

The Backyard of the Universe

Project Description /
Inspired by a *National Geographic* article, this infographic goes a little deeper, with the big bang and the beginning of the universe added to the story. The designers wanted to show how small our planet is in the context of the whole universe.

Client / *Infografika*
Design Agency / Infografika Magazine
Designer / Nonna Khismatullina
Completion / 2013

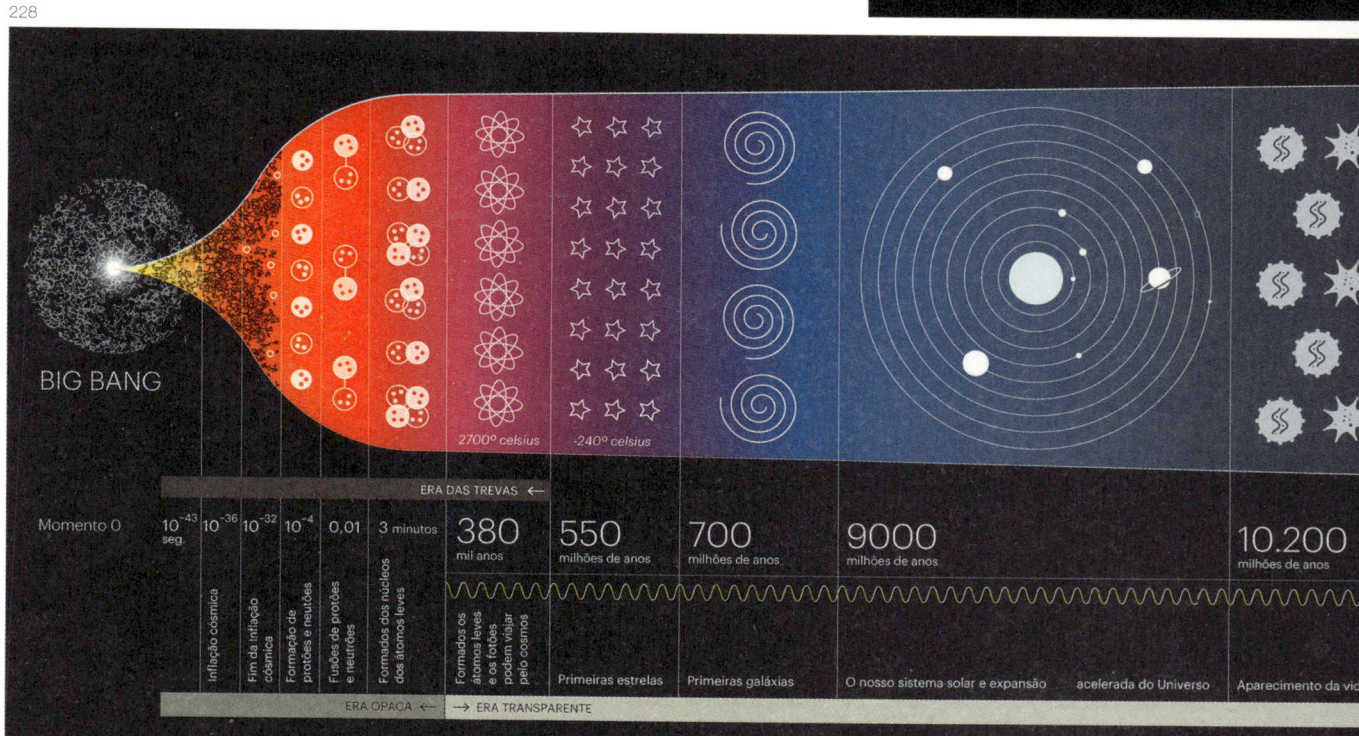

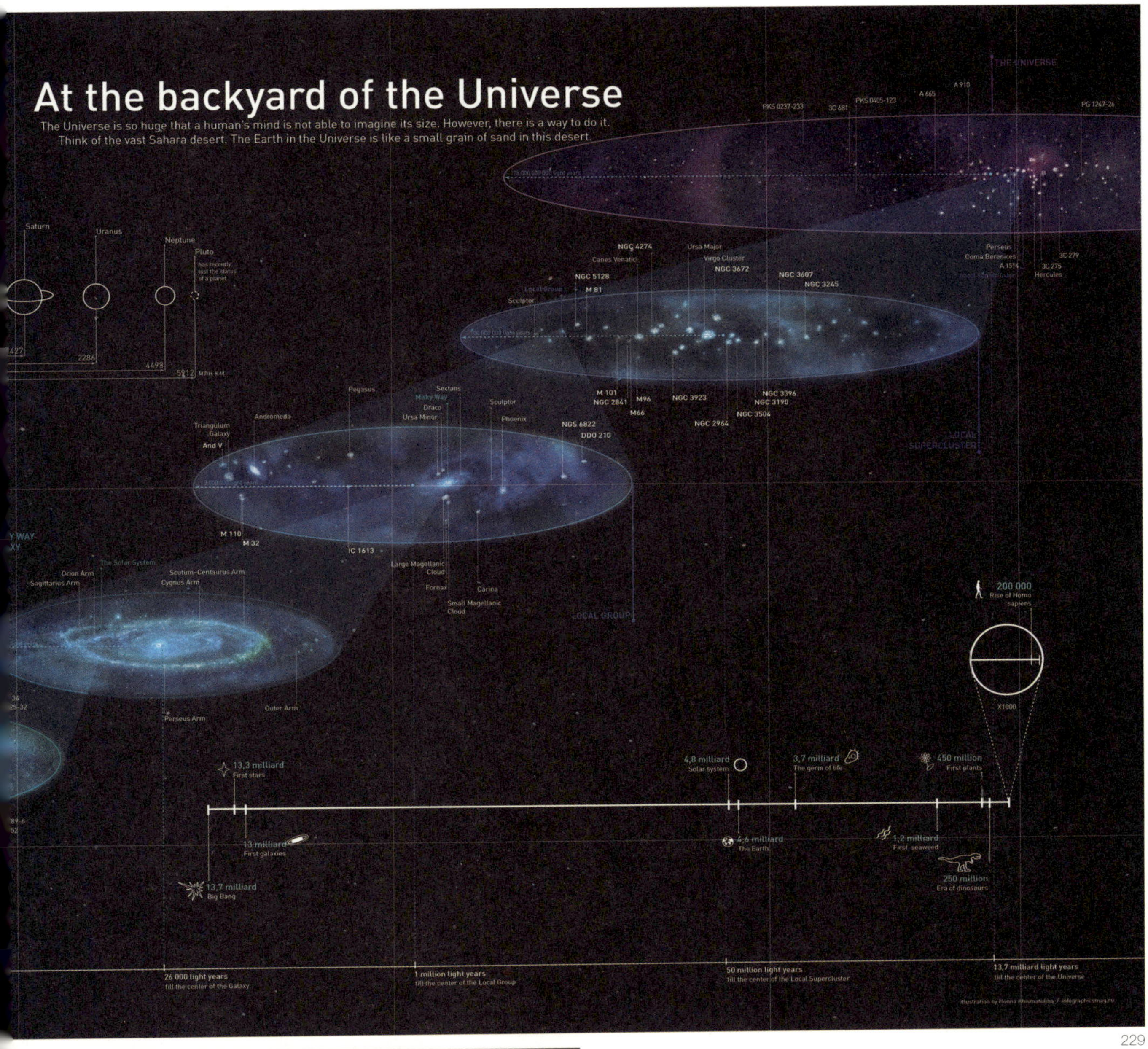

At the backyard of the Universe

The Universe is so huge that a human's mind is not able to imagine its size. However, there is a way to do it. Think of the vast Sahara desert. The Earth in the Universe is like a small grain of sand in this desert.

13.800
milhões de anos

Universo actual

The House of the Romanovs

Project Description /

Few people know very much about who ruled the roost in Russia between Peter the Great and Nikolay II, so the designers decided to make an infographic about the Russian royal family, the Romanovs. The goal was to explore how different imperators were connected to each other.

Client / *Infografika*
Design Agency / Infografika Magazine
Designer / Nastya Mikheeva
Completion / 2012

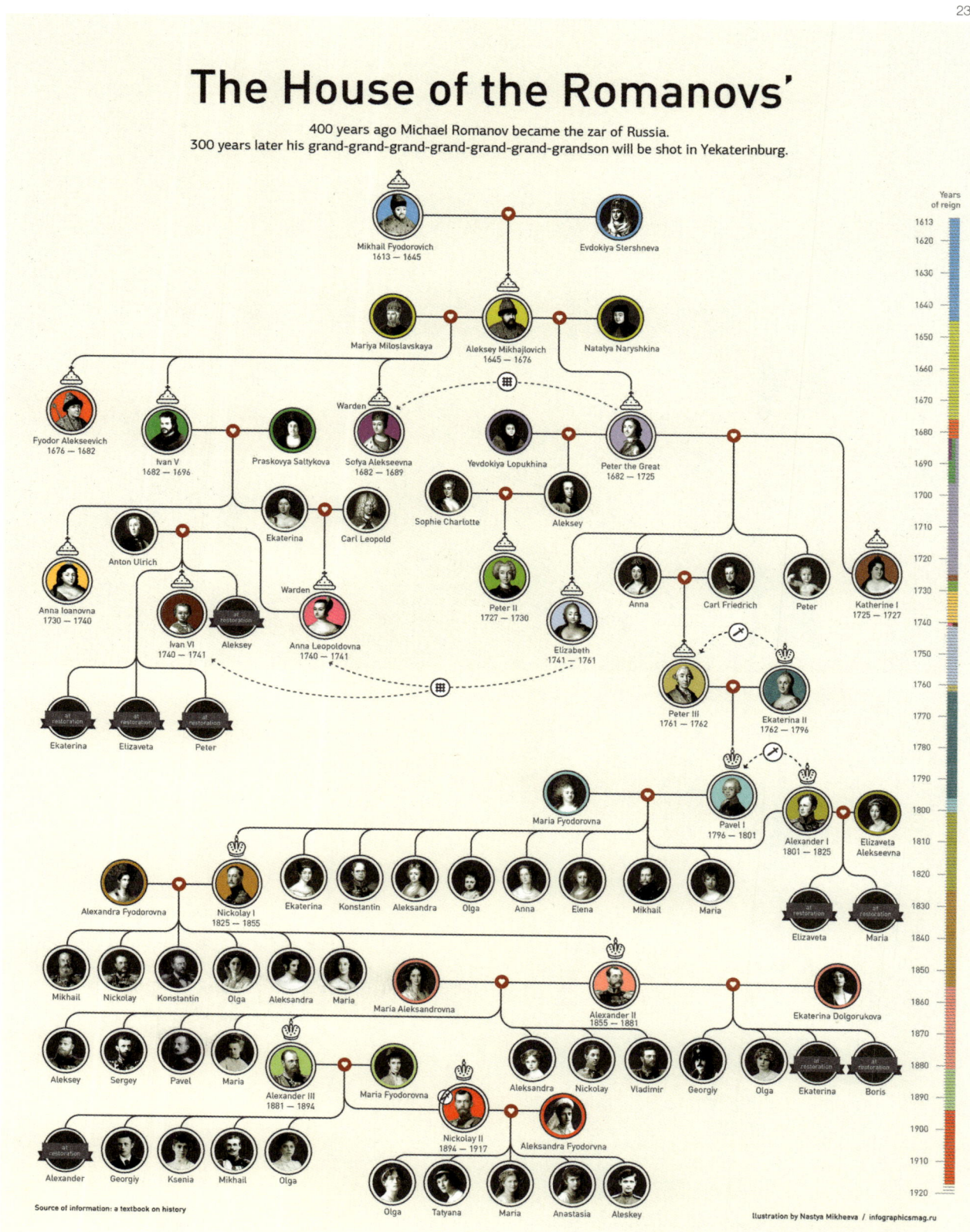

Fluffy Crystal

Project Description /

New Year's Eve had come and gone, but there still wasn't any snow at all in Saint Petersburg. Russians love snow and its absence was a widely discussed topic, so the designers decided to create an infographic about it. They used hand-drawn snowflakes to explain that a snowflake was a single crystal whose form and size depended on the humidity and temperature of the air.

Client / IInfografika
Design Agency / Infografika Magazine
Designer / Dmitri Gorelyshev
Completion / 2014

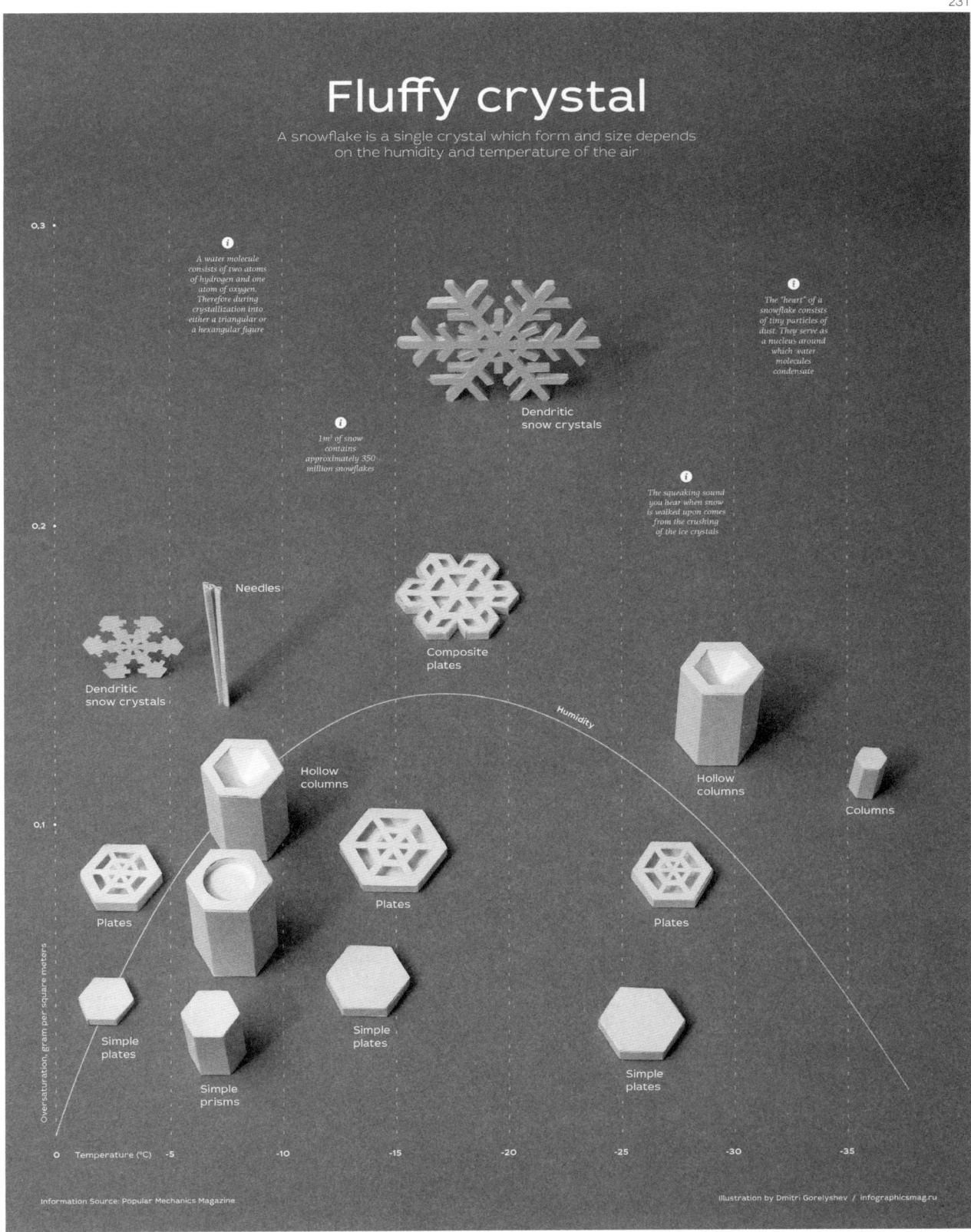

INDEX

A

Adonis Durado
www.behance.net/adonisdurado
PP 18, 118-126

Adriano Attus
adriano.attus.it
PP 34-38, 40-41

Alejandro Colmenárez
newspagedesigner.org/profile/
AlejandroColmenarez
PP 78-79

Alejandro Meraviglia
www.ajmeraviglia.freeiz.com
P 49

Andriy Nemchenko
www.behance.net/info2visual
P 223

Annalisa Varlotta
www.behance.net/avarlotta
P 161

Anton Osipov
medium.com/@TonyOsipov
P 84

Antonio Farach
www.behance.net/antoniofarachd05c
PP 28, 76-77, 88, 127, 160

Ashley Davis
www.behance.net/ashleyv_davis
PP 138-139

B

Bárbara Villoslada
www.behance.net/barbaravilloslada
P 208

Beutler Ink
www.tiffanyfarrant.com
P 150

C

Carlos Gámez Kindelán
carlosgamezkindelan.es
P 15

Carol Cavaleiro
www.behance.net/carolcavaleiro
PP 23, 116-117

Catherine Fields
www.catherinefieldsdesign.com
PP 146-147

Cátia Mendonça
www.behance.net/catianmend02f4
PP 234-235

Cees Mensen
cmontwerp.nl
PP 194-195

Chotiga Chotisorayuth
cargocollective.com/chotigac
P 59

Ciaran Hughes
www.ciaranhughes.co.uk
PP 89, 126, 154

Corriere Della Sera Infographic Newsroom
www.behance.net/nvargas
PP 62, 86, 198-202, 233

D

David McCandless
www.informationisbeautiful.net
P 104

David Santos
www.behance.net/david_t_santos
P 232

Diana Estefanía Rubio
www.behance.net/dianaestefaniarubio
PP 29, 100-101, 151

Duaa R. Hattab
www.behance.net/DuaaH
PP 156-157

E

Eduardo Asta
www.flickr.com/photos/easta
P 75

Emy Gariepy
www.behance.net/emy_gariepy
P 140

Erik Nylund
www.eriknylund.se
PP 65, 67-68, 111, 130, 225,

F

Francesco Franchi
www.francescofranchi.com
PP 83, 153

G

Gianluca Seta
www.nascuto.com
PP 20, 96-99, 196

Giovanni Piemontese
www.behance.net/GiovanniPiemontese
P 159

Graphicacy
graphicacy.com
PP 112-113

H

Heather Jones
visual.ly/users/heatherjones
P 228

Henrik Pettersson
www.henrikpettersson.co.uk
PP 58, 60-61, 192-193

Hugo Camacho
www.behance.net/hugoc
PP 222-223

I

Infografika Magazine
infographicsmag.ru
PP 56-57, 87, 132, 176-179, 184-190, 234-237

Ingvar Meen
portfoolio.meeen.com
P 151

Ivón Guzmán Pérez
newspagedesigner.org/profile/IvonGuzman
P 82

J

Jaime Serra
www.flickr.com/photos/96120027@N03/page1
PP 134-135

John Velasco
issuu.com/john_v
P 81

José Luis Barros Chaparro
www.behance.net/jlbarros
PP 74, 85

Juan Colombato
newspagedesigner.org/profile/
JuanColombato
P 108

Jude Buffum
www.judebuffum.com
P 204

Julieta Bernstein
www.behance.net/julietabernstein
PP 180-183

K

Karolina Kot
www.behance.net/kotillustration
P 158

Kata Kerekes
www.behance.net/kekerekeskata
P 44

L

Lana Bragina
www.ulani.de
PP 63, 131

Laura Cattaneo
www.halfpastwelve.com
PP 102, 230-231

Ligia Saenger
www.behance.net/ligiasaenger
P 105

Lizaveta Bukreeva
www.behance.net/LizavetaBukreeva
PP 52, 191

Lucille Umali
lucilleumali.blogspot.com
P 80

M

Mário Malhão
newspagedesigner.org/profile/
MarioRuidaSilvaLopesMalhao
PP 30, 42-43, 69-73, 133, 141

Marta Carvalho
cargocollective.com/martacarvalho
PP 53, 109

Matías Cipollatti
infograholics.blogspot.com
PP 92-95

Maxine Koen
maxinekoen.com/
P 209

Mayuresh Patole
www.behance.net/mayureshpatole25
P 166

McKenzie Smith
mckenziesmithstudio.com
PP 210-213

Miguel Ulloa Maciel
newspagedesigner.org/profile/MiguelUlloa
PP 90-91

Mónica Serrano
monicaserrano.com
PP 167-171

Mosettig Tamara
www.behance.net/tamose
P 197

N

Nicola Gubernale
cargocollective.com/nicolagubernale
P 129

Nicolas Verrier
eclairagepublic.net/
PP 50-51, 142-143, 155, 162

Norberto Baruch
visualoop.com/blog/30602/portfolio-of-the-week-norberto-baruch
P 128

O

Oleksandr Guzenko
www.behance.net/alex94
PP 48, 110

P

Pratyush Gupta
visual.ly/users/pratyush89
P 66

R

Rafael Cordoba
www.behance.net/rafaelcordoba
PP 214-215

Rahadyo Widyastomo
www.behance.net/rahadyo_widyastomo
P 27

Raj Kamal
www.flickr.com/photos/rajkamalaich
PP 64, 216-221

Renée Mak
reneemak.com
P 152

Rodrigo Fortes
www.flickr.com/photos/rodrigofortes/sets
PP 89, 161

Russel Daniela
www.behance.net/danielarussel
P 224

Russell Tate
www.russelltate.com/
PP 39, 163

Ryan MacEachern
www.ryanmaceachern.com
PP 148-149

S

Sajeev Kumarapuram
newspagedesigner.org/profile/sajeevkumarapuram
P 203

Sangseob Lee
www.behance.net/vvlss7
PP 206-207

Santosh Kushwaha
www.flickr.com/photos/kushwahasantosh
PP 15-16, 46-47

Sheikh Parvaiz Ahmad
newspaperdesign.in/profile/SheikhParvaiz
PP 45, 103

Simon Ducroquet
cargocollective.com/ducroquet/ESQUEMA-CACHOEIRA
PP 106-107

Spencer Shores
spencershor.es
P 229

Stephanie Halpern
cargocollective.com/blinkdesigns
P 164

T

Tamer Koseli
www.tamerkoseli.com
PP 136-137

Tien-Min Liao
www.tienminliao.com
PP 172-175

V

Valentina Teleschi
www.behance.net/vteleschib898
PP 226-227

Veronica Clarin
cargocollective.com/veronicaclarin
P 205

Vesa Sammalisto
vesa-s.com/filter/infographic
PP 144-145

Vitaliy Turov
www.behance.net/turov
PP 54-55

Y

Yael Shinkar
eaylis.com
PP 114-115, 163, 165

Published in Australia in 2015 by
The Images Publishing Group Pty Ltd
ABN 89 059 734 431
6 Bastow Place, Mulgrave, Victoria 3170, Australia
Tel: +61 3 9561 5544 Fax: +61 3 9561 4860
books@imagespublishing.com
www.imagespublishing.com

Copyright © The Images Publishing Group Pty Ltd 2015
The Images Publishing Group Reference Number: 1199

All rights reserved. Apart from any fair dealing for the purposes of private study, research, criticism or review as permitted under the Copyright Act, no part of this publication may be reproduced, stored in a retrieval system or transmitted in any form by any means, electronic, mechanical, photocopying, recording or otherwise, without the written permission of the publisher.

Title: Visual Storytelling—Infographic Design in News
Author: Edited by Liu Yikun and Dong Zhao
ISBN: 9781864706499

For Catalogue-in-Publication data, please see the National Library of Australia entry

Coordinated, edited and designed by Images Publishing, Shanghai (China) office.

Printed by Toppan Leefung Printing Limited

IMAGES has included on its website a page for special notices in relation to this and our other publications. Please visit www.imagespublishing.com.

Every effort has been made to trace the original source of copyright material contained in this book. The publishers would be pleased to hear from copyright holders to rectify any errors or omissions.
The information and illustrations in this publication have been prepared and supplied by the contributor/s. While all reasonable efforts have been made to ensure accuracy, the publishers do not, under any circumstances, accept responsibility for errors, omissions and representations, express or implied.